T0320316

CONTEMPORARY
CHINA

CONTEMPORARY CHINA

The dynamics of change at the start of the new millennium

edited by

P.W. Preston and Jürgen Haacke

LONDON AND NEW YORK

First Published in 2003
by RoutledgeCurzon
11 New Fetter Lane, London EC4P 4EE

Simultaneously published in the USA and Canada
by RoutledgeCurzon
29 West 35th Street, New York, NY 10001

RoutledgeCurzon is an imprint of the Taylor & Francis Group

© 2003 P.W. Preston and Jürgen Haacke for editorial matter and selection; contributors for individual chapters

All rights reserved. No part of this book may be reprinted or reproduced or utilised in any form or by any electronic, mechanical, or other means, now known or hereafter invented, including photocopying and recording, or in any information storage or retrieval system, without permission in writing from the publishers.

British Library Cataloguing in Publication Data
A catalogue record of this book is available from the British Library

Library of Congress Cataloging in Publication Data
A catalog record for this book has been requested

ISBN 0-7007-1637-8

Contents

China: Social and Political Change

China: Developments in External Relations

China: Conclusions

List of Contributors

Dr David Dickinson, Department of Economics, University of Birmingham, UK

Dr Zhang Zhichao, Department of East Asian Studies, University of Durham, UK

Prof. Tong Jiadong, Director, Centre for European Studies, University of Nankai, People's Republic of China

Assoc. Prof. Xing Aifen, Department of Philosophy, Beijing Normal University, People's Republic of China

Prof. Hsiao-hung Nancy Chen, Dean, College of Social Sciences, National Chengchi University, Taiwan

Prof. Guan Xinping, Department of Sociology, University of Nankai, People's Republic of China

Dr Gudrun Wacker, Stiftung Wissenschaft und Politik (Berlin), formerly at the Bundesinstitut fur Ostwissenschaftliche und Internationale Studien, Köln, Germany

Dr Christopher R. Hughes, Department of International Relations, London School of Economics, UK

Dr Zhao Chenggen, Department of Political Science and Public Administration, Peking University, People's Republic of China

Dr Ngai-Ling Sum, Department of Politics, University of Lancaster, UK

Dr Caroline Rose, Department of East Asian Studies, University of Leeds, UK

Dr Paul Lim, European Institute for Asian Studies, Brussels, Belgium

Dr Jürgen Haacke, Department of Political Science and International Studies, University of Birmingham, UK

Prof. P.W. Preston, Department of Political Science and International Studies, University of Birmingham, UK

Preface and Acknowledgements

That China has been undergoing significant change since embracing reform in the post-Mao period is to state the obvious. What this volume seeks to do is to provide an account that attempts not only to identify and chart the contours of this change, but also to examine the dynamics that are driving change within China. The volume does so in relation to a wide range of areas of intellectual inquiry: monetary and foreign exchange policy, the foreign trade regime, state-owned enterprises, regional economic development, social welfare reform, the Internet, cross-Strait relations, political governance, the post-Asian crisis high-tech strategies in 'Greater China', and China's foreign relations.

The idea for this book emerged after the Asia Research Centre of the University of Birmingham invited distinguished researchers from the People's Republic of China, Taiwan, continental Europe and the UK to debate developments and trends within China and to clarify the extent and drivers of change. This volume builds on the original workshop proceedings organised in June 2000, but contributors were asked to update their chapters to take account of developments up to the end of 2000. What has emerged is a comprehensive book on the scope and dynamics of change affecting China that brings together scholars offering significant expertise in their respective areas of study. It is hoped that the volume will contribute to illuminating an agenda of inquiry adequate to the present patterns of change within China as the country moves into the new millennium.

As editors of this book, we would like to thank first and foremost the contributors to this volume and all those colleagues who attended the workshop. We also gratefully acknowledge the generous financial support received from the School of Social Sciences at the University of Birmingham. Special thanks go to Xing Aifen and Qiu Ying for the assistance provided. Finally, we would like to acknowledge the support and advice offered by Peter Sowden who took on this book as commissioning editor.

Introduction

Chapter 1

Change in Contemporary China

P.W. Preston and Jürgen Haacke

Introduction

This book is concerned with analyzing change in contemporary China. Change has been a constant theme in the political history and economy as well as in the foreign relations of the People's Republic of China. Whereas change in China has nearly always impacted in some way on the human condition within the country and shaped its involvement with other parts of the world, the domestic and international implications of change in China at the beginning of the new millennium are potentially greater than ever before.

Social science: approaches, divergences and commonalities

Making sense of change is not straightforward. One reason for this is that the field of contemporary social science is very diverse. A mere casual look at the available stock of works in the social sciences reveals a wide range of competing approaches, theories, bodies of results and stances in regard to the production of knowledge (Anderson et al. 1986; Skinner 1990; Hollis and Smith 1991; Fay 1996). A number of efforts have been made over the years to bring order to this diversity. A particularly popular research strategy (itself pursued variously) – routinely summed up and dismissed as 'positivism' (Bernstein 1976; Bryant 1985) – has been to appeal to the model of the natural sciences. It might reasonably be asserted that approaches building on the model of the natural sciences remain the default setting across much of contemporary social science even now. However, the period from the 1970s to the 1990s also saw the emergence of 'post-positivism' in many disciplines, not least International Relations. For the purposes of this book, we shall not regard epistemological, theoretical, and methodological diversity as evidence of a failure to agree on an approach (or a failure to measure up to the model of the natural sciences). Instead, we shall take it as given, routine, inevitable and (if creatively ordered) beneficial in respect of the task of uncovering the 'truth' of matters social (Habermas 1989; Holub 1991). Irrespective of the outcome of philosophical debates about the nature of the social sciences, we hold that it is possible and a convenient strategy for the purposes of this volume to think about theoretical diversity in terms of a dialogue between models for understanding and explaining.

The notion of dialogue lets us look at the spread of the social sciences in terms of a wide range of arguments that are differently located, conceived and oriented. We can nevertheless order this diversity by characterizing lines of argument making. In the first place, perhaps most obviously, we can speak of disciplines; the institutionally vehicled spheres of concern which mark out different areas of intellectual inquiry within the social sciences. It is clear that the self-definitions of practicing academics will be varied, but typically we are invited to fit ourselves into an established discipline. Then, secondly, we can also speak of distinctive intellectual traditions. The ideas that animate the work of European thinkers will tend to draw on the intellectual histories of that continent, as similarly the work of colleagues from East Asia is generally shaped by their own intellectual histories. The ways in which recognizably social scientific areas of enquiry are construed and thereafter pursued are bound by historical intellectual contexts. Of course, this is an old point, but one that in the context of the recent enthusiasm over 'globalization' is perhaps worth reiterating. Then, third, the diversity of different intellectual traditions can be approached in a related, but distinct, fashion by speaking of 'national' traditions. Arguing this point may risk repeating a mere cliché, but the point that 'national' communities develop distinctive agendas nevertheless seems worth making. There is, for example, a stronger leaning on the European continent toward history/hermeneutics than there is, say, generally speaking, in the United States. In East Asia the picture is perhaps more complicated given the different degrees of fusion of domestic intellectual traditions and Western philosophy and theory. It is likely that we would find further ways to consider the diversity within the social sciences but, for now, it is enough to again note the point that this book is based on the premise of the possibility of ordered dialogue irrespective of the boundaries that have been drawn.

In this text, this ordered dialogue centres on the process of rapid and pervasive change that has affected the People's Republic and that appears to have accelerated at the turn of the millennium. The text consists of a collection of works from colleagues in the United Kingdom, continental Europe and China. The contributors to this volume draw on various disciplines such as Financial Economics, Trade Economics, Development Economics, Political Administration, Political Science, International

Relations, Political Sociology, Foreign Policy Analysis and European Studies. Although the contributors thus inhabit various intellectual traditions and are preoccupied with different sets of questions and concerns, there is a clear area of overlap, a concern around which the chapters revolve. As will be shown in the individual chapters, this area of common concern is how change has affected China at the level of the economy, politics, society and foreign relations. It will also explore the notion of there being drivers of change. Before exploring the empirical question of how manifest change is in contemporary China, and what drives this change, it is useful to briefly discuss the notion of change itself.

Some thoughts on the notion of change

We can think about change in a number of ways. One can, for instance, follow those, who, in the popular press and elsewhere, link change to new fashions, discourses and shifts in cultural likes and dislikes. However, much of the familiar rhetoric in relation to such change, ever more rapid change, is arguably simply vacuous, little more than the routine background noise of consumerism and its associated mass/popular culture. Following Ernest Gellner we can also think about change in a more substantive way. According to Gellner, the core questions for contemporary social science revolves around 'being and becoming industrial' (Gellner 1964: 36). This could lead us to explore macro-historical patterns of change, the broad sweep of history, changing structural patterns and the ways in which social agents variously acted. In the case of Europe, one might thus, for example, focus on the long process of the shift from essentially agrarian economies towards trading and thereafter industrial economies. This tale, as we know, would involve discussing the geographical relocation of centres of activity, as new patterns of trade developed and as new centres of industry emerged. (Clearly, one could unpack this tale in a variety of ways.) We might also focus on dealing with these macro-histories in terms of the development history of particular areas. Then, we might explore how different peoples of an area 'shifted' into history and later 'shifted' again into the modern world (Preston 1998). If one speaks of the development history of an area, it is also possible to examine but discrete periods or phases. This might involve discussions of the industrial revolution and its subsequent development in Britain, discussions of the Meiji Restoration or discussions of the drawn-out collapse of the Qing dynasty. Significantly, despite the above invocation of Gellner and his useful focus on the 'industrial', we do not necessarily assume that he has a monopoly on understanding the nature and dynamics of change. Other accounts that focus, say, more explicitly on capital accumulation or norm 'rationalization' processes may be equally relevant in understanding the important issue of the dynamics of change.

If the usefulness of distinguishing change according to macro patterns, discrete phases and the present day may not be immediately obvious (Preston 1996; Sztompa 1993), we should perhaps recall how other disciplines have thought about time-scales within which to examine events. The historians of the Annales School, for example, differentiated between (1) the secular or *longue durée*; (2) the immediate or *événementiel*, and (3) the intermediate or *conjuncturel*. As Fred Halliday (2001: 3) has noted, 'the secular may be too long to evaluate except in retrospect'. However, as he puts it, 'the immediate is not to be discounted, especially if it involves wars, revolutions or economic crises'. Still, for Halliday, it is the conjunctural trends that we should first and foremost seek to examine. This book, with its focus on contemporary China, seeks to focus our attention on both the immediate and the conjunctural trends. As regards the immediate, however, we again caution against mistaking for significant change that change which in essence may be but the routine froth of the industrial capitalist form of life or an emerging discourse. In this vein, we thus think that certainly the collapse of the Soviet Union was a significant political event. However, it is not at all clear that we can already take for granted the rise of a 'New Economy', the end of the business cycle, etc. We are also somewhat sceptical of the notion that change has never been more rapid, not least by virtue of today's contemporary access to communication technology (in relation to this point with reference to East Asia, also see Clammer 1997; Robison and Goodman 1996).

The nature and dynamics of change in the PRC: overview

If one wanted to get a feeling for the change undergone by the People's Republic of China, one might do worse than noting – in official parlance – the summary achievements of the three generations of leaderships that have ruled the country since its founding in 1949. As reprinted in *The China Quarterly* (no.164, December 2000: 1107–8), the first generation of leaders is said to have eliminated 'imperialism, feudalism and bureaucrat[ic] capitalism'. The second generation is regarded as having stood for 'reform, opening up and building socialism with Chinese characteristics'. Meanwhile, the third generation of Chinese leaders are seen to have 'consolidated and developed socialist undertakings in China under complicated domestic and international situations, developed Marxism and Deng Xiaoping Theory in the course of practice, and put forward the new ideology of the "three representatives"' (which is further discussed below).

What this summary suggests is that since its establishment, the People's Republic of China has undergone significant domestic political upheaval and economic transformation. As a country emerging from civil war, the immediate attention of leaders focused on economic reconstruction and development. Although initially reliant on established entrepreneurs, models of socialist development were soon imported from the Soviet Union. The spectre of revisionism in China prompted Mao to continue the revolution and to argue that political movements could significantly raise production. In the event, the 'great leap forward' proved an immensely costly and sobering exercise. However, while the worst of the economic consequences and distortions were rectified in the early 1960s, the reform agenda of the 1950s was embraced and put into practice only as Mao's hold on political power finally slipped for good. The sobering experience of the Cultural Revolution, which had seen the life of Mao's political opponents and countless others disrupted or even curtailed, with economic development stalled, made the Dengist reformers vow to prevent anything similar from ever occurring again. The interim Hua Guofeng years already saw the adoption of a measure of change even if policy shifts remained cloaked in Maoist rhetoric. The subsequent reform period under Deng then witnessed a determined effort to enhance efficiency and productivity, to modernize and make strong the People's Republic, and to make more prosperous its citizens. To be sure, the nature and pace of economic reforms under Deng's stewardship proved contentious within the leadership, leading to *fang/shou* cycles, cycles of liberalizing reform and subsequent attempts to regain control (Baum 1994: 5). However, Deng's 1992 southern tour, organized at a time when political and economic conservatives found themselves in the ascendancy following the violent suppression of street protests in June 1989, provided a strong stimulus for further economic reforms. The direction and nature of these reforms have since been met by the occasional criticism from conservative ideologues and those worried about social justice, but have nonetheless continued unabated. The third generation of leaders, with Jiang Zemin at the 'core', has continued Deng's legacy, but has increasingly also had to face up to the adverse social consequences of fostering a 'rapidly marketizing economy'. At the same time, leaders of the Chinese Communist Party (CCP) see their party as now formally representing the interests of advanced forces of production.

The foreign relations of the People's Republic have equally experienced almost seismic shifts. Having been forced to 'lean to one side' to achieve military security and assistance with economic construction, Mao Zedong fundamentally disagreed with the 'revisionist' turn of Moscow under Khrushchev that prompted the Sino-Soviet split. Following a period during which Beijing confronted both Washington and Moscow, Chinese leaders eventually decided on a strategic alignment with the United States against the Soviet Union. Since Beijing's rapprochement with Moscow in the 1980s, the PRC has sought to preserve maximum strategic flexibility and an independent foreign policy. The bloody suppression of street protests in 1989 forced the PRC to overcome international ostracism and isolation, an objective achieved not least by successful efforts to deepen relations with states in Pacific Asia and by fostering an interest of Western companies in the vast China market. In more recent years, China has opposed 'hegemonism' and 'power politics' in favour of multipolarity and co-operative security.

Dynamics of change

The dynamics underlying change, as well as its nature and extent, have clearly been varied. China has not been immune to developments in world politics and the global economy and some of these developments have prompted resistance, while others have proved to be the harbingers of domestic change and foreign policy re-orientation. The search for security has been important in understanding shifts in strategic alignment. The struggle for respect has informed both China's domestic and foreign policies in myriad ways, not only under Mao, but also under Deng and Jiang. However, turning China into a country that is 'rich and strong' remains the essential goal of the post-Mao 'collective leadership'. The outcome of domestic power struggles and the transition from one generation of leaders to the next have, so far, also decisively influenced the speed and extent of change within the People's Republic. In more recent years, concerns about regime survival have increasingly underpinned decisions to take bold steps in accelerating economic reforms, while the same concerns have also seen a slow but selective process of political reform, not least in the form of more village-level democracy and accountability.

The issue of regime survival has in recent years been at the heart of many new policies introduced by CCP leaders. Such concerns have also made the leadership's attempt to instil (but at the same time contain) a sense of patriotism or popular nationalism in a people that has mostly tired of communism as a legitimating ideology and resents the widespread and occasionally dramatic (economic) abuse of power by party officials. For a significant number of Chinese people, meanwhile, new possibilities of 'getting rich' have also proved a propellant for taking greater personal risks, even if that has only meant changing work places. Undoubtedly, higher living standards of many Chinese have also seen the (re-)introduction of social practices that create pressures for further change, particularly in areas such as family law. While the dynamics of change have thus been diverse, it is notable that reform, at least in the last two decades, has not always been a matter of successful design. Much change decreed from above has involved an approach relying on trial and error. This is especially the case in the area of economic and legal reforms. However, it is equally important to recognise that not all change has occurred by way of reform from above. Significant pressures from below, arising from discontent and justified grievances, for instance, have also given rise to a whole series of reform measures. The return to family farming in the early period of the reform period represents just one such example.

Contemporary China: the extent of change

It is a commonplace to note that China (including Taiwan and Hong Kong) has vastly changed over the last two decades or so. It is nevertheless worth briefly sketching here just how vast that change has been.

Ideology and China's political economy

Deng Xiaoping's criticism of Mao encompassed several points, not least that the latter had overlooked 'objective economic laws', possessed an 'inadequate understanding of the laws of economic development', and 'overestimated the role of man's subjective will and efforts' (Schell and Shambaugh: 29–49). Deng also disagreed with Mao's analysis that the principal contradiction in Chinese society faced by CCP leaders was that between the proletariat and the bourgeoisie. Hence, for Deng, there was no need for a continuation of the revolution. Instead, Deng saw China's principal contradiction to be 'between the growing material and cultural needs of the people and backward production'. For reformers like Deng, overcoming 'backward production' entailed changes in the relations of production. This was ideologically justified with reference to the emergence of socialism in China 'from the womb of a semicolonial, semifeudal society'. By implication, economic reformers asserted that China had to go through a 'very long primary stage'.

Although China's leaders have steadfastly reiterated their claim to be promoting a socialist economy, they have perceived a need to invoke ever-widening interpretations of the meaning of socialism to justify new reform measures. Notwithstanding the increasing lack of popular appeal of socialism as an overarching ideology, the leadership has at a declaratory level clung to this concept because it has perceived a failure to do so as further undermining its legitimacy. Not surprisingly, the official retreat from public ownership, which has usually been heralded, albeit not necessarily very convincingly, as the mainstay of socialism, has proved particularly awkward. Notwithstanding the difficulties, the leadership has over time expanded the role of the 'private economy'. While the public economy was still meant to play the 'principal part' under former Premier and CCP General Secretary Zhao Ziyang, it subsequently was merely designed to 'play a leading role' in the economy. The Fourteenth Party Congress in 1992 called for the establishment of a 'socialist market economy', a term integrated into the PRC constitution. It also continued contending that China was in the 'primary stage of socialism'.

Prior to the 15th National Party Congress, in response to criticism that resorting to the shareholding system to reform state-owned enterprises amounted to privatization, Jiang defended the shareholding system as a 'form of realization' of public ownership. Unofficially, this defence of the shareholding system was labeled, albeit again not necessarily persuasively, as a 'third thought liberation'.[1] A 1999 amendment to the constitution declares 'socialist public ownership of the means of production, namely, ownership by the whole people and collective ownership by the working people' as the 'basis' of China's socialist economic system. The stress on economic efficiency rather than equity was recently reinforced by the concept of the 'three representatives'. The latter is portrayed as a development of Deng Xiaoping's theory on 'building a socialist road with Chinese characteristics' and said to mark an aim for the party, a formula for governing the country, as well as a source of power. The 'three representatives' holds that the CCP should be representative of the 'development requirements of China's advanced productive forces, the progressive course of China's advanced culture, and the fundamental interests of the Chinese people'. The significance of the 'three representatives' is that it allows the Party to represent the interests of those economic and cultural forces that traditionally were often considered suspect. Implicitly, the 'three representatives' further legitimize changes in the relations of production that were so forcefully rejected by Mao.

Political, institutional and legal change

In contrast to the change inherent in the steps taken to legitimate the market and new forms of ownership, political change in the PRC has been more modest. The People's Republic remains an essentially Leninist party-state in the sense that the members of the Standing Committee and Politburo of the Central Committee of Chinese Communist Party continue to enjoy *de facto* monopoly power and are not accountable to political or judicial constraints. Bold calls in the 1980s for political reform aiming for a separation of functions of Party and government have to date proved less than a full success. The leadership has encouraged the development of democracy within the system of people's congresses. On the other hand, People's Congresses are not in a position to hold the government politically accountable, as only Party members may convene the former. There have also been efforts to strengthen the legal system.

Legal reforms, as we shall see below, have in many ways outpaced political reforms. As Pitman Potter (1999: 173) has argued, 'law-making and institution-building have reached impressive levels.' To be sure, however, legal reforms have not undermined state power. Indeed, the People's Republic has, up to now, embraced the 'rule through law' rather than the 'rule of law'. Former National People's Congress (NPC) Chairman Qiao Shi may have struggled to win acceptance for changes that would make the NPC and its Standing Committee supervise enforcement of the Constitution, the work of state organs and give it real responsibility for the enactment of laws. As it stands, however, the Party retains a *de facto* leadership role during law-making processes.

Particularly impressive has been the output of laws designed to foster economic development and to attract foreign capital. A comprehensive overview over laws relevant to economic reform is beyond the scope of this volume. It should be noted however that the PRC has not merely recognised private property rights, but has also integrated this recognition in the Constitution. Notably, the NPC has also adopted a series of administrative reform measures and legal avenues that are intended to provide citizens with possibilities to appeal decisions of the bureaucracy. However, the new regulations and law may still have limits in so far as they do not allow for the review of discretionary decisions. Nor do citizens have leeway to appeal against Party decisions. In criminal law, the crime of counter-revolution has been deleted from the statute books in response to longstanding international criticisms and increasing domestic pressures. However, citizens may now face being charged for the crime of endangering state security.

Some steps to more democratization have been taken as, for example, CCP leaders have allowed direct, secret and competitive election of the village head and the village council as well as the establishment of a village representative assembly. At the same time, however, opposition parties remain illegal as illustrated by the banning of the Democratic Party. Also, the PRC still does not boast independent media or autonomous trade unions. Its civil society is little more than embryonic, yet, as Tony Saich has suggested, 'multiple models of state-society relations may be operating [in China] at the same time' (Saich 2000: 138), that may involve state repression, co-optation and even state encouragement of the societal forces in question. Ultimately, however, the party-state continues to rely on security services and the People's Armed Police to maintain social stability.

'Rational bureaucratic rule' and instances of mobilization (*dongyuan*) have replaced mass political campaigns (*yundong*). Examples in case concern the efforts to address the problem of corruption and the threat posed by the Falungong. Party cadres remain subject to 'mobilization' such as the 'three stresses' (*san jiang*), initiated under Jiang Zemin, which seeks to enhance the self-understanding and mutual understanding of cadres by promoting study, politics, and healthy trends.

Economic change

The PRC may in some sense still be a developing country, but its economy has dramatically expanded in size. Depending on the assumed growth figure China's economy is set to overtake that of Japan in the medium long-term. Moreover, not only has the PRC joined the ranks of East Asia's Newly Industrializing Economies, it is also perceived by some, although not necessarily the Chinese leadership itself, to be on the threshold of joining the G8 states.

The Chinese economy continues to register high growth figures. In the first half of 2000, growth was estimated at 8.2 per cent, following a 'paltry' figure of 7.1 per cent in 1999. Notably, in view of sustained low levels of domestic consumption on the one hand and the perceived requirement of strong economic growth on the other hand (see below), the government has in the last few years adopted expansive fiscal policies.

As illustrated by its overall trade volume and the diversity of its import and export destinations, China has turned from a largely autarkic society during Mao's rule to a highly interdependent state. The CCP leadership's determination to join the major financial and trade institutions was again underlined by the concessions granted to the United States and the European Union in the bilateral accords that were reached to ensure China's accession to the World Trade Organisation (WTO).

Meanwhile, as regards China's domestic economic and industrial restructuring, collectively owned enterprises have converted into share-holding companies or private firms or joint ventures. Thousands of state-owned enterprises (SOEs) have implemented mergers and bankruptcies. There has been a strong shift from public and collective employment to private sector employment, with an increasingly diverse pattern of ownership. Notably, agricultural employment, as a percentage of the total labour force, has fallen to below 50 per cent.

Social changes and externalities of reform

The social changes as well as the 'externalities' accompanying economic reforms have proved enormous. The following are but a few examples. First, the realities of surplus labour and the demand for labour flexibility have in effect undermined the household registration system. Quotas for household registration (*hukou*) have been abolished in small cities and towns throughout China.

Second, during the hitherto reform period the rigid urban–rural divide characteristic of the Mao era has been partially overcome, even as the income disparity between rural and urban areas has grown. The urban population now stands at about 1/3 of the total population. At the same time, the disparity between wealthy and vibrant coastal regions and the vast and impoverished hinterland has become ever more conspicuous. Also on the more negative side, many working practices of those employed in the private sector amount to outrageous forms of exploitation. Significantly, China has not only seen the demise of the 'iron-rice bowl' and the re-emergence of social inequality and class divisions. It is also dealing with a huge 'floating population' that does not enjoy the same benefits as those that hold legal urban registration. Increasingly, successes in promoting gender equality are qualified by processes entailing the 'commodification' of women.

Military modernization

In military terms, the People's Republic is far from possessing the capabilities enjoyed by major Western industrial countries, particularly the United States or Japan. Indeed, there is a consensus that the capabilities of the People's Liberation Army (PLA) lag ten if not twenty years behind the state of the art in most categories. Military modernization has nevertheless implied the professionalization of the PLA, the upgrading of its hardware, command and control systems, changes to its force structure, training, and military doctrine. As regards the latter, the PLA has abandoned people's war and embraced instead a doctrine of limited war under high-tech conditions and active defence. Notwithstanding its evolving process of professionalization, the PLA retains its role as the guardian of the party-state.

Taiwan and Hong Kong

Taiwan was historically a somewhat remote and neglected part of China until it was ceded to Japan in 1895 and developed as a colony. Following the end of the Pacific War and against the background of their impending defeat by PLA forces, the Chinese nationalists retreated to the island and proceeded to establish their rule. The Kuomintang ruled Taiwan in an authoritarian manner until a political reform process was set in train in the 1980s. As one of the original four Asian 'tiger economies', Taiwan has for some years now enjoyed the status as a major trading state which successfully borrowed and adapted Japan's model of economic development for its own purposes. Notably, Taiwan was one of the first authoritarian states to initiate a process of political reform that culminated in the first direct 'presidential elections' in 1996. With the government in Beijing being hostile to any moves towards Taiwanese independence and suspicious about the development of a distinctive Taiwanese identity, along with the consolidation of Taiwanese democracy, cross-Strait developments are of crucial significance to the future of the island and the region.

Hong Kong also emerged as one of the four 'Asian tigers'. Economic interaction with mainland China developed on a massive scale with the onset of economic reforms in the PRC (such that almost the entire Pearl River delta now constitutes virtually one continuous urban-industrial complex). The 1984 Joint Declaration between London and Beijing paved the way to the transfer of sovereignty over Hong Kong to Beijing under the 'one country, two systems' formula. The actual hand-over, but not the run-up to the transfer of sovereignty in 1997, proceeded smoothly (Patten 1999). While the record of 'one country, two systems' has been relatively impressive in so far as Beijing has largely desisted from moves that would be incompatible with its commitments under the Basic Law, some questions about the extent of the territory's autonomy have nevertheless arisen. These have, among other, centred on a decision of the Court of Final Appeal that would have granted the right of abode in Hong Kong to more than 1.6 million mainland residents. In the event, the decision was overturned when the NPC Standing Committee re-interpreted the relevant article of the Basic Law. Other challenges have arisen in connection with the freedom of the press and the activities in Hong Kong of the Falungong sect. Significantly, the elections in September 2000 to the Legislative Council produced a strong swell of support for the leading pro-China party, the Democratic Alliance for the Betterment of Hong Kong. This reflected the abiding concern of the majority of voters in the territory with the latter's economic prospects and future living standards. Following the sobering economic decline in the wake of the Asian financial crisis, the executive-led government around Chief Executive, Tung Chee Hwa, has sought to turn the Hong Kong Special Administrative Region (HKSAR) into a 'knowledge-based and economy-led society' building on its 'four advantages'. These are identified as the propinquity to the mainland, the unique mix of Chinese and Western cultures, Hong Kong's tradition as a liberal and open society, and its highly developed institutions.

Overall, then, the economies, societies and polities of China, Taiwan, and Hong Kong have seen remarkable change since the end of the Pacific War. The patterns of economic advance and consequent social and political change have moved ahead ever more rapidly in the years following the initiation of the reform process in China. It is likely that change will continue to unfold as China integrates more deeply into the regionalized and internationalized global system. The chapters in this collection will focus, in the main, on the People's Republic of China and will consider the economic, social, political and strategic dynamics which are driving change within China at the start of the new millennium.

The contributors to this volume

The chapters in the volume are organized thematically. They focus, first, on economic change; second, on social and political change; and, third, on Beijing's evolving external relations. The opening section comprises six papers. These deal with core aspects of China's economic situation: financial sector reforms, reform of the foreign exchange and trade regimes (the key to linkages with regional and global systems); the continuing reform of state-owned enterprises, and approaches to address problems related to regional disparities in economic development.

David Dickinson and Zhang Zhichao deal, respectively, with changes in monetary policy and exchange rate policy. In the context of a process of domestic marketization which is paralleled by a strong international drive towards a similar implied end-point (all the talk about globalization), an economically rational financial system is a necessary condition of further successful advance. One might wish to interrogate the notion of 'rational' but, for the present, we might merely note that the powerful within the global system set the rules and at the present time the relevant powerful actors are those western countries, particularly the United States. It is western models of financial systems which are in the ascendant and to which the Chinese authorities must perforce look.

Dickinson considers the overall reform process within China and notes that substantive reforms – to industry, trade and so on – were the initial focus, with financial reforms apparently rather neglected. In the past the government has asserted strong control over the financial sector. However, in the context of advancing marketization such a solution to the problem of assembling an appropriate financial architecture raises questions for professional economists in Europe or America. In particular the question is whether such direct government control of the financial sector is likely to achieve optimal efficient solutions. Dickinson notes that in the 1980s and 1990s a government bond market has grown and non-bank financial institutions are developing. The issue of control of the financial markets is thus important and market oriented mechanisms need to be established (with the government retreating to a regulatory role). The problems for policy makers are difficult. It is not merely a matter of moving towards an independent central bank (which is not likely to happen in the near future), with the associated task of controlling a market-based financial system, but the sector of private commercial banking must also be developed. The technical problems are severe and are compounded by the practical (political) problems of disentangling the large state-owned enterprise (SOE) from the state which is presently simply rolling over commercially unviable debt. Dickinson notes that these issues are under-researched and suggests that, for the present, given the risks of instability, that reform be undertaken slowly.

In the subsequent chapter Zhang Zhichao notes the 'unfailing orientation' of Chinese leaders towards allowing ever more, but still limited room for market forces in the country's foreign exchange system. He traces the evolution of that system from the days when the State Planning Commission formulated an annual foreign exchange plan with a view to matching the foreign exchange income to import needs. He also shows how problems of chronic overvaluation then led to the adoption of an Internal Rate for Trade Settlements, as a form of selective devaluation, followed by the devaluation of the official rate. This was followed by a gradual liberalization of access to foreign exchange through the swap market that emerged with foreign exchange retention schemes. Zhang shows how in the swap market domestic units could sell notional foreign exchange quotas first to banks, and then among other parties. He explains that the swap market has served different uses, but also entailed a multiple exchange rate regime that became associated with rent-seeking activity and corruption. Zhang recounts how chaos on the swap market in the early 1990s, as well as capital flight and widespread currency substitution led the PRC government to 'full foreign exchange surrendering with convertibility on current account'. This entailed the unification of the dual exchange rate and the adoption of a managed floating rate based on market supply and demand, as well as the establishment of an inter-bank foreign exchange market (among others). Zhang explains that the latter remains subject to government intervention and that the uses of foreign exchange control are now effectively covered by trade restrictions. Zhang, in view of the recent Asian Financial Crisis, sees only a likelihood of 'conditional convertibility on the capital account' for some time.

The issues of monetary and foreign exchange rate policy lead into the topic dealt with by Tong Jiadong, namely the foreign trade regime. Tong begins by arguing that the economy used to be centered upon the SOEs and that enterprises were not encouraged to act on their own initiative. This being the case, foreign trade did not figure very highly in policy debates. However, the issue has become steadily more important, and Tong notes three phases: (i) 1979–87, when there was some deregulation of SOEs; (ii) 1988–90, when bonus payments were related to value/volume of production; and (iii) 1991 to the present day, when the policy focus moved towards the idea of encouraging markets and private businesses. In other words as the Chinese economy has been marketized, the role of foreign trade has begun to look more like the pattern found in other capitalist countries. Tong points out that enterprises trade and that the value of trade has grown dramatically, from US$24 billion in 1978 to US$360 billion recently, with average growth rate in recent years of some 15 per cent. The growth has, as might be expected, generated certain problems, in particular as new private firms advance and engage in trade there is less of a role for the SOEs, whose future looks increasingly problematical. The future is likely to hold further awkward problems, in particular the further integration within the global trading system will require the dismantling of protection mechanisms for Chinese firms (and once again the issue of reforming the SOEs is raised).

Peter Preston and Xing Aifen consider directly the situation of the SOEs. The development of these production units is considered, as is their distinctive character as centres of production, social and welfare provision and consumption. The SOEs constitute a large part of the more traditional Chinese industries and their role in the emerging new economy is not too obvious. Indeed, they stand in need of extensive reform, to their technological bases, their product ranges, their marketplaces and, most awkwardly, to their mode of operations. Any reform of the SOE sector will need a parallel process of employment creation and social welfare reform. It is evident that their reform is technically difficult, economically urgent and socially and politically sensitive.

One of the byproducts of the marketization programme thus far achieved is an increase in inequality, both as between social classes and between different regions of the country. Nancy Chen pursues these issues in the final analytical paper devoted to the changing Chinese economy. Chen notes that the Chinese economy has been run as a socialist planned economy for some fifty years and that there has long been talk of the spatial distribution of economic growth and its benefits within the country. The market reforms inaugurated by Deng Xiaoping involved the encouragement of foreign direct investment (FDI) and development of coastal Special Economic Zones (SEZs) and later the opening up of fourteen coastal cities. The result is well known, rapid dramatic economic growth. The problems are also known and the familiar disbenefits of rapid growth have been in evidence. However, a particularly resonant problem has arisen, namely the regional mal-distribution of FDI and the related mal-distribution of the experience of economic growth. The coastal areas are still advancing, whilst the inland western areas are still lagging behind. There is now an active debate amongst policy makers about how to deal with these regional disparities. It is clear that the spatial distribution of economic advance will be a key issue in the upcoming period of Chinese economic reform and development.

The dynamism of the economy generates a wide spread of social and political consequences. It is to the social and political consequences of these changes with which the second part of this text is concerned. Chapters focus on social welfare reform, the implications of the Internet, the implications of the March 2000 elections in Taiwan for unification of the mainland and Taiwan, the prospects of rational authoritarianism in the PRC and the discursive construction of a revitalized high-tech Greater China.

Guan Xinping considers the pressing issue of social welfare reform. The state has had a central role in organizing the provision of welfare, typically through the workplace unit. However, with the reform programme in the economy the provision of welfare has also been subject to wide-ranging changes, both in the philosophy and manner of provision. In terms of provisions and vehicles for these provisions a distinction can be drawn between urban and rural areas. In urban areas, the state now looks to provide a minimum level of welfare, increasingly leaving its citizens to pay for more and more forms of welfare provision. There are new bodies involved in delivering welfare, local organizations, NGOs, and, for some matters, the market is used. In rural areas, in contrast, there is arguably more continuity with the old workplace-centered system, fewer provisions and a greater role for private activity. Guan points out that these changes reflect a shifting understanding of welfare, where there is a shift away from family and enterprise in pursuit of universal coverage towards a reliance on the wider social sphere coupled to a much greater selectivity in state distribution. The goals too are changing, away from socialism and justice towards efficiency, cost reduction and stability. It is clearly a difficult task to engineer, and it is likely, notes Guan, to become more awkward in the future as China endeavours to translate into effective practice promises made in the context of WTO accession.

Gudrun Wacker argues that the Chinese government's attitude toward the internet has oscillated between explicit support and political mistrust, with the latter feeding on the perception that the internet could be a threat to political stability and to the Party's monopoly of power. Accordingly, the government has sought to encourage the use of the Internet while at the same time seeking to control this use. Support for the development of the internet has been given because leaders see the technological and IT revolution as underpinning the PRC's future comprehensive power, and, as such, as vital for the country's future economic development. In putting forward this argument, Wacker shows how the number of users of the Internet (in absolute numbers) has soared within only a few years, making it one of the top 15 countries in terms of Internet usage. She also shows how creating an environment for the internet has involved processes of reorganization and streamlining on the ministerial level and how the telecommunications infrastructure as well as the current Internet networks reflect the competing and often conflicting interests inherited from the former bureaucratic structures. Wacker examines in considerable depth the constantly changing set of Internet rules that aim at eradicating unwelcome information spread over the Internet, and protecting traditional news media from unwelcome competition. She cautions against the widely held belief that the popularity of the Internet and its increasingly widespread use in China make for a persuasive argument of 'convergence' with the West.

Christopher Hughes analyses the challenges and opportunities for cross-Strait unification in the aftermath of the victory of Chen Shui-bian of the Democratic Progressive Party (DPP) in the March 2000 election. Hughes shows how Chen Shui-bian has gradually re-assessed the DPP's China policy. Crucially, he argues that Chen has already taken the latter beyond the party's longstanding insistence on a referendum and declaration of independence toward embracing the status quo of 'no independence, no unification' in view of the various constraints that impinge on Taiwan's policy toward the mainland. These constraints are constitutional, a limited political support base and the likely need to respond to pressure by disaffected party members. Ultimately, Hughes is cautiously optimistic that Taiwan's democracy is not antithetical to future unification.

Zhao Chenggen considers the situation of the People's Republic and suggests that the state's affirmation of the goal of socialism is now little more than a routinely affirmed official ideological truth as it does not animate government policy. Zhao argues that Deng's reforms, which have been oriented to the marketization of the economy, are slowly impacting upon the Chinese political system. He demonstrates how the appeal of old

Marxist categories (such as class struggle) and goals (such as equality and social advance) has in practice long given way to a concern for rational bureaucratic activity. Zhao suggests that the Chinese authoritarian state has been institutionalized, that is, routinized. A concern for the 'rational' administration of the economy, society and polity, Zhao argues, is increasingly evident. After detailing the many political and institutional reforms, Zhao speculates that in the very long run China may well become a democracy in the usual sense.

It is, finally, to the dynamics of the wider system, or at least to one manner in which these might be construed, that Ngai-Ling Sum turns in a piece which looks at the siliconization of Greater China. Sum argues that the sphere of Greater China (in particular Shenzhen, Taiwan and Hong Kong) escaped some of the worst problems of the Asian financial crisis. There were some short term responses – measures to control and/or reassure the local financial, share and property markets and some ameliorative activity for some firms – and thereafter there was a response oriented to the longer term, cast in terms of radically upgrading local economies through the establishment of novel high-tech industries and operations. Sum details the broad enthusiasm for high-tech which was evident throughout the region in the late 1990s amongst entrepreneurs, policy makers, politicians and ordinary citizens. The whole complex of responses, Sum argues, amount to the attempt to articulate and implant a new discursive construct, a siliconized Greater China. As to the future, Sum, speculates that we may see the emergence of counter-discourses, but what is clear is that the siliconization strategy of Greater China has involved changing identities and governance mechanisms.

The next section, comprising four chapters, focuses on some of the core bilateral relationships of the People's Republic. The first explores the dynamics and issues underlying Sino-U.S. Relations. Jürgen Haacke argues that by the end of 2000, ties between Beijing and Washington had improved somewhat since reaching a nadir after NATO's bombing of the Chinese Embassy in Belgrade. However, he argues that at a fundamental level, relations between the elites of both countries are characterized by instability and uneasiness. This is illustrated with reference to divergent views of the future regional security architecture in East Asia, the Taiwan issue, and the possible deployment of National Missile Defence/Theatre Missile Defence. Haacke argues that the PRC's dependence on U.S. market access, capital and technology is likely to provide something of a floor in bilateral relations. However, he suggests that this dependence notwithstanding, friction in the economic dimension should be expected and future conflict will not necessarily be averted.

Caroline Rose examines whether Sino-Japanese relations constitute a 'weak link' in the new strategic triangle formed by the United States, Japan and the People's Republic of China. She argues that bilateral ties between

Beijing and Tokyo are imbued with an underlying stability, irrespective of periodic problems. Rose thus distances herself from the argument that either history *per se* or security issues that originate from mutual images based on historical experiences pose a significant obstacle to stable relations between the PRC and Japan. Indeed, in contrast to Sino-American relations, Rose notes that there are no irreconcilable differences between Tokyo and Beijing. She suggests that bilateral co-operation at various levels will further improve, allowing both sides to move forward and to leave the history issue behind them, thereby necessitating a re-assessment of the Sino-Japanese axis within the new strategic triangle.

Jürgen Haacke then explores developments in China–ASEAN relations in the aftermath of the Asian Financial Crisis. He argues that the PRC has sought to give ties with ASEAN as well as individual member states a boost in the context of the evolving triangular relationship among Beijing, Washington and Tokyo. Haacke illustrates the argument, inter alia, by providing a textual analysis of the joint statements that China signed or issued with all ASEAN member states from 1999 to 2000. He suggests that the joint statements signed, for instance, between Beijing and Bangkok or Beijing and Jakarta do reflect attempts to develop deeper or closer relations, expressed in terms of improvements in the economic, political and to some extent security dimension of bilateral ties. However, he cautions against interpreting the joint statements as heralding a major shift in the general strategic orientation of Southeast Asian countries at this point in time. Indeed, Haacke argues that regardless of the many interests shared by China and ASEAN states, differences between them remain. This argument is substantiated with reference to issues affecting China–ASEAN co-operation in the context of the so-called ASEAN plus Three-process and, if only very briefly, in relation to the South China Sea issue.

Adopting a different approach, the final piece of this section by Paul Lim attempts to examine the politics underlying developments in the relationship between the European Union and the People's Republic. Lim's argument is that the European states, notwithstanding their political discourse, are particularly interested in reaching a higher plane of economic co-operation with China, often at the expense of human rights and other political considerations. Lim shows that Chinese leaders have been relatively forthcoming in meeting Europe's economic interests. His account traces the complex politics of the EU–China relationship from its earliest days of trade agreements in the 1970s through to the deepening relationship of today.

Conclusion: an agenda for the new millennium

With a large and growing economy and a leadership dedicated both to domestic reform and the further integration into international society and the world economy, China is facing important challenges at the local, regional and international levels. There is no doubt that these challenges require examination and evaluation. While touching on an array of issues, and at the same time contributing to a dialogue across academic disciplines, this volume is necessarily a limited endeavour. Nevertheless, it is our hope that the chapters collected here will go some small way towards both illuminating the core dynamics which are driving change within China, and clarifying the key issues which are likely to concern scholars, policy analysts and political agents in the opening years of the new millennium.

Note

1 The first two so-called 'thought liberations' (*sixiang jiefang*) are associated with Deng Xiaoping. The first one was Deng Xiaoping's 'practice is the sole criterion of truth' slogan, which countered the slogan of the 'two whatevers' popularized by Hua Guofeng. The latter had read: 'Whatever decisions that Chairman Mao had made, we resolutely defend; whatever directives that Chairman Mao had issued, we forever follow.' The second thought liberation was 'achieved' by invoking the so-called 'three favourables' (*san ge youliyu*). The 'three favourables' constituted a set of criteria by which it would be possible to judge whether economic reform measures should be adopted or not. Whether or not an economic reform measure was favourable, Deng argued, depended on it (1) developing production, (2) enhancing the country's state power, and (3) improving living standards. By asking these questions Deng had sought to detract attention from the question of whether proposed economic reforms were 'surnamed capitalist or socialist'. See Lau (1999) and Chen (1999).

Bibliography

Anderson, R.J., Hughes, J.A., and Sharrock, W.W. 1986 *Philosophy and the Human Sciences*, London: Croom Helm.

Baum, R. 1994 *Burying Mao: Chinese Politics in the Age of Deng Xiaoping*, Princeton, NJ: Princeton University Press.

Bernstein, R. 1976 *The Restructuring of Social and Political Theory*, London: Methuen.

Bryant, C. 1985 *Positivism in Social Theory and Research*, London: Macmillan.

Chen Feng 1999 'An Unfinished Battle in China: The Leftist Criticism of the Reform and the Third Thought Emancipation', *The China Quarterly* 158: 430–446.

Clammer, J. 1997 *Contemporary Urban Japan: A Sociology of Consumption*, Oxford: Blackwell.

Fay, B. 1996 *Contemporary Philosophy of Science*, Oxford: Blackwell.

Gellner, E. 1964 *Thought and Change*, London: Weidenfeld.

Habermas, J. 1989 *The Structural Transformation of the Public Sphere*, Cambridge: Polity.

Halliday, F. 2001 *The World at 2000: Perils and Promises*, Basingstoke: Palgrave.

Hollis, M. and Smith, S. 1991 *Explaining and Understanding in International Relations*, Oxford: Clarendon Press.

Holub, R. 1991 *Jürgen Habermas: Critic in the Public Sphere*, London: Routledge.

Lau, Raymond W.K. 1999 'Left and Right in China's Economic Reform in the 1990s and the Facade of the Third Thought Liberation', *The Pacific Review* 12(1): 79–102.

Patten, C. 1999 *East and West*, London: Pan.

Potter, P. 1999 'The Chinese Legal System: Continuing Commitment to the Primacy of State Power', *The China Quarterly* 159: 673–683.

Preston, P.W. 1996 *Development Theory*, Oxford: Blackwell.

Preston, P.W. 1998 *Pacific Asia in the Global System*, Oxford: Blackwell.

Robison, R. and Goodman, D. (eds) 1996 *The New Rich in Asia: Mobile Phones, McDonalds and Middle-Class Revolution*, London: Routledge.

Saich, Tony 2000 'Negotiating the State: The Development of Social Organizations in China', *The China Quarterly* 161: 124–141.

Schell, Orville and Shambaugh, David (eds) 1999 *The China Reader: The Reform Era*, New York: Vintage.

Skinner, Q. (ed.) 1990 *The Return of Grand Theory in the Human Sciences*, Cambridge: Canto.

Sztompa, P. 1993 *The Sociology of Social Change*, Oxford: Blackwell.

Yahuda, M. 1995 *Hong Kong: China's Challenge*, London: Routledge.

China: Economic and Regional Change

Chapter 2

Monetary Policy and Structural Changes in the Financial Sector in China

David Dickinson

Introduction

Since 1979, China has undergone an economic transformation which has seen double digit annual rates of growth in output and relatively stable (if somewhat high) inflation. The gradualist process of economic reform which China has adopted has been extremely successful and has led to favourable comparisons with big bang transitions as practiced by, particularly, Russia (see for example, Chen (1992), Gelb (1994), McMillan and Naughton (1992), Sachs and Woo (1994)). Whether 'big bang' or gradualism is better is not something which concerns us in this chapter. However the process of gradualism has meant that reform of certain sectors of the economy (especially agriculture) and the creation of private incentives across the economy to encourage increased output, have been a priority, whilst reform of state-owned enterprises and the banking system has been persistently delayed. Hence there is still a considerable amount of work to be done in resolving the problems of state-owned enterprises and reforming the banking system and developing a broad-based financial system. Indeed some authors (see Lardy, 1998) argue that the reform of the financial sector is the next great challenge for China's policy-makers. The reasons why this reform has been delayed are very clear. The financial sector lies at the heart of the support for the institutions which are the surviving element of the old 'planned' economy, the state-owned enterprises (SOEs). The need to reform this sector of the economy has been a politically difficult issue, not only for ideological reasons but because many of the poorer regions of the country rely on the old SOE industries for employment and social support. As a result the financial sector (i.e. the banks) has been required to channel sufficient funds to keep these enterprises afloat. Therefore a consequence of gradualism has been to protect these industries and a related effect has been to delay financial sector reform. However, there now appears to be a general view emerging among policy makers in China that reform is necessary, spurred on by the increasing integration of China's economy into the global economic system, as exemplified by Beijing's WTO accession.

Given that change is going to take place, this chapter considers how the process of financial sector and state-owned enterprise reform, and the consequent development of the financial sector will have an impact on the operation of monetary policy in China. It is clear that such changes are going to make monetary policy difficult to operate and for targets of monetary policy to be achieved. The argument which we pursue in this chapter focuses on the need for the monetary policy authority to be able to conduct policy in a flexible way to ensure that the objectives of monetary policy are met. But flexibility brings with it problems of credibility. If the monetary policy maker wishes to use monetary policy instruments to achieve both output and inflation goals, in an environment where monetary policy can be used to bring short-term output and employment stability, there will be an inflation bias which makes the equilibrium rate of inflation greater than is optimal from the policy maker's perspective.[1] Various mechanisms can be used to overcome this problem including the decision to make the central bank independent (Walsh 1998). In interpreting these ideas in the case of China we will suggest that the problems for policy conflict are substantial. Hence we propose that the only way for China to smoothly adjust to the challenges faced by reform of the financial sector is to develop policy-making structures which are adaptable but which do not suffer from the lack of credibility which is often seen to arise when policy objectives are in conflict with each other.

The chapter is divided into four sections. Firstly we discuss what monetary policy should do and how conflicting objectives can create a credibility problem which can hinder the achievement of low rates of inflation. In section two we review the reform process in China so far and discuss how policy has been directed towards the creation of an efficient and broad-based financial system. In section three we present a discussion of China's monetary policy operation, while in section four we consider the challenges facing monetary policy makers in the future in China. A final section provides a short summary of the main ideas of the chapter and its conclusions.

What should monetary policy makers do?

In the long run, money determines the general price level. Technically the level of aggregate demand in the economy is determined by real money balances. In the long run, the level of aggregate demand should be at the level consistent with equilibrium in the real economy and hence changes in nominal money must create changes in the general price level to ensure that this condition is satisfied. When we put this reasoning into a framework of changing variables then we have the famous proposition that excessive growth in the money supply will generate inflation. Since inflation creates distortions in the economy (at least when it is high) the long run objective of monetary policy should be the maintenance of low or even zero inflation.

However, in the short run, when the economy is subject to price rigidities, changes in nominal money can have real effects. The key aspect here is whether the monetary change is expected or not. If it is correctly forecast then it will be incorporated into price setting behaviour and hence will not disturb the economy from its long run equilibrium. However if it is unexpected then changes in nominal money will not cause changes in prices which fully reflect the maintenance of long run equilibrium. As a result, real money balances, aggregate demand and the real economy will adjust in the short run. For example, an unexpected short run increase in nominal money will cause output and prices to increase in the short run and then prices will rise in the longer term as expectations adjust and output will fall back. We should therefore observe a positive relationship between observed output and inflation. This is exactly what has been observed in China (see Figure 1).[2]

A by-product of this reasoning is that monetary policy makers can use their ability to create surprise monetary growth to stabilise the economy. Suppose that the economy has been subject to a sudden fall in aggregate demand. Monetary policy can react by creating a positive money supply surprise which will counteract the effects of the fall in aggregate demand and hence push the economy back close to its long run equilibrium. Of course, in order to operate such a policy successfully, there are a number of requirements for accurate and timely information which it is not obvious will be met but we shall assume that such requirements are met. In this case it would seem that monetary policy has two tasks, one to keep the price level stable in the long run while using monetary surprises in the short run to counteract the negative effects of shocks.

However such a policy response may not be feasible. The argument for this observation is as follows. Suppose that monetary policy makers have a long-term commitment to (say) zero inflation which economic agents believe. Hence they will expect the rate of inflation to be zero. But policy makers may also be known to have a predilection to pushing output above its long run equilibrium (for example because they are politicians and hence can increase their chances of staying in power). They will therefore have an incentive to create surprise inflation so as to stimulate output. The rest of the economy knows that this is the optimal response of the policy maker to expectation of zero inflation and hence they will increase their forecasts of inflation to a level such that it is not in the interests of the policy maker to push inflation higher (because although they like output above its long run level they dislike even more high rates of inflation). The result is an inflation bias because a commitment to a zero inflation policy is not credible. Such reasoning has been at the root of the trend towards making central banks (at least, operationally) independent of the government with a single responsibility to achieve a low rate of inflation.[3]

We can summarise that whilst it would be optimal to have policy flexibility, the need to make the commitment to low inflation credible removes any room for manoeuvre which policy makers would like to have to respond to shocks which hit the economy. In order to see what these arguments imply for China as it moves down its road to full economic reform we present, in the next section, a brief overview of what reforms have taken place to this time and then, in section three, go on to discuss in detail the current operation of monetary policy and analyse what are its effects on the real economy. We will then be in a position to examine the monetary policy dilemmas which China faces and hence provide recommendations as to how it should plan to operate monetary policy in the face of the future structural changes which are going to hit the financial system.

A brief review of economic reform in China

The first moves towards introducing market discipline into resource allocation can be identified in policy introduced in 1979. At this time, the agriculture sector represented the predominant employer with over 80% of the population involved. The collective farm was the main form of industrial organisation. The characteristics of a planned economy, five-year plans financed by a central bank within a monobanking system, for example, were also present.

In the period 1979–1984, a number of key policy changes provided impetus to a gradual process of economic change. These related to the agricultural sector and were designed to give farmers the opportunity to escape the rigours of the planned system. Allowing farmers to take control over their land through leasing gave them the incentives to create surpluses and assisted in the development of free-markets in food. Relaxation of foreign trade also permitted the beginning of the integration of the Chinese economy into the world economy. The creation of special economic zones, designed to attract foreign direct investment, was the third major plank of the reform process.

In 1984 to 1987 the next stage of reforms concentrated on the industrial and financial sectors. Much greater autonomy was given to the managers of state owned enterprises, with encouragement to the creation of a free market integrated with the state-owned sector of the economy (the estimate of the share of the state sector in total output is now less than 50% and continuing to decline). In the financial sector, there was a major overhaul of the banking system which involved the break-up of the monobank to create a commercial banking network and a central bank. The new commercial banking system involved the creation of four 'specialised banks' which became the main instruments of policy for planning purposes – they formed the bulk of the new banking sector with over 80% of deposits. In addition, there were a number of comprehensive banks formed which were joint-stock companies, owned in varying proportions by central, provincial and local governments and by state-owned enterprises. These banks were to act with profit in mind and had no recourse to the central bank to cover their losses (unlike the specialised banks). The central bank was given responsibility for managing monetary policy and controlling the activities of the financial sector. In 1987 there was the creation of the first non state-owned bank, Shanghai's Bank of Communications, formed through the issue of share capital. Recent developments have meant that four of the 'commercial banks' have over 130,000 branches, with other regional banks and rural and urban cooperatives (over 60,000 branches) forming the basis of a market-led commercial banking system. In addition, there was the re-establishment of stock markets, with the expected burst of publicity, and markets such as insurance were opened to foreign companies.

In 1993, there were a series of financial reforms which were designed to commercialise the banking sector further.[4] In the spirit of gradualism these have taken a long time to come to fruition, reflecting, it can be argued, the political difficulties of facing up to reform of the state-owned enterprises. The proposed reforms of the financial sector represented an attempt to separate the policy lending (emanating from the state plan) and the commercial lending which banks would wish to undertake for normal profit-making purposes. The specialised banks were to become commercial banks while policy loans would be separately administered (using three policy banks, the State Development Bank, the Agricultural Development Bank of China and the Import and Export Bank of China). There was also attention paid to the development of a more competitive banking system with encouragement given to the creation of other commercial banks and to the development of non-bank financial intermediaries. There is a commitment to create fully-functioning money markets, starting with the market for short-term bills and moving onto longer-term assets (through an inter-bank market). Further development of the securities market was to be encouraged by expansion of the treasury bond market and the Central Bank will be able to initiate open market operations through this market. The responsibilities of the People's Bank of China (PBC) were to be refined to (i) preserving the stability of the RMB and (ii) ensuring proper supervision of the banking system. The latter objective will be facilitated by appropriate legal reform. The former will be achieved by the targeting of monetary aggregates and the use of indirect monetary instruments – in particular interest rates, the liberalisation of which is therefore a key part of the new policy.

The overall economic environment showed a remarkably successful response to the reforms which were introduced. Figure 2, in the appendix, shows the path of output and inflation from 1980–99. Economic growth was spectacular and whilst there have been periods when overheating has been obvious and inflation has been a problem this has not disturbed the overall pattern of relative macroeconomic stability accompanied by high economic growth. Whether this can be sustained is a crucial question. In recent periods there has been evidence that the economy is starting to run out of control, experiencing periods of inflation and deflation and indeed there appears to be some increasing uncertainty about the introduction of further reforms (for example, those related to China's membership of the WTO).

Looking to the future, progress on the financial sector has been undoubtedly slow. One particular development, of potential value in the reform of the financial system, is membership of the WTO, which should provide an impetus to the entry of foreign competition into the banking and other sectors. However in doing so it is likely to create policy dilemmas. Firstly, foreign banks entering a new market where domestic expertise is at a low level, typically will both improve the overall efficiency of the sector while at the same time picking up the most profitable segments of the market for themselves. It should be noted that this is of positive benefit to consumers of financial services and to the economy as a whole if, as is very likely, economic growth increases. Hence, whilst there are arguments for delaying entry of foreign banks, or limiting their ability to grab market share, on balance there seems no reason to protect the domestic industry once they are fully commercialised.[5]

Beyond this, and as the market is further liberalised there will be the need to provide an institutional framework for policy making which will be flexible enough to assist the development of the financial sector. This implies allowing market forces to play their role while ensuring that monetary policy can operate effectively in securing low inflation.[6] Of course this means that the reforms of the SOEs, and the way in which their losses are financed, is crucial. But beyond that it also means that the PBC should be independent of any further political pressure which could jeopardise its ability to credibly secure low inflation. As we shall argue below this has the added benefit of providing the central bank with additional instruments for achieving the aims of monetary policy.

Monetary policy in China

In a developed market economy, monetary policy works through adjustment of liquidity (or its price) in the money markets (which commercial banks use to cover their short-term needs for cash). These liquidity effects have consequences for the level of interest rates generally which impact on aggregate demand (directly on investment and through exchange rates on the trade balance and capital flows).[7] In such an environment it is known that structural change (as brought about, for example, by financial innovation) can make monetary policy difficult to operate when the money stock is used as an intermediate target. This results from instability in the relationship between liquidity in the money market and money stock and between money stock and the final target variable (normally inflation). In the face of such uncertainty, typically monetary policy makers have moved away from targeting the money stock towards using inflation targets directly (or selecting an alternative monetary target such as the exchange rate).

However, despite moves towards creating indirect methods of monetary control of the sort observed in the developed economies, the process of monetary policy operation is still very different in China. A number of authors have looked at this issue, particularly in the context of the use of monetary policy to achieve macroeconomic stability. In reviewing the operation of policy during the first 15 years of the reform process, McKinnon (1994) has argued that China's gradualist reforms were successful because high real growth rates produced large increases in savings. These ensured that there was sufficient growth in bank deposits to finance both government and SOE deficits while at the same time leaving sufficient resources outside of the banking system to finance acquisition of fixed assets in the liberalised sector (Figures 3 and 4 in the appendix show how bank deposits have been growing relative to output while at the same time the investment of state-owned enterprises, both in absolute terms as well as relative to total investment, has been static or declining; such a pattern is consistent with the contention above given that private enterprises obtained very little finance from the state-owned banks). Allsop (1995) also considers the issue of macroeconomic control. He points out that China has periodically, during the reform process, had inflationary periods. However there seems to be a change in the cause of this. Whilst he sees the inflation of 1989/90 as due to supply shortages, he identifies the 1993 inflation as due to asset price inflation. Clearly this may result from structural changes which have taken place in the Chinese economy (we present one possible reason later). He points out that fiscal policy does not offer much opportunity for stabilisation since expenditure has been on a declining trend for the whole of the reform period and is reaching its lower feasible limit.[8] Hence monetary policy takes the burden of ensuring that macroeconomic stability is preserved. Monetary policy involves both interest rate adjustment and restriction on credit.[9] The PBC has direct control over both these policy instruments. Allsop argues that interest rates are raised in order to encourage savings. He then sees the control of investment through the restrictions on credit as crucial to maintaining macroeconomic control (this point is echoed by Hussain and Stern, 1992). Yu (1997) has undertaken formal empirical analysis of the effects of tight monetary policy. He finds that it has had effects on real output but not, paradoxically, fixed investment. Furthermore, whilst he finds that monetary aggregates can predict fixed asset investment, he finds no similar results for credits although total credit does predict industrial output. One of the problems with the Yu analysis is the use of dummy variables to represent a tightening of monetary policy. Further work by Liu and Dickinson (2000) using a similar empirical methodology but deriving monetary policy shocks endogenously, finds an important relationship between bank credit and output. Furthermore they identify a change in behaviour pre- and post-1990 and argue that this is due to the development of the government bond market (specifically treasury bills/bonds). Hence the transmission mechanism of monetary policy may not be the one described above. Bennett and Dixon (1998) propose a model which highlights the importance of the provision of working capital in the credit plan and show that this implies significant deviations from a conventional view of the impact of monetary policy. We shall return to this point later.

One of the problems that the PBC has had to face is that, increasingly, it is unable to control overall financial conditions through operations on the banking sector. The activities of the non-bank financial institutions (NBFIs) have become much more significant. Girardin (1997) considers the way in which NBFIs (e.g. Investment and Trust Corporations, Urban Credit Co-operatives, Rural Credit Co-operatives) have usurped control over the banking sector. De-centralisation of the production and lending decision (to local authorities) has created a situation where central control no longer works effectively. However he suggests that monetary policy is effective in restrictive periods; this is because most new deposits go into state banks (SBs) which are then tightly controlled in their lending. Furthermore direct controls on SOE investment plans have immediate dampening effects on aggregate demand.

We can consider some of the policy responses to the inflationary periods in 1989/90 and 1993 in order to see how the PBC is responding to the problems with monetary policy it has faced. One particular mechanism the monetary authorities used was reserve requirements. This strengthened the PBC's financial power by increasing the leverage of its lending operations. Central bank lending to SBs is part and parcel of the system of directed capital and is aimed at providing state owned banks with the means to finance their loans while providing a mechanism for monetary control.[10] The first type of lending is made annually with maturity from one to two years. The second type is made up of seasonal loans, daily loans, and through the rediscounting of commercial paper. Each bank has access to PBC lending up to some quota which is a function of the projected increase in its deposits and in its credit requirements. For example, the required reserve ratio of both banks and non-bank financial institutions were raised from 12 to 13 percent from 1 September 1988. In 1989, even more strict reserve requirements were adopted. The rate of required reserves on demand and time domestic currency deposits were set uniformly, at 13% in 1994.[11] In the latter part of the 1990s, when the PBC was faced with increasing problems of control over its regional branches (which saw themselves closer to the local governments than to their bosses Beijing) they introduced a re-structuring which was designed to centralise power much more. They re-defined the geographical limits for each regional branch so that they no longer corresponded with the regional and local government and also reduced the number of regional power-bases at the same time.

Hence we see a model of monetary policy operation which focuses very much upon quantities as a target of monetary policy. Interest rates are used to control flows of savings and can be used to encourage greater levels of savings (and hence less consumption) in a period of inflation while investment is controlled through credit restrictions and through direct controls over the state-owned enterprises. However this very rigid system has run into difficulties given the ability of the financial system to find ways of subverting the system. As a consequence the PBC is finding increasingly difficult to maintain a proper monetary discipline with the tools available. But they have shown the ability to adapt to changing circumstances and the reforms proposed in 1993, though still to be implemented, indicate a willingness to move away from the current rigid structure which is inhibiting competition and efficient resource allocation and towards a more market-based system (see Pei (1997) for an interesting discussion of the political economy aspects of the banking reforms in the mid-1990s).

We now return to the issue discussed at the start of this section, namely what exactly is the mechanism through which monetary policy transmits its influence on the overall economy. Clearly monetary policy operates through two main instruments, credit restrictions and interest rates. But a significant part of bank credit is used by SOEs as working capital (60% of planned loans according to World Bank (1996)) and hence credit constraints are very likely to impinge on current operations rather than future investment plans. This contention is supported by empirical analysis in Yu (1997) and Liu and Dickinson (2000). Fixed investment plans may be altered as a result of direct instructions to SOEs (Allsop, 1995) but not as a reaction to monetary tightening. The impact of interest rates seems to be more on levels of savings (which are then channelled through the banking sector) than on levels of investment. Interest rate movements will however impinge on SBs since many of their interest rates are determined by the PBC. Increases in deposit rates without a corresponding increase in lending rates will squeeze the current SBs.[12] In a more market-driven environment this would clearly have an impact upon the activities of the banking system. But the current operation of monetary policy implies that the stance of monetary policy is responsible for the (underpinning the lack of) financial health of SOEs. Hence working capital can be seen to encompass not only the operations of the SOEs but also to fill the financial deficits these enterprises incur. Therefore decline in output in response to tighter monetary conditions results from the SOEs' inability to maintain their levels of operations in the face of a decline in working capital.[13]

Furthermore we have observed that the mechanism through which monetary policy operates changes character as structural changes take place. The linkages between monetary policy actions and financial aggregates and between those financial aggregates and target variables is unstable in the face of institutional changes. Theoretical work by Fung et al. (2000) provides a rationale for this empirical observation. They argue that a rise in government bond funding of the deficit will reduce investment in the state sector since there will be less bank deposits to fund this expenditure. However the decline in state sector output will encourage more private sector investment. Other effects also generate ambiguity, so overall it is not possible to determine the exact effect.

What then are the structural changes which will affect monetary policy in China in the future? Essentially there will be a move from direct to indirect control, based upon the development of short-term money markets. The PBC will have the ability to use its operations in these markets to control interest rates and hence influence the path of aggregate demand. The major changes which will be needed to achieve this reform are (in no particular order):

(a) the development of liquid money markets;
(b) the removal of interest rate controls;
(c) the dropping of the credit plan;
(d) the reform of the state-owned enterprises;
(e) the full commercialisation of the banking system;
(f) proper system of bank regulation.

The first two of these changes will ensure that monetary policy can operate through indirect methods, the next three will mean that monetary policy will operate on aggregate demand whilst the economy as a whole responds in an efficient manner. The final element will provide confidence in a fully liberalised banking system and is crucial given the recent experience of some East Asian economies (S. Korea, Indonesia, Thailand are key examples). Note that capital account liberalisation is not listed as a major change. However when it does occur it will significantly alter the way in which monetary policy operates and we will also consider this in the next section.

Monetary policy and structural change

The analysis of monetary policy in China, contained in section two, has shown that it operates in a very specific way. We have highlighted the structural changes necessary for a more conventional, market-driven, monetary policy to operate in China. In this section we wish to use that discussion to highlight some key ways in which structural change will impact upon monetary policy and hence provide an analysis of appropriate monetary policy strategies for China in the next few years. Our basic presumption is that the PBC will wish to operate monetary policy in such a way as to stabilise the economy while ensuring high growth rates. The question we pose relates to the optimal choice of monetary policy target in the face of structural change.

As discussed in section two the current structure of monetary policy involves: credit controls which operate to influence output through working capital (or via investment); interest rates which are used to encourage savings; while SOEs are subject to periodic cutbacks in their investment plans when the economy is over-heating. The future plans for monetary policy involve a move towards using manipulation of interest rates and stabilization of the economy through the influence on aggregate demand. Let us consider the structural changes which are required in order to move to this indirect system of monetary control.

First we consider the development of mechanisms for the PBC to operate monetary policy through interest rates. In the early stages of financial development the alternatives are rather limited. However it often falls to government short term debt to play the role (see Fry, 1997) and, in this regard, China is developing a treasury bill market. The process of financial sector development is enhanced by increasing use of financial markets by governments to cover for fiscal deficits (see Tables 1 and 2 in the appendix). The mechanism through which monetary policy operates involves using short term financial assets to influence the price of liquidity, either through open market operations or via a re-discount mechanism. The ability of central banks to use such a mechanism to manipulate aggregate demand requires first that demand for the short term liquidity is predictable and relatively stable; secondly that the relationship between interest rates and aggregate demand is also predictable and relatively stable. However it must be questioned whether such a situation is likely to arise. For example, participants in the new money markets are likely to be relatively inexperienced and consequently there may be a lot of speculative activity. Given that the economy has been controlled through direct intervention in bank lending decisions it will take time for bank customers to become used to the new system. There is the possibility of a consumer boom fuelled by borrowing in newly created markets.

Another major plank of monetary policy reform is that of interest rate de-control. Clearly monetary policy in the form outlined above will not work unless short term interest rates can influence the whole structure of interest rates particularly, given the predominance of banks in the financial system, deposit and lending rates. But this requires flexibility of interest rates and, except in exceptional circumstances, giving banks the freedom to set interest rates. But such a change, of itself, will lead to instability in the relationship between money market rates and other interest rates at least in the transition period (for example, banks will have little experience of managing their interest rate structures and are likely to make more mistakes as a result). In addition, if the PBC is not clear in its monetary policy objectives, banks may respond uncertainly to any movements in the money markets. Furthermore, given that banks are so dominant there will be substantial opportunity for them to use their monopoly power to raise interest rates and maintain them at high levels irrespective of the developments in the provision of short term liquidity. Beyond this we also must recognize that interest rate rises could have potentially perverse effects as interest rate rises generate both moral hazard and adverse selection problems (see Fung et. al (2000)).

In order to allow interest rates to impact upon aggregate demand it is crucial that banks can allocate credit in a free and flexible manner. This requires dismantling of the credit plan and a move towards bank determination of their lending decisions. But, as with interest liberalization, banks are unlikely to have the necessary skills, initially, to develop proper mechanisms for assessing the risk of lending and hence setting appropriate risk premiums. Thus we are likely to find instability in the relationship between movements in short term interest rates and aggregate demand. Furthermore, as we have already noted, the vast majority of lending is currently to support the SOEs. This is something which cannot continue in a liberalised environment and will mean that banks are lending to new (private) enterprises or lending to the newly liberalised SOEs who are familiar but who are operating in a new profit-orientated way.

This discussion leads us naturally to consider the impact of SOE reforms on the monetary policy process. That these are a necessary complement to the use of interest rates to manage monetary policy is clear since, without them, a move to indirect monetary policy instruments will generate insolvency among SOEs and hence the SBs themselves. Without reform the SBs would still be expected to support the SOEs and as a result would continue to lend at low interest rates to failing enterprises. Given the crucial role of the banks, a collapse of the financial system would result. At one level it is not absolutely necessary to privatise the SOEs, just to put them onto a sound financial footing (by transferring their indebtedness to central government) and to remove any implicit government guarantee which loans to them are seen to have.[14] But, specially in regard to the second requirement privatization may be necessary since any involvement of government may create moral hazard and resulting losses at both SOEs and SBs. Note however that the process of SOE reform will create instability in the relationship between interest changes and overall macroeconomic activity.

A theme which has arisen a number of times in the discussion above is that beyond the need to reform the SOEs a key aspect of the move to a new market-led system of monetary policy is the commercialization of the banking system. We have already argued that banks may struggle in the early stages of the reform process to set appropriate interest rate and make lending decisions which show a proper regard to the trade-off between risk and return. Requiring banks to pay heed to profitability is important, but control of their risk-taking activities by regulation is also crucial. The development of a proper regulatory regime is relatively straightforward, with lots of experience elsewhere in the world to be drawn upon. However ensuring that banks manage their activities appropriately in the face of the regulatory regime is more difficult. As indicated banks may take excessive risks. But in the face of a tough regulatory regime they may be too risk averse. Hence this may create further instability in predicting the effects of monetary policy on bank behaviour and hence on the aggregate economy.

Overall we can observe that introducing indirect monetary policy instruments is associated with a number of problems in the face of structural changes in the economy and the financial system. This process of reform is going to make monetary policy difficult to operate. One can envisage a situation where interest rates react perversely to policy changes, where credit does not respond appropriately to interest rate changes and that both interest rate and credit changes have uncertain impacts upon aggregate demand and the trade off between real growth and inflation. Hence monetary policy makers will have to adopt an approach to reforms which does not prevent their beneficial effects but which allows them to actively manage the overall levels of credit and hence aggregate demand. They will need to keep a number of different instruments with which to exert overall macroeconomic control. They should prepare to intervene directly, both in terms of price and quantity. Reserve powers to impose credit ceilings, the use of regulatory reserve ratios, and intervening directly in the setting of interest rates will need to be available.

The danger that such a policy framework presents is that it creates the potential for conflict between the objectives faced by the central bank. These conflicts will be particularly acute if there is no clear separation between political and economic policy-making. For example, if the central bank retains powers to curb the lending activities of the banking sector it is a short step to them issuing control over the allocation of that credit, by allowing certain types of lending and imposing controls over other categories. Similarly with the potential for setting interest rates there is the opportunity to manipulate the policy environment in favour of preferred borrowers. We have already observed that China has experienced increasing growth rates while at the same time observing higher rates of inflation while requiring significant recessions in order to bring inflation down (see Figures 1 and 2 in the appendix). Such an environment is consistent with the idea that monetary policy is losing its credibility and that an upward inflation bias will appear over time. This is likely to get worse as a result of the pressures created by financial reform.

Hence there is a strong argument for separating the central bank from the political process, at least at the operational level, in order to ensure that policy conflicts of the type above do not occur. This would make policy-making a much more transparent process and would assist in creating more stability in financial markets as traders became used to the predictable actions of the central bank in pursuit of their objectives. Note that an independent central bank does not have to be one which only cares about inflation. A total abstinence from policy designed to stabilize the economy would certainly deliver a lower rate of average inflation but, as long as the central bank is given the right objectives, there is no reason why it cannot credibly commit to a low average inflation rate while at the same time achieving optimal stabilisation of the real economy.

Conclusions

The arguments presented above suggest that China needs to be bold with its financial sector reforms. However such action will bring problems for monetary policy, particularly in the early stages of the reform process. Structural reform brings with it the danger that monetary control cannot be maintained without adopting a very severe policy stance. Failure to do this will lead to a loss of monetary policy credibility which will impose a higher average rate of inflation on the economy. Almost certainly this implies that there is a greater volatility of output as the central bank is unable to meet any output objectives without threatening its anti-inflation reputation. Hence there is a need to provide the tools so that the central bank can adopt a flexible policy response, to meet output as well as inflation targets. But the access to these policy tools will then create a further credibility problem which will potentially negate their use in achieving low rates of inflation without prejudicing output stability.

To resolve this dilemma a further important aspect of the reform process is to hand the central bank its operational independence. This does not imply that economic policy-making is taken away from the political process since targets (for inflation) can be set by the government and the central bank will need to conduct policy in a transparent manner and can be required to report formally on the success of meeting its objectives to its political masters. However, in such an environment, monetary policy can credibly commit to low inflation while retaining the flexibility to stabilise the economy. This will be particularly important when structural changes make monetary policy particularly difficult to operate.

Of course, it can be argued that the reform process will be stymied by the maintenance of a policy regime (including direct as well as indirect controls) associated closely with an era of planning. This would be an obvious danger if the PBC was seen to be unprepared for the challenges it faces in making monetary policy work in a liberalized financial sector. But, in fact, it has been promoting reforms. Tying its hands by placing too much emphasis on a single monetary policy tool creates the danger that monetary policy will not be able to cope with the instability associated with structural reforms. Such instability is likely to make the reform process less feasible politically. Hence moving too fast by abandoning the old tools of monetary policy may actually hinder the reform process rather than promoting it. Note that it has been quite common for developed economies to use such interventionist weapons in the past as a way of exerting monetary control. Most have been abandoned in the face of increased liberalisation in financial markets but were certainly used extensively on the way towards a liberalised system. In addition, and as China has found, strict control of one part of the financial market generates the incentives to expand in other areas. So these controls must be used carefully and are an additional weapon beyond standard interest rate mechanisms for controlling the expansionary activities of the financial markets. Given that China has yet to embrace the global financial system, such controls are feasible as temporary measures to restore stability. Of course, the final target is to create a domestic financial system which has the ability to compete in the global financial system. Meeting this target will take time but the suggestion of this chapter should ensure that the process is relatively low cost.

Appendix

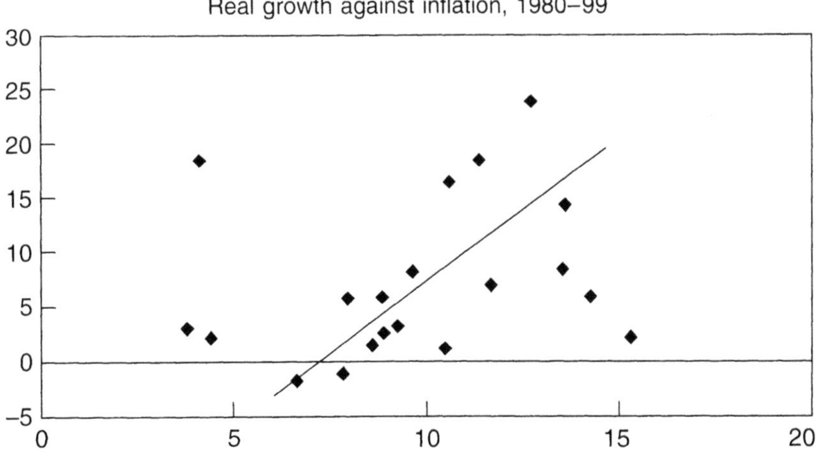

Figure 1 There is an output/inflation trade-off

Source: IMF, *World Economic Outlook*.

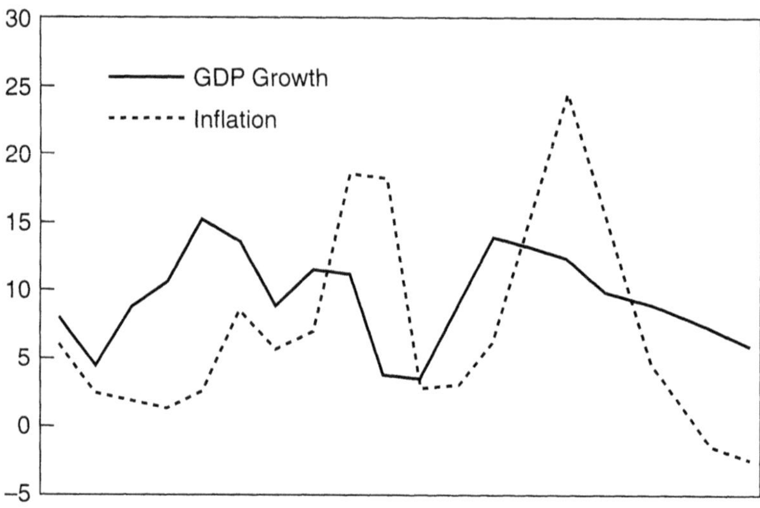

Figure 2 The growth and inflation performance of China, 1980–99

Source: IMF, *World Economic Outlook*.

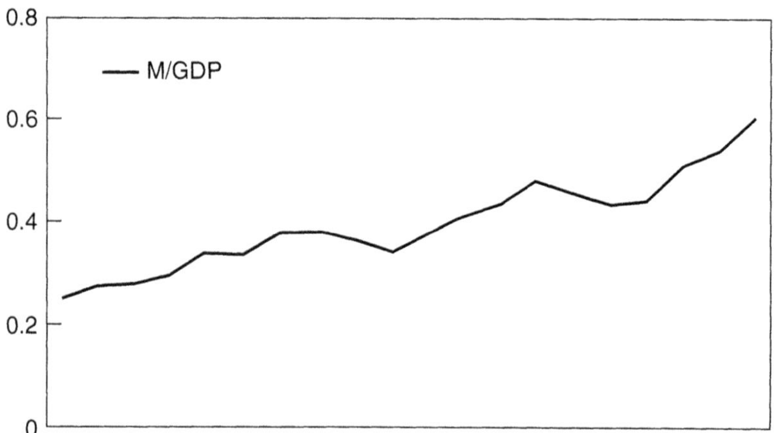

Figure 3 Ratio of narrow money to GDP (bank deposits are the main form of saving), 1980–99

Source: IMF, *International Financial Statistics*.

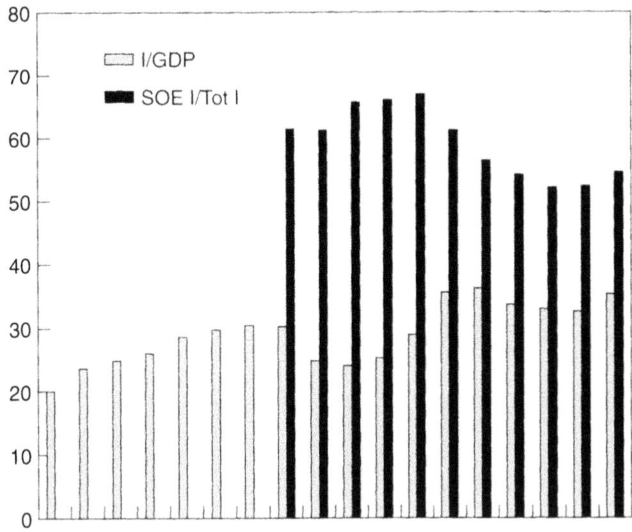

Figure 4 Investment ratios, 1980–97

Source: Datastream.

Table 1 Government expenditure and consumer expenditure in the GDP (1984–96)

Year	Total expenditure	Non-government expenditure	Percent	Government expenditure	Revenue (percent of GNP)
1978	2239.1	1759.1	79	480	
1979	2619.4	2005.4	77	614	
1980	2976.1	2317.1	78	659	
1981	3309.1	2604.1	79	705	
1982	3637.9	2867.9	79	770	
1983	4020.5	3182.5	79	838	
1984	4694.5	3674.5	78	1020	
1985	5773	4589	79	1184	
1986	6542	5175	79	1367	
1987	7451.2	5961.2	80	1490	21.0
1988	9360.1	7633.1	82	1727	18.7
1989	10556.5	8523.5	81	2033	18.4
1990	11365.2	9113.2	80	2252	18.7
1991	13145.9	10315.9	78	2830	17.8
1992	15952.1	12459.8	78	3492.3	17.4
1993	20182.1	15682.4	78	4499.7	16.2
1994	27216.2	21230	78	5986.2	12.2
1995	34529.4	27838.9	81	6690.5	10.7
1996	40171.7	32588.7	81	7583	

Source: *The Financial Outlook*, 1996. *The Almanac of Chinese Banking and Finance*, 1997.

Table 2 Government domestic debt issuance

Issuing year	Gov. domestic debt issuance	T-bill
1981	48.66	48.66
1982	43.83	43.83
1983	41.58	41.58
1984	42.53	42.53
1985	60.61	60.61
1986	62.51	62.51
1987	116.87	62.87
1988	188.77	92.16
1989	223.91	56.07
1990	197.23	93.46
1991	281.25	199.41
1992	460.78	395.64
1993	381.32	314.77
1994	1137.55	1113.93
1995	1510.81	1483.18
1996	2126.04	2092.79

Source: The People's Bank of China, *Quarterly Statistical Bulletin*, Volume VIII, 1993–4.

Notes

1 Figure 1 in the appendix shows that there is a trade-off between output and inflation where higher rates of inflation are associated with higher rates of growth. We discuss the reasons for such a trade-off in detail in later sections.

2 Our later discussion of the real effects of monetary policy in China does not suggest that the reason for the currently observed positive relationship is due to the argument above. However, as China liberalises its economy the mechanism for the positive relationship between output and inflation is likely to be explained in more conventional terms and hence we need to be aware of the policy implications of such liberalisation.

3 Once again this reasoning may not be applicable to China at the moment but certainly will become more appropriate as economic liberalisation continues. Indeed it can be argued that a zero inflation policy is not credible currently because of the benefits to the government of creating surprise inflation so as to reduce the real value of debt held by state-owned enterprises prior to full reform.

4 The reforms were approved (over the summer of 1995) by the National People's Congress to be introduced over a period of time. The aim was to create a properly functioning commercial banking system by the year 2000. However this target has been missed and continuing delays in dealing with state owned enterprise reform threaten development of a proper commercial banking system.

5 The economies of Central and eastern Europe have faced up to this reality and have benefitted from having much of their banking sector in foreign hands. In the case of China there is no reason to suppose that the domestic industry will collapse. Indeed China has the capability to be a significant player in international financial markets.

6 Note that similar considerations apply to the supervision of the financial sector.
7 In addition there may also be a direct credit channel which operates on the investment intentions of bank-dependent borrowers independently of any interest rate effects (e.g. see Mishkin (1995)).
8 The tax system is yet to be reformed.
9 Montes-Negret (1995) reviews China's credit plan and argues that the PBC uses bank credit as an intermediate target. Since the credit plan is underfunded there is always resort to PBC re-lending which allows the authorities to exert control over the level of credit extended. However he also notes that the state-owned banks margins are squeezed by controls over interest rates.
10 As we have already noted the credit plan is underfunded.
11 Beyond adjusting required reserves the PBC also use special required reserves as a way of freezing part of the excess reserves of the SBs.
12 Note the argument of Zou and Sun (1996), based on moral hazard ideas, that banks may choose to keep the lending rates low in order to maintain low risk investment.
13 Note that Fry (1996) argues that the Chinese financial system is being kept afloat by seigniorage revenue but that this cannot continue indefinitely without significant increases in inflation.
14 Note the difficulties created in selected Asian economies by such guarantees (see Krugman, 1998).

Bibliography

Allsop, C., 1995, 'Macroeconomic control and reform in China', *Oxford Review of Economic Policy*, 11(4): 43–53.

Bennett, J. and Dixon, H., 1998, 'Monetary policy and credit in China: a theoretical analysis', [*University of Wales Swansea*], discussion paper, March.

Chen, K., Jefferson, G. and Singh, L., 1992, 'Lessons from China's economic reform', *Journal of Comparative Economics*, 16: 201–25.

Dipchand, C.R., Zhang, Y. and Ma, M., 1994, *The Chinese Financial System*, Westport, CT: Greenwood Press.

Fry, M., 1996, 'Can seigniorage keep China's financial system afloat?', *IFG Working Paper IFGWP–96-09*, University of Birmingham.

Fry, M., 1997, *Money, Interest and Banking in Development*, Baltimore, MD: Johns Hopkins University Press.

Fung, M.K.Y., Ho, W-M. and Lijiang, 2., 2000, 'Stagflationary effects of government bond financing in the transforming Chinese economy: a general equilibrium analysis', *Journal of Development Economics*, 61: 111–35.

Girardin, E., 1997, 'The dilemmas of banking sector reform and credit control in China', *OECD Development Centre*, OECD, Paris.

Hussain, A. and Stern, N., 1991, 'Effective demand, enterprise reforms and public finance in China', *Economic Policy*, April, 142–86.

Krugman, P., 1998, 'What happened to Asia', mimeo, MIT.

Lardy, N., 1998, *China's Unfinished Economic Revolution*, Washington, DC: Brookings Institution.

Liu, J. and Dickinson, D.G., 2000, 'Monetary policy in China: the impact on the real economy in China', *University of Birmingham, Department of Economics Discussion Paper*.

McKinnon, R., 1994, 'Financial growth and macroeconomic stability in China 1978–92: Implications for Russia and other transitional economies', *Journal of Comparative Economics*, 18: 438–69.

McMillan, J. and Naughton, B., 1992, 'How to reform a planned economy: Lessons from China', *Oxford Review of Economic Policy*, 8: 130–43.

Mishkin, F. and others, 1995, 'Symposium on the monetary transmission mechanism', *Journal of Economic Perspectives*, 9: 3–96.

Montes-Negret, F., 1995, 'China's credit plan: An overview', *Oxford Review of Economic Policy*, 11: 25–42.

Pei, M., 1998, 'The political economy of banking reforms in China, 1993–1997', *Journal of Contemporary China*, 7: 321–50.

Sachs, J. and Woo, W.T., 1994, 'Reform in China and Russia', *Economic Policy*, 14: 101–45.

Walsh, C., 1998, *Monetary Theory and Policy*, Cambridge, MA: MIT Press.

World Bank, 1996, *The Chinese Economy: Fighting Inflation, Deepening Reforms*, Washington, DC: World Bank Country Study.

Yu, Q., 1997, 'Economic fluctuation, macro control and monetary policy in the transitional Chinese economy', *Journal of Comparative Economics*, 25: 180–95.

Zou, Liang, and Sun, Laixiang, 1996, 'Interest rate policy and incentives of state-owned enterprises in the transitional China', *Journal of Comparative Economics*, 23: 292–318.

Chapter 3

China's Foreign Exchange Policy in a Time of Change

Zhang Zhichao

Introduction

Foreign exchange reform has been a vital component of China's overall economic reforms. Since the late 1970s, China's foreign exchange system has undergone fundamental reform featuring consistent efforts to introduce market forces into foreign exchange allocation and exchange rate determination while improving the regulatory framework. The reform has shaken up the centralised regime of exchange controls in China and led to solid progress in foreign exchange liberalisation.

China's foreign exchange reform is an extensive enterprise. It encompasses reforms that affect foreign exchange pricing, foreign exchange allocation, currency convertibility, the institutional set-up, and the legal framework. As in other areas of China's economic reform, this reform has proceeded amid chaos yet with an unfailing orientation towards allowing more room for market forces in the foreign exchange system. Many interesting events have taken place during the process, which have passed largely unnoticed in the current literature. Given China's emerging economic power, it is critical to grasp the sweeping changes that have taken place in the Chinese foreign exchange system. Meanwhile, a better understanding of how China's foreign exchange system has evolved will also greatly help gauge the direction of future development in China's foreign exchange policy.

This chapter examines these reforms with special emphasis on how market forces have taken root in the Chinese foreign exchange system. It aims to shed light on the extent of foreign exchange liberalisation in China and the complexity of the reform process. Following this introduction, the second section reviews the pre-reform situation and sets the background against which the major reform events may be explored. The third section deals with China's first move in foreign exchange reform, i.e. the adoption of an internal exchange rate designed to mimic the effect of devaluation with a view to avoiding its possible negative consequences. This experiment brought forward a deeper issue – the necessity of liberalising the allocation of foreign exchange. China's response to this challenge is the theme of section four, where an interesting transition mechanism for the establishment of a free foreign exchange market, i.e. the emergence of the swap market, is examined. Section five discusses the exchange rate issues, including exchange-rate determination and the institutional arrangement thereof. Section five considers the most recent development in China's foreign exchange reform: the introduction of currency convertibility on the current account. The final section concludes the chapter with a general assessment of China's foreign exchange reform.

The bad old days

The starting-point of China's foreign exchange reform was the reign of the central planning system over the whole economy. In the foreign trade sector, the state had a complete monopoly over imports and exports. The function of trade was determined by the need to balance materials. The net import requirement was calculated by adding up import needs of each sector in proportion to the ad hoc planned growth target. Exports were perceived essentially as a means of financing such imports (Lardy 1992). Little room was allowed for price mechanism to serve its allocative function. Before 1978, prices of tradable goods in the domestic market were determined by administrative measures with little regard for international counterparts. The state simply treated the whole foreign trade sector as a single tax unit, leaving the Ministry of Foreign Trade to 'take imports to subsidise exports' within the system of foreign trade corporations. Because many trade corporations handled both imports and exports within a given sector, profits on imported goods were used to offset losses on exports. In consequence, trading corporations generally did not have, and did not need to have, independent financial accounts.

Before 1956, foreign exchange was controlled by the Central Financial and Economic Committee. Foreign exchange income had to be surrendered to the state banks; expenditure was subject to the approval of the People's Bank of China (PBC) and then had to be purchased from designated state foreign exchange banks (fifty-three in total). The foreign exchange distribution policy gave explicit priorities of the central government, industrial sectors and public enterprises over localities, commercial sectors and private enterprises. After 1956, the regime was further centralised with the principle of 'centralised controls and unified transactions'. The state had total monopoly power over the allocation of foreign exchange, the setting of the exchange rate, and related regulations. All foreign exchange business had to be conducted by state banks or non-banks (before 1979, the Bank of China only).

Central to the regime's policy was the annual foreign exchange plan formulated by the State Planning Commission after consultation with the Ministries of Trade and of Finance. It was characterised by the rigid separation of income and expenditure. Not a penny could be spent before it was surrendered to the exchange authority. All income and expenditure transactions had to be kept in separate accounts and were subject to different controls. This severed the last link between imports and exports with respect to foreign exchange.

To central planners, all that mattered was the matching of foreign exchange income to import needs. The planning targets were therefore formulated only in terms of the physical amount of foreign currencies, rather than of efficiency. Consequently, to earn a target amount of foreign exchange, productivity could be, and often was, sacrificed (Lardy 1992).

The plan was mandatory and exchange controls were enforced accordingly. In addition to the imposition of quantity controls, the exchange rate was strictly regulated. The exchange rate of the Chinese currency (Renminbi, RMB) played only an accounting role. Its principal role was to translate foreign trade transactions into domestic currency, and in this sense it served as an accounting device linking foreign trade and the domestic economy (Mah 1972). Economically, the RMB exchange rate was relevant only to non-trade transactions, such as foreign tourism, remittances from overseas Chinese, etc. Changes in the exchange rate could not directly affect the overall balance of trade since trade volumes were already fixed by the plan. While responsibilities for monitoring the exchange rate were vested in the Bank of China, a major change in the RMB rate required a decision of the State Council.

During the pre-reform period, China's exchange rate arrangement evolved through three stages. During 1949–55, China had a managed floating system. From 1955, it operated a fixed exchange rate regime with the RMB exchange rate frozen for almost 17 years. When the world financial system entered the era of general floating currencies in 1973, China pegged the RMB to a basket of international currencies.

The institutional rigidity and total severance from a market relationship inevitably made the RMB rate *outré*. Over time, the RMB rate became grotesquely overvalued. Yet, this was tolerated by the central planners. As an accounting device, the level of the exchange rate did not matter much, since its effect was only to scale up or down proportionately the balance. With imports and exports treated as a single tax unit, exchange rate levels might affect distribution of profits between two sub-items but not the total budget. And in any case, since domestic prices were set arbitrarily, trade profits or losses essentially were a matter of accounting manoeuvre. So overvalued or not, the RMB price was hardly a matter of concern. Rather, an overvalued RMB would make overseas tourists pay dear. In minor cases where foreign agents were allowed to hold accounts in domestic money, RMB's overvaluation meant that they would obtain less hard currency with a given balance in Chinese money.

Devaluation without tears: the experiment with IRTS

As everywhere, chronic overvaluation inevitably discouraged exports and caused import compression. With the launch of economic reforms and the open door policy, it soon became one of the first reform targets. In August 1979, the State Council decided to adopt an Internal Rate for Trade Settlements (IRTS), effective from 1 January 1981.

The driving force behind the scheme was the trade reform. As China began to open its economy in 1979, measures were taken to expand exports by decentralising trade and mobilising provincial initiatives. Some Ministries, local governments and enterprises were consequently granted access to foreign trade.

The practice that used import profits to subsidise exports became inoperative. Many new traders were specialised in either exports or imports and had separate accounts, and the Ministry of Foreign Trade was no longer willing or able to bear financial responsibility for provincial governments and other ministries. As the overvalued RMB rate frustrated export initiatives, pressure mounted for devaluing the unrealistic RMB rate.

A heated policy debate arose as a result. Provincial agents argued strongly that the RMB rate was overvalued since, at the time (1978), the national average cost of earning a unit of foreign exchange was 2.41 yuan/dollar, while the official exchange rate was only 1.6 yuan/dollar. The overvalued RMB meant that almost all exports ran at a loss while imports were extremely profitable. Opponents of the devaluation argued on the basis of a Purchasing Power Parity calculation since Chinese goods were cheaper than Western goods. A comparison between the value of a basket of goods in China and in some Western cities showed that the Chinese currency was undervalued rather than overvalued (Wu and Chen 1992).

The government faced a dilemma: in terms of external competitiveness, there was a manifest need for devaluation but a devaluation would give foreign currency more purchasing power, enhancing its ability to 'exploit' subsidised domestic prices. As a compromise, the government adopted the IRTS scheme under which a special rate was designed for trade settlements while the official rate was retained for non-trade transactions. It was essentially a selective devaluation scheme. Set at 2.80 yuan/dollar, the IRTS was based on the national average cost of earning a unit of foreign exchange plus a mark-up margin of 10–15 percent. The national export cost in 1979 was 2.40 yuan (or 2.65 yuan excluding oil exports) while the official rate was 1.5 yuan/dollar. Thus the IRTS rate represented an 87 percent devaluation of the RMB against the official going rate for merchandise trade.

At first glance, the scheme was not a radical departure from past practice since the old policy regime remained intact. The real significance of the scheme was greater than it appeared. First, the introduction of the IRTS was an acceptance of the role of price mechanisms in trade flows. The aim of the adoption of the IRTS, an internal price, was to provide incentives through price changes in contrast with the former trade-promoting practice which relied only on political persuasion with material bonus. Second, the devaluation embodied in the IRTS was an admission of the undesirability of overvaluation. This implied the removal of an important parameter of the old regime that related political correctness to a strong RMB. Hence, the devaluation through the IRTS scheme was a victory of economic realism over political fantasy.

The scheme's results were mixed. In the first years after its introduction, China's exports grew rapidly, from $18.12 billion in 1980 to $26.14 billion in 1984. Imports in the same period rose from $20.02 to $27.41 billion. In about 1984, however, its usefulness seemed to come to an end, and in 1985 China recorded a huge trade deficit. This was primarily attributable to changes in the macro environment. During the five-year period there was an upsurge of the general price level. At the start of 1984 the overheating of the economy became clearer. The high growth rate of China's GNP of 10.4 percent in 1983 increased to 14.7 percent in 1984 and remained high at 12.8 percent in 1985. The macro imbalance due to overheating overwhelmed any potential positive contribution to the balance of payments that the IRTS scheme might have had.

The managers of the IRTS scheme failed to adjust to the sweeping changes. The rate remained fixed throughout, implying that at best it was appropriate around 1979. In fact, the scheme's misfortune almost started at the beginning. The IRTS was based on the average foreign exchange cost in 1978, but became effective only on 1 January 1981. Even in normal years such a delay would have meant that the rate was already outdated; during the period of the first wave of China's economic reforms its divergence from the export cost became wider. As a result, the IRTS latterly became inadequate for exporters to recover their costs. There was also a flaw in the scheme itself: it was designed on the basis of the dichotomisation of trade and non-trade activities, yet in practice the dividing-line between them cannot be clearly defined. The price differential between the two invited rent-seeking activity and nurtured economic chaos.

Amid this confusion, China began in late 1984 to devalue the official rate towards the IRTS. On 1 January 1985, the official rate dipped to 2.8 yuan/dollar, on a par with the IRTS, which de facto abolished the scheme. Problems remained, however. The experiment with the IRTS highlighted the importance of adjusting the exchange rate to the rapidly changing economic environment. To achieve this, flexibility in the exchange rate regime was indispensable. On the other hand, the experiment showed that the positive effects of exchange reform might be constrained by inadequate reforms in other areas. How to find a way for the exchange reform to proceed with these constraints posed a challenge, for which China found an intermediate answer.

Turning to the market: swap market as a transitional mechanism

In a sense, the IRTS scheme was an experiment with 'getting the price right first'. The next problem was how to align the exchange rate with changing economic conditions. It turned out that, no matter how 'appropriate' it initially was, in a country where the whole economy was undergoing sea changes, the exchange rate was best left flexible. However, with central planning and the enforcing mechanism still in place at the time, government-sponsored adjustments of the exchange rate was effective as shown in the limited success of the IRTS scheme. The more sensible route was to liberalise supply and demand, at least to some extent, then let these forces decide the price in an interactive process. This was the route that China eventually followed, which ushered in a new phase in China's exchange reform featuring gradualistic liberalisation of access to foreign exchange through the swap market.[1]

The swap exchange market emerged from the foreign exchange retention schemes, which were introduced in 1979, along with the adoption of the IRTS. Designed to enhance export enthusiasm by linking import entitlement with export performance, the schemes allowed domestic units (including producers, trading organisations, and provincial governments) to retain a share of the foreign exchange they earned through export. To be exact, when domestic agents surrendered their foreign exchange proceeds to the government, in addition to receiving domestic money at the official exchange rate, they obtained entitlement to a proportion of foreign exchange. The proportion or the retention ratio was specified by the government, and was called the foreign exchange quota in China. The retention ratio was generally between 10 and 50 per cent in its early stages and averaged about 44 per cent overall for the whole period (Hoe 1993, also Lu and Zhang 2000. This section draws heavily from these papers). Initially only applicable to above-target exports, from 1988 the system was based on actual foreign exchange receipts (Liu 1993). In the early version, priority regions enjoyed higher retention ratios. For Special Economic Zones and minority regions (such as Tibet), the retention ratio was as high as 100 per cent. For Economic and Technological Development Areas in coastal cities, the ratio was 80 per cent. Guangdong and Fujian provinces were each given a retention ratio of 30 per cent because of their special policy status. Other provinces could only claim a ratio of 25 per cent. Later, priority products and sectors were given preference. From 1991 to 1994 (when the retention schemes ceased), all regions and sectors were given a uniform ratio of 80 per cent though in minority and less-developed regions preferential treatments were maintained.

While the usages of retained foreign exchange were specified by the government, imports financed by such retention quotas required no planning permit in general cases. In practice, imports under the schemes were fairly free. Given strict import rationing in China at the time, this was a significant liberalizing step.

The quotas were, however, initially not transferable, which limited their inducements. They became marketable in October 1980 when the Bank of China launched swap business in 12 cities. From August 1981, they could sell the notional quotas directly to the bank. In the beginning, the price of such notional quotas was at the IRTS rate with a margin of up to 10 per cent added or deducted. As of October 1985, this was changed, with the swap rate being set at one RMB yuan more than the official rate with a ceiling of 4.2 yuan per dollar. In October 1986, foreign investment enterprises (FIEs) were allowed to swap foreign exchange among themselves with the price to be decided freely by the parties involved. This gave rise to the emergence of swap centres exclusively for FIEs, separate from the swap market for domestic enterprises where the price was restricted. Further liberalisation occurred in April 1988. With the introduction of the contract responsibility programme in the foreign trade sector, the barrier segmenting domestic enterprises and FIEs on the market was lifted and the swap rate was allowed to move freely. Meanwhile, controls over the amount of retained foreign exchange that could be actually spent in a year were dropped. From 1 September 1989, private residents were gradually allowed to sell foreign currency on the swap market, implying that there were virtually no restrictions on sales on the swap market.

On the demand side, restrictions on the purchase of foreign exchange remained, reflecting China's cautious approach to foreign exchange liberalisation. Domestic buyers had first to be eligible to import, and then had to obtain foreign exchange approval from the local offices of the State Administration of Exchange Controls (SAEC). For licensed imports, enterprises had to obtain the licence in the first place. For non-licensed imports, SAEC approval was based on a 'Priority List' compiled in conformity with the national industrial policy. For products outside the list, mostly consumer goods, the restrictions applied were considerable although this varied between regions.

With the free price of retention quotas and an increased amount of retained foreign exchange, the swap market expanded dramatically. In 1988 the number of authorised local swap centres increased, and a national swap centre was created in Beijing to deal with swap business between ministries and between regional swap centres. By the end of 1993, there were 119 swap centres in China, with at least one swap centre in every province.

The dramatic development of the swap market was a milestone in China's exchange reform. One prominent aspect was its contribution to the reform of the foreign exchange price, i.e. the exchange rate. There is evidence that the authorities had used the movement of the swap rate to gather information about changes in the domestic cost of foreign exchange (Lu and Zhang 2000, and Chen 1992). When the authorities used this information to assess the prevailing exchange rate policy and to decide possible adjustment of the official exchange rate, the swap rate provided an intermediate link between the market system and China's exchange rate policy.

The swap market itself entailed liberalisation of foreign exchange allocation. As mentioned above, the foundation of the swap market was foreign exchange retention schemes that granted exporters easier excess to foreign exchange and hence lower costs due to reduced bureaucracy. Also, the schemes made it possible for exporters and local governments to import readily for their own needs that were not necessarily high in the central government's priority.

The swap market furthered the beneficial effects of retention schemes. The transferability of the retention quotas at a depreciated rate gave an implicit subsidy to exporters. As a result, the swap market operationally provided, at least partially, compensation for the general anti-export bias of the trade system. More fundamentally, it allowed the interactions between demand and supply, leading to the introduction of essential elements of a market system into China's foreign exchange allocation and so providing gains in terms of allocative efficiency.

Equally significant were its other educational functions, such as practical training opportunities for the Chinese dealers, brokers, and other personnel. Even the Central Bank had learnt how to monitor the market, what minimum legal and regulatory frameworks were required, and when and how to intervene if necessary.

On the minus side of the experiment, the market was frequently subject to administrative discretion in terms of entry qualification, usage restrictions, and price intervention. To make the problem worse, there were habitual interventions from local governments. To protect local interests, they often blocked the flow of foreign exchange between regions, invariably with administrative means. This problem was especially serious in less-developed regions and inland provinces, despite the fact that in these regions market spirit and institutions were actually most wanted. The resultant segmentation compromised the efficiency of the swap market.

The development of the swap market was, *a priori*, constrained by the gradual and experimental approach to the reforms adopted by the Chinese government. For a long time, the average retention ratio had been kept low, which limited the size and depth of the market, hence its liberalising effects.

Perhaps the most intractable problem was related to a multiple exchange rate regime. The more depreciated swap rate was tolerated by the authorities to redress overvaluation. To the government, it may have appeared to have a desirable effect in this regard, with less dramatic repercussions than a major official devaluation (Dai 1994). However, the multiple practice led to unpredictable discrimination, rent-seeking activity and corruption. The deleterious consequences gradually made the swap market a matter of wide concern and finally an object of further reform.

The government on the whole responded to these problems positively. Entry and usage controls were progressively relaxed, the retention ratio increased, and a national swap centre was created to reduce market fragmentation. Finally, the government unified the exchange rates and moved towards currency convertibility in 1994 that will be discussed below.

The exchange rate issues

Exchange rate determination

With the unfolding of China's exchange reform, in the early 1980s there emerged a new theory of exchange rate determination, which has since shaped China's exchange rate policy (Zhang 1986, Chen 1992, and Wang 1992).[2] This theory offers a new interpretation of the Purchasing Power Parity (PPP) relationship. According to this, the exchange rate between two currencies should, in a normative sense, be one at which the value that a certain amount of domestic currency has, or represents, is equal to that of a foreign currency. So, when a certain amount of domestic currency is exchanged for a given amount of foreign currency, the transaction should take place, on average, on the basis that the value exchanged is the same to both parties. The actual exchange rate may deviate from this rate in the short run, but in the long run this should be the norm.

The crucial assumption here is the value parity embodied in the comparable commodities. If prices are distorted, this assumption will become invalid. So the problem reduces to one of finding suitable goods whose prices are not distorted. Since tradable goods' prices are determined in international markets and are less distorted, they come close to meeting the requirement. As such, price ratios of tradable goods are the appropriate candidate.

It is essentially a theory of PPP in terms of tradable prices, which provides some plausible explanation of the foundation of exchange rate determination. In practical terms, it is capable of giving a simple and workable rule for setting the exchange rate; and the required data can then be made available. In fact, China has long collected data on domestic procurement prices of exportables and their selling prices in the world market for various goods, which can be used as proxies for relative tradable prices.

It is worth stressing that this PPP rule had been adopted by the Chinese communists in their guerrilla bases long before they came to national power. As early as the mid-1940s, they set the exchange rate of their guerrilla currency on the basis of the external PPP, which continued after 1949. Later, from 1949 to 1952, an index of the weighted average cost of earning a unit on foreign exchange of 80 export goods, whose volume represented 70 per cent of China's total exports at the time, was used as the main reference for adjusting the RMB rate.

This pursuit came to an end in the mid-1950s. Starting in 1953, the RMB rate was less frequently altered. From 1955 to 1972 the RMB rate against the US dollar was fixed. During that period, while the RMB–rouble rate for merchandise trade transactions was first based on the cross rate of the dollar and then on gold,[3] the non-trade RMB–rouble rate for the bilateral settlements account was calculated in December 1957 with reference to a weighted average of domestic price ratios of 47 categories of goods. These 47 goods and their weights were also applicable to the RMB rates against the currencies of North Korea, North Vietnam, Mongolia and Eastern European countries. In 1963, the commodity categories were increased to include 69 goods and services named in the Prague Treaty concerning the payment arrangement of non-trade transactions among 12 Eastern Bloc countries (Wang 1992).

When in 1979 the IRTS was proposed, it was based on the national average cost of earning a unit of foreign exchange through exports in 1978. However, the Chinese policy makers remained to be convinced. At this juncture, the emergence of the new theory helped the situation. The influence of this theory is to be found in the later developments of China's official exchange rate. In 1984, the RMB rate began to change frequently in the direction towards the IRTS rate, which was based on the relative tradable price. In subsequent major devaluations (January–October 1985, July 1986, December 1989, November 1990), the RMB rate was guided mainly by the tradable price ratios (Wang 1992). In 1990, it was officially revealed that changes in China's exchange rate were conditioned by three factors: the position of the balance of payments; the cost of earning a unit of foreign exchange through exports; and developments in international currencies (International Monetary Fund 1990). Later, Chinese sources further confirmed that the relative tradable price was the major consideration in changes in the official RMB rate (Yin et al. 1991).

Evolution of China's exchange rate arrangement

China operated a flexible exchange rate regime in the early 1950s. The RMB was first quoted against foreign currencies in Tianjin on 18 January 1949, followed by Shanghai on 10 June 1949 and Guangzhou on 6 January 1950. From 18 January 1949 to 1 July 1950, the RMB rate in Tianjin was adjusted

55 times, mainly depreciating. Sizeable variations of the rates existed between regions. On 8 July 1950, a unified national quotation for the RMB rate replaced regional quotations.

The Korean War ended this exchange rate policy. From 20 July 1950, all Chinese imports from the US were blocked, which eventually grounded all direct Sino-American trade. In 1952, China suspended publication of the RMB rate against the dollar; only the RMB rate against the pound was quoted. Nevertheless, internally a dollar rate was still used which fluctuated occasionally (devalued twice in December 1952 and January 1953). From 15 January 1955, the internal RMB–dollar rate was fixed at 2.4618 yuan per US dollar until the 1970s.

Consequently, from 1955 a fixed exchange rate regime appeared in China. Amid the demise of the Bretton Woods system, the RMB–dollar rate revalued from 2.4618 to 2.2673 yuan/dollar on 18 December 1971 when the dollar devalued by 7.89 per cent. With the thaw in Sino-American relations, China resumed quoting the RMB–dollar rate on 14 September 1972.

When the world entered the era of general floating rate currencies, the Chinese exchange rate regime underwent another change. After sterling's floatation on 23 June 1972, China pegged its currency to the French franc for a brief period and then to a basket of currencies. Because of the chaos in the international monetary system, China suspended public quotation of the dollar rate on 12–14 February when the US dollar devalued by a further 10 per cent on 12 February 1973. The RMB quotations were re-published on 15 February but suspended again on 2–16 March with an internal rate circulated to domestic units. On 17 March 1973, China resumed quoting RMB rates against foreign currencies by pegging them to a basket that initially consisted of 11 major currencies, later reduced to 7 and then to 5. From November 1975 to 1980, currencies from the dollar and Deutschmark groups became the main components of the basket. The weight of each currency in the basket was not determined, as generally believed, by the relevant country's weight in China's trade, but by an arithmetic average (Wu and Chen 1992). The prominent position of the Deutschmark in the basket reflected China's intention to make the RMB 'hard' for reasons of political prestige.

The general tendency of the evolution of China's exchange rate arrangement since 1979 has been towards a higher degree of flexibility. Basket pegging gradually gave way to managed flotation. From the early 1980s, exchange-rate adjustments were made by the authorities in response to changes in some key indicators. Because the rate was flexible but its adjustments were not automatic in response to selected indicators, the IMF has, since October 1986 classified China as having a managed floating regime. In fact, moves towards a managed floating rate regime began at least as early as 1984 when the RMB started to depreciate to the level of the IRTS. It was not until 9 April 1991 that China officially announced the adoption of a managed floating rate. Finally, there came the grand 1994 initiative that unified the two-tier exchange market and adopted a managed floating rate regime based on market supply and demand.

Towards a convertible Chinese currency

One feature of China's reform of exchange controls was the improvement of the regulatory framework. This included establishment of a national control board and a legal framework. As mentioned above, no well-defined regulatory body actually existed in China before the reform, a surprising fact considering the strictness and extensiveness of the controls. The old regime was multilateral, with the overall authority in the hands of the SPC. In addition to carrying out trade business, the state-owned trade corporations were also the superintendents. Under the contract with the PBC they supervised foreign exchange flows arising from merchandise trade. Non-trade foreign exchange flows were the responsibility of the Ministry of Finance, with the participation of the PBC (Yin et al. 1991). Considerable confusion and bewildering bureaucracy resulted in the overlapping of responsibility and undefined accountability.

In March 1979, the State General Administration of Exchange Controls was established to supervise all inflows and outflows of foreign exchange across the country. In August 1982, the SGAEC ended its association with the Bank of China and became a bureau of the PBC, renamed the State Administration of Exchange Controls (SAEC). In July 1988, the SAEC was put under the direct control of the State Council, with organisational affiliation to the PBC. In December 1989, the SAEC was promoted to vice-ministerial level. With this status, it was merged with the PBC in 1990 by a resolution of the People's Congress. The creation of this single supervisory institution helped to reduce bureaucracy and improve informational and institutional efficiency.

Along with these institutional reforms, there have also been legal improvements. In December 1980, the State Council promulgated the Preliminary Regulations Regarding Foreign Exchange Management (amended in April 1996). Later, a dozen bylaws and rules were issued. The old control system was based on the rule by man. Unpublished internal plus bureaucratic expedient were the main media through which all foreign exchange within the country was controlled. The system was thus prone to bureaucratic abuse. The effort of trying to regulate the controls with a legal framework represents a break with this tradition.

Of crucial importance is the issue of what to control. On the whole, the regime has gradually embraced liberalisation, as reflected in four changes: adoption of the retention schemes; development of the swap market; delusion of the monopoly power of the Bank of China in foreign exchange business, and granting of freedom for private holdings of foreign currencies.

As the retention schemes and the swap market have already been discussed, we now turn to the other two.

The pre-reform system of foreign exchange business in China was wholly monopolised by the Bank of China. In October 1979, the China International Trust and Investment Corporation (CITIC) came into operation and was awarded the franchise for foreign exchange business. In 1982, the Nanyang Commercial Bank (a Hong Kong bank) opened a branch in Shenzhen with the right to deal in foreign currency. From 1984, foreign or overseas Chinese-owned banks could extend their business and in October 1984, the Shenzhen branch of the China Industrial and Commercial Bank was accorded a licence for foreign exchange business. Since 1989 several other banks (the Bank of Communications, the Guangdong Development Bank, the Shenzhen Development Bank, the Xiamen International Bank, Fujian Industrial Bank, Shenzhen Zhaoshang Bank, CITIC Industrial Bank, and China Investment Bank) have been permitted to engage in foreign exchange business. By 1996, all domestic specialised banks have been granted the right to conduct foreign exchange business.

From 1985, private residents have been allowed to open foreign currency deposit accounts at designated banks. From 1988, private customers have been permitted to sell foreign exchange on the swap market and to buy foreign exchange for purposes like visiting overseas relatives, immigration, studying abroad, sending maintenance for overseas dependants. Pensions and redundancy allowances etc. in foreign currency may also be sent out.

However, the exchange reform was incomplete and piecemeal and considerable frictions emerged as a result. The chaotic situation on the swap market manifested the seriousness of the problem. Before 1994, there were actually three exchange rates in China: the official rate; the swap rate; and the black market rate. Differentials between the rates inevitably invited profit-seeking speculation and rent-seeking activity. Taking advantage of inadequate government supervision, large enterprises and trading corporations often manipulated the swap market, especially when the macro economy was in a state of imbalance (Ji 1993). In China's economy, a new round of overheating peaked in 1993. In anticipation of devaluation, big companies withheld their swap transactions, which led to a sudden shortage of supply. The swap rate began to dive; it depreciated by 50 per cent in 1992 and continued depreciating in the beginning of 1993. On 1 March 1993, the SAEC tried to cap the swap price but this merely brought the market to a standstill. After the capping was lifted on 1 June, the swap rate rocketed to more than 10 yuan/dollar. The alarmed government intervened again, but this time tried a different method. The first instance of government intervention occurred on 22 June (Li 1995). On 12 July, the central bank sold US$10 million on the market at a price 6.6 per cent lower than the then going rate. On 13 July, it poured another US$70 million onto the market at one cent less than the market rate. The amount of intervention was estimated at about US$300 million in June alone (Kaye 1994). For the whole period from June to the end of 1993, some Chinese sources indicated that the figure might be several billion dollars (Li 1994).

To reinforce the intervention, administrative measures were announced stipulating that enterprises could only hold for three months retention quotas obtained before 31 June, and for six months those obtained after 1 July. In July that year, a new PBC governor (Zhu Rongji) was appointed and the government launched a sixteen-point austerity programme to curb the overheating and to stabilise the domestic currency. The swap rate finally stabilised at 8.7 yuan/dollar.

Mirroring the disarray on the swap market, there emerged large-scale capital outflows from China. While some were normal business, many were illegal foreign exchange transactions by Chinese nationals, or capital flight. The Chinese government was apparently aware of their existence (Zhou 1995). International news coverage indicates that the Chinese agents involved in capital flight ranged from individuals to the state-owned travel agency and included army officers (Drumm 1995). State banks and other financial institutions were perhaps also involved (Lin 1994). Once the funds had left the country, they disappeared into personal bank accounts, overseas real estate, or were lavishly spent on extravagant lifestyles. Some were recycled into the country disguised as foreign direct investment in order to benefit from tax breaks, or to evade import tariffs or restrictions (Drumm 1995). The inefficient financial system and strict, though diminishing, exchange controls might also have played some role in causing the capital flight (Lin 1994). The size of capital flight, by definition, is difficult to detect and quantify. Estimates varied from US$8 billion to US$20 billion a year (Drumm 1995 and references therein). The Chinese official sources estimate it at least US$1billion a year (Zhou and Wang 1993). Recent studies from China indicate that in 1989 it was about US$8.3 billion, then rising to US$ 20 billion in 1990, US$26.6 in 1991, US$30 in 1992 and US$37.8 in 1993 (Li 2000).[4]

Domestically, regionalism was spreading. The region-based retention system provided a hidden subsidy for priority regions that worsened regional disparity with the result that inland provinces then turned to regional protectionism. When supply was short, they would block outside buyers from entering local markets and prohibit local foreign exchange from flowing out of their territory. The reverse occurred when demand was weak. Such regionalism existed not only between provinces but also between different districts within a province (Drumm 1995).

Further, there was the problem of currency substitution. In addition to the substitution of RMB into US dollars, a huge amount of Hong Kong dollars, estimated at HK$ 15 billion or 20–25 per cent of total cash HK dollars, was circulating in China. In some southern areas, such as Shenzhen, HK dollars used by local residents are estimated to amount to 40 per cent of the total money in circulation in the city (Jiao 1994). This situation is undesirable because it may imply low credibility of the RMB and tends to disturb the national economy.

The chaos on the swap market, capital flight, and widespread currency substitution sent a signal to the government, compelling changes. The government could have simply resorted to recentralisation that, as past experience shows, may temporarily ease the strains caused by exchange controls. However, the reformers gained the upper hand and pushed ahead with the market-oriented reform.

Three options were put forward to the government as a result of an internal policy debate. One involved full foreign exchange surrendering with convertibility on current account. According to this proposal, dual exchange rates must first be unified while all export proceeds are surrendered to the designated state banks. The state abolishes exchange controls and undertakes to sell foreign exchange to enterprises for merchandise imports. The second proposal was a more radical programme to allow economic agents to retain cash foreign currency instead of notional quotas, and for the swap market to be enlarged to achieve convertibility of the RMB. A third but minority group suggested starting the convertibility process with non-trade transactions on the current account (Zhongguo jinrong xuehui mishuchu 1993).

The government finally opted for the first proposal. On 29 December 1993, the PBC announced measures to further the reform of China's foreign exchange system. Effective on 1 January 1994, the package included: unification of the dual exchange rates and adoption of a managed floating rate based on market supply and demand; introduction of a full surrendering system with abolition of the retention schemes; abolition the compulsory foreign exchange plan and the granting to users of the right to buy foreign currency from designated banks on presentation of valid import documentation; termination of Foreign Exchange Certificates; and establishment of an interbank foreign exchange market.

The salient feature of the package was that it made the RMB convertible on the current account. The transition strategy focused on creating a price mechanism capable of generating a flexible but unitary exchange rate through an interbank market, with which allocation of foreign exchange can be decided by market-determined outcomes. To implement this strategy, on the supply side full surrendering was employed to ensure sufficient liquidity of the market, and on the demand side trade controls were retained to prevent euphoric importing while the compulsory foreign exchange plan was abolished. On the institutional front, on 4 April 1994, the Shanghai Foreign Exchange Transaction Centre (the interbank market) started business. The centre is electronically linked with 22 other cities to ensure uniformity in ask and bid prices and to speed up settlements of foreign exchange transactions (Zhu 1994).

The transition to the partial current account convertibility for the Chinese currency was smooth. In 1994 China's exports grew at a rate of 31.9 per cent while imports rose by 11.2 per cent resulting in a trade surplus of US$5.3 billion. More vigorous was the increase in official reserves that increased by US$30.4 billion. Foreign capital flooded into China, with the amount of foreign capital actually used totalling US$33.8 billion. The only noticeable disruption was perhaps the rush to spend FECs in the first few months (Kaye 1996). Since the partial convertibility the RMB exchange rate has been stable. During 1994, it fluctuated around 8.4–8.5 yuan/dollar. Contrary to government estimates, the rate appreciated rather than depreciated, to 8.4 yuan/dollar by the end of the year. The smooth transition continued in the following years.

Further liberalisation steps were taken after 1994. The 1994 programme preserved the swap business for FIEs, which caused some resentment. Compared with the freedom granted to domestic enterprises, FIEs felt that they were discriminated against because they still had to obtain the SAEC's approval for access to swap centres and pay a fee. It was also feared that the government might tighten the requirement for individual FIEs to balance their foreign exchange account (Drumm 1995). In response, the government abandoned the arrangement in July 1996 and allowed FIEs to buy foreign exchange freely on the interbank market.[5] In addition, from 1995 individuals have been able to buy $1,000 for one overseas trip ($600 to Hong Kong). From 1 January 1997, authorised foreign banks have been able to provide financial services in RMB in Shanghai, and later on in Shenzhen. With most current account transactions freed, China on 1 December 1996 officially notified the International Monetary Fund of RMB's convertibility on the current account.

China's next move will logically be the establishment of RMB's convertibility on the capital account. However, because of the Asian financial crisis that is believed by many Chinese economists to be largely related to the volatile movements of international capital, the Chinese government becomes more cautious about this issue. Government economists at the central bank have talked about an intermediate plan for the 'fundamental convertibility of the Chinese currency' (Jing 2000). This plan aims to achieve 'total convertibility on the current account but conditional convertibility on the capital account' for RMB, meaning that some long-term capital account transactions will be free but short-term capital movement will be prohibited, while current account transactions remain convertible. Some official suggested a timetable for the RMB to become fully convertible by 2015.[6] However, the governor of the Chinese central bank has resisted all the pressure to make any commitment to a specific timetable.[7]

Concluding remarks

China's foreign exchange reform has proved a success. Once a country with chronic overvaluation and foreign exchange shortage, China now holds one of the largest foreign exchange reserves in the world. Within about 15 years, its currency has established partial convertibility with a stable exchange rate. A rigid regime of exchange controls has given way to a new system in which the price mechanism plays a critical role in allocation of foreign exchange and in decisions about the exchange rate.

The reign of market forces over China's foreign exchange system is not complete. Currently, the interbank foreign exchange market is still subject to frequent government intervention and lacks competition due to, among other things, the exclusion of productive enterprises. Nonetheless, that country's major problem ahead is perhaps to further the RMB's convertibility. Although convertibility on the capital account can be a longer-term target as widely agreed, China's convertibility on the current account as it stands is yet to be desirable. Despite solid progress in reforming the exchange rate policy and foreign exchange allocation, trade restrictions linger on. It is true that the importance of trade planning is declining, but China still operates a relatively complex trade regime. In particular, imports are regulated through tariffs, canalisation (monopoly or limited import rights), licensing and direct controls (World Bank 1994). The new foreign exchange regime has transferred many of its assignments of foreign exchange controls to trade restrictions rather than entirely abolished them. As a result, not only are capital movements in and out of the country not free, but also, in relation to convertibility on the current account, China's exchange reform has only liberalised supply initiatives with the demand side being still at the mercy of state administration. In this sense, China's foreign exchange liberalisation is still only at the half way point.

Notes

1 This is actually a misnomer since it has no resemblance to the swap transactions on the world financial market. But the Chinese official term for the market – the Foreign Exchange Adjustment Center – is equally confusing. We use the term following the literature.

2 This theory first appeared in an internal report on the RMB exchange rate policy, which was commissioned by the Chinese Cabinet in 1982. Around the same time, there was another important article in the Chinese literature on PPP by Li (1985).

3 Before June 1951, the yuan–rouble rate was based on the cross-rate with the US dollar. After that, the yuan–rouble rate was determined on the basis of the rouble's gold content and China's domestic purchasing price of gold. But this rate had little practical significance from the mid-1960s when Sino-Soviet trade shrank drastically.

4 According to the author, capital flight from China reached US$47.7 billion in 1997. See also Yang and Chen (2000).

5 *People's Daily*, 21 June 1996.
6 *Mingpao* [*The Ming Newspaper*], 1 November 2000. This timetable was suggested by Dr Yi Gang, deputy secretary of the Central Monetary Policy Committee of China. A former vice governor of the Chinese central bank, Liu Mingkang made the same suggestion.
7 *Guoji Jinrong Bao* [*The Newspaper of International Finance*], 9 October 2000.

Bibliography

Chen, Biaoru (ed.) (1992) *Renminbi huilü yanjiu [Studies of the RMB Exchange Rate]*, Shanghai: Huadong Shida Chubanshe.

Dai, Quanding (1994) 'Guanyu tongyi duozhong huilü wenti' [On the issues concerning unification of multiple exchange rates], *Guoji jinrong* [*Studies of International Finance*], February, pp. 4–7.

Drumm, L. (1995) 'Changing Money: Foreign Exchange Reform in the People's Republic of China', *Hastings International and Comparative Law Review*, vol. 18. no. 2, pp. 359–95.

Hoe, Ee Khor (1993) *China's Foreign Currency Swap Market*, International Monetary Fund, Paper on Policy Analysis and Assessment, PPAA/94/1, Washington, D.C.

International Monetary Fund (1990) 'Exchange Arrangements and Exchange Restrictions', *Annual Report*, Washington, D.C.

Ji, Chongwei (1993) 'Wending renminbi huijia jixu shenghua gaige zonghe zhili' [To stabilize the RMB exchange rate requires deepening the reforms and a comprehensive cure], *Guoji jinrong yanjiu* [*Studies of International Finance*], July, pp. 3–4.

Jiao, Jinpu (1994) 'Renminbi "wailiu" yu gangbi "neiliu" de bijiao fenxi' [The 'outflow' of RMB and the 'inflow' of Hongkong Dollars: a comparative analysis], *Jinrong yanjiu* [*Financial Studies*], December, pp. 12–14.

Jing, Xuechen (2000) 'Lun renminbi jiben keduihuan' [On the fundamental convertibility of renminbi], *Caimao jingjin* [*Financial and Trade Economy*], August, pp. 28–33.

Kaye, L. (1994) 'This money has wings', *Far Eastern Economic Review*, July, p. 72.

—— (1996) 'Discipline restored', *Far Eastern Economic Review*, 9 September 1996, p. 58.

Lardy, N.R. (1992) *Foreign Trade and Economic Reform in China: 1978–1990*, Cambridge: Cambridge University Press.

Li, He (1985) 'Goumaili pingjia lun' [On the purchasing power parity], *Zhongguo shehui kexue* [*Social Sciences in China*], June, pp. 121–34.

Li, Jun (1995) 'Shilun woguo zhongyang yinhang dui waihui shichang de ganyu' [On the intervention of China's central bank in the foreign exchange market], *Jinrong yanjiu* [*Financial Studies*] September, pp. 21–4.

Li, Puming (1995) '1994 nian waihui he waimao gaige shuping' [Review of foreign exchange and trade reforms in 1994], *Gaige* [*Reform*], March, pp. 80–5.

Li, Xiaofeng (2000) 'Zhongguo ziben waitao de lilun yu xianshi' [Capital flight from China: theory and reality], *Guanli shijie* [*Management World*], April, 123–33.

Lin, Zhiyuan (1994) 'Renminbi zhiyou duihuan de tiaojian he duiche' [Conditions and measures for RMB's free convertibility], *Jingji yanjiu* [*Economic Studies*], February, pp. 33–8.

Liu, Changsheng (1993) 'Guanyu renminbi zhiyou duihuan de shikao' [Thoughts on RMB's free convertibility], *Guoji jinrong yanjiu* [*Studies of International Finance*], June, pp. 32–4.

Lu, Maozu and Zhang, Zhichao (2000) 'Parallel exchange market as a transition mechanism for foreign exchange reform: China's experiment', *Applied Financial Economics*, vol. 18. no. 2, pp. 123–36.

Mah, Feng-hwa (1972) *The Foreign Trade of Mainland China*, Edinburgh: Edinburgh University Press.

Wang, Huaqing (1992) *Zhongguo huilü de lilun yu shijian* [*Theory and Practice of the Chinese Exchange Rate*], Shanghai: Shanghai Renmin Chubanshe.

World Bank (1994), *China: Foreign Trade Reform*, Washington, D.C.: World Bank.

Wu, Nianru and Chen, Quangeng (1992), *Renminbi huilü yanjiu* [*Studies of the RMB Exchange Rate*], Beijing: Zhongguo Jingrong Chubanshe.

Yang, Haizheng and Chen, Jinxian (2000) 'Zhongguo ziben waitao: guji he guoji bijiao' [Capital flight from China: estimates and international comparisons], *Shijie jingji* [*World Economy*], January, pp. 11–15.

Yin Jieyan, Lei Zhuhua, Tao Xiang, and Wang Songqi (eds) (1991) *Zhongguo waihui yewu quanshu* [*Handbook of China's Foreign Exchange Practice*], Beijing: Jinji Guanli Chubanshe.

Zhang, Zhichao (1986) *Huilü lun* [*On the Theory of the Exchange Rate*], Shanghai: Xuelin Chubanshe.

Zhongguo jinrong xuehui mishuchu [Secretariat of the Finance Association of China] (1993) 'Huobi guojihua lilun yantaohui zongshu' [A Summary Report of the Conference on the Internationalisation of Money], *Jinrong yanjiu* [*Financial Studies*], July, pp. 60–1.

Zhou, Xiaochuan (1995), 'Renminbi Zhouxiang Keduihuan' [RMB's move towards convertibility], *Guoji Jinrong Yanjiu* [*Studies of International Finance*], February, pp. 4–9.

Zhou, Yeliang and Wang, Rensheng (1993) 'Jiakuai waihui shichang gaige yinjie fuguan de tiaozhan' [Speed up the reform of foreign exchange market to meet the Challenges of Re-entering the GATT], *Guoji jinrong yanjiu* [*Studies of International Finance*], September, pp. 34–7.

Zhu, Xiaohua (1994) 'Jiji wentuo tuijing waihui guanli tizhi gaige, heli tiaokong shouzhi, chushi waihui pingheng you yu' [Actively and steadily push the reform of foreign exchange management system, rationally adjust revenue and expenditure to keep the foreign exchange account in surplus], *Jinrong yanjiu* [*Financial Studies*], April, pp. 1–3.

List of abbreviations

FIE	Foreign Investment Enterprise
IRTS	Internal Rate for Trade Settlements
PBC	People's Bank of China
PPP	Purchasing Power Parity
RMB	Renminbi, the Chinese currency
SAEC	State Administration of Exchange Controls

Chapter 4

The Reform of China's Foreign Trade Regime in the First Decade of the New Millennium

Tong Jiadong

Introduction

The Chinese government has initiated a series of reforms in the country's foreign trade regime since 1979. It has slowly changed the regime from a highly centralized and mainly administrative system towards a much freer market regime. The traditional trade regime could be called a state monopolistic system. It is not an easy task to reform such a system. Indeed, while the reform of the Chinese foreign trade regime has been successful, the Chinese government has faced many difficulties in the process of implementing these reforms. The main issue in this regard has been how to reconcile the operation of state-owned enterprises (SOEs) with the workings of a market economy.

Removing state control over foreign trade

Before 1979 the Chinese government directly controlled the foreign trade regime. This meant that the central government could decide policies in respect of the exportation and importation of goods, both in the short run and the long term. In fact, China's entire foreign trade was conducted by fifteen state-owned enterprises. The trade system was organized in such a way that each of these companies had responsibility for a particular trading area; for example, all imports and exports of chemical materials and products were handled by the Chinese Chemistry Industrial Import and Export Company. The Ministry of Foreign Economic Relations and Trade directed the activities of these fifteen SOEs. The Ministry was an element within a wider government planning system; every year the Ministry was involved in discussing the import and export plans with the State Planning Commission. The organization is represented in Figure 1.

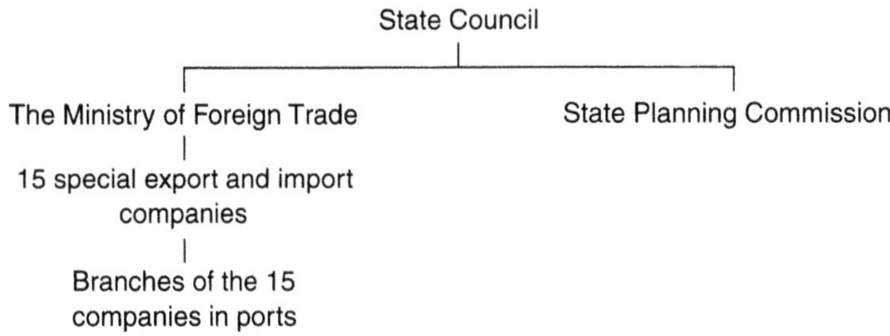

Figure 1

The above is a typical organizational regime under a state planning system. The activities of the firm have to be authorized by the relevant state officials. This regime does not encourage or help the enterprise to do business on the basis of the pursuit of maximum profit. This organization is indicative of the limited role played at the time by foreign trade in the overall economy. Consequently, it was difficult for the Chinese economy to realize the advantages of trade. Indeed, a reform of the foreign trade regime was necessary if China wanted to fully take advantage of trading opportunities on the basis of factor endowment. A series of reforms have thus been introduced. The reform process can be divided into three stages: (a) 1979 to 1987; (b) 1988 to 1990; and (c) the post-1991 period.

In the first period, from 1979 to 1987, the reform process focused on the deregulation in respect of the right to engage in foreign trade. The central government began to transfer such rights to local governments. The form of the state economic plan was changed from one revolving around the authoritative specification of schedules of production to a system that revolved around the issuing of more general guidelines. Emphasis was placed on the combination of guideline planning with market forces. The government moreover encouraged local governments and enterprises to look for ways to build cooperation between trade firms and industrial companies or the agricultural sector. This kind of reform was intended to make the trade enterprises more active and to expand foreign trade and, in particular, to encourage export activity.

In the second period, from 1988 to 1990, the main concern of the central government was that levels of remuneration (wages, or salary, and bonuses) were based on the volume and value of exports. The central government (represented through the Ministry of Foreign Economic Relations and Trade) stopped requiring a trading company involved in foreign trade to earn foreign exchange, to recover any foreign exchange used as well as to submit any residual foreign exchange holdings to the government. After the regulations were changed, the enterprise could retain part of their foreign exchange earnings. They could also use these reserves to make purchases to assist in their business. This is a very important point, not merely in terms of the effects on the ways in which firms operated, but also because it led to some local prices being set – to some extent – by wider market forces. Relatedly, in a further change, the branch operations of the foreign trade companies were transferred to local governments. The government tried to loosen control over foreign trade enterprises and let the market come more into play.

In the third phase, after 1991, the government tried to change systematically the foreign trade regime. The new reform measures focused on eliminating export subsidies, on making the foreign trade enterprises assume commercial risks, including ones relating to gains and losses. The government paid much more attention to the use of tariffs, and other economic measures, allowing enterprises to conduct trade in any goods they chose. This also meant that particular enterprises no longer had a privileged position in relation to the trade of particular goods. Clearly, by implementing these reform measures, the government sought to weaken the monopoly hold of old state enterprises. The government therefore also allowed the state enterprises to introduce a shareholding system, reorganizing the firm in the style of western companies. The government has authorized 320,000 companies to do business in the foreign trade sector.

The government has by now pursued reforms of China's foreign trade regime for twenty or more years. These reforms have made a lot of progress, albeit only gradually. The tariff and non-tariff barriers have replaced the authoritative plan, and related administrative tools, for guiding the economy. At the micro-level, state enterprises have been exposed to market forces. The government has encouraged enterprises to shift their business focus from one limited to particular goods to one that is no longer restricted in terms of the goods traded. Accordingly, more companies now play a part in foreign trade. Significantly, some companies now finance their business activities by raising capital on the stock market.

Chinese foreign trade is now conducted within the context of a regime in which the individual enterprise increasingly is in a position to decide on its own operations. The structure of the regime looks very much like one that one would expect in a market economy. First of all, central government adjusts foreign trade through tariff and non-tariff barriers. Secondly, there is no longer any broad plan for imports and exports. Most of the imports and exports are based on the decisions of enterprises. Thirdly, the structure of enterprise has changed greatly. State-owned foreign trade companies play an increasingly less important role in foreign trade.

The reform of the foreign trade regime has played a positive role in China's economic development. The statistics show that of the goods traded only 10% are controlled by the plan. It is now tariffs that are playing a more and more important role in foreign trade management. This is testified by a decrease in recent years in the average normal tariff level from 43% to only 17%. Also, at the end of 1999 there were 320,000 enterprises that had the right to conduct foreign trade. Meanwhile, 526 enterprises took the form of 'western-style companies', and many companies were listed on the stock market. The reforms have led to other significant change. The total value of trade has grown from US $20.64 billion in 1978 to US $360.6 billion in 1999. The average growth rate has been about 14%. It must also be noted that the structure of goods traded has seen a change from what mainly were raw materials to commodities, with the latter now making up 87% of total exports.

The problems of reforming the trade regime

While it can not be denied that the reform of the Chinese foreign trade regime has proved to be a great success, there still exist some limitations during the transition toward a more market-oriented trade regime. It is possible to summarize briefly the problems under two broad headings: (i) micro-level problems; and (ii) macro-level problems.

Micro-level problems

First of all, the decentralization of the right to conduct foreign trade has resulted in two problems. One is the fall in the level of profit made by state-owned enterprises as a consequence of the introduction of market competition. Lower profits make it difficult to keep afloat or support the big companies that were established in the days of the planned economy. The reason is that these enterprises have employed too many people and established too many departments. As was noted, 320,000 enterprises now have the right to conduct foreign trade in China. The foreign trade companies now face serious competition, and had to reduce prices further than they would in normal circumstances. This price competition, which has benefited above all the foreign consumer, has caused profit rates to decrease.

Second, because foreign trade companies have acted as intermediaries, workers employed in such enterprises increasingly risk being laid off, as the foreign trade company could not otherwise hope to make a profit. The point here is not that the incomes of the workers are high, but that it is the overall running costs of the companies that are too high. And, as noted, increasing competition has further reduced profits. Consequently, the system of intermediate companies has proved difficult to maintain. According to available statistics, only 10% of the value of foreign trade are now handled by way of such agency.

Third, the co-operation of trade and industrial companies as well as that between trade and technological companies has only extended from the trade stage to the production process. In these cases, the 'fusion' of activities of state-owned enterprise in the foreign trade sector with those in the industrial sector shows that foreign trade can become an integral part of industrial enterprises if this trade connects well with the business of the industrial enterprise and is successful. There may also be instances of course in which the shortcomings of state-owned enterprises are effectively inherited leading the coming together of the two types of companies to be unsuccessful, which will make the foreign trade company seek to co-operate with other industrial enterprises. Generally, private enterprises are likely to merge with the better companies, while state-owned enterprise comes together with other enterprises under government control. This shows that foreign trade enterprises are not obliged to operate independently. Equally, the establishment of huge trading companies is also not necessary.

Fourth, shareholding companies were meant to strengthen the incentive mechanism, the control mechanism and competition mechanism. The operation of these mechanisms is useful to avoid the loss of state capital. Also, these mechanisms make managers assume risk and responsibility when running the enterprise. This means that the enterprise could take independent decisions on the basis of profit considerations, i.e. without having to observe the central government plan or other government requirements. In the past, the government required state-owned enterprises to make available as much foreign exchange as possible. Under the current regime, this requirement could be dispensed with if the enterprise could get much more profit. The scale of the enterprise is based on the economy of scale, rather than an artificial target.

Companies established now to some extent are meant to obtain capital in the market. This capital would only be useful to save the life of state-owned enterprises in new form under the old regime, if the real market mechanism had not been established. The collective company is a good choice to link the interest of companies with private interests or with the interests of its employees. In other words, an employee is now able to buy and hold the firm's shares. In this case every employee can consider himself as owning the firm. So he can closely link his private interest with the firm's interest. But there are some preconditions. The preconditions are, first, that the company has a bright future, as otherwise the employees will not buy the stock or hold the shares or would just pay attention to the market value of the stock. The employees, then, must feel assured that they can get interest or profit from this kind of investment. However, most of the shares are held by the state. This means that private investors are primarily interested in the market price of individual stocks (for speculative reasons). Moreover, the employees may well lose interest in the stock if more and more new issues appear. Company reform is therefore only one kind of change for a state-owned enterprise to embrace. It may also just be the expression of a transitional form, if the company reform just takes the path of normal reform rather than real reform.

Macro-level problems

Turning now to the macro-side problems, the state-owned foreign trade enterprise continues to play the role of government servant even if the instances of administrative intervention are gradually decreasing. Foreign trade enterprises (still) assume a policy burden or pay some other cost. For instance, the government might ask the foreign trade enterprise to buy certain goods in order to ensure the survival of some industrial enterprise, irrespective of whether or not the foreign trade enterprise really wants to make these purchases. Ultimately, the government does not care whether the trade enterprise can then make a profit from selling on the goods in question. At the same time, foreign trade companies are required to pay interest on loans to the bank taken out perhaps just to make the original purchase. Moreover, foreign trade companies also assume other costs derivative of policy made by the central government. For instance, at one point in time, the government offered a refund of the export tax. However, the full amount of taxes due could not be collected given shortcomings of the taxation system. In this case, the government adopted a new policy that introduced but a partial tax refund. So the trade enterprise had to accept a partial rather than a full tax refund (in the region of perhaps 3%, or 6%, or 9%, when the full tax refund rate is 17%). This practice has increased costs for the enterprises concerned and weakened their price advantage. Not surprisingly, this kind of attitude by the central government has failed in encouraging the enterprise to operate independently. It has also harmed the firms' aim of maximizing profits.

A reform programme, which is not thorough enough, or not consistent across the foreign trade sector, will lead to a series of difficulties, especially operational difficulties. The enterprises lack mechanisms that encourage them to operate according to market principles, involving losses in operations, poor economies of scale and so on. Operational losses can be linked to losses resulting from the unclear demands made by government policy. This has offered an opportunity for managers to find an excuse for all losses. Consequently, the reform of the foreign trade regime should achieve two aims in the next decade. First, the enterprise must cut the economic linkage with the government (central government and local government). The foreign trade enterprise should operate independently, and identify different losses clearly. It must avoid the mixture between the two kinds of losses sketched above and no longer consider firms to be only government servants. The government should no longer have the right to issue orders to enterprises to do what the enterprises are not willing to do. The operation of enterprises should not be considered as a part of government performance, so as to avoid a weakening of the real objectives of any firm. Secondly, company reform should be pushed forward. The reforms should allow the companies to become real companies and gradually expose them to market competition.

The politics of reforming the trade regime

It is very difficult for the government to take the reform of state foreign trade enterprises to its logical conclusion. There are a number of reasons for this.

The main reason is that we must dispense with the target of total trade value when pursuing regime reform. From the angle of the government it would be good if firms could dispense with the aim of foreign trade volume (or foreign trade plan) irrespective of the trade regime. In the past twenty years, the average increase in China's foreign trade has been about 16%, but this rate of increase is not even. It was 3.2% higher in 1996 than it was in 1999. Notably, the growth rate achieved by joint ventures has steadily been at about 25–30%, compared with a negative rate of state foreign firms. It is a worry that the government could not require the joint ventures to meet the target that the central government set. And yet, state firms will not be able to meet the required target if the firms break free from government control in the wake of further reform since the aim of the firm will change from meeting the government's plan of foreign trade to making a profit.

Second, to complete the reform in the foreign trade regime would affect the growth in trade in the short run. The volume of trade may decline if the negative effects of reform outstrip the positive effect. In other words, the government must be careful with further reforms of the trade regime. Accordingly, the government may prefer gradual to fast reforms. Of course, it is likely that in practice foreign trade enterprises link up with industrial firms and that both will replace the single foreign trade firm and become ever more active, unless the authorized system for conducting foreign trade is maintained. But it is impossible for the government to keep still.

Third, state enterprise reform will weaken the government's powers. It will lead to the shrinking of government functions. Consequently, it is very difficult for the government to take relevant decisions of this nature. It is equally obvious however that the separation of firm and government will encourage the firm to do business, bringing company behaviour full circle. If this does not happen, it will be very difficult for the firm to exist in a market economy, especially if we keep the trading regime unchanged. In case the government retains the most significant levers of control, the firm cannot develop further. Therefore, the government faces a trade-off between allowing for the separation of state firms, which is likely to release new business energies, and controlling the firms, which will likely lead to their commercial failure. Many Chinese policy-makers and analysts hope that setting free new energies can be reconciled with retaining some form of control. This is illustrated by the state taking control of the reform process and the acceptance of the Chinese that the process will be gradual. As far as foreign trade firms are concerned, the government hopes that reform will make it more active than in the past while retaining control. This has been a longstanding principle in the pursuit of reforms in key fields. It has also encouraged the adjustment of the export structure from raw materials to manufactured goods, the move from labour-intensive to capital-intensive goods, trade liberalization, and the strengthening of competition. All are gradual reforms under the control of the government.

Conclusion

In China, the policy-makers and commentators tend to think that all reforms in relation to the foreign trade regime are from top to bottom, and gradual. This kind of reform shows that policy-makers and commentators always hope that the reform can be pushed forward under the control of the government. This suggests that the government is trying to 'plan a market economy', because this kind of reform could bring good results – and provide mutual support in the areas of reform and development. Optimistic elite members think that China could move beyond the preliminary stage in the transition to a perfect market economy, one that combines the invisible and visible hand.

I think it will take time to achieve this goal as it will take time to train people to operate in a market economy environment. It is hard for firms to establish the machinery for existence and development. Accordingly, the remainder of the reform depends on real change of the relation between the government and state firms. When this happens, perhaps in the next decade, it seems to me that China should no longer conduct reform from top to bottom (from government to firm). That means all the reform steps are initiated and taken by the central government and the state firms just follow and implement them step by step. The aim of the central government is to find a way to maintain their power over the state-trading firm. So this is not real reform. Indeed, in the past twenty years, China's reforms just developed on the basis of such thinking as well as trial and error. What China should do is to allow for reform to develop from the bottom to the top. In other words, the government should allow every state firm to look for its own way, so that it can earn money and make profit. In essence, then, I think it is difficult for a market economy to be generated from the concept of the planned economy. We should allow foreign trade firms to be able to test various forms of state ownership. It would be good if the reform process could be accelerated. In 1999, the Chinese government took some important steps to push forward reform of the foreign trade regime. These have not been effective yet. We have to wait for a little while longer.

Bibliography

Beijing Center for Chinese Economic Studies (1995) *Economics and the Reform of Chinese Economy* (Shanghai: Shanghai People's Press).

People's Daily, December 20th 1999.
Song, Hong (1999) 'A Comprehensive Cost-Benefit Study of China's Entering into the WTO', *International Economic Review* 7–8.
Tong, Jiadong (1998) 'The Reform of Chinese Foreign Trade Regime', *Nankai Journal* 1.
Tong, Jiadong (2000) 'WTO and Economic Reform in China', *Herald of Open Economy* 5.
World Bank (1987) *World Development Report 1987*, Washington, D.C.
Yearbook in Chinese Economy 1999, Beijing.
Yearbook in Chinese Foreign Trade 1999, Beijing.
Zhang, Jun (1998) *Rethinking and Analysis of Chinese Economic Reform* (Shanxi: Shanxi Publishing House).
Zhang, Zhenyu (1995) 'Trade Policy Choice under Economic Development', *International Trade Review* 7.

Chapter 5

State-Owned Enterprises

A Review of Development Dynamics, Contemporary Problems and the Shape of the Future

P.W. Preston and Xing Aifen

Introduction

Cast in the very broadest of historical terms, the shift of China into the modern world has been peculiarly long drawn out and difficult. Beginning with the depredations of European and American traders in the nineteenth century, a long-drawn-out episode of gross and violent exploitation, reaching its nadir in the years of Imperial Japanese invasion, successive Chinese governments have had to deal with both their own populations and the outside world from positions of weakness (Moore 1966). At the present time, this long-endured situation is easing rapidly as China continues along the path sketched out by Deng Xiaoping – the pursuit of a distinctly East Asian-style development – and re-enters, thereby, once again (Frank 1998) the wider global system, this time as an economically and culturally powerful equal to those already established modern countries.[1] In our view, three elements are crucial to this situation: first, the results of the 1937–49 period when a series of wars resulted in the expulsion of foreign powers from China (for the first time since the Opium Wars against the British in the early nineteenth century); second, the drive for domestic solidarity and development pursued by Mao Zedong; and third, the pragmatic, piecemeal and finally sweeping reform programme inaugurated by Deng Xiaoping. All these matters are ongoing. In this chapter we will consider one crucial aspect of the current situation, that is, the reorganization of the state-owned enterprise (SOE) sector of the Chinese political-economy. The SOEs have stood at the heart of Chinese development strategies and their reorganization (which has economic, social and political significance) is central to the contemporary elite-sponsored political project, the shift from the autarchic state socialism of Mao into the unfolding territory of Deng's 'socialism with Chinese characteristics', a trajectory reaffirmed by Jiang Zemin and Zhu Rongji.

From Mao Zedong to Deng Xiaoping

The logic of particular historical conjunctures will present key agents with the framework within which they can orient their political-cultural projects. China entered the modern world late and, after Sun Yat Sen's 1911 republican revolution collapsed into warlordism, progress remained chaotic up until 1949. Thereafter, there was very significant advance coupled to further domestically engineered short-term chaos (that is, the Great Leap Forward and the Cultural Revolution). The political model affirmed, socialism, was distinctively modern, one of the key European models generated in the nineteenth century. In 1949 the ideal of socialism provided a persuasive political programme. The leadership of Mao Zedong oversaw the autarchic pursuit of a Chinese variant of socialism in one country which looked to reform peasant agriculture, in communes, and develop heavy industry, in particular via SOEs. The project took place within the context of US-sponsored post-Bretton Woods liberal trading project, coupled to a cold war-vehicled counter-revolution aimed at any and all dissenters from its project. However, in East Asia an adjunct to cold war politics was an unexpected and unambiguous economic success, subsequently characterized as the rise of an East Asian model of industrial-capitalism, a state-centred communitarian development (Johnson 1982, 1995; Wade 1990; Amsden 1989). This became a model available for the Chinese leadership to adopt. In the 1980s Deng Xiaoping inaugurated a series of cautious reforms, a controlled state-sponsored marketization, in rural and urban sectors, moving beyond both the rural commune strategy and urban state-owned enterprise model. The reforms have been very successful. The new regime of Jiang Zemin and Zhu Rongji has moved the reform programme forward. There are a series of concerns: first, to increase the rate of growth; second, to improve efficiency, and here the SOEs remain a problem; and third, to reorganize the banking system which is probably insolvent as a result of credits to SOEs (Dernberger 1999: 612–3). Looking to the future, we can note both the difficulties of further reform and the technocratic nature of the leaders – they belong to the post-long march generation (Dernberger 1999: 615).

The reforms to the Chinese economy in the period 1949–1976 took place in the shadow of the influence of Mao. The early policy debates were how to interpret Marx who, clearly, had focused his analyses of the logic of capitalism on the countries of Europe, the UK in particular. In the early period a radical line prevailed, which argued for immediate pursuit of the construction of socialism, whereas the revisionists suggested it was too soon and the productive forces would have to be developed first (Christiansen and Rai 1996: 188). It can be characterized as a debate between those who stressed political mobilization and creation of socialist structures and those who looked to individual motivation and the demands of economic efficiency (Christiansen and Rai 1996: 188). The socialist economy was introduced in the early 1950s – a key element of the CCP's programme.

The economy was modelled on the Soviet Union. The key policy instrument was the state plan, which had a series of time horizons – one, five and ten years – and which specified the inputs and outputs of enterprises, sectors and regions. The system required a large administrative apparatus, a complex bureaucracy. It was an hierarchical system. A key element was the work unit, which served both an economic function and a crucial social role, as it was the particular institutional linkage of individual citizen and the developing socialist political economy (Christiansen and Rai 1996: 190). In the economic sphere state ownership was distinguished from collective ownership (Christiansen and Rai 1996: 193), and SOEs were the central instrument of the drive for development.

The SOEs were owned by the whole people, organized within a ministerial line of command and located at a particular place in the hierarchy. The SOEs could be run by various levels of the bureaucracy (national government, provincial government, city government or county level government) (Christiansen and Rai 1996: 193). The managers were civil servants, so to speak, and the enterprise would have a director and functional subordinates. In addition each enterprise had its own party committee and worker's congress (Christiansen and Rai 1996: 204). The SOEs' activities would be oriented to fulfilling the plan requirement, consequently the key to success for an enterprise was how well it could function within the bureaucratic environment (and conflicts emerged between technical specialists and administrators) (Christiansen and Rai 1966: 205). The enterprises were work units and thus provided a permanent job, housing and welfare. In this social environment patronage relations developed; there was never a western-style workers versus management culture (Christiansen and Rai 1966: 206). Finally, it might be noted that the industrialization drive took place in the 1950s at the height of the cold war, and strategic concerns meant many very large industries were located in remote areas of China.

The development of industry demanded financing and in the early phases this entailed a transfer of resources from rural areas to urban areas, in theory without creating inequality of rural distress (Christiansen and Rai 1996: 194). The plan divided urban and rural areas in order to control labour and migration and to foster industrialization. A series of key factors can thereafter be considered: labour; materials; markets; capital; and food. Labour was ordered from around 1957 in the context of the household registration system. In theory this allocated persons to either urban or rural status and their employment was secured either through the Labour Administration Bureau or via the system of rural People's Communes, but the situation was very complicated and it worked to the extent it did because the state controlled all access to the necessities of life (food, accommodation, welfare, and so on[2]) (Christiansen and Rai 1996: 198). Raw materials were monopolized by the state, markets were controlled and prices set by the state. The supply of investment capital was controlled and the system redistributed capital to the industrialization drive. And, finally, food was controlled, supplied mostly by rural communes with an intermittently tolerated private supply. In brief, in the language of development theory, the system had a strong urban bias.

As the CCP took over, the urban economy comprised a melange of traditional, modern and international elements. The CCP changed the economy slowly. First the resources left by retreating Kuomintang, the urban gangs and international holdings were seized and reorganized. The local small traders were encouraged to form cooperatives. The state emerged as the dominant owner and the key area of investment was in large enterprises (Christiansen and Rai 1996: 203). The SOEs were central to the state plan-specified drive to industrialize. The enterprises were large integrated operations, and their workers were an elite. A further element were the urban collective enterprises, involving a diversity of small activities, and in time these began to look rather like SOEs. By contrast, in 1949–53, in the rural economy there was a process of land redistribution from landlords to peasant households (Christiansen and Rai 1996: 208). The development of communal activity was encouraged, at first via control of credit, and thereafter more directly. Mao favoured people's communes which concentrated production and were read in terms of a rapid move to socialism. These efforts were redoubled in the Great Leap Forward, which took place in 1957–8. The policy failed and famine followed in 1960–1. Thereafter people's communes were stabilized through the 1960s, with private plots permitted and some rural industry and trade (which developed quickly when it was permitted by the state) (Christiansen and Rai 1996: 213).

Until 1976 the economy was driven by the political project of radicals who were committed to a rapid movement towards socialism. Mao died in 1976 and Hua Guofeng took over. Hua affirmed that everything Mao had said was correct and also reaffirmed an idea from Zhou Enlai – the 'four modernizations'. Once again the key state strategy was to be large-scale projects. Several were inaugurated but foreign currency was drained away and ideas had to be curbed. (Christiansen and Rai 1996: 216). The same predilection for the large scale found expression in rural development plans. The production unit was too small, as was the production brigade; so attention focused on entire people's communes which were to become agricultural factories (Christiansen and Rai 1996: 216). But the leadership could not agree and the four modernizations were dropped. An austerity period followed under leadership of Deng Xiaoping and a more pragmatic line ruled Chinese development.

Deng took power in December 1978 and set out to change the direction of development of economic structures. The reforms were introduced gradually. The grand policy visions were out, and pragmatism was preferred. The pragmatists were undoubtedly communists, but pushed the realization of the vision far into the future and discarded egalitarianism in the present in favour of practical results – the colour of the cat does not matter. The economic reforms inaugurated by Deng can be construed as the core of the recent Chinese political project, a reorientation from the state directed pursuit of egalitarian socialist development to a new model, a state sponsored communitarian development, a Chinese variant of the East Asian model. A key move in the debate, introduced by Hu Qiaomu prior to Deng's return, was the idea of contracts. These contracts were to regulate relationships within the planned system so as to better allocate resources, and they were to penetrate all levels of activity (Christiansen and Rai 1996: 218). The procedures for negotiating and enforcing contracts grew out of existing procedures within the plan system (Christiansen and Rai 1996: 218). Further development of the law was necessary to attain these goals, and an Economic Contracts Law was established in 1981, a Law on Court Procedures in Civil Cases was established in 1982 and a Law on Inheritance was established in 1985 (Christiansen and Rai 1996: 219). Thereafter reforms have involved the first moves in the construction of a recognizably modern financial system.[3] The reforms have involved changes in the production sector of the economy, both changes to the SOEs and the encouragement of new private firms. These reforms, in turn, have entailed change in the social and political spheres. The role of the SOEs in providing welfare means that the issue of welfare reform is vital. It bears directly upon the changing ways in which society and economy are articulated. As the state and the work unit move into the background, or past, the provision of social networks and support systems moves into the foreground and represents, it might be thought, the future. Finally, in the political sphere the implications of change can be unpacked domestically, as class patterns, life-style and ideas about participation all change, and within the wider regional and global systems where the increasing openness of China offers further evidence of the unfolding implications of the choice for a new historical development trajectory.

The first sphere to be reformed under Deng was agriculture. The first step was to reassure producers (some prices were adjusted, some administrative abuses/problems resolved and land was distributed to peasants in poorer areas) and the effects were immediate and output rose (Christiansen and Rai 1996: 220). In 1978/79 the leadership could not agree on land redistribution but it started to happen anyway at provincial level, and thereafter the leadership embraced the idea. The impact was great and the ways in which land was redistributed were various. The whole ensemble of patterns came to be summed up as the 'Household Responsibility System for Agricultural Production' (Christiansen and Rai 1996: 221). The control of land was returned to the level of peasant households and non-land assets (such as large animal production units and machinery) were auctioned off.

The prices were cheap and the process had the effect of creating a group of rural entrepreneurs (Christiansen and Rai 1996: 221). The result was something of a development free for all and negative effects in land use had to be curbed (Christiansen and Rai 1996: 222). The rise in production of basic grains embarrassed the state (which had to buy it all) and the system of decentralized production took some time to mesh with the system of central production targets (Christiansen and Rai 1996: 222). In subsequent years the move towards a free market system advanced whilst the state involved itself in a familiar spread of agricultural extension services (Christiansen and Rai 1996: 224). In this process of reform, rural industries grew very rapidly. The rural areas had lots of labour, lots of encouragement and good links with urban areas. In time a vast spread of activities developed (Christiansen and Rai 1996: 233).

In the urban areas the reforms inaugurated by Deng impacted directly upon the SOE sector. A key shift was the 1982 move to allow enterprises to keep profits but pay tax. In this new situation enterprise leaders looked to profitable investments and enterprises began to operate as profit centres. This was a key move towards wider reliance on the mechanism of the market. In the early 1990s those enterprises which had not responded were further encouraged to shed unproductive labour (Christiansen and Rai 1996: 229). The SOEs turned out to be key players in the emerging market economy (Christiansen and Rai 1996: 229). Duckett (1996) has shown that state bureaux quickly became involved in the emerging market economy. On the debate about the state and the market (where neo-classical economics and the 'new political-economy' have argued that marketization is the remedy to all ills, and alternative lines associated with the developmental state have not been able to reply to neo-liberal charges that state involvement necessarily distorts the market (Duckett 1996: 181)), research in Tianjin shows that state bureaux can respond to developing market situations (Duckett 1996: 182). In Tianjin the state bureaux have involved themselves in pursuing a range of market opportunities – a line of argument which seeks to disaggregate the developmental state and to look at how it works at local level (Duckett 1996: 189).

In the urban economy a sphere of private enterprise grew (Christiansen and Rai 1996: 225). The state gave support to this 'individual economy'. Thus work units were encouraged to rent out unused space, banks were encouraged to make loans and local government was invited to be supportive (Christiansen and Rai 1996: 225). The encouragement of private enterprise was fostered both by the desire to pursue growth and also the problem of mopping up surplus labour (who under the Household Responsibility System were entitled to jobs) (Christiansen and Rai 1996: 226). A series of measures were taken from 1970 onwards, but this was not a free labour market and the problems of mopping up labour continued. In the 1980s and 1990s the pressure on enterprises to shed unproductive labour grew, and people started to leave. The concern of SOE managers for profit turned out to be significant in the overall move towards the market (Christiansen and Rai 1996: 227).

A related aspect of the reforms, whose lessons were to feed back into the wider economy, was the establishment of a series of special economic zones (SEZs). They were a key experiment which proved very successful, in particular in Guandong province. The new city of Shenzhen, which lies on the border with Hong Kong, has seen a great inflow of money and people (in particular educated people from other parts of China). Shenzhen has become a boom area (Christiansen and Rai 1996: 237). After the SEZs fourteen coastal cities were given similar status; then Hainan in 1987/88 became a province, in effect an SEZ; likewise Shanghai; likewise the Three Gorges Dam project (Christiansen and Rai 1996: 239).

The Chinese economy is ever more diverse – problems notwithstanding. The market-oriented reforms in China have seen both success and difficulties. There has been periodic economic overheating, confusion of economic roles within the changing economic structure (as the state withdraws in favour of the more dispersed patterns of power associated with market systems – in particular, the situation of the large SOEs may be cited) and in places outright corruption. At the same time, the rapidly changing economy has generated new patterns of wealth and consumption; it has also drawn inward migration from rural areas and led to social problems such as urban dislocation and crime. In addition there are problems with inequality, as between social groups and between different parts of the country. An old familiar distinction – coastal China and inland China – is being presented again: the western inland areas of China are poor, relative to the burgeoning areas along the coast. The changes are very broad and in political and policy terms quite problematical. The path of market-oriented reforms (projected to lead in short order to Chinese accession to the machineries of the WTO (with all the broad swathe of problems and prospects associated with the putative process of globalization)) have already involved interlinked changes in economic, social and political patterns. These changes involve both patterns of change deliberately engineered (as, for example, with the establishment of SEZs) and other patterns which might be read as entirely unintended consequences (e.g. the flow of migrants to the towns). In a period of such deep-seated change it is to be expected that individuals and groups will be discomfited; that people will find their ordinary life expectations challenged and undermined. The consequences of such structurally occasioned instability are potentially dangerous – not merely in the sphere of economic or social dislocation, but also in political breakdown. It might be argued that the events of Tianenmen Square are an extreme example of these tensions and problems; but more routinely we might find these matters acknowledged in the government's continuing 'rational authoritarian' preference for stability.

The processes of reform within China are wide-ranging, challenging and problematical. The projects of Mao and Deng evidence both similarities and dissimilarities. When Mao came to power, China adopted a variant of the Soviet model. Mao stressed self-dependence and rather cut off the economy from wider influences. Yet 'from 1952 to 1975 China's gross domestic product grew at an average annual rate of 6.7 per cent and the secondary sector (industry) increased its share of GDP from 20.9 to 45.7 per cent' (Dernberger 1999: 608). However the Maoist programme was running out of steam and the death of Mao allowed new leaders and new policy to emerge. Deng moved to reform agriculture and later urban economic activity. The reforms moved incrementally. The new regime of Jiang Zemin and Zhu Rongji has moved the reforms forward (Dernberger 1999: 611).

Jiang Zemin, Zhu Rongji and the further reform of the SOEs

After the death of Deng Xiaoping in February 1997 Jiang Zemin and Zhu Rongji came to power. They moved forwards along policy lines which they and Deng had already established – the continuing drive for a socialist market. In this context, during the 1990s, policy makers in China had placed two contentious issues on the agenda: ownership and labour (Solinger 1999: 629). The autumn 1997 Party Congress was a watershed and the debates cut to the heart of what socialism meant in China. Solinger (1999: 630) reports that 'Party General Secretary Jiang Zemin put forward two essential chores at the 1997 congress: to "adjust and improve the ownership structure" and to "accelerate the reform of state-owned enterprises"'.[4] The result was a 'surge in privatization, in fact if not name' (Solinger 1999: 630).[5]

In the early 1990s there had been a wave of deregulation, marketization and headlong bubble growth (Naughton 1999: 211). In 1997 Zhu moved to inaugurate macro-economic restraint and regulatory reform (Naughton 1999: 211). The macro reforms shifted the balance of power from enterprises to the banks and they moved to hold down inflation (Naughton 1999: 211). The banking laws and regulations were reformed, overall budget constraints were hardened and this discipline was passed on to the SOEs and their local government patrons (Naughton 1999: 212). The regulatory reforms strengthened the legal structure supporting marketization, and again this bore down on SOEs as vague ideas of ownership and responsibilities became clearer (Naughton 1999: 231). In consequence there was a wave of enterprise reform, known as 'enterprise restructuring' (Naughton 1999: 215). The SOEs cannot now use state finances easily; they must perform more like profit centres. As local governments moved to reorganize their SOEs there was 'a wave of sales, privatizations and bankruptcies' (Naughton 1999: 216).[6] Solinger (1999: 631) comments that lay-offs became familiar. The role of the work unit is being radically changed and, as unemployment rose sharply, welfare became an issue. The reforms are still unfolding but the relative decline of the SOEs in production and employment has now turned into an absolute decline (Naughton 1999: 215). Solinger (1999: 639) comments that all this represents a dramatic change from the early days of Mao where precisely the opposite course was followed.

Naughton (1999: 216) remarks that 'up until 1997, an extremely coherent economic policy configuration prevailed. Macro-economic austerity, combined with regulatory reforms, was being used to drive a substantial downsizing of the state sector'. However, in late 1997 the Asian financial crisis erupted. The most important impact of the crisis on China was that it made Zhu's policy package unsustainable. The reform programme had addressed the issue of urban workers, the SOEs, the privileged group; and enterprise restructuring has had a dramatic impact on their conditions of work – for example, the numbers of unemployed and laid-off has risen (Naughton 1999: 217). The crisis meant that this process had to be slowed.[7] In 1997/98 a series of policies were begun to maintain gross domestic product (GDP) growth, relaxing the financial austerity (Naughton 1999: 217). A new concern for welfare appeared (Naughton 1999:219). Nonetheless the policy remains in place. It would seem that the Asian financial crisis has reminded the leadership of the dangers of reform and the need for control (Naughton 1999: 223).

The Asian financial crisis broke in late 1997 and there were reasons to expect problems. The share of exports in GDP has risen from 12% in 1988 to 22% in 1994 (Naughton 1999: 204). In the years since 1993 China has been a large recipient of foreign direct investment, with 80% coming from East Asia (Naughton 1999: 204). The pattern of investment has been similar to that in ASEAN countries, and China now produces a roughly similar spread of goods (Naughton 1999: 204). China had also informally pegged the yuan to the US$ but had devalued in 1994. And, like the crisis-affected countries, China had outgrown its financial system (Naughton 1999: 206). However, there are crucial differences. Firstly, the Chinese system is much more closed, economically and politically. In the reform process foreign direct investment was liberalized, but not other forms of inward investment: so there have been no flows of speculative money (Naughton 1999: 206). The yuan is only convertible on current account, that is, to finance specific trade contracts, and not on the capital account where money is moved for non-specific reasons. This blocks speculation against the currency (Naughton 1999: 206). The openness of the economy to foreign trade is narrow (it is a processing trade) and imports into the Chinese market are restricted (Naughton 1999: 207). Once again, links with the wider global system are controlled. Then, secondly, the Chinese government has been conservative and has maintained a balance of payments surplus and built large reserves (Naughton 1999: 207). As the crisis developed there was an expectation amongst western financial commentators that yuan would be devalued, but it was not.[8] The country thus absorbed pressure on its exports caused by the devaluations of competitor countries. Godement (1999: 30) remarks that 'the politburo members ... turned out to be better economic strategists than other governments of fast-track Asia'. Overall the crisis was a warning and opportunity for China, as it strengthened Chinese leadership in East Asia and reinforced the view of the leadership that keeping control of reform is vital (Naughton 1999: 209).

Identifying the benefits, coping with the consequences

The benefits are clear. Chen (1995: 8) looks at collective action within the decision-making system and notes the interplay of reason, competition, collusion and consensus building. At the start of the reforms it is suggested that there were three political groups: conservatives, who wanted no change; authoritarians, who wanted change in the economy; and democrats, who wanted change in both economics and politics. Subsequent events show how these three lines of policy preference have interacted with each other and with society in general. The overall record is broadly very good (Chen 1995: 9). Chen (1995: 19) points out that: 'During 1978–1993, per capita real income grew at 7.1 per cent per annum for Chinese rural residents, and 6.4 per cent for urban residents ... although the income growth has been closely correlated with the economic reform, different policy changes induced different responses.... The growth of rural personal income was primarily the result of the increase of agricultural productivity under the decollectivized farming and the development of rural township and village enterprises (TVEs), while the urban income growth could be attributed mainly to the increasing influence of workers of state-owned enterprises over their own remunerations and the ineffectiveness of reforms in terms of enforcing financial accountability of enterprises.' Nonetheless, the reforms continue. Chen (1995) suggests that serious problems abound with escalating inflation, regional fragmentation and post-Deng uncertainty, but there has been increasing infrastructural investment, and a more heterogeneous society with overall stability and advance.

The consequences are difficult. The 1980s' and 1990s' rapid growth was not planned in advance; rather 'crossing the river by groping for stones' (Perry and Selden 2000: 1). The reforms have attracted lots of favourable commentary; but the consequences have not been so extensively considered, nor have the conflicts (e.g. riots, strikes, and demonstrations). The reforms officially began in December 1978 (Third Plenum of the Eleventh Party Congress), but the roots go back to the early seventies when the key moves were the de-communization of agriculture (the rise of the Household Responsibility System), and the emergence of new light industries and private industries of all types (which often linked up with urban enterprises and foreign firms), later summarily tagged as 'township and village enterprises' (Perry and Selden 2000: 3). The level of economic activity in the rural areas increased quickly. The household registration system has been eased, but not ended, and there has been a significant rural–urban migration, such that there is now an urban 'floating population' (Perry and Selden 2000: 4). The reforms in urban areas were more difficult. In particular, the situation of the large SOEs.[9] The reforms to the SOEs meant greater risk for workers and a loss of social status. As reforms have advanced it is the older workers, the less skilled and women who have been dismissed (Perry and Selden 2000: 4). There is now significant unemployment and little by way of welfare. In this situation, given the scale of change, it is not surprising that conflict has developed. In some ways it resembles conflicts of earlier periods: there are outbreaks of protest and violence, routine resistance and quite unexpected forms (as with messianic religions) (Perry and Selden 2000: 9). The state, too, is changing as it retreats from its mobilizing involvement in the detail of everyday life (Perry and Selden 2000: 11).

A key problem is employment and unemployment. A problem of the reforms has been lack of enterprise restructuring (Chen 1995: 95). The reform of the commune system revealed disguised unemployment, and although TVEs have created jobs there have not been enough. The urban SOEs also have significant disguised unemployment. The urban collectives seem rather more flexible (Chen 1995: 105). Overall, labour allocation is still tightly controlled and anxieties about opening up the labour market include principle (not making labour a commodity), fear of instability (an open labour market requires wide changes in enterprises and their environment, that is, social welfare, housing, unemployment pay and pensions) and there is always the problem of large numbers (Chen 1995: 108–12). There has in fact been significant labour protest since the 1990s. The labour reforms have borne heavily on SOEs, a key area of support of the regime. At the outset of the reform process they were the elite, comprising 42% of the industrial workforce and producing 75% of the total industrial output (Lee 2000: 42). The reforms have increased growth and fostered new industrial activity, but SOE workers have been overall losers.[10] The workers have responded with a series of 'weapons of the weak', the territory of 'everyday resistance', strikes, moonlighting, protests, demonstrations and violence (for example, attacks on managers) (Lee 2000: 45–51). In some cases the old work unit has been the vehicle of protest, and old socialist slogans have been appropriated by protesters (Lee 2000: 52). All these problems have been worse in those areas where SOEs are concentrated – the interior provinces. However, organized protest generates a sharp reaction from the state (Lee 2000: 55). Lee (2000: 59) suggests that the road ahead could be rocky unless the state acknowledges these problems more directly.

As economic reforms have swept onwards, the issue of welfare has moved up the political agenda. It is clear that Chinese people regard welfare as an entitlement. The urban workers had been used to extensive provision through their work unit, but as SOEs are pressured, and as the private sphere develops, the old style of welfare provision is declining and changing (Croll 1999: 687). There is now an urban poor without welfare (Croll 1999: 688). In the rural areas there was weaker provision and the economic growth of the rural areas has allowed better provision at local level; but as with cities it is 'cellular' (Croll 1999: 691), which is to say that provision is patchy, dependent upon economic success and not universal. The government's policy reform has looked to a new welfare system separate from enterprises, a process of socializing welfare (Croll 1999: 692). There is a hesitant move towards a national system – but little progress. The provision remains cellular, and family and local community are becoming more involved. In the future it is likely that the present collage of provisions will continue. However, it is now realized that economic growth and social welfare are intertwined (Croll 1999: 698).

Wider problems and possible new directions

The economic advance of China continues apace. The economy is now one of the largest national economies. There are extensive links to the powerful economies in Hong Kong, Taiwan and thereafter to the networks amongst the Overseas Chinese diaspora (in Southeast Asia, North America and Europe). A familiar spread of issues surrounding economic growth might be noted, in particular:

(i) the policies necessary to ensure sustained rapid growth;
(ii) the policies necessary to combat the problems of pollution (urban and rural);
(iii) the policies necessary to foster sustainable development in western China;
(iv) the development of trade linkages within the sphere of Greater China;
(v) the relationship between 'Chinese' and 'Japanese' capital;
(vi) the unfolding implications of the Asian financial crisis; and
(vii) the implications of membership of the WTO.

China has looked to the East Asian developmental model. The model disaggregated would include: (i) Japan (with its large government-linked keiretsu); (ii) Korea (with its government-linked chaebol); (iii) Taiwan (with its economy of state activity and smaller firms); (iv) Hong Kong (small firms, central role for state); (v) Singapore (with its extensive state holding companies); (vi) Malaysia (with its state holding company); and also the poorer economies of Southeast Asia (with a variety of state/economy patterns). The model has offered lessons for China; but the role of SOEs in a Chinese variant of the East Asian model is not clear. Any socialist central plan variant of the SOE would look odd in this context. But it is clear that the state is centrally involved in the economies of East Asia. It is also clear that the Asian financial crisis has not destroyed this model (notwithstanding a froth of self-serving neo-liberal commentary (Pempel 1999)).

In the social sphere, the employment and welfare consequences of the economic growth in China present acute challenges to the current leadership. In Hong Kong, Taiwan and the diaspora, it might be noted, many people are rich, enjoy high levels of consumption (and display the peculiarly associated problems). The levels of living amongst the diaspora offer a continuing readily available 'good example' to the growing middle classes in China (an example whose availability is heavily underscored by the developing patterns of travel by the Chinese and the rapidly developing new forms of communication, in particular the internet and the broadcasts of commercial satellite television). In China the following issues continue to be of particular concern:

(i) the loss of guaranteed employment possibilities;
(ii) the loss of guaranteed welfare provisions;
(iii) the consequent problems of urban instability;
(iv) the displacement of population, with inward migration to the cities;
(v) the problems of health, security and social order;
(vi) a rise in social problems (for example, low level corruption and crime); and
(vii) a growing focus on consumption patterns as central to life, with the consequent rise in visible inequality between rich and poor.

In the political sphere there is a complex mixture of issues to consider, as contemporary national problems, the legacies of the cold war and the novel demands of regionalization and globalization all bear down upon political actors of all kinds. The pressures of economic advance and social change will place heavy demands on the existing political structures. The following issues might be noted:

(i) the dynamics of the internal elite politics of the CCP (as the generation which has direct recollection of the formative pre-revolution years leaves the scene);
(ii) the shifting nature of the political goal affirmed by the CCP (from Maoist peasant-vehicled socialism to Deng's market socialism, and now the Jiang–Zhu position which mixes a drive for economic development with an opportunistic nationalism);
(iii) the wider issue of the structural reform of the political system, a key problem in China (and the root of many other problems (which would challenge any leadership)), where the demand for change is high but the difficulties of effective advance are severe and order is an ever-present concern;
(iv) the nature of the response of the wider population to the claims of the authorities and the demands of systemic economic and social change;

(v) the continuing foreign and security problems (Taiwan, South China Sea and various boundary problems); and
(vi) the developing demands of the regionalized and internationalized post-cold war system.

Conclusion

It took the Chinese many years, following the failure of the later years of Mao, to decide that they could safely engage with the regional and wider global system. This outward-oriented development strategy has been an economic success. The upshot has been the rapid integration of coastal China into the regional economy. Yet the economic success has been achieved at some cost: in particular, inter-regional and intra-regional inequality has grown; the difference in levels of living between rural and urban areas has grown; there has been massive rural–urban migration; and there is significant social dislocation attached to still unfolding marketization programmes (as with the reform of the SOEs). In brief, the country has recorded sustained high economic growth rates but has done so at some social cost. These costs have created the base for political instability, as people used to the ordered society of a centrally planned socialist system confront the problems attendant upon rapid structural change. It is clear that there is no great drive for any western-style democracy and, indeed, the more familiar concern at elite level is for order, read as a necessary condition of regime survival and further national advance.

It is clear that China is emerging as a significant regional power, economically, politically and militarily. It has been argued that the Chinese will not seek to establish an hegemonic position within the region. A series of constraints on their room for manoeuvre could be cited, including lack of economic resources, military strength and the continuing presence of the USA. China is in many respects still poor. The real question for China's neighbours becomes one of how best to engage so that all might prosper. Western thinking has been cast in terms of 'containment' versus 'engagement'. But the various Western countries are all pursuing their own policies; in other words, there is no organized response. It is noticeable that economic concerns are coming to the fore for the European Union, whilst this is perhaps not quite so clear with Bush's America. It is likely that economics will be the key axis around which China's relationships with the region will revolve, as the WTO regime establishes itself in the sphere of trade.

Notes

1 Angus Maddison (*Chinese Economic Performance in the Long Run*, OECD, 1998, reported in the *Economist*, October 22 1998, accessed via Economist.com) argues that from 1820 to 1952 world economic output rose eightfold whilst

China's output per head fell. Over the same period China's share of world GDP fell from one third to one twentieth. Income per head fell from the world average to only one quarter of it. Hence the concern to recover.

2 The CCP analysed society in class terms – individuals were allocated a class status/family background – this allocation to category determined significantly the person's subsequent life chances (Christiansen and Rai: 190). The work unit is a key institution – fits person into economy and society – a definite place in the social system – provided employment and welfare – clientilistic – solidaristic (against state) – cuts against political participation in public sphere – will slowly change as economy does but is proving resilient (Christiansen and Rai: 123–4).

3 The reforms involve a hierarchy of functional units (central banks, commercial banks, development banks, non-bank institutions, and so on), new patterns of control (the shift from centralized secret control towards a decentralized open dispersed marketized pattern) and a spread of new policy areas and action (monetary policy, foreign exchange, foreign trade regimes).

4 The reform of the SOEs is hugely complicated – their size, workforces and social role – however, their outmoded debt-ridden character is seen by many western commentators as obliging change (see *Economist*, September 11 1997, accessed via Economist.com).

5 A key element was the reform of the SOEs, under the slogan, 'manage the large, let go the small' – the 118,000 industrial SOEs, the bulk of the total, are divided into small and large and 100,000 small SOEs can be let go leaving the larger ones to be managed (and here the idea of Chinese chaebols has been mooted). The SOEs employ two-thirds of China's urban workforce yet contribute 33% of industrial output as against 75% in 1981 (*Economist*, May 1 1997, accessed via Economist.com).

6 A spectacular example of failure was that of the Guandong International Trust and Investment Corporation (GITIC), owned by Guandong Province government, which was allowed by the central government to fail in January 1999 causing consternation in domestic and foreign financial circles – it was understood as a sign of the central government's determination to curb unconstrained growth and the debt burdens of SOEs and the banking system (Guardian Unlimited Archive, January 11 1999). However, the confusion of the pursuit of growth and problems of adjustment of the economy continue (see Guardian Unlimited Archive, January 22 1999).

7 The *Economist* (July 16 1998, accessed via Economist.com) commented that Zhu was putting key elements of the reform on ice – as policy makers and population digested the implications of the Asian financial crisis.

8 Martin Jacques notes the pressures to devalue and the high domestic costs of not doing so – employment, welfare and possible conflicts (Guardian Unlimited Archive, February 7 1999).

9 The *Economist* (September 28 2000, accessed via Economist.com) returned to the problems of SOE reform, noting the headline figures (employment, unemployment, debt, and so on) and the structural problems. SOEs are economic operations embedded in social and political systems; and trying to turn them into western liberal market disembedded operations is not simple and is fraught with possibilities for severe conflict.

10 The changes have hurt women. In the Maoist period women enjoyed official equality and a measure of practical equality (Zheng 2000: 63) – the expansion of 1980s onwards has included women (Zheng 2000: 64) but the SOE sector lay-offs have involved women disproportionately (Zheng 2000: 65) – old gender stereotypes have reasserted themselves (Zheng 2000: 66) – yet as new modern

industrial and urban activity develops women have been involved but patterns are gendered (Zheng 2000: 71) – there has been differentiation of women's experience in the job market (Zheng 2000: 81) – overall, it looks like downward mobility (Zheng 2000: 81).

Bibliography

Amsden, A. 1989 *Asia's Next Giant: South Korea and Late Industrialization*, Oxford: Oxford University Press.

Chen, Kang 1995 *The Chinese Economy in Transition*, Singapore: Singapore University Press.

Christiansen, Flemming and Rai, Shirin 1996 *Chinese Politics and Society*, London: Prentice Hall.

Croll, Elizabeth J. 1999 'Social Welfare Reform: Trends and Tensions' in *China Quarterly* 159, September.

Dernberger, Robert F. 1999 'The People's Republic of China at 50: The Economy' in *China Quarterly* 159, September.

Duckett, Jane 1996 'The Emergence of the Entrepreneurial State in Contemporary China' in *The Pacific Review* Vol 9 No 2.

Far Eastern Economic Review 1999 *Asia 2000 Yearbook*, Hong Kong: Review Publishing Co.

Frank, A.G. 1998 *Re-Orient: Global Economy in the Asian Age*, Berkeley: University of California Press.

Godement, Francois 1999 *The Downsizing of Asia*, London: Routledge.

Johnson, C. 1982 *MITI and the Japanese Miracle*, Stanford: Stanford University Press.

Johnson, C. 1995 *Japan: Who Governs?*, New York: Norton.

Lee, Ching Kwan 2000 'Pathways of Labour Insurgency' in Perry and Selden 2000.

Maddison, A. 1998 *Chinese Economic Performance in the Long Run*, Paris, OECD.

Moore, B. 1966 *Social Origins of Dictatorship and Democracy*, Boston, MA: Beacon Press.

Naughton, Barry 1999 'China: Domestic Restructuring and a New Role in Asia' in Pempel 1999.

Pempel, T.J. ed. 1999 *Politics of the Asian Economic Crisis*, Ithaca, NY: Cornell University Press.

Perry, Elizabeth and Selden, Mark 2000 'Introduction: Reform and Resistance in Contemporary China' in Perry and Selden 2000.

Perry, Elizabeth and Selden, Mark eds 2000 *Chinese Society: Change, Conflict and Resistance*, London: Routledge.

Solinger, Dorothy J. 1999 'Demolishing Partitions: Back to Beginnings in the Cities' in *China Quarterly* 159, September.

Wade, R. 1990 *Governing the Market: Economic Theory and the Role of Government in East Asian Industrialization*, Princeton, NJ: Princeton University Press.

Zheng, Wang 2000 'Gender Employment and Women's Resistance' in Perry and Selden 2000.

Chapter 6

Regional Economic Development Strategies in China

Hsiao-hung Nancy Chen

Introduction

In China, regional economic policy has for many years been made as part of the macroeconomic policy. Political considerations have played a major part in the formulation of Beijing's policy stances with regard to regional economic development. Regional industrial structure and regional industrial specialization have been controlled by the central government, while local governments have been treated only as implementation units. This kind of centralized planned economy, though it may be conducive to overall capital accumulation and industrialization, also made free flow and/or union among regions almost impossible.

China's once unbalanced growth strategy, which was adopted for military reasons, brought about a type of vertical specialization that made the central and western regions of China focus mainly on resource development, whereas the eastern region concentrated on manufacturing and processing industries. The economic development of China's central and western regions has therefore been stifled and depended heavily on government financial subsidies. Under the PRC's indicative planning system the economic development of the country's eastern region did not necessarily proceed any better, because the tax policy that regulated the amount of revenue that had to be contributed to the central coffers often discouraged the eastern provinces from seeking further economic development.

The PRC's open-door policy, inaugurated in 1978, marked a big change in terms of regional economic policy. Since then an unbalanced regional development policy, which favors the eastern region, has been pursued. The economic disparities among regions have ever since also become one of the policy concerns in China. This is evidenced not only by China's eleventh Plenary meeting that made 'anti-poverty and solving the east–west regional

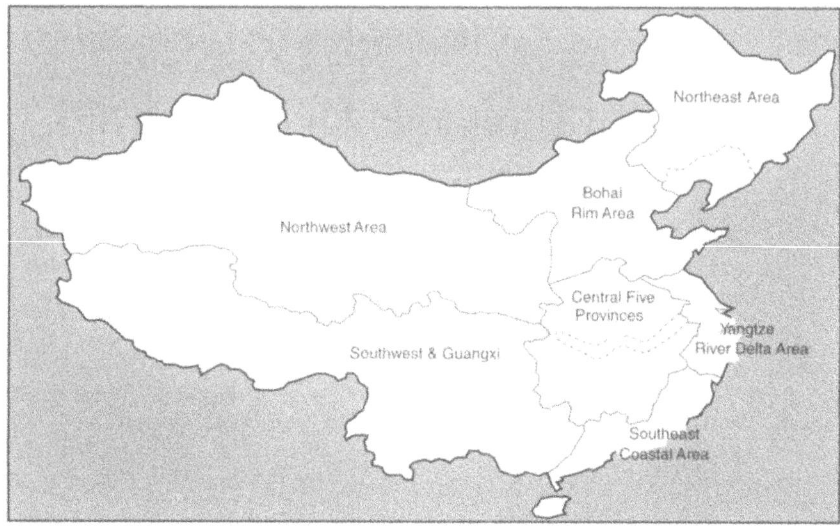

Chart 1 The distribution of the seven economic zones in China

Source: Various sources, but mainly derived from Tze-liang Hu and Sui-chin Rou, 1999, 'China's regional economic differences & economic planning', in Nora N. H. Chiang and Yi-lin Sung (eds.), *China's population, urban and regional development,* Taipei: Population Study Center, National Taiwan University, p. 66.

Table 1 Key indicators of the seven major regional economic development zones in China

Economic zone	Area (%)	Population 1997 (%)	GDP 1997 (%)	GDP (Hong Kong included) (%)	Growth rate of GDP (1978–1997) (%)
1. Yangtze River Delta and Surrounding Area	2.2 3.4	10.6 14.7	19.1 23.7	16.1 19.9	9.8
2. Southeast Coastal Area	3.5	9.0	13.9	27.6	13.6
3. Bohai Rim Area (including Liaoning)	9.9 11.6	17.8 21.7	20.2 24.8	17.0 20.9	9.5 8.9
4. Northeast	13.1	9.5	10.7	9.0	7.7
5. Five Central Provinces	9.1	26.0	19.4	16.3	9.7
6. Southwest and Guangxi	27.1	20.0	12.0	10.0	9.0
7. Northwest	35.1	7.1	4.7	4.0	7.9
Total	100.0	100.0	100.0	100.0	9.7

Source: Derived from Tze-liang Hu and Sui-chin Rou, 1999, 'China's regional economic differences & economic planning', in Nora N. H. Chiang and Yi-lin Sung (eds.), *China's population, urban and regional development,* Taipei: Population Study Center, National Taiwan University, p. 63.

economic disparity' top policy priorities, but also by the ninth five-year economic development and 2010 plans. These divide the country into seven economic zones (Chart 1 and Table 1). The seven economic zones which were divided by the ninth five-year economic and 2010 plans are the Yangtze River Delta area, the Bohai Rim area, the South-East coastal area, the South-west and HuaNan areas, the Northeast area, the Five Central Provinces and the Northwest areas. If a massive scale plan could be implemented, its impact on China's regional economy would surely be tremendous.

Guiding reasonable regional economic specialization has become one of China's key economic development tasks in the next 15 years. This chapter intends, first, to review China's regional economic development strategies over time. It then focuses on the present stage of China's regional economic specialization, in both sectoral and spatial terms. Finally, the chapter touches upon some related measures that ought to be adopted if such a grand plan were to be realized.

Regional economic development strategies at different development stages

Prior to the 1978 reform era: unbalanced growth strategy

Basically speaking, the Chinese government adopted a relatively unbalanced growth strategy prior to the 1978 reform era. The central and western regions gained relatively more government resources at the time due mainly to the following considerations:

(1) Being a socialist state, the government tried to rectify the then biased development pattern which overemphasized the development of the few eastern coastal cities; and
(2) Mao's perspective on the nature of world politics made him extremely cautious about the possibility of war. For strategic reasons, he therefore decided to relocate major industries from the north-east to the central and/or western regions,[1] especially after the conflict between China and the Soviet Union intensified in the early 1960s.

The post-reform era (1978–1990): development strategy biased towards the eastern region

The aim of this strategy was, first, to develop the eastern region which boasted better infrastructure and then to spread the effects of the development generated to the central and western regions. Deng Xiaoping's adage to 'let some segments of society get rich first, and let some region flourish first' was a clear endorsement of this development pattern. It is also true that because of the implementation of this strategy, China has since witnessed its highest economic growth along the eastern coastal areas.

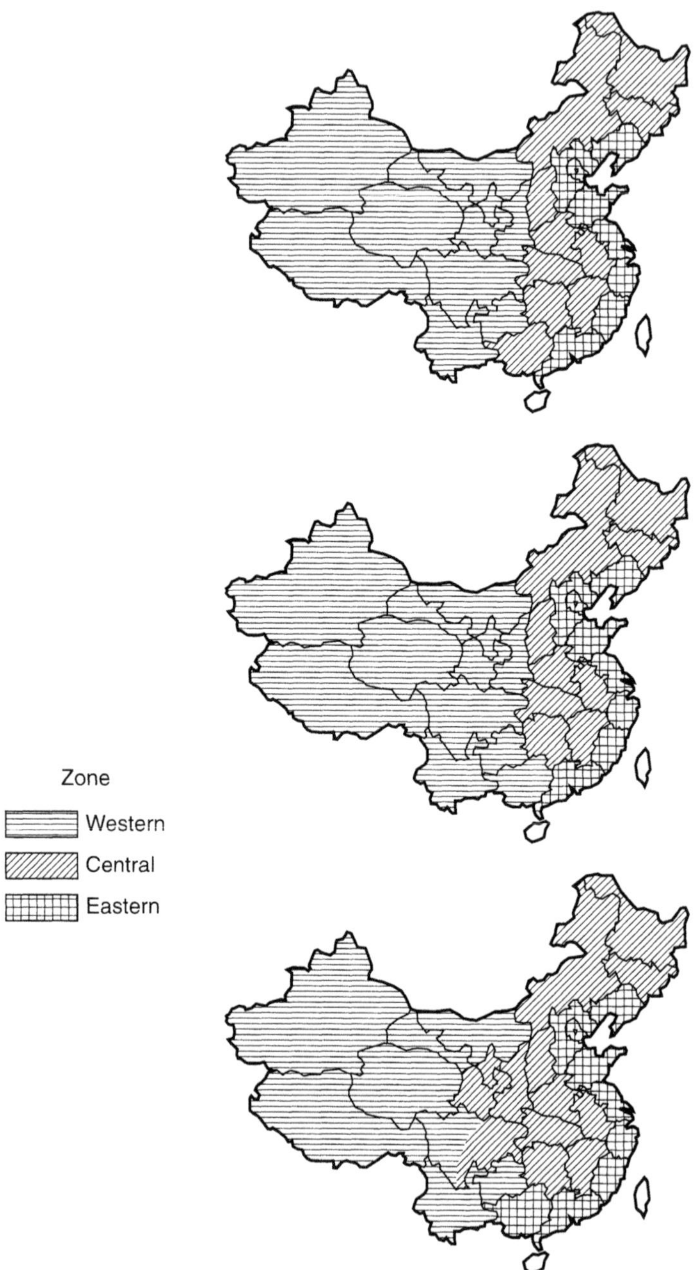

Chart 2 Division of economic zones (three versions)

Source: Derived from Li, Wen-yan, 'Contemporary spatial issues', in G.J.R. Linge and D.K. Forbes (eds.), 1990, *China's Spatial Economy: Recent Developements and Reforms*, Hong Kong: Oxford University Press, p. 69.

Table 2 Basic indicators of three regions in China, 1995

Indicators	Eastern	Central	Western
Regions %	16	27	57
Population %	41.3	35.8	22.9
GDP %	58.2	27.6	14.2
GDP per capita	807	442	355
Direct Foreign Investment %	85.7	9.9	4.4

Source: Compiled by author.

Table 3 Comparison of GDP growth of three major regions in China

Indicators	Eastern	Central	Western
GDP in the whole country (1978) %	52.8	30.7	16.5
GDP in the whole country (1995) %	58.2	27.6	14.2
GDP change during 1978–1995 %	+5.4	−3.1	−2.3
Average growth of GDP (1978–1995) %	10.4	9.0	8.8

Source: Compiled by author.

However, the policy also led to growing regional disparities, unbalanced regional investment, growing contradictions between the central and local governments, as well as trade conflicts and resource battles among the provinces. Chang's study has pointed out that at least 40% of the resources allocated by the central government to the western regions have flowed back to the eastern region.[2] The policy whereby the central government has tried to loosen price controls generally, while maintaining strict control over the price of raw materials, put the central and western regions in an awkward situation.

As a result, it is believed that from 1980 to 1993 the level of disparity among the eastern, the central and the western regions increased by the factors 9, 11.1 and 6.1 respectively in terms of their share of total GDP. They grew by the factors 7.7, 8.9 and 4.2 respectively in terms of their share in GDP per capita. Chang and Wu's study has concluded that after 1985 the disparity among provinces is growing both in absolute and relative terms.[3]

Chart 2 shows the then most widely used versions of regional classification. Tables 2 and 3 provide some basic indicators and a comparison of GDP growth of those three regions.

The post-1990 era: growth pole and growth region strategy

This strategy, patterned after the concept of 'growth pole' introduced by western scholars,[4] has aimed at developing some leading industries in a

Table 4 The changing Chinese administrative-economic regions (1949–1990s)

Stage	Year	Key measures
1	1949–	1. Six Administrative Areas (Economic Regions); 2. Inner Mongolia as a self-governed Territory; 3. Tibet.
2	1954–	1. Reduction of the original 49 provinces, Taiwan included, into 32 provinces; 2. Abolition of the former six Administrative Areas (Economic Regions) and Tibet.
3	1958–	1. Establishment of seven Economic Development Coordination Areas; 2. Establishment of the 'Economic Coordination Commission'; 3. Establishment of the Economic Planning Office.
4	1961–	1. Establishment of the six Economic Coordination Areas; 2. Abolition of the 'Economic Coordination Commission'; 3. Establishment of the Central Bureau of Ministry of Civil Affairs.
5	1970–	Establishment of ten Economic Coordination Areas.
6	1978–	Establishment of six Primary Economic Development Systems.
7	1982–	The National Planning Committee and The Bureau of Statistics divided the whole country into two major areas: Coastal and Inland.
8	1981–1985	Seven Economic Coordination Areas were established consecutively: 1. The Huabei Area (1981) 2. The East-North Area (1983) 3. The Huatung Area (1983) 4. The West-South Area (1984) 5. The West-North Area (1984) 6. The Central-South Area (1985) 7. Shandong Area
9	1986–	Divide the country into three major Regions (the Eastern, the Central and the Western) during the Seventh Five-year Economic Planning Era.
10	1990s	Seven major Economic Development Regions were established consecutively.

Source: Mainly derived from Z.P. Huang, 1998: 25–27.

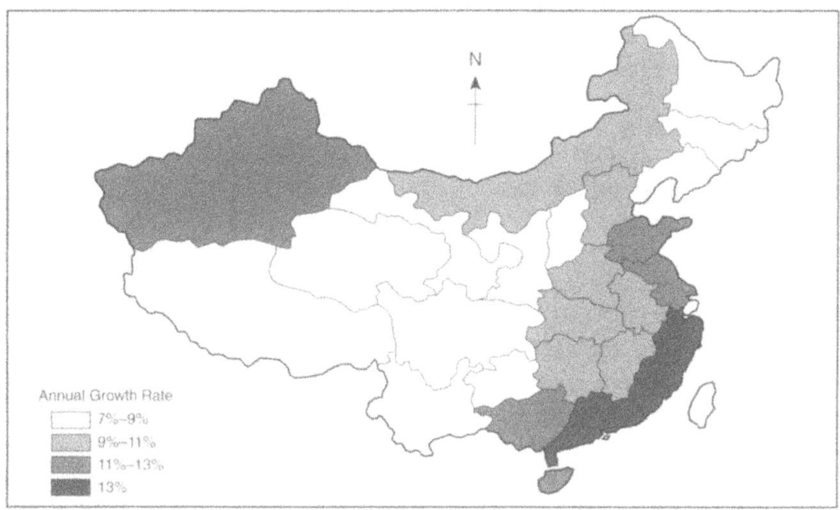

Chart 3 Annual growth rate of GDP in China (1978–1995)

Source: Compiled by author.

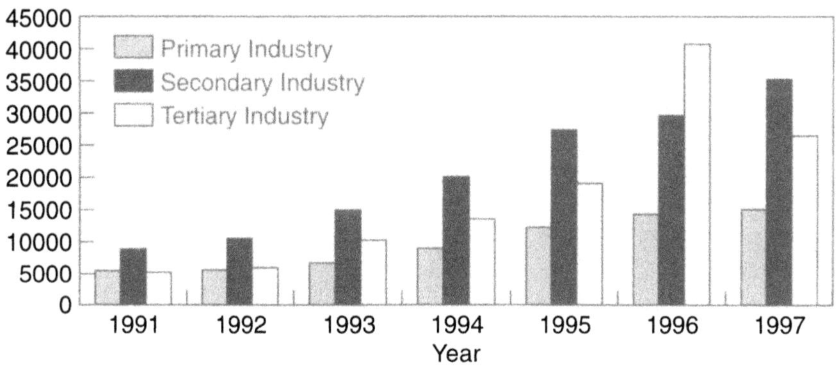

Chart 4 The industrial structural change in China (1991–1997)

Note: It is generally held that there are two main reasons for the decline of industrial production in 1997: (1) affected by the Asian financial crisis, the overall economic performance is declining; (2) the huge decline of the tertiary sector.

Source: Compiled from *Statistical Yearbook of China*, 1991–1997.

particular region in the hope that it will create linkage effects for adjacent regions. In the event, the growth pole and growth region strategy has focused on the coastal and river basin areas, such as the development of Pudong and Shanghai, in the expectation that it would also lead to the development of the Yangtze River Delta area. The government has planned to develop water resource-, natural resource-, mining resource- and environmental resource-oriented industries in the central and/or western regions along the same lines.

When further dividing the regional economic development strategies in China from an economic development plan period point of view, one may discover that during the first five-year economic development plan period (1953–1957), most strategic industries were located in inland areas. However, the second five-year economic development plan period (1958–1962) witnessed a more balanced allocation to both coastal and inland areas. The third five-year development era (1963–1967) again saw the shifting of industries into inland areas. The pendulum swung back to a more balanced development pattern during the fourth five-year development plan period (1968–1972). However, beginning with the fifth five-year economic development plan era (1973–1977), the trend was yet again reversed in favour of the eastern coastal regions. Statistics show that during 1984 to 1990 the proportion of export generated from the eastern region amounted to 80.6%, far ahead of the total produced by the central and the western regions. Furthermore, all economic indices of the interior showed that it was here that a total of 70% of China's population lived, whereas 80% of her land accommodated less than half her total population.

Table 4 (above) illustrates chronologically the changing picture of the Chinese administrative-economic regions from 1949 up to the 1990s. Charts 3 and 4 (above) give some idea as to how the annual growth of GDP and industrial composition of China have changed since reform.

Debates over different strategies for regional economic development

Different regional economic development strategies have been heatedly debated ever since 1978. In this section we shall look at what underlies the ethos of four different development strategies as applied to the People's Republic.

The biased development strategy

The idea behind the biased development strategy is simply that, given the better infrastructure of the eastern region, it was only pragmatic to concentrate the government efforts on the development of the coastal area first, before gradually shifting the focus of the development strategy to the central and western regions. Although this idea has been broached by using different terminology, the strategy is very similar to the idea of the 'unbalanced growth strategy' put forward by Albert Hirschman.[5]

The anti-biased development strategy

In contradistinction to the biased development strategy, the anti-biased development strategy holds that, even though the existing infrastructure in the eastern region is far better than that in western areas, the growth and development speed in the western regions might exceed that of the former. This strategy builds on the fact that in the western regions there are abundant natural resources, and operates on the premise that appropriate technology could be brought in. It is therefore suggested that mining and electronic industries should be located closer to where the resources are.

Unlike the preceding strategy, the anti-biased development strategy holds that development does not necessarily follow the notion that the advanced regions control the advanced technology which then, step by step, permeates into those areas where it is most suitable to adopt the intermediate and traditional technologies. According to the advocates of the anti-biased growth strategy it is possible to develop an area exclusively on the basis of its natural resources.

The multi-wave development strategy

The multi-wave development strategy actually is a strategy acknowledging China's reality, where the eastern region is more developed than the central and western regions, notwithstanding that the western region is richer in natural resources. Accordingly, this strategy holds that future regional economic growth may actually derive from a multi-wave development strategy whereby the eastern and the western regions would be developed concomitantly.

The strategy of restructuring the industrial composition

This strategy contends that in working out the regional economic development strategy for China, one has to take note of the country's long-standing 'dual structure'[6] and 'inadequate price mechanism'.[7] In other words, one has to note that past practices created the so-called 'double profits' phenomenon in the eastern region and the 'double squeeze' phenomenon in the central and western regions. Concrete measures proposed have included encouraging industries to move to the western region and allowing certain industries to move to agricultural areas.

In addition to the aforementioned strategies, improving the quality of human resources in the western regions and developing the tourist industry are included among some of the other concrete tactics proposed.

Up to now, there would not appear to be a consensus as to which strategy is the best suited to meet China's regional economic development needs. However, it is generally agreed that while the biased development strategy may be the least costly, it seems to neglect the possibility of resource-centered development patterns. The anti-biased strategy is criticized for its lack of a 'cost' concept. The third and the fourth strategies are generally regarded to be the most pragmatic, though moving industries may also turn out to be costly. The ideas on improving the quality of human resources and developing the tourist industry have, however, gained the least support so far.

Proposals for the industrial distribution in China's three major regions

Since the reorganization of China's industrial composition has been taken as the most viable strategy for regional economic development, how should China's industries be distributed regionally? Scholars such as Tsao[8] have suggested that readjustment may need to be made within the following dimensions: technology-orientation, structure-orientation and resource-orientation.

To be more specific, Tsao[9] has proposed that the eastern region should focus on technology-oriented industries such as information technology, biological engineering, optical appliances, oceanic development, aviation industry and nuclear industry, etc. He further suggested that the eastern region should develop small-scale, multiple products that are energy-efficient, possess high added value, and are environmentally sensitive. The computer, electronics, information software, semi-conductor and satellite industries would be among the right choices.

Tsao has moreover suggested that the central region should concentrate on attracting capital-intensive industries such as chemical engineering, mechanical engineering, etc. To avoid limitations in relation to the raw materials shortages, inadequate transportation and environmental pollution that are likely to result from the practices of these industries, he also mentioned that a model combining restructuring and technology would be a better strategy.

As regards the western region, resource-orientated or labor-intensive industry should be encouraged. Agricultural, textile and petrochemical industries could thus be considered.

Related measures ought to be taken to bring about regional economic development in China

Theoretically speaking, regional economic development not only relies on investment in the right types of leading industries, but also demands sufficient raw materials, water, energy supply and supplementary industrial development. Besides, adequate infrastructure in both a hardware and a software sense is also desperately needed. For a country as huge as China, some other measures, as illustrated below, therefore also deserve special attention:

Interregional industrial structure coordination

Interregional industrial structure coordination implies the coordination of industrial structures among the eastern, the central and the western regions. Tsao (1997) suggested that if the western region were to transport raw materials and natural resources to the eastern region, while the eastern region were to move some high energy consumption industries to the western region, a good combination of the eastern technology and western resources might ensue. By itself, this would be an important step toward the integration of the eastern region's development with the western region's exploration. Meanwhile, the central region is seen to play the intermediate role. In other words, if the eastern region is taken to be the 'export promotion' area, the western region is treated as the 'resource exploration' area; leaving the central region then to be viewed as a 'comprehensive development' area. Only when the three regions are well coordinated, can the resource or market wars that occurred in the past be avoided.

Coordination between regional development policy and international open policy

It is fully recognized that if China expects to become a developed country, she has to work hard on reforming her industry, agriculture and infrastructure simultaneously. An 'export promotion' strategy that aims at involving her in the international market and solving problems associated with the agricultural surplus labor and high technology problems is naturally a must for the eastern region. On the other hand, an 'import substitution' strategy geared to address the problems encountered in upgrading the industrial structure have laid down the foundation for basic heavy industrial development that seems to provide the right developmental answer for the central and western regions. It is expected that the coordination of China's regional development needs, and its international open-door policy, will allow China to develop from an inward-looking economy into an outward-looking one.

Emphasis on the 'unbalanced mutual compensation and coordinated growth strategy'

The trade-off between the 'balanced' and 'unbalanced' growth strategies propounded by western academics has also caught the attention of Chinese scholars. According to Tsao (1997) adopting a 'balanced growth strategy' may bring about interregional equity without however achieving greater resource allocation efficiency. By contrast, the adoption of the 'unbalanced growth strategy' may promote resource allocation efficiency without however achieving interregional equity. In order to strike a balance between economic efficiency and social equity between regions, an 'unbalanced mutual compensation and coordinated growth strategy' has to be worked out.

'East–West Union' and 'West–West Union'

Tsao (1997) proposed that, in order to rectify the 'double squeeze' problem mentioned above, the government should reform its taxation, fiscal and administrative systems to bring about proper coordination in development between the eastern and the western regions. In addition, in order to bring about 'economies of scale', the western regions should jointly develop some of the industries that enjoy an (international) comparative advantage such as energy and mining industries. Jointly constructing and improving the inter-regional transportation networks is another good case in point. In short, if the 'east–west union' can be understood as one type of vertical specialization, the 'west–west union' might then be understood as one type of horizontal specialization.

Appropriate regional development strategy under the long-standing 'dual structure'

Given the long-standing 'dual structure' in China, various scholars have argued that, in addition to the familiar regional economic development strategies, the following ideas on possible development directions deserve special mention:

(a) A balanced approach needs to be taken between regional economic development and ecological equilibrium;
(b) Human resources development should be kept in line with technological advancement;
(c) A balance should pertain between industrialization and the market economy; and
(d) Urban élites should be formed so as to realize the 'growth pole' ideal.

The necessity of pursuing both a regional open policy and an international open policy

It is suggested that the 'regional open-door policy' should start in the eastern regions of China, gradually moving toward the central and the western regions. This approach is called the 'Three-along policy'.[10] As regards the international open-door policy, it is said that the country should gradually shift from a spatial open-door policy to an industrial open-door policy to truly transform itself from a 'closed economy' into an 'open economy'.

Planned industrial and spatial change: a sketch of regional development within the realm of the ninth five-year economic development plan and the 2010 plan in China

The ninth five-year economic development plan and the 2010 plan were promulgated during the fourteenth plenary meeting in 1992. 'Two basic changes', 'nine major guidelines' and 'twelve relations', introduced by Chairman Jiang Zemin, made up the core of these plans. The 'two basic changes' hold that China is heading away from the planned economy towards a market economy. Moreover, the economic growth pattern is pointing more toward agglomeration rather than along the previous dispersion path. Among the 'nine major guidelines', the one relating to 'insisting on regional economic coordinated development and gradual improvement of 'regional disparity' relates most closely to this chapter. And among the 'twelve relations',[11] the substance of the fifth, eighth, and the tenth relations also relates to this chapter.

In order to address the problem of disparity among regions, the ninth five-year economic development plan stressed that regional economic development should follow the market economy principle, while taking into account the natural geographical characteristics, and moving beyond the administrative boundaries to develop some cross-provincial/district/city economic zones. The planned zones mentioned above include: the Yangtze River Delta and River Basin economic zone using Shanghai as the core; the Zhujiang Delta and the Southeast Fujian coastal area economic zone; the Bohai Economic Rim composed of the Liaodong and Shandong Peninsulas, Beijing, Tianjin, and Hebei province and the Euro-Asia Corridor. In short, the focus with regard to the eastern coastal area development will not see much change in the future. At the same time, the following measures were brought up to promote the development of the central and the western regions:

- reform the financial system;
- prioritize the resource-related and infrastructure development in these regions;
- encourage foreign direct investment into such regions; and
- adopt further price reforms.

We may further summarize the ninth five-year economic development plan from the regional economic development point of view as follows:

Guangdong's open-door policy

It is said in the plan that Guangzhou, Shantou and Zhanjiang, given their comparatively good locations, would be made the three major growth poles in Guangdong Province. The already designated special economic zone of

Shenzhen will be developed into a center for banking, information, trade, transportation, tourism and, not least, a high-tech center.

Southeast area/Fujian province

The development model for this area seeks to combine the outward-oriented and unbalanced, yet coordinated, development strategies. There are several key areas that need to be developed under this strategy. For instance:

(a) On the issue of Fujian–Taiwan coordination the idea is to integrate the four provinces of Fujian, Guangdong, Hainan and Guangxi to form an industrial coordination circle, in order to gradually make these areas part of the international economic division of labor in the Pacific Rim;
(b) As regards pole-line coordination, the idea is to develop those small townships with economic growth potential, then connect these poles together through the Fuzhou–Xiamen highway;
(c) It is proposed to turn Fuzhou and Xiamen into two major growth poles which can generate spread development effects in the whole of Fujian province;
(d) It was decided to strengthen the development of China's central region; and
(e) Also proposed has been the structural upgrading, which implies turning some regions from labor-intensive areas into capital-intensive ones.

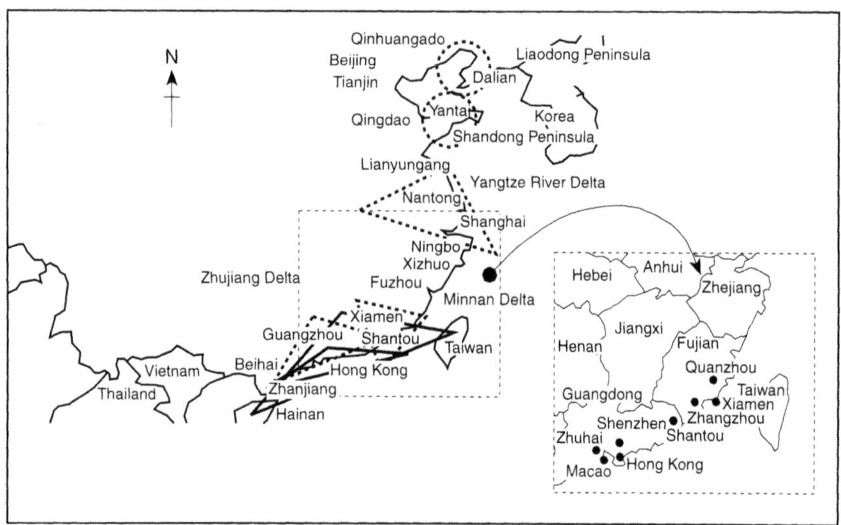

Chart 5 Special economic zones, open cities and economic development areas along the coastal area of China

Source: Derived from Linge and Forbes, 1990, p. 17.

Southwest development: surrounding the Baipuwan economic development circle

This plan aims at the utilization of the unique geographical situation surrounding the southwest area – India, Bhutan, Sikkim, Nepal, Cambodia, Vietnam, etc. – and of the abundant natural resources, to ensure the regional development of China's Southwest, Hainan, and west Guangdong.

Chart 5 indicates the planned special economic zones, open cities and economic development areas along the coastal area of China.

The Yangtze River Delta development

The expansion of Yangtze River Delta is by far the most important development plan. Shanghai, Wuhan and Chongqing are singled out as the three growth-poles along the lower, middle, and upper Yangtze River region respectively. Outward-looking and high-tech industries will be the focus for the lower Yangtze River area, while resource-orientated and basic industries will be the focus of the upper Yangtze River region. The petrochemical industry, as well as intensive agriculture, is the focus for the central Yangtze region. In short, Shanghai, Nanjing, Wuhan and Chongqing are the four major growth poles in the region; it is hoped that positive developmental effects will result from these cities' expansion that may then permeate the whole region.

Charts 6 and 7 contrast both the planned Yangtze River economic belts and city belts with other world major urban galaxies.

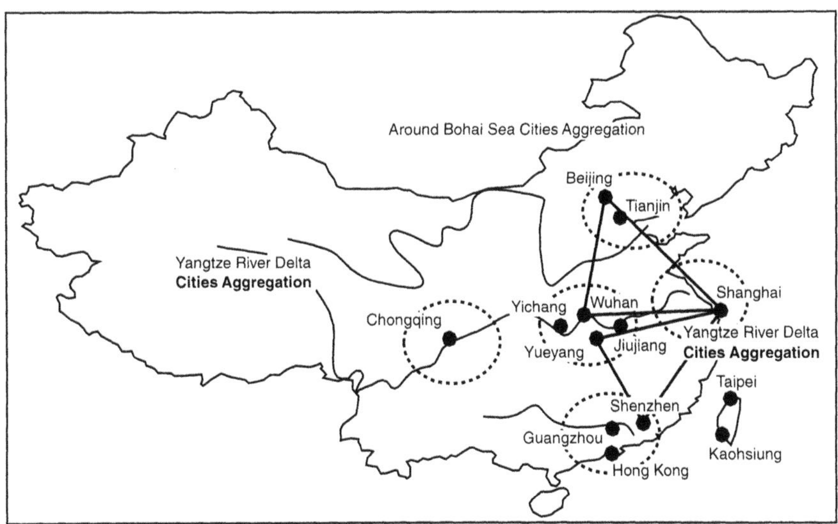

Chart 6 Yangtze River economic belts and city belts

Source: Compiled by author.

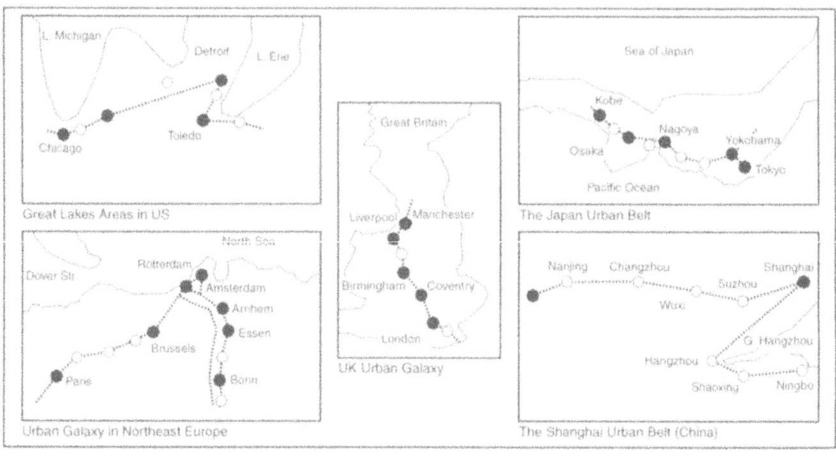

Chart 7 World major urban galaxies

Source: Derived from Terry G. McGee, 1991, 'The emergence of "Desakota" regions in Asia: Expanding a hypothesis', in N. Ginsburg, B. Koppel, and T.G. McGee (eds.), *The Extended Metropolis: Settlement Transition in Asia*, Honolulu: University of Hawaii Press, pp. 3–25.

Harbin–Dalian economic development zone

Harbin and Daqing are chosen as the two major growth poles which, it is hoped, will be able to bring about spillover effects to its adjacent cities, thus leading to the overall development of Heilongjiang.

Bohai economic development zone

The Bohai economic development zone covers four major provinces – Hebei, Shandong, Shanxi, and Liaoning. It constitutes 7% of the country's area and 20.5% of China's population. Additionally, from northern Dandong to Qingdao, the area covers almost 1/3 of China's coastal line, boasts more than 40 different harbors and contributes to 60% of the total import/export volume. With its huge hinterland, and by virtue of its proximity to the new Euro-Asian Corridor, this area is more than qualified to lead to the development of the center of Northern China.

From an international development point of view, given that this area is located at the center of Northeast Asia, close to both Japan and Korea, decisions on how to exploit international economic links will certainly affect whether this area can be fully developed in the future.

The new Euro-Asian Corridor (Chart 8): main line for the economic development of China's central and western regions

Basic heavy chemical and energy industries will be made the lead industries in the development of this region. It is expected that dispersion effects can be generated through the expansion of these industries.

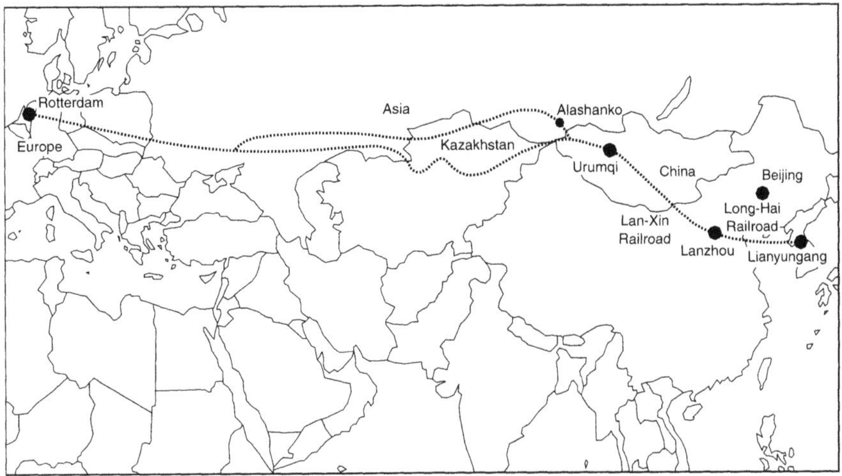

Chart 8 New Euro-Asian Corridor

Source: compiled by author.

Tumen River economic growth triangle

This triangle represents for the special economic zone that brings together border regions of China, Russia and North Korea. Mongolia, South Korea and even UNDP are all interested in getting involved in this development plan. It is estimated that 20 years and a total of US$300 thousand million will be required to realize such a plan.

To summarize, through the ninth five-year economic development plan and the 2010 grand plan, China expects to adopt a full-fledged development strategy that integrates the development of all coastal and river basin as well as border regions. The Bohai Rim, Yangtze River and Zhujiang Deltas will be the foci of the coastal development plan that is intended to integrate Taiwan, Hong Kong, Macao, and other overseas markets. Shanghai's Pudong will be the leading area for Yangtze River basin development. The new Euro-Asian Corridor is meant to create new international trade routes for China. And finally, the encouragement of developing border trade seeks to bring about regional economic cooperation with neighboring countries such as Russia, India, Nepal and the continental Southeast Asian countries.

Chart 9 summarizes overall the planned economic growth triangles in China.

Prospects for China's regional economic development trends

From what has been stated above, there is no doubt that China is determined to enter into an era in which both export-promotion and import-substitution

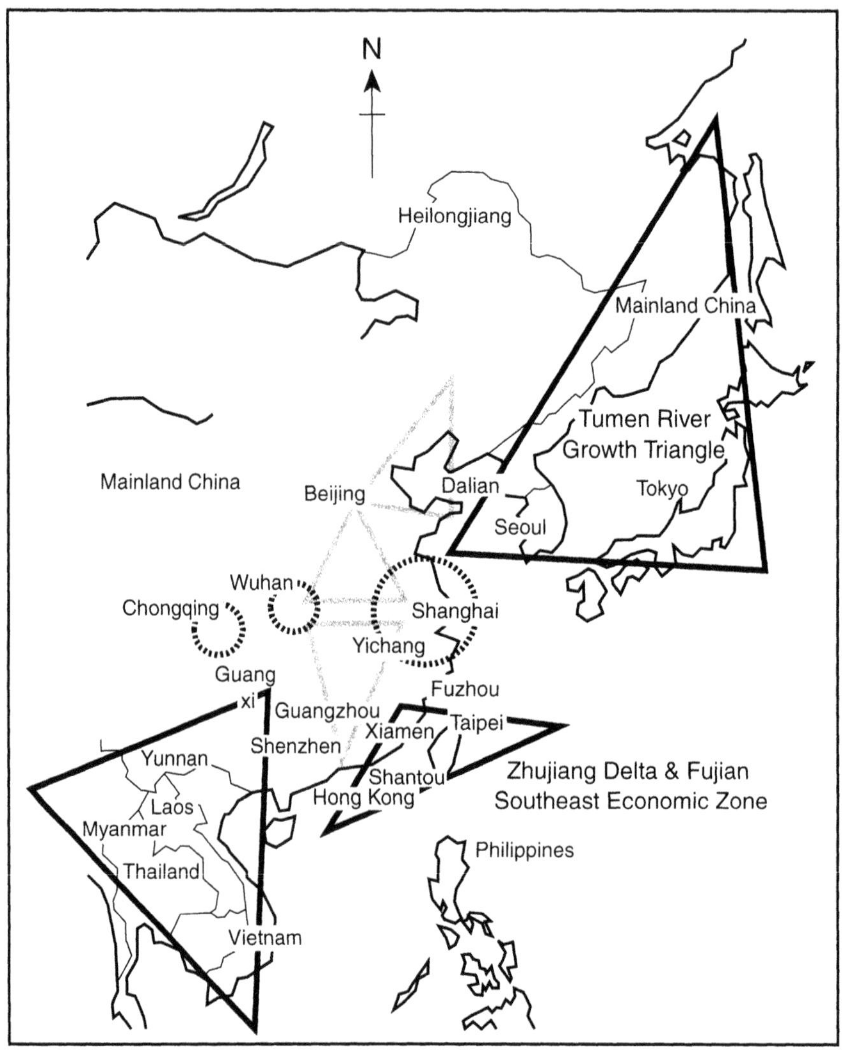

Chart 9 Economic growth triangles in China

Source: Compiled by author. Also consult Xiangming Chen, 1993a, 1993b and 1995.

strategies will be emphasized, both industrial and service sectors will be addressed and, most importantly, regional economic development will be pushed forward. It is exactly in this vein that the following trends have been forecast (Chang and Wu 1995a, 1995b):

(i) the relative disparity between the eastern and the western regions will decline while the absolute disparity will widen;
(ii) more attention will be paid to the integration of industrial structural transformation and the regional economic development

plan (as it is the goal of China that the country will be able to solve her basic development needs within ten years, to reach the take-off stage within another ten years and achieve modernisation within yet another ten years, it is therefore imperative that China transforms her industrial structures and restructures urban–rural relations); and

(iii) the central and the western regional development will receive more attention, including improvements in infrastructure, greater foreign direct investment, loans for investors and government investment – and it is hoped that through such tactics the autonomous region of Xinjiang, as well as the regional cities of Xining and Lanzhou, can be developed.

Concluding remarks

This chapter has demonstrated that, as of 1990, China has adopted a regional economic development strategy which combines both efficiency and equity consideration, planning and market mechanisms, as well as unbalanced and co-ordination policies. However, given various historical, geographical and policy constraints, it is believed that, in the foreseeable future, regional imbalances will continue. Some scholars[12] have even pointed out that, only when the growth rate of the inland areas exceeds that of the eastern region by 73%, can the absolute disparity be narrowed. Further, Rou Chang has also held that, only when the growth rate per capita of GDP in the central and western regions is higher than that in the coastal area, is there a possibility of narrowing the relative disparity between the two.

In conclusion, this author believes that the ideals embedded in both plans can be realized only if huge amounts of direct foreign investment can be poured into China, and domestically vertical and horizontal specializations are accomplished. Therefore, the questions of how to develop internal regional development networks and how to grasp international cooperation opportunities in an ever-changing world economic system are likely to pose almost unavoidable challenges and bring with them significant responsibilities.

Notes

1 This is widely known as the 'Third-Line' area or 'Third Front' or 'Defensive Heartland' which was created in the remote mountainous hinterland in the central region of China where defense facilities could be hidden, sometimes even in caves.
2 For details, please consult Chang (1996).
3 Please see Chang and Wu (1995a, 1995b).
4 The concept of 'growth pole' was introduced by French economist Perroux during the mid-1950s. Later, it caught the attention of scholars such as J. Boudeville, J. Friedmann, N. Hansen, W. Alonso, A. Kuklinski, H. Richardson and many others. As of 1970, it was widely applied as one of the available regional development policy measures.

5 For details, please see Hirschman (1958).
6 The 'dual structure' stands for the rural–urban dichotomy or, better still, the barriers which have created various kinds of inequality that have existed in China ever since the country was established.
7 The concept of 'inadequate price mechanism' implies that there exist price differences between the agricultural and industrial products, such that the prices of the former are normally unreasonably low compared to the prices of the latter. This price differential is due to government policies which often favour the industrial sector and the eastern region where most industries are concentrated.
8 For details, please consult Hsin Tsao (1997: 10).
9 Please see Tsao (1997: 10).
10 The 'Three-along policy' stands for 'along the coastal area', 'along the river basin' and 'along the border line' policies which were to be implemented sequentially as China's regional development strategies in the 1990s.
11 The 'Twelve relations' include: Relationship among reform, development and stability; Relationship between efficiency and effectiveness; Relationship among economic construction, population, resources and environment; Relationship among primary, secondary and service sectors; Relationship between the eastern region and the central–western regions; Relationship between market and planning mechanism; Relationship between public and private ownership; Relationship among state, enterprise and individual in terms of income distribution; Relationship between open policy and self-sufficiency; Relationship between central and local government; Relationship between military and economic construction; and the Relationship between physical and mental construction.
12 For details, please consult Rou Chang (1995a: 27–30, 35).

Bibliography

Chang, Lou-chen and Tze-tsai Wu (1995a) 'Trend analysis on China's regional economic disparities', *Economic Science*, Vol. 3: 32–36.

Chang, Lou-chen and Tze-tsai Wu (1995b) 'China's regional economic disparities trend analysis and policies', *China's Economic Problems*, pp. 19–24 for details (in Chinese).

Chang, Rou (1995a) 'Regional economic development policy: theories and practices revisited', *Economic Dynamics*, Vol. 1, pp. 27–30, 35.

Chang, You-su (1996) 'The historical account of regional economic development strategies', *Finance-Economic Science*, No. 6: 54–56 (in Chinese).

Chen, Xiangming (1993a) 'China's growing integration with the Asia-Pacific economy: subregional and local dimensions, determinants, and consequences', in Arif Dirlik (ed.), *What Is in a Rim? Critical Perspectives on the Pacific Region Idea*, Boulder, CO: Westview Press.

Chen, Xiangming (1993b) 'The new spatial division of labor and commodity chains in the greater south China economic region', in Gary Gereffi and Miguel Korzenewiez (eds), *Commodity Chains and Global Capitalism*, Westport, CT: Greenwood Press.

Chen, Xiangming (1995) 'The evolution of free economic zones and the recent development of cross-national zones', *International Journal of Urban and Regional Research*, Vol. 19, No. 4.

Chinese Geography and Environment: A Journal of Translations, Special Issue on Territorial Planning and Management, Summer 1990, New York: M. E. Sharpe, Inc.

Fujita, Masahisa, Paul Krugman, and Anthony J. Venables (1999) *The Spatial Economy: Cities, Regions, and International Trade*, Cambridge, MA: The MIT Press.

Hirschman, Albert C. (1958) *The Strategy of Economic Development*, New Haven, CT: Yale University Press.

Linge, G. J. R. and D. K. Forbes (1990) 'The spatial economy of China', in G. J. R. Linge and D. K. Forbes (eds), *China's Spatial Economy*, Hong Kong: Oxford University Press, pp. 10–34.

Linge, Godfrey (ed.) (1997) *China's New Spatial Economy: Heading Toward 2020*, New York: Oxford University Press.

Scott, Allen J. (2000) *Regions and the World Economy: The Coming Shape of Global Production, Competition, and Political Order*, New York: Oxford University Press.

China:
Social and Political Change

Chapter 7

Social Welfare Reform in China

The Impact of Globalisation

Guan Xinping

Introduction

Since the late 1970s, many countries have seen moves towards welfare reform. This is also the case in China. In spite of the many differences from country to country, not least in terms of the extent of the reforms undertaken, the basic direction of reform has been very similar in all countries concerned. From the post-war welfare state model, which was based on the ideology of social justice and equality, we are moving towards the neo-liberal welfare model, which is based mainly on economic efficiency. A number of social and economic factors have influenced this shift but two are fundamental: economic globalisation and the introduction of market reforms.

Social welfare reform in China in the past two decades

In the first 30 years of the People's Republic, China enjoyed a high level of social welfare provision, especially when compared with its relatively low level of economic development. During this period, responsibility for social welfare in urban areas was assumed by both the government and the state enterprises, and by collective economic organisations in rural areas. As a result of the reform measures introduced as of the early 1980s, China's social policy has undergone significant change.

China's welfare system before the reform

China's socialist welfare system dates back to the early 1950s. The first legislation in the field of welfare policy were the 'Labour Insurance Regulations of the PRC', promulgated in 1951. In the following three decades, the governmental welfare system in urban areas and the collective welfare system in rural areas were gradually extended to include almost all the welfare provisions that European welfare states provided to their citizens (Guan 2000). The Chinese welfare system in that period had the following characteristics:

(a) full employment: almost all urban labourers were assigned a job by the government and they were not laid off after taking up employment. In the countryside, rural workers were granted full access to collectively-owned farmland in rural villages;
(b) a rationing system in the context of the distribution of subsistence foodstuffs and goods such as grain, cooking oil and clothes for the urban residents. These goods were subsidised;
(c) public services in health care, education, public housing for urban residents and personal services for urban and rural residents;
(d) social assistance in urban and rural areas; and
(e) various insurances for state workers and other staff, including pensions, medical insurance, occupational benefits, etc.

In summary, China's social welfare system prior to the introduction of social welfare reforms amounted to a multiple-tier system. At its most basic level it was a 'safety net' which, in the case of urban residents, was open for all those in full employment and provided access to a supply of basic foodstuffs. In rural areas, access was given to collective farm land. At the next higher level, China's social welfare system boasted a social assistance scheme for those urban and rural residents who were unable to seek employment or to obtain family support. At the highest level, an exclusive welfare system was reserved for urban state workers and government staff. This covered welfare provisions such as pensions, free medical care and public housing.

Although the Chinese welfare system has been criticised for its shortcomings, not least its differentiation between those living in rural and urban areas, it functioned well in the centrally planned economy. All Chinese people enjoyed basic social security and China as a whole was able to make significant achievements in its overall social development measured in terms of a rising average life expectancy, lower illiteracy rates, and a relatively equitable standard of living.

The early stage of welfare reform

China's social welfare system has undergone reform since the early 1980s. In its early phase, this reform was a response to the then ongoing reforms of the country's economic system.

The first step in the urban economic reform was aimed at the decoupling of state enterprises from the government's financial system. The fundamental new objective of state enterprises henceforth focused no longer on simply carrying out the government's productive plan but on making profit. As a result, differences in the average age of workers and in the numbers of those who had retired from a state enterprise became key issues for the latter's management. This was so because the associated costs of workers and pensioners had an impact on the economic performance of the enterprise. In response to the economic reform measures, systems that pooled pension and free medical benefits were set up from the early 1980s to replace the old individual-enterprise-based labour insurance system.

The introduction as of the mid-1980s of a contract employment system entailed the abolition of China's rigid employment system. Workers henceforth taking on jobs at state enterprises were no longer guaranteed permanent employment as had been more senior workers previously. In response to the new risks of becoming unemployed, the government set up an unemployment insurance system in 1986. This was extended to all state workers as of the early 1990s.

As a consequence of the economic reforms, urban enterprises were transformed from 'socio-economic organisations' into 'economic organisations'. Their role as a provider of social welfare services was gradually weakened. To make up for this functional loss in the provision of social welfare services, urban residents' communities began to be reinforced to undertake this task from the late 1980s onwards.

Briefly, then, social welfare reform in China in the 1980s mainly affected urban areas, as it constituted an institutional adjustment in response to the institutional imbalances that had opened up between the existing welfare system and the economic reforms newly initiated. The basic aim of welfare reform in this period was to reinforce existing welfare functions by introducing new mechanisms that would compensate for the functional weakening of the levers of the traditional welfare system.

Social welfare reform in the 1990s

In the past decade China has experienced a fundamental shift in welfare policy, in line with her embrace of the market as well as her increasing interdependence with the global economy. The reform of China's social welfare system has been comprehensive and significant. The main aspects of this reform can be summarised as follows:

The urban welfare system

The abolition of the old rationing system in basic subsistence goods meant that the government no longer subsidised food and other basic necessities for urban residents. The latter are now required to purchase their food in the market place.

Before the reforms, the Chinese government pursued a policy of full employment, or at least a policy of low unemployment. Lay-offs happened only seldom, especially in the state sector. After the reforms, the government has tended to pursue a labour market policy under which urban labourers' employment is no longer arranged by the government. As has been noted above, the individual labourers' experience of stable employment has been replaced with the labour contract practice. In practice, employees now face a much higher risk of being laid off.

As regards pensions, the state operated a legal insurance scheme in state enterprises before the introduction of welfare reforms. This was a non-contributory benefit. After the adoption of social welfare reforms, a social insurance model has come into practice. This is a contributory benefit, which is paid for by both employees and employers.

Prior to welfare reform the state workers and governmental staff benefited from free medical care, and other urban residents benefited from cheaply priced hospital services as well as medicine provision. With the onset of a contributory model of social insurance, residents are now faced with a semi-commercial hospital system and commercial medicine provision.

Before the reforms, the country boasted a social relief system which provided assistance to those urban residents who did not have the capacity to work, had no family support and no income. This system only had a narrow coverage. After the reforms began, this system was changed to a subsistence level security system, aimed at all urban families whose income falls below a certain threshold. The coverage of this new system is much wider.

Prior to the initiation of social welfare reforms, welfare housing provision was made in the urban state sector. This included public investment in the construction of such housing and the so-called 'welfare house-distribution system' through which state workers and governmental staff were assigned a flat free of charge at low rental costs. With reform, the housing provision system has become commercialised. While this has implied both public and private investment in the construction of new housing, residents now need to pay for their housing at market prices or close to that level.

Moreover, before the onset of welfare reforms in China's welfare system, there were government-financed homes for the elderly, disabled, and orphans. Following welfare reform, private investors and NGO/NPOs are encouraged to participate in providing relevant services.

As regards other welfare facilities and services, it can be noted that before the reforms began substantial public investment went into improving the infrastructure for urban residents that raised the level of their standard of living and their cultural environment. Urban residents could use relevant public facilities free of charge or at very low prices. After the adoption of reforms in the welfare system, not least due to insufficient public finances, many urban facilities are now running on a commercial basis, and the residents need to pay a market price for the services rendered.

The rural welfare system

Before the introduction of welfare reforms almost no pension system worthy of note existed in rural areas. Now, in some rich villages, a pension programme modelled along the social insurance scheme of the urban areas has come into existence.

On the issue of social assistance, rural areas in the past benefited from the so-called 'five-guaranteed household' (*wu bao hu*) system. This system provided basic security in five areas: food, clothes, fuel, medical care and funeral costs. The assistance was granted to elderly people who were not or could not be supported by their family. In the wake of welfare reforms there has been an attempt to maintain this basic social assistance, but it is now run at the level of the county to allow for funds for the above purposes to be pooled.

As regards the provision of health services, a co-operative medical system prevailed before the onset of welfare reforms. This was based in the rural collective economic organisations. In the aftermath of reform, the co-operative medical care system has been disbanded in about 90 per cent of all villages. It has been replaced by a private medical care practice.

From the above, four general trends of social welfare reform – in both urban and rural areas – can be identified: first, the 'societalisation of social welfare'; second, the rise of selectivity; third, a change in the basic philosophy of welfare provision; and fourth, changes in the basic objectives of welfare provision.

General trends in China's social welfare reform

The most significant characteristic of the welfare reform concerns the trend towards the 'societalisation' of social welfare. This term summarises two kinds of change in the provision of welfare. First, the government is no longer taking full responsibility for providing social welfare. Instead, other actors, including local community organisations and various non-governmental organisations, have been encouraged to participate in its provision. Individual labourers are required to pay for their social security as well as more generally in many other areas traditionally labelled social welfare. Second, economic entities, including state enterprises, also no longer serve a strong function in the provision of welfare. Indeed, their traditional role and responsibility as a welfare provider have been passed on to other social organisations, e.g. the local community.

The reform of China's welfare system has brought about a move from a universal model to a selective model of welfare provision. The new system targets the poor and those who are most in need. This trend is illustrated by the extension of means-tested urban social relief and the end of the government's universal provision of pensions, medical care, housing and other services.

In terms of its ideological underpinning, the traditional social welfare system in China was based on 'socialist ideology', which meant that social protection and social equality were the core objectives. After the introduction of welfare reform, however, there has been a shift in the basic ideology underlying the provision of welfare. Economic efficiency is now being given priority over social justice.

Turning towards the changes in the economic and social goals of the social welfare system after the reform, emphasis has focused on reducing labour costs in order to have a 'more efficient economy' by restricting the government's social welfare expenditure. This stands in contrast to the main economic goal before the initiation of welfare reform which was to increase the employees' work enthusiasm by providing them with good social services. Moreover, while in the past the social welfare system served to maintain social justice through what was called the 'socialist distribution system', and to increase the quality of life of Chinese citizens through higher public expenditure, the supreme social goal of the new social welfare system is now different. The main social objective now is to provide sufficient basic welfare benefits to maintain social stability in the People's Republic of China.

In summary, the main task of China's current social welfare policy is to provide a basic 'safety net' that will avoid social unrest, while limiting the growth in social expenditure in order to allow China to become more competitive. In practical terms, the result of this policy shift has been a reduced benefit level in China's social welfare. While welfare principles of the old days have become less important in the economic reform period, market principles and commercial services have been increasingly encouraged. Similarly, as the roles of the government and state enterprises in the provision of welfare have been reduced, those of the local communities and non-governmental organisations have become more important.

The causes of change in China's welfare system

Many researchers tend to explain the above changes as a consequence of the adoption of market reforms in the economic system. That is to say, they see a correlation between the shift from a centrally planned economy to a market economy and the shift from traditional principles and institutional arrangements in social welfare to those that have been institutionalised since welfare reforms began.

It is true that institutional co-ordination as described above has been an important consideration in China's social welfare reforms, especially in the early stage of reform. However, it is also possible to identify another factor that has played a similarly, if not more important role in accounting for the changes in China's welfare system: the impact of economic globalisation.

To make this point clearer, we might want to examine what happened to the welfare provision in other countries. In the first two decades following the end of the Second World War, the Western developed countries, as well as the Eastern socialist countries, including China, all enjoyed a measure of achievement in their respective social welfare development, notwithstanding differences in their political and economic systems. As we know, many countries with higher than average welfare provisions found themselves in a so-called 'crisis of the welfare state' at the end of the 1970s.

Turning to the reasons as to why such a crisis arose, two factors have by and large been identified. First, it has been argued that the post-war European welfare state, given its generous welfare provisions, has suffered from market distortions. The argument here is that the generous welfare provisions spoilt people's working motivation and led to higher unemployment as well as lower economic efficiency. As a result, governments had to raise their expenditure for social programmes. This further harmed economic efficiency. Second, the demographic trends in these developed countries increasingly imposed a higher burden on the financial resources of the welfare state, a point not considered by the original designers of the welfare state.

From the early 1990s, however, more and more researchers have begun to focus on a third explanation: economic globalisation. As many researchers (for instance Deacon, with Hulse and Stubbs, 1997, Ramesh 1998) have indicated, economic globalisation has been one of the main factors that has pushed the European welfare state into crisis. The golden age of the European welfare state existed under the mantle of a protected economy. However, since the 1970s, trade and capital flows have increasingly been liberalised. When capital can move freely to any place were labour is much cheaper, and cheaper goods can move freely from country to country, both governments and trade unions lose the key means to bargaining for better welfare provision. Faced with globalisation, European welfare states have met more and more problems and the workers in the countries concerned have faced increasing cutbacks in their social welfare provision (Deacon, with Hulse and Stubbs, 1997).

Many researchers in developed countries have been focusing on the negative effects of economic globalisation on their respective domestic social policy since the early 1990s. By contrast, governments and scholars of developing countries have, generally speaking, been more likely to focus on the unequal international economic order between developed and developing countries, which has been further aggravated by economic globalisation. In spite of the fact that some researchers have paid attention to international factors when explaining, for instance, Latin-American social policy reform after the debt crisis in the 1980s, the effects of globalisation on developing countries' domestic social welfare have, comparatively speaking, attracted less attention. Judging by China's case, however, it seems possible to suggest that globalisation has had negative effects on the social welfare development in developing countries more generally.

Under Mao, China had a highly closed economy, which, before the late 1970s, was only seldom affected by the global world economy. As a result of China's open-door policy, however, more foreign capital has entered into China, international trade has increased, and the Chinese economy has become, step by step, a part of the globalising world economy. It is this change that has exercised a strong influence on China's social welfare development in at least two ways. First, as more foreign goods have been imported and as more foreign investment funds have been attracted – enhancing China's competitiveness – the state sector's lower efficiency has proved a major obstacle to the continued survival of the regime and China's further development. This is the reason why the government has tried its best to boost economic efficiency of the state sector by, for instance, reducing its payroll expenses. Consequently, a lot of state workers have lost their job and poverty has become an increasingly serious problem. Second, under the pressure of international economic competition, the government has sought to control the growth of labour costs in an effort to create a more attractive environment for foreign investors. To attract additional investment, the government is keen to limit increases in social expenditure and to curb expenditure in areas of social security, housing, health services, education, etc.

In short, in a more open economy, the government faces pressure from two sides. On the one hand, the government has extended the social welfare programmes that are necessary to deal with the increasing problems of urban unemployment and poverty, in part a consequence of the pressures of international competition. On the other hand, the government seeks to reduce its social expenditure in order to strengthen the economic competitiveness of the People's Republic. China's social welfare reforms thus provide an example of how joining the globalising economy creates social problems in a developing country which may then be forced to transform its social policy.

Possible challenges to China's social policy after WTO accession

One of the most important events in China's economic and social life in the late 1990s has been the country's attempt to step up its efforts to enter the WTO. To secure China's membership, Beijing has had to negotiate with current WTO member states on precise accession criteria. There have been many debates within China about whether the country would 'win' or 'lose' as a consequence of WTO membership. However, academic discussions have mainly focused on the economic consequences of China's WTO membership and, in particular, on the likely impact on China's various industries. Less discussion has centred on the likely social effects that will emanate from WTO membership. Although a detailed analysis of the latter may need more empirical data and systematic research, I propose to set out here some ideas about the possible impact of economic globalisation on Beijing's social policy after China enters the WTO.

Global trends in economic and social situations

Before we further discuss the possible influences of economic globalisation on China and the possible social policy responses to these after China's accession to the WTO, I suggest that we consider the following matters.

International economic competition will increase. Entering the WTO means that the Chinese economy will be more than ever a part of the global market, i.e. she has to open her market to international competitors, while Chinese enterprises will have more opportunities to access international markets. Without doubt, the Chinese economic actors will face stronger competition as a consequence of this development. As to whether China will experience a net gain or a net loss as a result of WTO accession will depend on the extent to which the economic sectors can enhance their respective competitiveness.

Inequality and poverty will also increase. After joining the WTO, economic competition between China and other countries will have two dimensions. One involves competing against developed countries in hi-tech industries. This competition is for the most part also a competition for highly educated young talents who have to be offered high incomes. We may want to describe this as a competition in the 'race to the top'. The other dimension is about competition against countries in international markets for a larger share of international investment and trade in goods produced by labour-intensive industries. To win this competition, both the Chinese labour-intensive industries and its international competitors may have to keep labour costs low. We may want to describe this competition as a 'race to the bottom'. As a consequence, China is likely to experience more social inequality, especially if measures designed to maintain social protection are not implemented. Moreover, as a result of a higher unemployment rate that results from enterprises cutting down on staff in their drive for greater economic efficiency, and the government's deregulation in this area, the poverty rate in China will possibly grow substantially. This will happen even if the average income may increase as a result of good performance achieved by enterprises operating in the free market.

Demands for social protection will also increase. In a situation in which unemployment and poverty are growing, demands for greater social protection are bound to increase. The demands of this nature will concern not only social security (social insurance and social assistance), but also other aspects of the social services such as education, medical care, housing, and personal services.

Economic reforms will continue to be implemented, leading to further social transition. China's economic reforms will probably accelerate after Beijing joins the WTO. Further reform is likely to occur along two trajectories. The first is the further marketisation of China's economic system in order to increase the country's economic competitiveness. The second focuses on the adjustment of its regulatory system so as to better co-ordinate between China on the one hand and the WTO's regulatory system. The regulatory adjustment is likely to happen not only in the economic sector, but also in the social sector.

China's social welfare development and the near future

Two overriding objectives of the government have shaped welfare reforms: social and political stability on the one hand and economic development on the other. China's future social welfare development should be analysed in the light of the continued relevance of these two goals or principles, provided that the political system does not undergo major change. In other words, any changes to China's social welfare policy will take place within the policy space provided by the above two principles, as in other policy areas. Put differently, the above two principles or objectives will set the upper and lower limits for the further development of social policy in the People's Republic. Welfare provision by the government will not exceed the point at which economic efficiency will be threatened; but neither will it fall below a point deemed essential to prevent social unrest.

New challenges after WTO accession

As stated above, China's social policy will in future depend on the government's ability to balance policies in two directions at the same time: to accelerate economic growth and to maintain social stability. Following China's accession to the WTO, we may expect challenges to arise with regard to both objectives.

First, upon entering the WTO, China will face much fiercer international economic competition. Given its ambitious economic developmental strategy, which focuses on catching up with the developed countries, the goal of social justice may be kept on the back-burner or at least in secondary place among the core state objectives for a long time. Even if the government's social policy was based on considerations other than social stability, the intense pressure stemming from international economic competition may not give Beijing enough room to balance its economic and social objectives.

Second, as a result of the increasing social inequality in the People's Republic, there is a possibility of a strong negative response to 'liberal reforms' by those people who have been made worse off by them. Resistance to social welfare reform has already been in evidence. Under these circumstances, the likelihood of further 'liberal reform' of the social welfare system will depend on the government's ability to maintain effective social control. Considering China's socialist and egalitarian traditions, the road ahead is fraught with difficulty.

Third, China's social policy – while still considered to be an internal affair of the national government – will increasingly become the subject of international intervention. Such international intervention may take two forms: ideological challenges spreading from other countries and international concerns about 'fair competition' raised by other countries' economic interactions with China. Given that changes in China's social policy may exert effects on the country's economic condition, social policy as a traditionally domestic affair may become more of an international issue in an era of globalisation.

The need to establish basic social protection standards among developing countries

The decline of the social welfare state in both developed and developing countries is, to a large extent, a consequence of closer international interactions in an increasingly interdependent world economy. Efforts to improve social welfare will therefore only be successful if they are not limited to 'domestic action' by single countries. Some Western scholars have pointed out that international co-operation is necessary to prevent social welfare standards from deteriorating further. The European Union's social protection co-ordination mechanism within the European integration process has – in the past few decades – given an example of what international co-operation in social policy might look like in order to address the harmful effects of economic integration. Since the issues are unlikely to be resolved even at the level of regional international negotiations, however, some scholars have gone yet further to propose an 'international welfare state' (Townsend 1996), i.e. a global social welfare system that includes both developed and developing countries. International action of this nature is not unknown in many international organisations, such as the World Bank, or the United Nations, etc. Some developed countries have proposed that issues of labour standards be linked to questions of international trade and dealt with in the WTO.

The efforts by developed countries to force developing countries to accept basic labour standards by linking these with questions of international trade has so far been rejected as a protectionist move by the latter. Most, if not all, developing countries consider that accepting the proposed labour standards would raise their respective production costs and reduce their economic competitiveness *vis-à-vis* the developed countries. This attitude of developing countries in relation to low labour standards is rooted in the basic understanding that the developing and developed countries are competitors in the global world economy and that one of the very few advantages enjoyed by the former is cheaper labour forces. Arguably, this analysis is nevertheless too simple.

In a globalised world economy, there are two kinds of international competition that concern developing countries. One concerns competition against developed countries in the high-tech sectors; another area of competition is among developing countries in the labour-intensive sectors. In the competition of the high-tech sectors a cheaper labour force is by no means an advantage. Indeed it is rather a disadvantage because the consequence of this will lead to a 'brain drain' of local talents to the developed countries. In the labour-intensive sectors of the economy, competitiveness of individual countries might (temporarily) be strengthened on the basis of a cheaper labour force. However, in the medium term this will result in a 'race to the bottom' as other developing countries pursue the same approach. As such, the initial advantage enjoyed by one will over time disappear for all. In other words, all developing countries will become losers in this 'zero-sum game', leaving transnational corporations and international investors as the only winners.

In summary, globalisation implies a 'prisoner's dilemma' for developing countries in so far as any countries attempting to maintain a cheap labour force by reducing social protection may find its approach being copied by other developing countries. This will inevitably lead to the interest of all labourers in all of the countries concerned to be harmed without any advantage to the country in its respective international economic competition. In such a situation, no single country can pursue a high standard of social protection. Indeed, no country is probably even capable of maintaining the level of social welfare previously enjoyed by its citizens if others reduce their respective social welfare provision. The only way to escape from this dilemma is to set up a basic social welfare standard and to establish an international co-ordination mechanism in the field of social protection that will prevent developing countries from engaging in a 'race to the bottom'.

Conclusion

In sum, then, if we move away from notions of 'competition between developed and developing countries' to 'competition among developing countries', discussion of a regional or even global standard of social protection becomes meaningful for developing states. Only if joint efforts are made toward its realisation, can developing countries expect to have adequate social protection while maintaining or even enhancing their economic competitiveness *vis-à-vis* the developed world.

Bibliography

In English

Deacon, Bob, with Michelle Hulse and Paul Stubbs, 1997, *Global Social Policy: International Organizations and the Future of Welfare*, London: Sage Publications.
El-Agraa, Ali M. ed., 1998, *The European Union: History, Institutions, Economics and Policies*, New Yersey: Prentice Hall, Chapter 18 pp. 389–422.
Esping-Anderson, Gosta, ed., 1996, *Welfare States in Transition: National Adaptations in Global Economies*, London: Sage Publications.
Guan, Xinping, 2000, 'China's Social Policy: Reform and Development in the Context of Marketization and Globalization', in *Social Policy & Administration*, Vol. 34, No. 1. Pp. 115–30.
Gupta, Satya Dev, with Nanda K. Choudhry, 1997, *Dynamics of Globalization and Development*, Dordrecht: Kluwer Academic Publishers.
Hantrais, Linda, 1995, *Social Policy in the European Union*, Basingstoke: Macmillan Press.
Midgley, James, 1997, *Social Welfare in Global Context*, London: Sage Publications.
Pieters, Danny and Jason Alan Nickless, 1998, *Pathways for Social Protection in Europe*, Helsinki: Ministry of Social Affairs and Health.
Ramesh, Mishra, 1998, 'Beyond the Nation State: Social Policy in an Age of Globalization', in *Social Policy & Administration*, Vol. 32, No. 5. Pp. 481–500.
Swaan, de Abram, 1994, *Social Policy Beyond Borders: The Social Question in Transnational Perspective*, Amsterdam: Amsterdam University Press.
Townsend, Peter, with Kwabena Donker, 1996, *Global Restructuring and Social Policy*, Oxford: The Polity Press.

In Chinese

Cui Ying and Gao, Fulai, eds, 1999, *Zhongguo jiqi zhoubian guojia yu diqu de jingji* [The Economies of China and Its Surrounding Countries and Regions], Beijing: Shoudu jingji maoyi daxue chubanshe [Capital Economic & Trade University Press].
Guo, Shizheng and Ge Shouchang, 1998, *Zhongguo shehui baoxian gaige yu yanyiu* [The Reform and Research of China's Social Insurance], Shanghai: Caijing daxue chubanshe [Shanghai Finance and Economics University Press].
Li Peilin, 1993, *Zhongguo shichang zhuanxing zhong de shehui fenceng* [Social Stratification in the Market Transition of China], Shenyang: Liaoning renmin chubanshe [Liaoning People's Press].
Li Qiang, ed., 1993, *Dangdai Zhongguo yu liudong* [Social Stratification and Mobility in Contemporary China], Beijing: Zhongguo jingji chubanshe [China Economics Press].
Li Xuezeng and Cheng Xuebin, 1997, *Zhongguo chengshi ge jieceng liyi chaju fenxi* [A Quantitative Analysis of the Interest Gaps among Chinese Urban Social Strata], Beijing: Zhongguo shehui kexue [Chinese Social Sciences].
Liu Minghui and Chen Junhui, 1998, *Shehui baozhang lilun jiqi gaige shijian* [Social Security Theories and Its Reform Practices], Harbin: Dongbei caijing daxue [Northeast Finance & Economic University Press].

M Huaizhong, 1998, *Zhongguo shehui baozhang shidu shuiping yanjiu* [Studies on the Proper Level of Social Security in China], Shenyang: Liaoning daxue chubanshe [Liaoning University Press].

Ru Xin, *et al.*, eds, 1999, *Zhongguo 1999: shehui xingshi de fenxi yu yuce* [China in 1999: Analysis And Forecast of Social Situation], Beijing: Shehui kexue wenxian chubanshe [Social Science Literature Press].

Wang Lie, ed., 1998, *Quanqiuhua yu shijie* [Globalization and the World], Beijing: Zhongyong hianyi chubanshe [Central Compilation and Translation Press].

Xu Dianqing, *et al.*, eds, 1999, *Zhongguo shehui baozhang tizhi gaige* [Social Security Reform in China], Beijing: Jingji kexue chubanshe [Economic Science Press].

You Hongbing, 1998, *Zhongguo shouru fenpei chaju yanjiu* [A Study of the Income Inequality in China], Beijing: Zhongguo jingji chubanshe [China Economics Press].

Yu Keping, ed., 1998, *Quanqiu shidai de shehuizhuyi* [Socialism in the Global Age], Beijing: Zhongong bianyi chubanshe [Central Compilation and Translation Press].

Zhang Hongming, *et al.*, 1998, *Zhufang jingji xue* [Economics of Housing], Shanghai: Shanghai caijing daxue chubanshe [Shanghai Economics and Finance University Press].

Zhang Shipeng, 1998, *Quanqiuhua shidai de zibenzhuyi* [Capitalism in the Global Age], Beijing: Zhongyong bianyi chubanshe [Central Compilation and Translation Press].

Zhao Man, 1997, *Shehui baozhang zhidu jiegou yu yunxing fenxi* [An Analysis of the Structure and Operation of Social Security], Beijing: Zhongguo jihua chubanshe [China Planning Press].

Chapter 8

Behind the Virtual Wall

The People's Republic of China and the Internet

Gudrun Wacker

Introduction

The World Wide Web, e-mail and 'dotcom' companies have become popular in the People's Republic of China during the last few years, and even electronic commerce has been developing. Since 1998 the number of Internet users has doubled every six months, and registration of domain names under 'cn' for China has been growing dramatically. A broad range of information, statistical data and news on China are provided in electronic form by Chinese government agencies and Chinese-language portals, and Chinese newspapers and magazines strengthen their presence via the Internet.[1] The opening of the telecommunications service sector, including the Internet, to foreign enterprises played a major role in negotiations with the United States and the European Union on China's WTO entry.

Speaking at the opening of an international computer congress in Beijing in August 2000, President Jiang Zemin underlined the central importance of information technology for China's future economic development, while at the same time warning of the dangers and negative aspects of the Internet (*CITTR* 2000d). It is symptomatic of China's attitude with respect to the Internet to oscillate between these two poles of explicit support, on the one hand, and political mistrust, on the other.

Such an ambiguous attitude is not new in China's history. When the Chinese leadership decided in December 1978 to transform the country into a modern economy, this also implied opening up China to the outside world. In a way, this decision brought back an old dilemma the Middle Kingdom had been basically facing from the 18th century onwards. It can be phrased as follows: how can China import and adopt those technologies, methods and ideas from abroad that are considered positive and useful, while at the same time filtering out apparently negative and harmful foreign influences?

The traditional Chinese solution to this problem is associated with the formula: *Zhong ti Xi yong* – 'Chinese for essence, Western for usage'. In the past, more often than not this selective approach proved difficult if not impossible to put into practice, since in the medium to long term the 'usage' tended to alter the 'essence'.

Modern communication technology, acquired and introduced to make business transactions more efficient, has also proven to be a double-edged sword. It cannot be shut off at will when deemed desirable for ideological or political reasons. An early demonstration of this problem were fax transmissions to China by Chinese students abroad to distribute information on the events happening on Tiananmen Square in May and June 1989.

The Internet has added another dimension to this basic problem and presents the Chinese Communist Party with a new challenge. The Chinese leadership is well aware that a modernising China cannot afford to ignore the new forms of communication, but at the same time the Internet is perceived as a threat to political stability and to the Party's monopoly of power. As a consequence, the Chinese authorities have attempted both to encourage the development of the Internet and to control everything related to it. Ideally, at least part of China's leadership would like to connect the country by a giant intra-net and build an electronic or virtual 'Great Wall' around all of China, with a limited number of heavily guarded gateways to the outside world.

This chapter will provide a brief overview of the development and the current state of the Internet in China. The following questions will be addressed: Who and where are China's *netizens*? Who are the major players in providing the necessary infrastructure and setting the framework for the Internet in China? How does the state encourage or discourage the diffusion of the Internet and by what means does it try to minimise the perceived risks for political and social stability? It will be argued in this paper that the popular belief in the West which attributes magical powers to the Internet as a carrier of democracy and gravedigger of authoritarian rule has to be revised in view of China's actual and virtual reality.

The development of the Internet in China

China entered the age of electronic communication networks relatively late, namely with an academic network in 1988. A first permanent satellite link to Stanford University was established in 1993, and TCP/IP connectivity started later in the same year. In the following years, academic institutions became the main engines for popularising the Internet and setting standards.[2] Since the mid-1990s, dissemination of the Internet has picked up speed, and from 1998 on, growth rates have been dramatic.

There has been an explosion in terms of computers with Internet access as well as in terms of registered Internet users (see Tables 1 and 2).

Table 1 Number of computers on the Internet

	Total	On-line	Dial-up	Change per cent)
June 1998	542,000	82,000	460,000	
Dec. 1998	747,000	117,000	630,000	+ 37.8
June 1999	1,460,000	250,000	1,210,000	+ 95.4
Dec. 1999	3,500,000	410,000	3,090,000	+ 139.7
June 2000	6,500,000	1,010,000	5,490,000	+ 85.7

Sources: Derived from CNNIC reports, July 1998, January 1999, July 1999, January 2000, July 2000. The CNNIC reports are available on-line in Chinese under http://www.cnnic.cn.[3]

Table 2 Number of Internet users

	Internet users	On-line	Dial-up	Both	Change (per cent)
June 1998	1,175,999	325,000	850,000	n.d.	
Dec. 1998	2,100,000	400,000	1,490,000	n.d.	+ 78.6
June 1999	4,000,000	760,000	2,560,000	680,000	+ 90.5
Dec. 1999	8,900,000	1,090,000	6,660,000	1,150,000	+ 122.5
June 2000	16,900,000	2,580,000	11,760,000	2,560,000	+ 89.9

Sources: Derived from CNNIC reports, July 1998, January 1999, July 1999, January 2000, July 2000. For the first time in July 2000, the CNNIC report listed the number of users accessing the Internet by other means than PCs (590,000), e.g. mobile phones.

According to official statistics, the number of *netizens* (Chinese: *wangmin*) grew from about one million to almost seventeen million between July 1998 and July 2000. Continually high growth rates are expected in this sector for the years to come (*ChinaOnline* 1999a).

The figures in Tables 1 and 2 are data provided by CNNIC, an institution of the Chinese Academy of Sciences which has been conducting surveys on Internet usage in China semi-annually since 1998 with authorisation of the State Council. As is practically always the case with Chinese statistics, there has been much debate about the reliability of these figures, especially since CNNIC supplies only a rough outline of what methods it applies in gathering the data. For example, it is unclear how an Internet user is defined, namely, how frequently one has to access the Internet in order to be considered a user. Some Western studies assume a much smaller number of Chinese Internet users – according to a survey conducted by a Hong Kong-based company, for example, there were only about twelve million users in June 2000 rather than the almost 17 million identified by CNNIC (Olesen 2000). By contrast, other sources argue that the figure provided by CNNIC is too low, because in a developing country like China, where PCs and Internet access fees are relatively expensive, Internet accounts are likely to be used by more than one person.[4]

No matter how many people in China are online, there can be no doubt that the number of *netizens* or *wangmin* has been growing fast over the last years. In international comparison, China is doing well. A Western study conducted in 1998 showed China ahead of India in pervasiveness, sectoral absorption, connectivity and organisational infrastructure as well as sophistication of use (Press et al. 1998). China ranked as 14th among the top 15 countries of Internet users worldwide in 1998 (Computer Industry Almanac Inc. 1999) and was among the top ten with respect to registration of domain names in 1999 (Mooney 2000).

Despite these overall positive results, the level of development of the Internet in China is still very low. What looks impressive in terms of absolute numbers is put in perspective by the size of China's population: if we assume about 17 million users by mid-2000, not even two per cent of China's population had access to the Internet. Thus, the country lags far behind other Asian countries like South Korea (21 per cent) and Japan (15.5 per cent) or Western industrialised nations like the US (45 per cent), Finland (38 per cent) or Germany (19 per cent).[5] China is a developing country, and this is true with respect to the level of Internet penetration as well.

The digital divide

To reduce the gap between China and more developed countries is one of the declared objectives of China's political leaders. Since technological capacity and the 'IT revolution' are perceived as constituents of the country's 'comprehensive power', it has been ascribed prime importance (Feng 2000). But a 'digital divide' exists not only between a developing nation (China) and industrialised nations (US, Japan, Europe), but also at the domestic level within China itself.

In the 1980s, the Chinese leadership acknowledged that electronics and modern information technology would be vital for the country's future economic development. Therefore, during the 1980s and 1990s, considerable funds and resources were channelled into building and modernising China's telecommunication infrastructure. Due to the measures taken on the central and regional level, telephone networks have been dramatically expanded and improved within the last decade of the century: telephone density increased from only one per cent in 1990 to 12.6 per cent by the end of 1999 (Gesteland 1999). In September 2000, the number of telephone subscribers in China reached 200 million, of which 135 million were fixed-line and 65 million mobile phone subscribers (*ChinaOnline* 2000t). However, telephone penetration in cities is still more than double that in rural areas: by mid-2000, the nationwide telephone density was 14.7 per cent, while it had reached 32.1 per cent in urban areas (*CITTR* 2000i, *ChinaOnline* 2000u).

Internet usage is also not spread evenly throughout China (see Table 3) (Lu 2000a; Michaels 2000). It is hardly surprising that Internet users as well as domain name registration are concentrated in the big urban centres and in the economically more advanced coastal provinces. Thus, Internet usage in China reflects the regional disparities that have characterised the country since the 1980s. A 'digital divide' is firmly in place: residents of Beijing, Shanghai and Guangdong alone account for more than 40 per cent of China's Internet users and for 60 per cent of the hosts registered under the domain name 'cn'. Moreover, all international data transmissions[6] are handled through communication outlets in these three regions (CNNIC 2000b). Beijing is not only the administrative centre of China, but the city also has the highest number of universities and colleges. In addition, hundreds of electronics and IT companies, part of which are spin-offs founded by universities, are concentrated in Beijing's Zhongguancun, often

Table 3 Regional distribution of users and domain names

	Users (%)			Domain (%)		Users (%)			Domain (%)
Region	June 1998	June 1999	June 2000	June 2000	Region	June 1998	June 1999	June 2000	June 1999
Beijing	25.30	21.02	18.72	38.2	Anhui	2.60	1.53	1.16	0.7
Guangdong	11.50	11.77	12.82	13.9	Chongqing	0.60	1.45	1.84	
Shanghai	7.80	8.71	10.79	8.6	Jiangxi	1.80	1.19	0.91	0.4
Jiangsu	6.10	6.76	6.76	4.3	Jilin	2.00	1.06	1.40	0.7
Zhejiang	3.90	5.97	4.92	4.1	Yunnan	0.50	1.03	0.70	1.4
Sichuan	2.80	5.11	3.35	2.5	Shanxi	0.80	0.93	0.95	0.6
Shandong	4.00	4.19	8.53	4.2	Xinjiang	0.60	0.92	0.64	0.7
Hubei	4.10	3.74	4.64	1.7	Gansu	0.40	0.72	0.56	0.3
Fujian	3.10	3.72	1.94	2.4	Inner Mongolia	0.40	0.65	0.43	0.4
Liaoning	5.00	3.43	3.34	2.4	Overseas	0.58	n.d.		
Shaanxi	1.40	2.76	2.83	1.3	Hainan	0.40	0.44	0.27	1.8
Hunan	1.60	2.23	2.05	0.9	Guizhou	0.30	0.31	0.36	0.2
Heilongjiang	2.60	2.16	1.67	0.9	Ningxia	0.10	0.19	0.18	0.2
Hebei	2.70	2.09	2.22	1.6	Qinghai	0.20	0.10	0.07	0.1
Tianjin	2.40	2.05	2.79	1.6	[Hongkong]		0.07	n.d.	1.0
Guangxi	1.60	1.56	0.91	0.8	Tibet	0.00	0.02	0.03	0.1
Henan	3.40	1.54	2.22	2.0	Total	100	100	100	100

Source: Derived from CNNIC reports.

called China's Silicon Valley. The strong position of Beijing in domain names can at least in part be attributed to the 'government online' project launched in 1999.[7]

Table 4 shows the correlation between population and the number of Internet users in China's regions (column 5) and the respective density of Internet usage (column 8). It also becomes clear that the level of Internet dissemination is related to GDP.

It is important to note that there is not only the digital divide between urban and rural areas, but Internet usage in China declines also from East to West (*ChinaOnline* 2000k). Within the broader context of the 'go West' strategy propagated by the Chinese government and intended to attract investment to the underdeveloped hinterland, attention has also been drawn to the technological gap that exists at the domestic level. Therefore, preferential conditions (mainly tax reductions) were announced for Chinese enterprises or joint ventures which engage in the manufacturing of telecommunication equipment, and in value-added telecommunication and Internet services in these regions (*ChinaOnline* 2000l). Provision of the necessary telecommunication infrastructure, however, is left to the state-owned telecommunication enterprises.

In theory, the Internet, as a 'space-shrinking technology', can be used as a means to alleviate developmental gaps between different regions and between urban centres and rural areas.[8] Under the condition that the necessary telecommunications infrastructure is in place, it would be possible to supply even remote and underdeveloped areas with educational or health services via the Internet or interactive TV. Apparently building on this assumption, the Chinese Ministry of Education drafted a programme for online education in 1994, which was run on a trial basis by six universities and colleges and later expanded to thirty institutions of higher learning. By the year 2010, China is planning to have an up-to-date distance-education system in place (*ChinaOnline* 2000m, *ChinaOnline* 2000o).[9] However, apart from lacking the modern infrastructure, many additional obstacles make such plans difficult to put into practice: the training of tutors and teachers, drawing up teaching materials, lack of computer literacy and the learning habits of Chinese students, to name only a few. It is too early to tell whether the ambitious programme will really contribute to bridging, or at least narrowing, developmental gaps.

China's WTO agreement with the US reflects the existing digital divide by providing for an opening up of China's telecommunications sector to foreign direct investment (FDI) and foreign equity shares in several stages: the big urban centres Beijing, Shanghai and Guangzhou will be first. Chengdu, Chongqing, Dalian, Fuzhou, Hangzhou, Nanjing, Ningbo, Qingdao, Shenyang, Shenzhen, Taiyuan, Wuhan, Xiamen and Xi'an will follow in the second stage, and the rest of the country in the third and final stage.[10] Due to these geographic restrictions, foreign investments will have

Table 4 Correlation between regional population, per capita GDP and Internet users (Dec. 1999)

Province	Population (1998) million	Percentage of population	Number of users*	Correlation users/ population	GDP (1999) bn. Yuan	GDP per capita	Users per 10,000 population
Beijing	12.46	1.01	1,890,360	21.03	216.60	17,408	1,517
Shanghai	14.64	1.19	1,151,660	9.42	403.50	27,561	681
Tianjin	9.57	0.78	997,690	3.44	145.00	15,152	249
Guangdong	71.43	5.80	525,990	2.23	845.90	11,842	161
Zhejiang	43.43	3.53	401,390	1.28	535.00	12,319	92
Liaoning	41.57	3.38	267,000	1.26	413.60	9,949	91
Jiangsu	71.82	5.83	461,910	1.01	770.00	10,721	73
Fujian	32.99	2.68	295,480	1.00	362.80	10,997	73
Hainan	7.53	0.61	239,410	0.80	47.20	6,268	58
Shanxi	31.72	2.58	380,030	0.76	163.10	5,142	55
Shandong	88.38	7.18	92,560	0.72	766.20	8,669	52
Hubei	59.07	4.80	306,160	0.69	385.80	6,531	50
Jilin	26.44	2.15	147,740	0.70	167.00	6,316	50
Hunan	65.02	5.28	230,510	0.65	340.70	5,240	47
Heilongjiang	37.73	3.06	238,520	0.54	289.70	7,678	39
Hebei	65.69	5.33	119,260	0.49	455.70	6,937	35
Shaanxi	35.96	2.92	187,790	0.36	148.80	4,138	26
Guangxi	46.75	3.80	86,330	0.35	200.20	4,282	26
Ningxia	5.38	0.44	169,100	0.36	24.20	4,498	26
Jiangxi	41.91	3.40	101,460	0.34	196.70	4,693	24
Xinjiang	17.47	1.42	133,500	0.33	116.90	6,691	24
Sichuan	115.53	9.38	56,070	0.32	519.90	4,500	23
Henan	93.15	7.56	174,440	0.28	458.00	4,917	20
Gansu	25.19	2.05	41,830	0.28	93.20	3,700	20
Inner Mongolia	23.45	1.90	50,730	0.26	127.10	5,420	19
Anhui	61.84	5.02	44,500	0.19	291.00	4,706	14
Yunnan	41.44	3.36	43,610	0.19	185.00	4,464	14
Qinghai	5.03	0.41	40,940	0.20	23.80	4,732	14
Guizhou	36.58	2.97	14,240	0.15	90.70	2,479	11
Tibet	2.52	0.20	7,120	0.15	10.30	4,087	11
Chongqing	[30.6]	(included under Sichuan)	2,670	[148.8]			
Total	1,231.690	100.00	8,900,000	1.00	8793.60	7,139**	161**

Sources: Calculations are based on CNNIC statistics (2000a) and *Jingji Ribao*, Feb. 29, 2000, cited from *China aktuell*, April 2000, p. 393. *If the number is >1, the region is 'over-represented' in terms of Internet users; if the number is <1, the region is under-represented. **National average

to concentrate for several years on cities which are already better supplied, and thus foreign involvement after China's WTO entry is likely to intensify the problem of uneven development.

The framework: the telecommunications sector, Internet networks and Internet Service Providers

Creating the environment of the Internet in China has been largely a top-down process with the Communist Party and the central as well as the regional governments as the main actors. The 'informatisation' of China became an important component of China's economic reform from the 1980s onwards. In order to lead the country into the age of electronic networks and online banking, three so-called 'Golden Projects' were launched in the early 1990s:

(i) the 'Golden Bridge' – interconnecting economic databases nationwide. Originally under the auspices of the Ministry of Electronics Industry (MEI), the State Information Centre and JiTong Corp;
(ii) the 'Golden Card' – electronic money project; intended to accelerate the development of banking and credit card systems; the target was to create a credit card verification system and an inter-bank, inter-regional clearing system by 2000 (the People's Bank of China, the former MEI, the Ministry of Internal Trade and the Great Wall Computer Company participated in this project); and
(iii) the 'Golden Customs' – linking China's customs offices in a computer network.

More 'Golden Projects' were launched in the following years.[11] Various players pursuing their own respective interests have been involved not only in these programmes for the 'informatisation' of China, but also in the telecommunications sector in general. Up to 1998, several ministries and other government institutions, each of them directly controlling several enterprises, were in charge of parts of the telecommunications infrastructure and the IT industry. The most powerful players and competitors were the Ministry of Post and Telecommunications (MPT) with its commercial arm China Telecom, on the one hand, and the Ministry of Electronics Industry (MEI) in alliance with some other ministries, which succeeded in getting permission to establish a second telecommunication enterprise, namely China Unicom (*Zhongguo Liantong*), in 1994.[12] Moreover, other institutions like the Ministry of Railways built their own dedicated networks. And on the regional and local levels, paging services came into being, operated, for example, by the People's Liberation Army which commercialised frequencies originally reserved for military purposes. Competition, if it existed at the time, was due to rivalries between government agencies or administrative units rather than market forces (Mueller and Tan 1997, p. 59).

Due to its growing economic importance, a restructuring of the entire IT and telecommunications sector was begun in the late 1990s. Reform measures affected government institutions as well as the enterprises under their jurisdiction. In March 1998, the National People's Congress decided to merge the MPT, the MEI and parts of the Ministry of Radio, Film and Television into a new super-ministry. Postal and telecoms administration was separated, the MEI was dissolved, and the remains of the Ministry of Radio, Film and Television were reorganized as the State Administration for Radio, Film and Television (SARFT). The newly established Ministry of Information Industry (MII) was supposed to act as *the* regulator for the entire telecommunications industry (*ChinaOnline* 1998a; Chen 1999). Since the MII was the direct successor of the MPT and absorbed the MEI including its IT enterprises, the reorganisation was interpreted as a victory of the more conservative MPT[13] over the MEI (Heilmann 1999).

Despite this reorganisation and streamlining at the ministerial level, the telecommunications infrastructure as well as the Internet networks that exist in China today still reflect, in part, competing and often conflicting interests inherited from the former bureaucratic structures. As a result of the importance ascribed to the telecommunications sector, on the one hand, and the need to balance persisting rivalries between government agencies, a new commission, the 'Leading group for informatisation' (*Guojia xinxihua gongzuo lingdao xiaozu*), was set up in December 1999. This leading group brings together representatives from all the administrative bodies involved.[14] Its main task is co-ordinating issues of computer networks and information security.

The process of restructuring the telecommunications enterprises was accompanied by long negotiations mainly between China's Premier Zhu Rongji and the MII under Minister Wu Jichuan. While Zhu Rongji apparently sought to separate government and enterprise functions and to introduce more competition into the telecommunications sector in view of China's impending WTO accession, the main objective of the MII seemed to be protecting the state-owned enterprises (SOEs) under its supervision, in particular China Telecom, from foreign as well as domestic competitors as long as possible (McGill 2000b; Rasin 2000).

By fall 2000, there were basically five state-owned telecommunications enterprises in China, all of which either already offered Internet services or planned to do so in the future.

The dominant enterprise was and still is China Telecom (under the MII). It used to be the commercial arm of the MPT, and until 1999 held the monopoly for fixed-line, long distance and international telephone services. During 1999 and 2000 the telecom giant was split up into separate entities for landline, satellite, and mobile telephone services. As a result of these measures, China Telecom kept the fixed-line services and control of ChinaNet, its commercial Internet network. China Mobile Communications specialises in mobile services. The provincial networks of China Mobile and its publicly listed subsidiary China Mobile Hong Kong are the biggest providers of mobile phone services in China. Satellite services of the former China Telecom, which operate under the name China Satellite Communications Corp. (ChinaSat), formally started business in October 2000. (*CITTR* 2000k). The different off-springs of former China Telecom are supposed to act as 'real' enterprises, i.e. independently of their former owner, the MII. However, through long-standing ties between their personnel, the Ministry and the telecom companies remain closely entwined (Rasin 2000). For example, it was reported that in Gansu province, employees of the local postal and telecommunications administration still got their wages from China Telecom (*ChinaOnline* 2000q).

The fourth telecommunications SOE is China Unicom or *Liantong*. Founded in 1994 on the initiative of several ministries led by the former MEI, Unicom is now also under the supervision of the MII. It is supposed to become the main competitor of China Telecom, but due to its late start and lack of strong official backing, it is still no real match for China's telecommunications giants. With the reorganisation of China Telecom completed, China Unicom became the only telecommunications enterprise in China with licences for fixed-line and mobile telephone services – based on GSM and CDMA standards[15] – as well as IP telephony (i.e. phone calls via Internet), Internet and paging services. China Telecom's former paging service *Guo Xin* was also incorporated into China Unicom.[16] To improve Unicom's position vis-à-vis China Mobile and to enable it to gain a greater share of the market, it was permitted to offer its services ten per cent cheaper than China Mobile.

The fifth telecommunications SOE, China Netcom Corporation (China Network Corporation), was founded in April 1999. Its four shareholders are the Chinese Academy of Sciences, the Ministry of Railways, the State Administration of Film, Radio and Television and the Municipal Government of Shanghai. President Jiang Zemin's son Jiang Mianheng is indirectly involved in the enterprise (Forney 1999). China Netcom Corporation started business by connecting cities on the Chinese east coast with a system of fibre-optic cables to offer IP-based telephone and broadband Internet services. Of all telecommunication enterprises in China, Netcom is the only one whose management is modelled on American computer companies. This fact, together with the official backing enjoyed by the new enterprise, is widely considered as a good starting position for the future prospects of the company (Kynge 1999; *ChinaOnline* 2000z).

JiTong Communications, the enterprise that had been involved in the 'Golden Bridge' project, has been authorised to offer not only Internet but also IP telephone services (*ChinaOnline* 2000e).

At the time of writing, the telecommunications sector in China was still in a state of flux. For example, it was widely expected that the MII would grant another mobile licence to China Telecom to further strengthen competition in the field (*ChinaOnline* 2000s; *CITTR* 2000k).[17] The plan to incorporate the dedicated network connecting China's train stations, built and run by the Ministry of Railways, into China Unicom was put on hold. The State Council decided instead to authorise the Ministry of Railways to launch its own telecommunication enterprise (ChinaRailcom) and postponed its decision on the merger for three years (*CITTR* 2000c; Wang and Ma 2000).

Most of the above-mentioned telecommunication SOEs have launched a commercial network offering Internet services. The largest net is China Telecom's CHINANET (also called 163-Network, because 163 is the dial-in number of this network). China Unicom operates UNINET. China Netcom's CNCNET (China Network Communications Public Interconnection Network), approved in July 1999, started offering Internet services in November 2000. And the fourth commercial network, which provides Internet connections mainly to corporations and government agencies, is CHINAGBN (Golden Bridge Information Network), the network operated by JiTong Communications.

In addition to these four commercial networks, there are two public ones. The first of these is CERNET, the campus network connecting China's universities, colleges and eventually China's middle schools. The other is CSTNET which was launched by the Chinese Academy of Sciences and connects research institutes.[18]

Table 5 shows the respective international bandwidth of these networks. China is directly interconnected with the United States, Canada, Australia, Great Britain, Germany, France, Japan and South Korea. A project to upgrade domestic interconnections between several networks to 155 Megabits per second (Mbps)[19] was finished in spring 2000. The lack of bandwidth capacity is still a major bottleneck and is responsible for slow access speed to the Internet and data congestion in China. In March 2000 MII announced that it would triple the existing bandwidth of 351 Mbps to 1 Gigabit per second by the end of the year (*ChinaOnline* 2000c; *CITTR*

Table 5 Bandwidth distribution by network (capacity Mbps)

	CSTNET	CHINANET	CERNET	CHINAGBT	UNINET	CNCNET	Sum	Growth
June 1998	2,128	78,000	2,256	2,256			84,640	
Dec. 1998	4,000	123,000	8,000	8,256			143,256	+69.3%
June 1999	8,000	195,000	8,000	18,000	12,000		241,000	+68.2%
Dec. 1999	10,000	291,000	8,000	22,000	20,000		351,000	+45.6%
June 2000	10,000	711,000	12,000	69,000	55,000	377,000	1,234,000	+251.6%

Source: Derived from CNNIC reports, July 1998, Jan. 1999, July 1999, Jan. 2000, July 2000.

2000b; Greenberg 2000). Despite these efforts, the situation has not been decisively improved, since the number of users has grown even faster than bandwidth capacity (Qiu 1999/2000).

To use PCs and modems for dialling into the telecommunications networks is still the predominant method of accessing the Internet in China. However, there are two alternative ways to get on-line: (1) with television sets and cable TV networks; and (2) with mobile phones using WAP (Wireless Application Protocol).

With more than 80 million subscribers, cable TV is one giant albeit fragmented network already in place in China which could, under certain conditions, be used for providing Internet access.[20] Until fall 2000, this possibility was outlawed by the so-called 'convergence ban',[21] which prohibited telecom and cable TV operators from interfering in each other's business spheres (*ChinaOnline* 1999d). Reportedly the restriction had to do with violent incidents in some regions involving employees of cable companies and telecom operators,[22] but it was widely suspected that the real issue had to do with a struggle between MII and SARFT for control over cable infrastructure. In some localities the rule was apparently ignored – cable TV operators continued to offer value-added telecom services and telecom operators were offering TV programming and VOD (video on demand).[23] Statements from the MII in fall 2000 were inconsistent: while Minister Wu Jichuan repeated in late September that SARFT would not be allowed to enter the telecom sector to offer Internet services, later announcements from the MII seemed to point to a relaxation of the 'convergence ban' (*CITTR* 2000j; *ChinaOnline* 2000x; *ChinaOnline* 2000zb). The trend to integrated multimedia networks combining telecommunication, broadcasting, data and voice transmission will inevitably lead to a lifting of the restriction sooner or later (*ChinaOnline* 2000w). The questions to be solved concern not only the distribution of authority over infrastructure and contents between Chinese government institutions, but also the consequences for foreign involvement having to conform with China's WTO commitments.

Another alternative to access the Internet was launched in China on a trial basis in May 2000. But in contrast to Japan, where Internet access via mobile phones became extremely popular within a short period of time,[24] WAP (Wireless Application Protocol) has so far failed to meet the high expectations that had accompanied its introduction in China. Loading speed is still too slow and there is simply not enough information yet adjusted to the small display of a mobile phone to attract a large number of customers. In order to change these deficiencies, telecom carriers, vendors and Internet content providers have formed alliances to offer useful services like Yellow Pages, etc. At some point in the future, however, WAP could lead to a major upsurge[25] in Chinese Internet usage (Watts 2000; *ChinaOnline* 2000y).

Unlike basic telecommunications, Internet Service Providers (ISPs) can, at least in theory, operate as private enterprises in China. But the structure of the telecoms sector does not encourage independent ISPs, since China Telecom has charged them extremely high fees for line-rental in the past (*ChinaOnline* 1999c; *ChinaOnline* 1998b; *ChinaOnline* 1999e). By leasing bandwidth to ISPs, China Netcom as well as China Railcom could challenge China Telecom's dominant position. Meanwhile some ISPs forged alliances with foreign partners, which, strictly speaking, is not legal. The unfavourable conditions notwithstanding, 204 ISPs were granted business licences in 1998 and 520 in 1999 (*ChinaOnline* 2000h; *ChinaOnline* 2000n).

The entire telecommunications and Internet sector in China has been and still is in a phase of restructuring and transition. The recent adjustments must be seen against the background of China's WTO accession. The agreements between the United States and China (signed in November 1999) and between the EU and China (signed in May 2000) on China's WTO entry[26] contain passages providing for a gradual opening of the telecommunications sectors for FDI and foreign equity shares. This prospect sparked a domestic discussion on the necessary measures China would have to adopt in order to be ready for WTO entry. Delegates of the National People's Congress formulated a petition in March 2000 favouring the acceleration of the liberalisation of the domestic telecom market and related value-added services in order to prepare the country for the competitive environment in the future (*ChinaOnline* 2000b; *CITTR* 2000a). Such radical deregulation cannot be expected any time soon, however, at least not as long as Wu Jichuan, who has established a reputation for trying to protect the vested interests of his Ministry and the SOEs under its jurisdiction, is a key decision-maker. Nevertheless, new players have been permitted to enter the field, and this has introduced some competition in telecommunications services. Indeed, while fixed-line telephone services are still firmly in the hands of China Telecom, China Unicom's overall position has somewhat improved via-à-vis China Mobile.

In sum, the prospect of joining the WTO produced external pressures and thereby has acted as a catalyst for reform in the telecommunications sector. The MII's overall strategy is to strengthen its own position and the enterprises under its jurisdiction. Even after China's accession to the WTO, the opening of the telecoms market to foreign competition will be stretched over three to five years and Chinese SOEs will keep a 51 per cent share, at least in all 'basic' telecommunications services.

China's Internet users, Internet portals and e-commerce

The questionnaire which CNNIC sends out to gather Internet data contains information on gender, age, education and income of Internet users in China. According to the results of the July 2000 survey,[27] the majority of *wangmin* were between 18 and 30 years old (46.8 per cent between 18 and 24, 29.2 per cent between 25 and 30). Their level of educational attainment was above average (two years of college or bachelor degree are the rule). The income of the majority of users in June 2000 ranged between 500 and 1000 RMB (around 29 per cent), or between 1000 and 2000 RMB per month (around 36 per cent). Considering the high costs of computers and Internet access, it is not surprising that in most cases their incomes were clearly above average. Thus, the majority of Chinese Internet users were young urban male professionals. In this respect China is not much different from the rest of the world. However, by comparing figures over several years, the following trends can be noted:

(i) the percentage of female users has grown from 7 per cent in June 1998 to 25.3 per cent in June 2000;
(ii) the percentage of students among users has increased;
(iii) Internet cafes have become more popular; and
(iv) more and more *netizens* pay for their Internet access from personal funds, rather than using facilities at their workplace.

The average time spent online per week was 16.5 hours. The popularity of e-mail in China is unbroken: in June 2000, it was still the most frequently used service (88 per cent),[28] followed by search engines (56 per cent) and up- and downloading of software (51 per cent). Electronic chat rooms and bulletin boards (BBS) were also very popular. The top three reasons for accessing the Internet were 'gathering information' (82 per cent), education ('learning about computers and other new technologies') (59 per cent) and entertainment (51 per cent). As main reasons for dissatisfaction with the Internet, users in China complained about the slow access speed (48 per cent) and high costs (35 per cent), followed by 'insufficient information in Chinese' (6 per cent) – in comparison to earlier surveys, users clearly saw less reason to complain about this last point.

In each survey conducted by CNNIC it has asked respondents to identify the most popular Web sites in China. This part of the survey was quite controversial, since it turned out to be an incentive for Chinese-language portals to produce fake responses in order to improve their ranking.[29] Due to the objections raised, CNNIC announced in November 2000 that it would discontinue the ranking (*ChinaOnline* 2000zd). The most widely-known Chinese Internet portals during 1999 and 2000 were Sina, Netease and Sohu.[30]

Electronic commerce, business-to-customer (B2C) as well as business-to-business (B2B), is still in an embryonic stage in China. In June 2000, the vast majority of the Internet users (84 per cent) had not ordered anything online. China has made progress in developing a credit card system and delivery services have improved, but people have no trust in the security of online transactions, in the quality of items bought via the Net or in after-sales service. Although the number of e-commerce platforms is increasing and there were about 800 online shopping sites and 100 auction sites by March 2000, the volume of shopping conducted via the Internet accounted for only 0.018 per cent of the total retail volume in 1999.[31] An official of the State Economic and Trade Commission saw three major obstacles for e-commerce in China: in the small number of Internet users, the small number of high-quality Chinese e-commerce sites and the lack of local e-commerce product development (*ChinaOnline* 2000v).

Efforts of control

In addition to providing the infrastructure necessary for Internet access, the Chinese Party-state wields other instruments by which dissemination and contents of the Internet can be directly influenced. First, the MII decides – in coordination with the Ministry of Finance – on fees for the installation of telephones, phone calls and other telecommunications services (MII 2000). Fees for registering domain names are also set by the MII. Second, non-financial obstacles for market entry can be erected, e.g. by ruling out online businesses for 'pure plays' (Internet companies that only offer electronic services) or by requiring that Internet providers and Internet cafes hire security staff for monitoring ongoing activities. While the above-mentioned fees have generally been lowered in the last few years, the second category of measures has been applied and incorporated in legislative decrees.

Although some lawsuits related to the Internet were settled on the basis of other laws,[32] the necessity to regulate and standardise the booming telecoms and Internet sector has become more pressing in recent years. As has been the case in other areas of the Chinese economy and society, the government approaches this problem in a trial-and-error fashion. First, provisional or interim regulations are issued, sometimes on a local basis. Then, after a period of experiment, the provisional rules are amended. The final aim is to draw up a comprehensive telecoms law on the basis of these regulations. Since fall 1999, a whole series of new regulations have come into force.[33] Apart from the MII, which is responsible for telecoms infrastructure, the IT industry and ISPs, many other ministries and government institutions have been involved in formulating policies and regulations concerning different aspects of the Internet: the State Secrets Bureau, the Ministry of Public Security (cyber crime), the State Administration for Industry and Commerce (advertisements on the Internet), the Securities Regulatory Commission (online brokerage), the Ministry of Education (online education) and Ministry of Health (online selling of pharmaceuticals and medical instruments), to name only a few. To supervise Internet Content Providers (ICPs), the State Council's Information Office established a special 'Internet Information Management Bureau' (*Guowuyuan Xinwen Bangongshi Wangluo Xinwen Guanliju*) in April 2000. This institution not only supervises ICPs, but also has the task of stepping up the online presence of traditional media to make them more attractive.[34]

Between September and November 2000 alone, four new important regulations concerning telecommunications and Internet services came into force.[35] It would appear that the Chinese government accelerated its efforts to have rules in place before the country joined the WTO. While some have criticised the new rules as 'realising worst fears' (Kynge 2000), others have greeted them as adding clarity to the confused situation (Hui and Ng 2000). Representatives of Chinese Internet companies claimed to be unsurprised by the new rules, because most of the details had been widely circulated for months before publication (*ChinaOnline* 2000za).

The new regulations identify a fixed set of contents that are prohibited. Since this list of illegal contents seems to present the standard wording for now, it is cited here in detail. The following information is forbidden:

(i) material which contradicts basic principles of the constitution;
(ii) material which endangers national security, leaks state secrets, subverts the government, undermines national unity;
(iii) material which is detrimental to the honour and interests of the state;
(iv) material which instigates ethnic hatred or ethnic discrimination or undermines the unity of [China's] nationalities;
(v) material which undermines the State's religious policy, preaches evil cults or [feudal] superstition;
(vi) material which spreads rumour, disturbs social order, undermines social stability;
(vii) material which disseminates lewdness, pornography, gambling, violence, homicide, terror or instigates crime;
(viii) material which insults or slanders other people, infringes upon other people's legitimate rights and interests; and, finally,
(ix) any other information that is forbidden by the law or administrative regulations.

This list is not new: it bears a very strong resemblance to the 'Regulations for the management of publishing' issued in early 1997 (State Council 1997, Article 25). This means that content accessible in the Internet is basically subject to the same restrictions as in the Chinese media in general. It is important to note that the formulations are not very specific and leave a lot of room for interpretation. And this vagueness is not accidental either. The term 'state secret', for example, can be applied to almost any information in China – even data on the last grain harvest can be declared a state secret.[36] Thus, the responsible administrative institutions have an instrument to shut down almost any Web site if they deem it necessary.

Even more importantly, China emulates a principle we find in Singapore's Internet regulations: the providers of Internet services and content are held liable for all electronic activities conducted within their business sphere. This, it was pointed out, could be compared to holding the postal service liable for the contents of letters and parcels it accepts for transportation and delivery (Rodan 1998, pp. 80–83). Internet providers are to remove every bit of information immediately from their servers that does not comply with the rules and to notify the authorities. The regulations issued in autumn 2000 went one step further by stipulating that records are to be kept for 60 days of every user logging in, the time spent online, the user's account number, the telephone number mainly used for logging in, and the Internet addresses or domain names of the sites visited. These data have to be disclosed to the authorities 'upon demand in accordance with the law'. By this method, self-censorship of Internet providers is strongly encouraged. For Internet companies that want to stay in business it is also recommendable to enter alliances with official State media. A US representative of Sina.com described the situation of his company as a 'balancing act' between users and government.[37]

Western media generally tend to attribute a more conservative and restrictive attitude to the 'ideological' departments within the Chinese government and the Communist Party, and a more liberal attitude to the 'economic' departments. However, the fault lines are not that clear-cut. The protection of vested interests (for example of the official 'traditional' media that want to strengthen their presence on the Web) and sources of revenue and power are strong motives for government institutions, no matter whether they fall under the 'ideological' or the 'economic' category. In addition to that, regulations can be handled in a very flexible fashion in China, as was demonstrated in the case of the encryption rules issued in December 1999. The encryption rules, which stipulated registration of every item containing encryption technology, were considerably toned down shortly after coming into force. It was explained that the regulations applied only to appliances in which encryption technology is the core, and did not apply to mobile phones, Windows software and browser software (Marlow 2000). Whether the directives will hinder the development of the Internet or not depends largely on how strictly they are implemented and enforced.

There have indeed been cases which, at least from the perspective of China's political leaders, provide proof of the dangers and the destabilising potential lurking in the Internet. The most striking example of this 'subversive' potential of the Internet was Falungong, a spiritual movement whose leader lives in the United States. It must have been a shock for the Chinese political elite to find that, one morning in April 1999, thousands of Falungong members had gathered silently in front of Zhongnanhai, the very centre of political power in Beijing. The demonstration had been organised mainly via e-mail. Not only did the Chinese government ban Falungong and launch a traditional campaign of criticism, but it also used the Internet as one of the battlefields to fight Falungong (Smith 1999; *VirtualChina* 1999c). Chinese citizens were also arrested for selling e-mail addresses or for posting politically controversial material on Web sites (*VirtualChina* 1999a; *VirtualChina* 1999b; *BBC News* (online) 2000). Reportedly special 'cyber police' units have been organised to fight all sorts of illegal electronic activities and to provide security services, like warning of new viruses (*VirtualChina* 1999a; *ChinaOnline* 2000p; Schwankert 2000).

But in the era of global networks China's IT security is also perceived as being threatened from abroad. Foreign hackers have attacked Chinese Web sites several times (*VirtualChina* 1999a). One problem from the perspective of the Chinese leadership is the country's dependency on foreign (Western) software. The markets for operating systems and especially security software are dominated by firms from the USA. Repeatedly there have been official statements underlining the necessity to build up a domestic software industry. The open source operating system 'Linux', of which various Chinese-developed versions exist, was officially recommended for government and administrative units. One reason for this is the lower price; but another is the fear of becoming vulnerable to 'cyber-attacks' from abroad if mainly US-developed software and computer equipment are used.[38] However, Western companies are keen to get their share of China's IT security market. It is an irony that the Western press criticises China for 'cracking down' on the Internet and crippling its budding development, while most of the equipment for doing so is supplied by Western firms.[39]

Conclusion

Proponents of the Internet in the West praise the Internet as inherently democratic in nature and, due to its decentralised and non-hierarchical character, as a threat to authoritarian regimes.[40] Such beliefs apparently find support within China's leadership, albeit as negative trends to be prevented at all costs. Systematic research on the Internet in China and the impact it could have on China's society and political system has only just begun. The few Western studies on the topic come to the conclusion that matters are not quite as simple as suggested, for example, by then US President Bill Clinton in March 2000, when he compared cracking down on the Internet to 'trying to nail Jello to the wall'.[41] There is, at least for now, no clear evidence, that dissemination of the Internet renders the Chinese Party-state helpless against the free flow of information and will inevitably weaken or undermine one-party rule.[42]

Ever since December 1978, when China embarked on the journey of reform and modernisation, there have been conflicting and often contradictory views within the Chinese leadership on the question of how far the process of opening China to the outside world should go. The Party-state has attempted to keep macro-control and to ensure social stability; but it should not be forgotten that the first steps towards decentralisation of power were initiated from above – despite the ensuing risks for the ideological foundations of the Chinese state and society.

When assessing the control measures initiated by the Chinese government, it is important not to lose perspective. Laws and regulations with respect to telecommunications and the Internet are not automatically or primarily intended to hinder its development, and they are not exclusively directed against political adversaries of the Chinese political system. Efforts to fight new forms of crime and misuse of electronic media, to standardise technical procedures and regulate business transactions conducted via the Internet and to protect consumers are legitimate. This is not to say that China's leaders do not strive to restrict the flow of information by outlawing unwelcome content and filtering or blocking foreign Web sites. With the regulations issued in 1999 and 2000 the authorities have an instrument to discipline Internet companies and individuals. This instrument can be implemented in a lenient or a strict way. By treating the Internet like other media and stipulating that Internet companies can only publish news from officially approved media, the government tried to kill two birds with one stone: the rules aim not only at eradicating unwelcome information spread over the Internet, but also at protecting the traditional news media from unwelcome competition.

Decisive obstacles to a wider diffusion of the Internet in China are the underdeveloped state of its telecommunications infrastructure, especially in the countryside, an administrative-organisational structure that provides fertile ground for struggles for power and revenues, and a system of state-owned telecoms enterprises which is not apt to encourage innovation and true competitiveness, at least not yet. And last but not least, due to the low standard of living, the purchase of a PC and Internet access are still out of reach for the overwhelming majority of the population. However, Internet access via TV sets and via WAP-enabled mobile devices could help in popularising the Internet.

The fast growth of the Internet in recent years would not have been possible without the active support of the responsible institutions within both the Party and the government. This support is based, among other things, on the conviction in parts of the leadership that it also has something to gain from the new technology. It would be an oversimplification to see the Internet in China as a technology which directly undermines Party control and is mainly utilised by democrats or political dissidents for spreading their ideas. The majority of Chinese *wangmin* are young urban professionals with an above-average income. This social group is likely to be more interested in acquiring information on the stock market, life style and entertainment than in using the Internet for activities seen as subversive and dangerous by their political leaders.

This does not mean, however, that the Internet will not have an impact on Chinese society in the long term. In 1995 the late Gerald Segal stated in his article 'Asians in Cyberia': 'The new information technology is a challenge to old authority because it adds new strands of pluralism to politics, but that challenge is, in fact, greatest where the running of the economy and the development of new social trends are concerned' (Segal 1995, p. 6).

Therefore, the real 'dangers' emanating from the Internet might be less direct and less easy to grasp than China's political leaders, as well as some Western observers, would like to think. The application of modern information and communication technology has brought new ways of doing business, and new possibilities of entertainment and of interacting with each other, into the daily lives of the Chinese people, thereby gradually changing their thinking and their values. The Internet has added one more dimension to the more fundamental dilemma that has accompanied the process of reform in China and the opening-up of the country from the beginning – that the 'usage' tends to change the 'essence'. However, it should not be taken for granted that these processes necessarily lead to more 'convergence' with the West.

Notes

1 For an overview of the sources see Fravel (2000b).
2 On the beginnings of China's Internet see Thomas (1999) and Qiu (1999/2000, pp. 6–7).
3 The following reports are accessible in English: CNNIC 1998, CNNIC 1999a, CNNIC 1999b, CNNIC 2000a. The last report (July 2000) was used in the Chinese version (CNNIC 2000b).
4 See e.g. Chang (2000). CNNIC seems to work on the assumption of multiple users per computer. A calculation of the ratio between users and computers with Internet access on the basis of Tables 1 and 2, however, provides no coherent picture: for June 1998, e.g., we get 2.2 users per computer, for December 1998 2.8, 2.7 for June 1999 and 2.5 for Dec. 1999.
5 Figures for spring 2000. For these and other countries in the world, see the Internet surveys of NUA (2000).
6 For China's international bandwidth capacity see Table 5.
7 On this project and first results see *People's Daily Online* (1999). In the meantime, China Telecom started promoting 'enterprises online' and 'home online' (in co-operation with Yahoo!China and Sinohome), see MacLeod (2000).
8 On some initiatives on the international level (G7 Summit in Okinawa, World Economic Forum in Davos, World Bank) to bridge the digital divide, see Chanda (2000).
9 The carriers of this system are CERNET, the Internet network connecting China's campuses and schools, and Chinese Educational TV (CETV) (*ChinaWeb* 2000).
10 Details of the agreement concerning telecommunications can be found on the Web site of The White House (2000).

11 On the 'Golden Projects' see Tan (1995) and Lovelock (1999). Lovelock's description of the three original projects is different from Tan's.

12 For the history of Chinese telecommunications up to 1996 see Mueller and Tan (1997).

13 The MPT's Minister Wu Jichuan was also appointed head of the new MII.

14 The group is headed by Vice-Premier Wu Bangguo. On the members and responsibilities of this group see State Council (2000a).

15 On the background and the political significance of GSM and CDMA in China see Forney (2000); Forney and Dean (2000): China Unicom was authorised to build China's only mobile network based on CDMA (Code Division Multiple Access) technology. The question of GSM (Global System for Mobile Communication) and CDMA played a role during China's WTO negotiations with the US and the EU. While CDMA was developed by US companies, European suppliers concentrated on GSM. US companies lobbied for CDMA standard in China. In order to satisfy at least in part American wishes, a joint venture between the Chinese Army (who happened to own the necessary frequency for CDMA) and the former MPA called 'Great Wall Communications' was founded in 1995. This JV built and operated small CDMA networks on a trial basis in Beijing, Shanghai, Xi'an and Guangzhou. But because the MPA itself wholly owned the frequency used by GSM networks, it supported the roll-out of GSM through its commercial arm China Telecom. Thus, GSM became the dominant standard in China's mobile market. When in 1998 the Chinese Army was ordered to give up its commercial activities, it also had to withdraw from Great Wall Communications. With Zhu Rongji's personal backing, China Unicom was authorised to build a CDMA network, including Great Wall Communication's networks. During the summer of 2000, China Unicom seemed to have given up all plans for a CDMA network, but by the fall CDMA was back on Unicom's agenda. At the time of writing, details about the network's size etc. were not clear.

16 In fall 2000, there were 1,479 registered operators of paging services in China and more than 70 million subscribers. *Guo Xin*'s share was more than 50 per cent (*ChinaOnline* 1999f; *CITTR* 2000g; *ChinaOnline* 2000zc).

17 In some regions, China Mobile and its former parent have already become competitors. Since China Telecom has no license for mobile services, it started offering – not quite legally – wireless local loop services with cordless phones. One such case was reported from Lanzhou, where Lanzhou Mobile protested against the use of PHS and cut the connection of the PHS phones to its mobile network. In retaliation, Lanzhou Telecom disconnected mobile users from its fixed-line network. Similar incidents happened in Tianjin and other localities (*CITTR* 2000e).

18 For a good overview of the different Internet networks see *ChinaOnline* (1999f).

19 155 Mbps are the minimum for a broadband network.

20 In addition to upgrading the existing cable networks for two-way interconnectivity, special set-top boxes for TV sets are required for Internet access.

21 Official Chinese text MII, SARFT (1999). Shanghai was officially exempted from the ban.

22 According to the reports, the 'battle' started after employees of a local cable company chopped down telephone poles in Hunan (*ChinaOnline* 2000x)

23 One reported case referred to struggles between Zibo Telecom and Zibo Radio, Film and Television in Shandong province. The latter company had offered broadband Internet services to individual customers and Internet cafes at a much lower price than Zibo Telecom (*CITTR* 2000j).

24 Nusbaum (2000) explains the success of WAP-enabled mobile phones by two facts: Only very few Japanese have a PC at home, while mobile phones are extremely popular, and specialised services (iMode) were offered by NTT DoCoMo, the Japanese mobile operator.

25 Forecasts predict that the number of Chinese accessing the Internet via mobile phone will soar from 0.3 million in 2000 to almost 80 million in 2005 (and mobile phones to 254 million) (*CITTR* 2000h).

26 For a comparison between the US and the EU agreements, see Laprès (2000).

27 For the report in July 2000, CNNIC received 570,000 responses that were assessed as being valid. (CNNIC 2000b)

28 There was an astonishing number of more than 65 million registered e-mail accounts in China, of which 56 million were free of charge.

29 Some Internet companies even generated small programmes to fill out online questionnaires with random user data (Lu 2000b). The Chinese version of the most popular Web sites in June 2000 can be found under CNNIC (2000c).

30 All 'top three' portals are publicly listed, although they had to go through a complicated restructuring in order to secure the MII's permission for their IPOs. With the exception of Chinadotcom, the Internet portals had to turn their assets on the Chinese mainland into separate companies. The mainland assets – considered to be the most valuable part of these enterprises – were excluded from listing abroad (e.g. *ChinaOnline* 2000d). Chinese 'dotcoms' have also been affected by the sharp decline of Internet shares on the international stock markets. Many observers predicted that 80 per cent of the domestic Chinese Internet companies were nearing bankruptcy in 2000 and would sooner or later go out of business or be bought up by stronger players. Lay-offs of employees and take-overs of smaller Internet firms have become frequent in China too (*CITTR* 2000f; MacLeod 2000; *ChinaOnline* 2000g).

31 For the year 2000, the volume of online shopping was predicted to grow by 200 per cent (*ChinaOnline* 2000f).

32 One reported case had to do with a Web site providing financial and tax information. It had falsely claimed to be supported by 'leaders of the State Council' and other high government officials and was penalised in accordance with the law against unfair competition (*ChinaOnline* 2000j).

33 Some English translations of important legal texts can be found under: http://www.chinaonline.com/refer/legal/laws_regs/important_documents.asp. State Council (1999); State Bureau of Secrets Protection (2000); Ministry of Culture (2000); China Securities Regulatory Commission (2000a); China Securities Regulatory Commission (2000b); Beijing Municipal Administration of Industry and Commerce (2000a); Beijing Municipal Administration for Industry and Commerce (2000b); State Council (2000b); Ministry of Information Industry (2000a); State Council Information Office and Ministry of Information Industry (2000); Ministry of Information Industry (2000b).

34 A portrait of the new bureau and its activities can be found under *ChinaOnline* (2000i). In spring 1999, the 'traditional' state-run media formed an alliance against the growing competition from Internet portals, which provided interesting news up-to-date and other features attractive to the users. Among other things, the official media demanded government intervention against piracy of news (*ChinaOnline* 1999b). It was reported that one billion Renminbi (US$121 million) were earmarked by the government to support the online presence of important media like Xinhua News Agency, *China Daily*, *People's Daily*, and China International Broadcast Station (Fravel 2000a).

35 They are: State Council (2000b); Ministry of Information Industry (2000a); State Council Information Office and Ministry of Information Industry (2000); Ministry of Information Industry (2000b).
36 Implementation rules for the Law on State Secrets of 1988 were issued in 1990. They define the circumstances under which information is considered a state secret. One of the points listed here is '[...] undermining the consolidation and defence of state political power, and undermining state unification, national unity and social stability' (*ChinaOnline* 2000a).
37 'We are playing that role, to let people talk about sensitive issues but also to help the government manage the flow of ideas' (McGill 2000a).
38 Such fears have been expressed with respect to Microsoft products, but also to Intel chips. The security issue was one reason for slowing down the 'government online' programme in late 1999 (*ChinaOnline* 2000r).
39 Western surveillance software was on display at a business fair devoted to the 'Golden Shield' project, which was launched by the Ministry of Public Security to monitor activities in cyberspace (*FEER* 2000). On this question see also Sieren (1998).
40 For a discussion of these views and literature, see Rodan (1998, pp. 63–64).
41 Cited in Drake, Kalathil and Boas (2000: 1).
42 On this question see also Qiu (1999/2000); Drake, Kalathil and Boas (2000); Hartford (2000).

Bibliography

BBC News (2000): China to Battle Internet 'Enemies', *BBC News* (online), Aug. 9, 2000, http://www.bbc.co.uk/hi/english/asia-pacific/newsid_872000/872407.stm (accessed Oct. 6, 2000)

Chanda, Nayan (2000): The Digital Divide, *Far Eastern Economic Review*, Oct. 19, 2000, pp. 50, 52–53

Chang, Leslie (2000): China's Internet Users Multiply, But E-Commerce Is Suffering, *Asian Wall Street Journal* [*AWStJ*], July 28–30, 2000, p. 2

Chen, Gary (1999): China's Booming Internet Sector: Open or Closed to Foreign Investment?, Oct. 8, 1999, http://www.chinaonline.com/industry/infotech/NewsArchive/Secure/1999/october/C9100519REV-SS.asp (accessed Jan. 9, 2000)

ChinaOnline (1998a): China Consolidates Telecom, Software, and Electronic Media Under One Super-ministry, May 1998, http://www.chinaonline.com/industry/infotech/newsarchive/Secure/1998/May/te14_.asp (accessed Jan. 10, 2000)

ChinaOnline (1998b): Chinese Internet Service Providers Lack Connections, Dec. 28, 1998, http://www.chinaonline.com/industry/infotech/NewsArchive/Secure/1998/December/it_b8121120.asp (accessed Feb. 2, 2000)

ChinaOnline (1999a): Internet Users in China Will Number 6.7 Million This Year, 33 Million by 2003, June 29, 1999, http://www.chinaonline.com/industry/infotech/newsarchive/secure/1999/june/it_c9062522.asp (accessed Oct. 24, 1999)

ChinaOnline (1999b): China's Print Media Concerned Over New Internet Portals, Sept. 22, 2000, http://www.chinaonline.com/issues/legal/currentnews/open/C9092180e-SS.asp (accessed Oct. 24, 1999)

ChinaOnline (1999c): China Cuts Internet Access Fees to Spur Online Growth, Oct. 26, 1999, http://www.chinaonline.com/industry/infotech/Archive/Secure/1999/october/C9102207.asp (accessed Jan. 9, 2000)

ChinaOnline (1999d): China Decides Not to Integrate Cable Radio, TV, and Telecom Networks, Nov. 18, 1999, http://www.chinaonline.com/industry/infotech/NewsArchive/Secure/1999/november/B2–99111630-SS.asp (accessed Jan. 9, 2000)

ChinaOnline (1999e): Beijing ISPs Can't Pay Their Bills, Dec. 1, 1999, http://www.chinaonline.com/industry/infotech/newsarchive/Secure/1999/December/b9113015.asp (accessed Feb. 23, 2000)
ChinaOnline (1999f): China's Telecommunications and Internet Sectors Experience Rapid Growth, Dec. 14, 1999, http://www.chinaonline.com/industry/infotech/newsarchive/secure/1999/december/b9120920–46-ss.asp (accessed Feb. 21, 2000)
ChinaOnline (2000a): Bureau for the Protection of State Secrets (State Secrets Bureau), Jan. 28, 2000, http://www.chinaonline.com/refer/ministry_profiles/Secrets–3-S.asp?nav=ref (accessed Jan. 31, 2000)
ChinaOnline (2000b): China's Telecom Sector Should Be Open to Private Competition – Petition, March 7, 2000, http://www.chinaonline.com/topstories/000307/1/C00030603.asp (accessed March 10, 2000)
ChinaOnline (2000c): China Aims to Triple Internet Bandwidth to 1 Gb/s, March 9, 2000, http://chinaonline.com/topstories/000309/2/C00030801.asp (accessed March 10, 2000)
ChinaOnline (2000d): Peel Off China Assets Before Listing Abroad – Internet Regulator, March 29, 2000, http://www.chinaonline.com/topstories/000329/1/b200032907.asp (accessed March 30, 2000)
ChinaOnline (2000e): China Jitong to List on NASDAQ, SEHK, April 25, 2000, http://www.chinaonline.com/topstories/000425/2/C00041908.asp (accessed April 26, 2000).
ChinaOnline (2000f): Ecommerce in China: The CCIDnet Survey (April 27), May 5, 2000, http://www.chinaonline.com/issues/internet_policy/newsarchive/secure/2000/may/c00050213.asp (accessed May 16, 2000)
ChinaOnline (2000g): The Party's Over: China's Growing Tech Wreck Fears, May 11, 2000, http://www.chinaonline.com/topstories/0005011/top/C00051121.asp (accessed May 12, 2000)
ChinaOnline (2000h): China's MII Ready to Delegate ISP Authority, May 16, 2000, http://www.chinaonline.com/topstories/000516/1/c00051505.asp (accessed May 17, 2000)
ChinaOnline (2000i): Internet Information Management Bureau (IIMB), May 30, 2000, http://www.chinaonline.com/refer/ministry_profiles/IIMB.asp (accessed Nov. 2, 2000)
ChinaOnline (2000j): China Fines Net Co. for Untruthful Statements, June 1, 2000, http://www.chinaonline.com/topstories/000601/1/c00053101.asp (accessed June 2, 2000)
ChinaOnline (2000k): Study: China Web Use – and Security Fears – Soars, June 7, 2000, http://www.chinaonline.com/topstories/000607/1/B100060533.asp (accessed June 8, 2000)
ChinaOnline (2000l): China to Open Western Regions' Telecom and Energy Sectors, June 26, 2000, http://www.chinaonline.com/topstories/000626/1/c00062202.asp (accessed June 27, 2000)
ChinaOnline (2000m): Ministry of Education Unveils Plan for Furnishing Teachers with Net Training, June 30, 2000, http://www.chinaonline.com/topstories/000630/1/C00062805.asp (accessed July 3, 2000)
ChinaOnline (2000n): MII Report Card: China's ISPs Demonstrate Weaknesses but Are Progressing, July 13, 2000, http://www.chinaonline.com/topstories/000713/1/C00070703.asp (accessed July 14, 2000)
ChinaOnline (2000o): Chinese Government Going the Distance to Expand Internet-based Education, Aug. 7, 2000, http://www.chinaonline.com/topstories/000807/1/B200080305.asp (accessed Aug. 8, 2000)

ChinaOnline (2000p): Cyber-sleuths: Web Police on the Beat in China, Aug. 8, 2000, http://www.chinaonline.com/topstories/000808/1/C00080713.asp (accessed Aug. 9, 2000)
ChinaOnline (2000q): Telecom Regulator Bans New Investment in Handyphone System, Aug. 17, 2000, http://www.chinaonline.com/topstories/000817/1/B200081612.asp (accessed Aug. 20, 2000)
ChinaOnline (2000r): China's Concern With Information Security on the Internet, Sept. 9, 2000, http://www.chinaonline.com/industry/infotech/NewsArchive/Secure/1999/september/C9080988s.asp (accessed Sept. 9, 2000)
ChinaOnline (2000s): China Telecom Hankering to Become 3rd Mobile Player, Sept. 25, 2000, http://www.chinaonline.com/industry/telecom/currentnews/secure/c00092209.asp (accessed Oct. 5, 2000)
ChinaOnline (2000t): Wu Jichuan: No Business Volume Limitations for Foreign Investors in Telecom, Sept. 26, 2000, http://www.chinaonline.com/industry/telecom/currentnews/secure/c00092619.asp (accessed Oct. 5, 2000)
ChinaOnline (2000u): Communications Industry Pulls in US$ 28.76 billion, Sept. 26, 2000, http://www.chinaonline.com/topstories/000926/1/B100092111.asp (accessed Oct. 5, 2000)
ChinaOnline (2000v): It's a Long Road to E-commerce, Says SETC Official, Oct. 2, 2000, http://www.chinaonline.com/topstories/001002/1/B100092825.asp (accessed Oct. 4, 2000)
ChinaOnline (2000w): Information Highway to Become Data Cloud, Oct. 19, 2000, http://www.chinaonline.com/topstories/001019/1/C00101801.asp (accessed Oct. 20, 2000)
ChinaOnline (2000x): Banding Together: China Opens Net to Cable TV Industry, Oct. 25, 2000, http://www.chinaonline.com/topstories/0010025/1/c000102556.asp (accessed Oct. 26, 2000)
ChinaOnline (2000y): China Mobile Subscribers in the Majority, Cell Phone Survey says, Oct. 27, 2000, http://www.chinaonline.com/topstories/001027/1/C00101910.asp (accessed Oct. 30, 2000)
ChinaOnline (2000z): Netcom Moves to Offer Internet Services, Nov. 8, 2000, http://www.chinaonline.com/industry/telecom/currentnews/secure/c000110856.asp (accessed Nov. 11, 2000)
ChinaOnline (2000za): Heads of Online Services React to New Regs, Nov. 9, 2000, http://www.chinaonline.com/topstories/001109/1/C00110803.asp (accessed Nov. 10, 2000)
ChinaOnline (2000zb): Lines Are Open: Cable, Phone Companies Get Go-ahead to Lock Horns After All, Nov. 9, 2000, http://www.chinaonline.com/topstories/001109/1/B2000110834.asp (accessed Nov. 11, 2000)
ChinaOnline (2000zc): MII Review of Mobile Communications Market Shows China Needs to Make Presence Known, Nov. 11, 2000, http://www.chinaonline.com/topstories/001101/1/B200102436.asp (accessed Nov. 2, 2000)
ChinaOnline (2000zd): Poll Vaulted: CNNIC to Halt Controversial Top-10 Ranking of Web Sites, Nov. 14, 2000, http://www.chinaonline.com/topstories/001114/1/C00111302.asp (accessed Nov. 15, 2000)
ChinaWeb (2000): Distance Education Opens Minds, Oct. 30, 2000, http://www.chinaweb.com/english/cw_html/itnews/internet_industry/BJ14100.html (accessed Oct. 31, 2000)
CITTR (2000a): NPC & CPPCC Urge China to Boost Cyber-economy and to Open Telecom Market, Vol.1, No.22, p. 1
CITTR (2000b): China to Speed up Network Construction, Vol.1, No.22, p. 6

CITTR (2000c): Railcom Likely to Gain Telecom License as Merger with Unicom Put on Ice, Vol.1, No.44, pp. 1–2

CITTR (2000d): Jiang Looks to Information Technology to Drive Economy, Vol.1, No.45, pp. 4–5

CITTR (2000e): Lanzhou Mobile and Lanzhou Telecom Penalized By MII After Feud, Vol.1, No.45, p. 4

CITTR (2000f): Chinadotcom Cuts China Staff by 10%, Vol.46, No.1, p. 11

CITTR (2000g): China Shuts Down 100 Wireless Paging Channels, Vol.1, No.46, pp. 16–17

CITTR (2000h): Intrinsic Statistical Handbook Maps China's Wireless Landscape, Vol.1, No.47, p. 11

CITTR (2000i): China's Telephone Subscribers Exceed 200 Mln on Sept. 20, Vol.1, No.49, p. 3

CITTR (2000j): MII: Radio, Cable TV Entities Not Allowed to Provide Internet Services, Vol.1, No.49, p. 4

CITTR (2000k): ChinaSat: China Telecom's Final Offspring, Vol.1, No.52, pp. 19–25

Computer Industry Almanac Inc. (1999): 150 Million Internet Users Worldwide Year-End 1998, April 30, 1999, http://www.c-i-a.com/199904iu.htm (accessed October 19, 1999)

Drake, William J., Shanthi Kalathil, Taylor C. Boas (2000): Dictatorships in the Digital Age: Some Considerations on the Internet in China and Cuba, *iMP: The Magazine on Information Impacts* (online), October 2000, 12 pp, http://www.cisp.org/imp/october_2000/10-00drake.html (accessed Nov. 10, 2000)

FEER (2000): Spy Systems on Show in China, Nov. 2, 2000, p. 10

Feng, Zhaokui (2000): IT geming: 'gengxin' zonghe guoli jingzheng (The IT revolution: 'Reviving' the competition for comprehensive national power), *Shijie Zhishi*, 2000, No.17, pp. 12–14.

Forney, Matt (1999): Chinese Leader's Son Builds an Empire, *AWStJ*, Nov. 3, 1999, pp. 1, 6.

Forney, Matt (2000): China Beckoned Qualcomm Twice – And Hung Up, *AWStJ*, July 14–16, 2000, pp. 1, 5

Forney, Matt, Jason Dean (2000): Personal Ties Aid Qualcomm in China, *AWStJ*, Oct. 20–22, 2000, pp. 1, 26

Fravel, [M.] Taylor (2000a): The Bureaucrats' Battle over the Internet in China, Feb. 17, 2000, http://www.virtualchina.com/news/feb00/021800-ministries-tf.html (accessed Feb. 19, 2000)

Fravel, M. Taylor (2000b): Online and on China: Research Sources in the Information Age, *China Quarterly*, No.163 (Sept. 2000), pp. 821–842

Gesteland, Lester J. (1999): China Ripe For IP Telephony, Says Clarent Corp Exec, Dec. 23, 1999, http://www.chinaonline.com/issues/internet_policy/currentnews/open/c9122351.asp (accessed Jan. 9, 2000)

Greenberg, Jonah (2000): China's Backbones: Not the Weakest Link, March 24, 2000, http://www.virtualchina.com/news/mar00/032400-backbone-jg-jsl.htm (accessed March 25, 2000)

Hartford, Kathleen (2000): Cyberspace with Chinese Characteristics, *Current History*, Sept. 2000, pp. 255–262

Heilmann, Sebastian (1999): Die neue chinesische Regierung: Abschied vom sozialistischen Leviathan?, *China aktuell* [*Ca*], March 1999, pp. 277–287

Hui, Yuk-Min, Eric Ng (2000): Rules Hailed for Adding Clarity as Shares Falter, Oct. 4, 2000, http://www.chinaweb.com/english/cw_html/itnews/internet_industry/HK12773.html (accessed Oct. 6, 2000)

Kynge, James (1999): China to Launch Third State Telecoms Company, *Financial Times* [*FT*], (online) Oct. 27, 1999

Kynge, James (2000): China sets internet rules, *FT*, Oct. 2, 2000.

Laprès, Daniel Arthur (2000): The EU–China WTO Deal Compared, http://www.chinabusinessreview.com/0007/lapres.html (accessed Nov. 21, 2000)

Lovelock, Peter (1999): E-China: Putting Business on the Internet, Oct. 18, 1999, http://www.virtualchina.com/infotech/analysis/index.html (accessed Oct. 22, 1999)

Lu, Peter Weigang (2000a): Internet Development in China: An Analysis on CNNIC Survey Reports, part 3, http://www.virtualchina.com/infotech/analysis/chinanet-cnnic-3.html (accessed March 23, 2000)

Lu, Peter Weigang (2000b): Internet Development in China: An Analysis on CNNIC Survey Reports, part 7, http://www.virtualchina.com/infotech/analysis/chinanet-cnnic-7.html (accessed March 23, 2000)

MacLeod, Calum (2000): China's Home Online Pitch: Let's Go Surfing Now, Oct. 3, 2000, http://www.chinaonline.com/topstories/001003/1/c00100355.asp (accessed Oct. 4, 2000)

Marlow, Kit (2000): China Softens Encryption Rules, March 14, 2000, http://www.chinaonline.com/topstories/000314/1/C00031430.asp (accessed March 15, 2000)

McGill, Douglas C. (2000a): Sina.com's Delicate Balancing Act, May 23, 2000, http://www.virtualchina.com/finance/stirfry/052300-stirfry-dcm-alo2.html (accessed May 25, 2000)

McGill, Douglas C. (2000b): Beijing Reaffirms Ban on Foreign Backing of Internet Companies, Stunning Investors Anew, Oct. 25, 2000, http://www.virtualchina.com/news/feature/102599-ban.html (accessed Oct. 25, 2000)

Michaels, R. J. (2000): Numbers say IT Is for Everybody; Reality Says Only the Rich Have Access, Aug. 15, 2000, http://www.chinaonline.com/industry/infotech/currentnews/secure/c00081530.asp (accessed Aug. 16, 2000)

Mooney, P. (2000): Master of His Domain: Network Solutions Exec on Net Names in China, May 30, 2000, http://http://www.chinaonline.com/topstories/000530/1/c00053053.asp (accessed May 31, 2000)

Mueller, M., Zixiang Tan (1997): *China in the Information Age. Telecommunications and the Dilemmas of Reform*, Westport, Connecticut, and London: Praeger, 1997 (= The Washington Papers, 169)

NUA (2000): How Many Online?, http://www.nua.ie/surveys/how_many_online (accessed April 17, 2000).

Nusbaum, A. (2000): Surge Reshapes Corporate and Cultural Landscape, *FT*, March 3, 2000

Olesen, A. (2000): China Internet Users Rise to 12.3 Million, June 7, 2000, http://www.virtualchina.com/news/jun00/060700-numbers-alo-dcm.htm (accessed June 10, 2000)

People's Daily Online (1999): Much Achieved by Government Online Project in China, People's Daily Online, July 13, 1999, http://english.peopledaily.com.cn/199907/13/enc_19990712001047_TopNews.html (accessed Nov. 10, 2000)

Press, L., et al. (1998): An Internet Diffusion Framework (executive summary), http://som.csudh.edu/fac/lpress/articles/acmfwk/acmfrwk.htm (accessed Jan. 11, 2000)

Qiu, J. Linchuan (1999/2000): Virtual Censorship in China: Keeping the Gate between the Cyberspaces, *International Journal of Communications Law and Policy* (online), Issue 4, Winter 1999/2000, 25 pp., http://www.ijclp.org/4_2000/ijclp_webdoc_1_4_2000.html (accessed Nov. 10, 2000)

Rasin, S. (2000): Great Netspectations: Chinese Government Has High Hopes for Information Revolution, May 18, 2000, http://www.chinaonline.com/topstories/000518/1/c00051840.asp (accessed May 19, 2000)

Rodan, G. (1998): The Internet and Political Control in Singapore, *Political Science Quarterly*, Vol.113, No.1, pp. 63–89.

Schwankert, S. (2000): China Deploys Internet Police, Aug. 8, 2000, *internet.com*, http://asia.internet.com/2000/8/0802-police.html (accessed Aug. 10, 2000)

Segal, G. (1995): Asians in Cyberia, *The Washington Quarterly*, Summer, pp. 5–16

Sieren, F. (1998): Von Netzen und Mauern. Über die Substanz chinesischer Internetphantasien, in: Klaus Leggewie, Christa Maar (eds): *Internet und Politik. Von der Zuschauer- zur Beteiligungsdemokratie*, Cologne: Bollmann, pp. 229–235

Smith, C. S. (1999): Falun Dafa Defies Authority By Preaching in Cyberspace, *AWStJ*, Sept. 10–11, 1999, pp. 1, 6

Tan, Zixiang (1995): China's information superhighway. What is it and who controls it?, *Telecommunications Policy*, Vol.19, No.9 (1995), pp. 721–731

Thomas, S. (1999): Das Internet in der VR China. Teil 1: Aufbau einer Informationsstruktur, *China aktuell* [*Ca*], May 1999, pp. 500–510

VirtualChina (1999a): The Cracker War on China, Jan. 15, 1999, http://www.virtualchina.com/infotech/perspectives/perspective-011599.html (accessed Jan. 2, 2000)

VirtualChina (1999b): Whither the China Net?, Feb 5, 1999, http://www.virtualchina.com/infotech/perspectives/perspective-020599.html (accessed Jan. 2, 2000).

VirtualChina (1999c): Falun Dafa and the Internet. A Marriage Made in Web Heaven, July 30, 1999, http://www.virtualchina.com/infotech/perspectives/perspective-073099.html (accessed Feb. 1, 2000)

Wang, Xiangwei, Michael Ma (2000): China Unicom Merger Plans on Hold, *South China Morning Post* [*SCMP*] (online), Aug. 15, 2000.

Watts, C. (2000): Do WAP: China's Internet Goes WAP Wireless, April 18, 2000, www.chinaonline.com/topstories/email/c000418wap-ss.asp (accessed April 19, 2000)

[The White House 2000]: Telecommunications, Feb. 15, 2000, http://www.chinapntr.gov/industry%20fact%20sheets/telecommunications.htm (accessed March 17, 2000)

Official Publications

Beijing Municipal Administration for Industry and Commerce (2000a): Notice on Protecting the Legitimate Rights and Interests of Consumers in Network Economic Activities, July 2000, see: Get the fraud out of the baud: Beijing issues laws to regulate e-commerce, *ChinaOnline*, July 13, 2000, http://www.chinaonline.com/topstories/000713/1/C00070709.asp (accessed July 14, 2000)

Beijing Municipal Administration for Industry and Commerce (2000b): Jingyingxing wangzhan beian dengji guanli zhanxing banfa [Provisional Regulations for the Registration and Filing of Business Web Sites], *ChinaOnline*, Sept. 1, 2000, http://www.chinaonline.com/refer/law_reg/C00082813CE.pdf (Engl. and Chinese)

China Securities Regulatory Commission (2000a): Interim Regulations for the On-line Securities Brokerage Sector, April 2000, see *ChinaOnline*: New China Laws Regulate Online Securities Brokerages, April 17, 2000, http://www.chinaonline.com/issues/internet_policy/currentnews/open/B2000414031.asp (accessed Dec. 13, 2000)

China Securities Regulatory Commission (2000b): Procedures for the Examination and Approval of Securities Companies Engaging in On-line Brokerage Activities, May 2000, see *ChinaOnline*: Text of China Regulations On Online Securities

Brokerages, May 11, 2000, http://www.chinaonline.com/issues/internet_policy/NewsArchive/Secure/2000/may/B200050901b.asp (accessed Dec. 13, 2000)

CNNIC (1998): *Statistical Report of the Development of the Chinese Internet (1998.7)*, http://www.cnnic.net.cn/englishdata/English(9807).html (accessed Oct. 22, 1999)

CNNIC (1999a): *Statistical Report of the Development of China Internet*, http://www.cnnic.net.cn/englishdata/English(9901).html (accessed Oct. 22, 1999)

CNNIC (1999b): *The Development of the Internet in China: A Statistical Report*, July 1999, http://www.virtualchina.com/infotech/resources/index.html (accessed Oct. 22, 1999)

CNNIC (2000a): *SemiAnnual Survey Report on Internet Development in China (2000.1)*, http://www.cnnic.net.cn/Develst_e/cnnic2000_e.htm (accessed Feb. 7, 2000)

CNNIC (2000b): Zhongguo hulianwang xinxi zhongxin [Centre for News on the Chinese Internet, CNNIC]: Zhongguo hulianwangluo fazhan zhuangkuang tongji baogao (2000/7) [Statistical report on the development and situation of the Chinese Internet (2000/7)], http://www.cnnic.net.cn/develst/cnnic200007.shtml (accessed July 27, 2000)

CNNIC (2000c): Zhongguo hulianwang xinxi zhongxin [Centre for News on the Chinese Internet, CNNIC]: Zhongguo hulianwangluo wangzhan yingxiangli tiaocha baogao (2000/7) [Survey report on the influence of Web sites in the Chinese Internet (2000/7)], http://www.cnnic.net.cn/develst/topten2000-7.shtml (accessed July 27, 2000)

Ministry of Culture (2000): Circular on Relevant Issues Concerning the On-line Business of Audio-visual Products, March 2000, see *ChinaOnline*: China Regulates Audio-Visual Online Commerce, March 28, 2000, http://www.chinaonline.com/issues/internet_policy/currentnews/open/C00032705.asp (accessed Dec. 13, 2000)

Ministry of Information Industry (2000a): Zhonghua Renmin Gongheguo dianxin tiaoli [Telecommunication Regulations of the People's Republic of China], Sept. 25, 2000, http://www.mii.gov.cn/news2000/1013_1.htm (accessed Dec. 2, 2000)

Ministry of Information Industry (2000b): Hulianwang dianzi gonggao fuwu guanli guiding [Provisions for the Managment of Electronic Announcement Services on the Internet], Nov. 7, 2000, *People's Daily Online*, Nov. 7, 2000, http://www.peopledaily.com.cn/GB/channel5/28/20001107/302408.html (accessed Nov. 8, 2000)

Ministry of Information Industry, State Administration for Radio, Film and Television (1999): [Xinxi Chanyebu, Guojia guangbo dianying dianshi zongju:] Guanyu jiaqiang guangbo dianshi youxian wangluo jianshe guanli de yijian [Opinions on strengthening the management of constructing broadcasting and TV cable network], Sept. 13, 1999, in: *Zhonghua Renmin Gongheguo Guowuyuan Gongbao*, 1999, No.35, pp. 1573–1575

State Bureau of Secrets Protection (2000): Jisuanji xinxi xitong guoji lianwang baomi guanli guiding [State Sectrets Protection Regulations for Computer Information Systems on the Internet], Jan. 25, 2000, http://www.chinaonline.com/refer/law_reg/C00012601CE.pdf (Engl. and Chinese)

State Council (1997): [Guowuyuan:] Chuban guanli tiaoli [Regulations for the management of publishing], *Zhonghua Renmin Gongheguo Guowuyuan Gongbao*, 1997, No.2, pp. 38–46

State Council (1999): Regulation of Commercial Encryption Codes (Directive No. 273, Dec. 1999), http://www.chinaonline.com/features/legal/newsarchive/secure/1999/december/c9101510-ss.asp (accessed Feb. 16, 2000)

State Council (2000a): [Guowuyuan bangongting:] Guowuyuan Bangongting guanyu chengli Guojia xinxihua gongzuo lingdao xiaozu de tongzhi [Circular of the State Council's Office on setting up the Leading group for informatisation], Dec. 23, 1999, in: *Zhonghua Renmin Gongheguo Guowuyuan Gongbao*, 2000, No.6, pp. 8–9

State Council (2000b): Hulianwang xinxi fuwu guanli banfa [Measures for Managing Internet Information Services], Sept. 20, 2000, *People's Daily Online*, Nov. 7, 2000, http://www.peopledaily.com.cn/GB/channel5/28/200010017/2557566.html (accessed Oct. 24, 2000)

State Council Information Office, Ministry of Information Industry (2000): Hulianwangzhan congshi dengzai xinwen yewu guanli zhanxing guiding [Interim Provisions on the Management of Publishing News on the Internet], Nov. 7, 2000, *People's Daily Online*, Nov. 7, 2000, http://www.peopledaily.com.cn/GB/channel5/28/20001107/302409.html (accessed Nov. 8, 2000)

List of abbreviations

AWStJ	*Asian Wall Street Journal*
Ca	*China aktuell*
CITTR	*China IT and Telecom Report*
GWYGB	*Zhonghua Renmin Gongheguo Guowuyuan Gongbao*
FEER	*Far Eastern Economic Review*
FT	*Financial Times*
SCMP	*South China Morning Post*

Chapter 9

Challenges and Opportunities for Unification after Taiwan's 2000 Presidential Elections

Christopher R. Hughes

Introduction

The victory of the opposition Democratic Progressive Party (DPP) candidate, Chen Shui-bian, in Taiwan's presidential election on 18 March 2000 was an event of great significance for Chinese politics for two reasons. First of all, it marked the first peaceful transition of power between political parties in Chinese history. Although uncertainties as to how much power actually resides in the presidency under the Republic of China (ROC) Constitution mean that such a claim has to be qualified, for the island of Taiwan this certainly marked a new stage in the process of democratisation that began with the establishment of the opposition party in September 1986. Although full elections for central and local government chambers had been held since 1991, the DPP had never managed to gain a parliamentary majority. In the first presidential election, held in March 1996, it polled a mere 21 per cent, failing to remove the incumbent KMT president, Dr. Lee Teng-hui. With the victory of the DPP in March 2000, therefore, it appeared that Taiwan's democratisation had taken another step towards 'consolidation'.

Secondly, the election marked a new stage in Taiwan's relations with the PRC. Although there is a strong commitment to independence among DPP leaders and activists, during elections in the 1990s this cause failed to build a broadly based nationalist movement built on a solid sense of Taiwanese national identity. Findings of opinion polls indicated that the majority of people preferred to maintain a status quo of 'no independence, no unification' in relations with the PRC, and this was borne out at the ballot box. Although the election in March 2000 did not signal a sea-change in popular attitudes to independence, it put the island for the first time under the leadership of a member of a party with the long term ambition of achieving a *de jure* independent Taiwan Republic.

The victory of Chen Shui-bian, then, will undoubtedly have profound long-term consequences for the shape of Taiwan's democratisation and for relations with the PRC. To gain some insight into how these will play out in the longer term, it is important to carefully analyse the way in which Chen Shui-bian achieved victory, his intentions for government, the constraints within which he will have to work, and responses from the PRC.

The fall of the KMT

The most important thing to note about the results of the 2000 presidential election is that Chen Shui-bian won with just over 39 per cent of the vote and a lead of just over 300,000 votes over the independent candidate, James Soong. What made victory with such a small degree of support possible was a combination of a first-past-the-post electoral system with the collapse of the vote of the ruling KMT. The party that had ruled Taiwan since 1945 and had until then seemed able to maintain an iron grip on power even under democratisation suffered a catastrophe at the polls, leading to a breakdown of the vote as follows:

Chen Shui-bian	(DPP)	4,977,737	39.3%
James Soong	(Independent)	4,664,932	36.84%
Lien Chan	(KMT)	2,925,513	23.1%
Hsu Hsin-liang	(Independent)	79,429	0.63%
Li Ao	(New Party)	16,782	0.13%
Total Votes:	12,486,671	Turnout:	82.69%

The adoption of a first-past-the-post system for a presidential election is quite unusual. Voting arrangements in other systems normally make provisions for indecisive outcomes by allowing either a second round of voting, or the counting of second preference votes. The anomaly of the Taiwan system, somewhat ironically, can be explained by the fact that it was decided during constitutional reforms steered by the KMT at a time when it had not expected to win over 50 per cent of the vote, but could have been fairly confident in polling more than the DPP. In March 2000 this carefully worked out strategy backfired on the ruling party.

The main reason why the KMT became the victim of its own voting system, was that the party split. Behind the division was the issue of who would succeed the incumbent president and party chairman, Lee Teng-hui. Two candidates had emerged for this role from inside the KMT: the 'native-Taiwanese' vice-president and former premier Lien Chan; and the 'mainlander' former party secretary and governor of Taiwan province, James Soong. The latter is by far the more charismatic of the two and, despite his origins in mainland China, had built himself a strong base of popular support during his time as provincial governor, a post to which he had been elected. When the Taiwan provincial government was dismantled and the governorship was abolished as part of the constitutional reform programme, however, Soong was left alienated from the party centre and without a position. His outspoken opposition to the abolition did little to endear him to the Lee Teng-hui leadership. The result was a bitter split between Soong and Lee Teng-hui, which left the far from charismatic Lien Chan as the only viable KMT candidate for the presidency.

This division at the top of the KMT was fatal. First of all, it split the party down to the grass roots, making it impossible for the leadership to exert control over the local party organisations upon which the centre relied to mobilise factional voting. To all effects, the KMT stopped functioning as a national party as its members had to make a choice between supporting Lien or Soong. The choice became more difficult as Soong began to campaign on a platform of clean politics, leaving Lien representing a continuation of the Lee regime which had fallen into disrepute due to rampant corruption.

The KMT tried to rescue the Lien campaign by directing most of its campaigning against Soong. A fatal blow was struck against Soong's campaign when his old party accused him of having embezzled party funds on a massive scale during his term as secretary general. However, aside from undermining Soong's overwhelming lead in the opinion polls, this also reinforced the message that the ruling party was rotten through and through and more concerned with intra-party factional struggles than with opposing the DPP. The last few days of campaigning thus saw the Lien and Soong camps spending most of their resources and energy on appealing to each other's supporters to either dump Lien and support Soong, or dump Soong and support Lien.

The split in the anti-DPP vote on polling day was thus ensured. The main casualty of the division was the KMT. This was a great shock to many, because the party had ruled the island since 1945 and appeared to have an unshakeable grip on power even under democratisation. Up until the last few days before the election, opinion polls had fuelled the widespread perception that the three main candidates were running roughly neck and neck, leaving about 25 per cent of floating voters to decide the outcome. The final result shows that none of those floating voters moved towards supporting the KMT when it came to polling day. This represented a defeat of the worst degree for the KMT, yet not enough of a swing to enable Soong to claim victory over Chen.

Moderation in the DPP

Yet the DPP victory cannot be explained in terms of the collapse of the KMT alone. Even with the ruling party divided, the opposition still had to do a lot of work to overcome its political credibility gap with the voters. This process had actually begun after the disastrous defeat suffered by the party in the 1996 presidential election, when the DPP's veteran secessionist candidate Peng Ming-min had polled a dismal 21 per cent of the vote. Since then, the party had held a series of conferences to re-assess its 'China' policy, and produced a formula that proved to be far more acceptable to voters than insistence on a referendum and declaration of independence. A conference on China policy in February 1998 brought together radical and moderate factions to produce a broadly acceptable slogan of 'strong base – westward advance' to characterise the new stance (Hughes, C. 1998: 13–18). This meant that the priority should be building a strong sense of loyalty to Taiwan, while simultaneously allowing investment and trade in mainland China. In 1999, China policy was moderated further when the party produced a document stating that it accepted that according to the present constitution the name of Taiwan was the Republic of China, and that there is no need to make a formal declaration of independence because it is already an independent state.

This moderation allowed key sectors of the population to move towards supporting the DPP. Among these were some 1.4 million young voters who had come of age since the 1996 presidential election, and whose impressions of China were forged by the PLA's missile tests off Taiwan ports at that time, rather than by the nationalist indoctrination of the KMT. Perhaps more significant, though, was the role played by a number of leading figures from industry and academia, who openly campaigned for Chen Shui-bian, forming a political advisory group that would help him to select a cabinet if he won the election. By far the most important of these figures, in a society where Confucian values still have a role to play, was Dr Lee Yuan-tse, a Nobel Prize-winning physicist and president of the prestigious Academia Sinica.

Lee Yuan-tse spoke for many of the leading figures who threw their weight behind the Chen campaign when he stated that a change of ruling party was the only way that corruption could be tackled in Taiwan politics. He also felt that the DPP had changed enough for it not to represent an unacceptable provocation to the PRC. Lee even envisioned figures such as himself playing a stabilising role in cross-Strait relations under a DPP administration. He has been a frequent visitor to the mainland and enjoyed good relations with CCP leaders. In an interview with the *China Times* (*Zhongguo Shibao*) he even stressed his sympathy with the nationalist feelings of the mainland Chinese, recalling his own childhood memories of celebrating the victory of the Allies over Japan in 1945. He even went so far as to claim that the DPP and the CCP should be able to work together because both have experience of combating KMT corruption!

This kind of support lent credibility to attempts to portray Chen Shui-bian himself as a Nixon-like figure who could break new ground in relations with the PRC because the people trusted that he loved Taiwan and would not sell out the island. Chen built on this moderate image by openly committing himself to what became known as the 'Four Noes' in his China policy, namely: no change of the national name, no change of the ROC constitution to include Lee Teng-hui's 'two-states theory'; no referendum on independence; and no declaration of independence unless Taiwan is attacked by China (*CT* 18 April 2000).

Such moderation did much to defuse the KMT campaign, which focused on delivering the message that a vote for the DPP was a vote for war with mainland China. Indeed, this type of negative campaign could be turned back on the KMT, when the DPP presented it as an attempt by the ruling party to stay in power by joining the PRC in threatening the population of Taiwan.

Portraying the KMT as being in cahoots with the PRC's attempts to intimidate the voters in Taiwan became increasingly credible thanks largely to the propaganda war that was unleashed against Chen Shui-bian by Beijing. The first round of this was launched on 28 January and was obviously directed at Chen, without naming him. It reached a new intensity when the State Council issued a White Paper on 21 February that warned, for the first time, that continuing to postpone negotiations on unification could be taken as a reason to using force against Taiwan. This successfully focused the election campaigns on cross-strait relations and national security, calculated to be Chen's weakest point, according to Xu Bodong, of the Taiwan Research Institute of the Beijing Union University (*Beijing lianhe daxue*) (*CT* 4 April 2000).

The PLA added to the psychological warfare by making bellicose statements about the inevitability of Taiwan independence leading to war. Finally, on 15 March PRC Premier Zhu Rongji gave a 90-minute news conference to mark the end of the meeting of the National People's Congress. Waving his fist, Zhu raised his voice in anger when asked about Taiwan, stating 'No matter who comes into power in Taiwan, Taiwan will never be allowed to be independent.' Referring unmistakably to Chen Shui-bian, he exclaimed that if 'the people who favour independence' win, 'it may trigger a war between the two sides and undermine peace'. Zhu threatened, 'We trust that our Taiwan compatriots will make a sensible choice', adding that if they did not, they might not 'get another opportunity'. If leaders in Beijing had thought such threats would alienate voters in Taiwan from Chen Shui-bian, they badly miscalculated. Instead, a wave of defiance developed just in time for voting day.

The ethos surrounding the competing parties seemed to be crystallised when they held massive campaign rallies on the evening before polling. The KMT had, naturally, bagged the most prestigious site for its rally, the Chiang Kai-shek Memorial Plaza. Yet if any doubt had been left in the minds of voters about the calibre of Lien Chan, it must have been dispelled by his appearance at this event, where he looked more like a lost schoolboy than a would-be president. Moreover, the whole procedure came over as distinctively Taiwan politics old-style, a political rally composed of people rather mechanically going through the motions of flag waving and cheering.

In contrast, the James Soong rally was vibrant, fuelled by the enthusiasm of highly-motivated grass-roots supporters. Yet even this seemed to pale when compared with Chen Shui-bian's rally, which was a well orchestrated sequence of speeches enhanced by music and special effects. The massive crowd was genuinely excited and the speeches rang with conviction, referring to the iconic figures and events of the Taiwanese struggle against foreign rulers. Previous party leaders/elders appeared on stage, many of them having spent years in the KMT's gaols. Yet even despite the strong flavour of Taiwanese nationalism that this produced, Chen Shui-bian's own speech was carefully calibrated not to alienate non-Minnanese speaking Taiwanese or voters afraid of the DPP's independence policy. He stressed that he would be a president of the whole people, would not take part in DPP activities after his inauguration, and would work for stability in relations with the PRC. The overall impression created was of a youthful and vibrant party with its roots solidly in Taiwan's modern history, and with a genuine commitment to the future of the island.

Chen's rally thus appears to have convinced enough undecided voters that he was the candidate to mark a new beginning in Taiwan politics. His promise was one of consolidating democracy by changing government, while not antagonising the mainland by going down the road of independence in the process. The ability to maintain such a balancing act will be the true test of his administration.

The future of party politics

The political dispensation in Taiwan following the presidential election provides both challenges and opportunities for Chen Shui-bian in achieving a balance of policies that will be popular enough to make his victory more than a flash in the pan for the DPP. Perhaps his greatest source of strength arises from the disarray of the opposition and a general uncertainty over the future dynamics of party politics. Most significant is the challenge for the KMT to reinstate discipline and find an ideology that can appeal to voters in Taiwan. Its first responses to defeat should not be a cause of great concern to the DPP.

Rather than embarking on a planned reorganisation, hasty measures were forced on the KMT leadership by grass-roots supporters enraged at what they believed to be Lee Teng-hui's division of the party by campaigning against James Soong, which ensured Chen Shui-bian's minority victory. Immediately after the election result was known, demonstrators made their way to the KMT headquarters to express their outrage, sometimes with outbursts of violence. After some prevarication it was agreed that Lee should stand down as chairman. Instead of this signalling the beginning of real reform, though, the leadership then diverted most of its energy into blaming the supporters of James Soong for the crisis and initiating a large-scale purge of members suspected of supporting him.

Instead of looking for fresh blood to take the top post in the party, Lien Chan was made chairman by the Central Committee. The only alternative, Ma Ying-jeou, the charismatic and youthful mayor of Taipei, was ruled out because he had played a prominent role in persuading Lee to stand down as chairman. Thus, unable to break from the influence and legacy of its former chairman, the KMT has shown no immediate signs of being able to rethink its role and mission in Taiwan politics, despite the fact that it retains control over massive financial resources and a majority in the Legislative Yuan.

What used to be Taiwan's most disciplined and richest party thus faces the serious risk of losing members and legislators to James Soong, who was quick to establish his own 'People First Party' on 31 March. Some indication of Soong's future strategy was given when he declared that one of the main causes of his new party would be to oppose the DPP declaring an independent Taiwan. Such a position can be carefully crafted so as to appeal not only to the dwindling number of voters still committed to unification with China, but more importantly to the majority who support maintaining the status quo of 'no unification and no independence' with China. Such a formula worked well for the KMT throughout the 1990s as a way to take the wind out of the DPP's pro-independence sails. Coupled with calls for clean and efficient government, which used to be the vote-winning platform for the DPP, the People First Party could have a potent political message as the party for good governance and political stability.

The People First Party has already shown that such a platform can gain the support of the old guard KMT, from the small New Party that split off from the KMT in the early 1990s, from urban intellectuals, and from ethnic groups such as the Hakkas and aboriginal groups. That there is the possibility for a broad grass-roots following is also indicated by the fact that Soong won majorities in all the northern counties and cities of Taiwan, barring the DPP stronghold of Ilan. With the new party lacking financial resources, however, it is uncertain whether such grass roots support will grow or dissipate as the excitement of the presidential election fades. Moreover, if Soong's new party is to look largely to disaffected KMT members for support, then it could be taking on many of the problems of corruption and factionalism that the KMT itself has been trying to shake off.

If Soong is successful in building his party, though, Taiwan could be heading towards a true three-party system that would alter the fundamental dynamics of future elections. In the immediate aftermath of the 2000 election Chen Shui-bian thus faces the task of consolidating support in a situation where the bases of support for political parties have become very fluid. Rather than his victory signalling a sea-change in support for the DPP, his majorities were confined to the southern counties of Taiwan, bar the northern DPP stronghold of Ilan. Overall he managed to achieve an increase of around 10 per cent on the usual DPP vote. If he is to maintain this beyond the 2001 Legislative Yuan elections, and through to his own re-election in 2004, he will have to avoid extreme policies.

Avoiding extremes, however, will be made difficult by the nature of the DPP itself. Many of its members, who have spent years in opposition waiting to realise their ideals of an independent Taiwan Republic, will not sit idly by as policy is watered down. This quickly became apparent when, just three weeks after the election, vice-president elect Annette Lu publicly vented her anger about not being consulted on the staffing of the new cabinet. She was quickly slapped down by chairman Lin I-hsiung, who pointed out that according to the constitution she actually has no powers. This, however, did not stop her making a number of public statements to the effect that she does not consider Taiwan to be a part of China.

Potential problems for Chen also began to appear at the grass roots when founding members of the radical pro-independence Nation Building Party attempted to disband their organisation on 7 April, arguing that its mission had been completed with the election of Chen. When stalwarts refused to disband, 23 senior members resigned, announcing that they would continue their political activities through pressure groups. At the same time, the father of the independence movement Peng Ming-min and members of the New Nation Alliance (*Xin Guojia Lianxian*) began to make known their intentions to return to the DPP fold. These developments are important because such former DPP figures left the party largely due to the frustration they felt during the move towards a more moderate China policy that took place under chairmen Shi Ming-teh and Hsu Hsin-liang. If the more radical factions of the DPP put pressure on Chen to take a more pro-independence stance in relations with the PRC, he will face a difficult balancing act indeed (*CT* 8 April 2000).

Constitutional constraints

Chen's weakness is also caused by the distribution of power in the ROC Constitution. This document was originally designed to prevent the emergence of strong-man government by putting in place parliamentary institutions of a cabinet (Executive Yuan), legislature (Legislative Yuan), and upper house (National Assembly). It has, however, been manipulated over the decades by leaders trying to concentrate more power in the hands of the president. When Chiang Kai-shek was in power in Taiwan he merely suspended the Constitution by declaring martial law. Under Lee Teng-hui, Constitutional balances were eroded by appending 'Additional Articles' to the Constitution, which swung power very much into the hands of the president at the expense of the other institutions. With Chen Shui-bian having come into power on such a small minority vote, however, there is a serious lack of clarity over just where supreme power lies. This problem is magnified by the fact that the KMT has a majority of members in the National Assembly and the Legislative Yuan.

Luckily for Chen, the National Assembly was not too much of a problem to deal with. This was because the upper house had undermined its own authority the previous year when it enraged the public by revising the constitution to extend its own term for another two years. With nobody able to defend the unpopular upper house, a cross-party consensus was built between DPP and KMT assembly members to strip the body of most of its powers from 19 May. It would convene for just one month at a time and only when called upon to do so by the Legislative Yuan in cases such as impeachment of the president or vice president or constitutional revision. Rather than members being appointed by election, they would be selected in proportion to the political parties in the Legislative Yuan. Opposition from inside the KMT was thus minimised because ideological implications regarding continuity with the 'Chinese' constitution were circumvented and members of the DPP could accept the arrangement as a temporary measure (*CT* 30 March 2000).

Dealing with the Executive Yuan and Legislative Yuan poses a much more difficult challenge for Chen. This is because the KMT, with 117 seats in the Legislative Yuan compared to the DPP's 71, has an overall majority of 10 seats. This creates problems because the ROC Constitution works as a presidential system when the Legislative Yuan and Presidency are controlled by the same party, but a cabinet system when they are controlled by different parties. The reason for this can be found in Additional Article 3, put in place by Lee Teng-hui. This allows the President to appoint his Premier without the consent of the legislature, but also permits the legislature to remove the premier if more than half its members support such a motion.

Facing this situation, Chen had to appoint a premier with the potential to gain cross-party support. He found such a figure when, on 29 March, he appointed outgoing defence minister Tang Fei. Born in 1932 in Jiangsu province, mainland China, Tang rose to prominence in Taiwan through a career in the air force, becoming defence minister in 1999. This KMT general was the ideal candidate because he was liked in Washington, where he had taken part in negotiations over arms purchases and the possibility of acquiring TMD for Taiwan. Equally important was that the appointment of a mainlander to this key position could be as a signal of conciliation to Beijing. Perhaps most important of all though, was that Tang had won credibility within the DPP for having steered a national security law through the legislature that requires the military to withdraw from all political activity. This is of great significance for the DPP, because the KMT made the armed forces the bastion of Chinese nationalism following the retreat to Taiwan. He also gained much credit for having denied claims made by Lee Teng-hui and other KMT leaders that if Lien Chan did not win Taiwan would be condemned to social unrest and invasion.

Both Tang Fei and Chen Shui-bian were careful to avoid dividing their own parties by presenting Tang's premiership as a move towards coalition government, however. The problem was circumvented by an agreement between the two that Tang would withdraw from all KMT activities on becoming premier. He also only accepted the post on condition that the KMT Central Committee agreed, and insisted he would only hold the premiership until the holding of the 2001 Legislative Yuan elections. The Central Committee agreed on March 31, after some debate, and the insistence of Chen Shui-bian that this was a 'government of all the people' (*quan min zhengfu*), rather than a party–party coalition, seeing as both Chen and Tang would withdraw from party activities. A refusal by the KMT would only have worsened its situation by presenting its leadership as putting party interests before the interests of the people.

Chen's strategy of creating a 'government of all the people' was also evident in appointments to the two most sensitive posts regarding foreign policy and cross-Strait relations, both of which were filled by non-party affiliated academics. Professor Hung-mao Tien, formerly director of the National Policy Research Institute and an internationally renowned expert on Taiwan's constitution, was made foreign minister. The directorship of the Mainland Affairs Council, which guides policy towards the PRC, went to Dr Tsai Ing-wen who specialises in international trade law at National Chengchi University and holds a doctorate from the London School of Economics. Although both Tien and Tsai are not affiliated to political parties, both have been close to the policy-making process as advisers to Lee Teng-hui. Tsai has a relatively moderate approach to cross-Strait relations, based on the assumption that increasing trade between the two sides will lead to a reduction in tension and pave the way for political solutions, providing that Taiwan's national security is not compromised. Her perceived role in helping Lee Teng-hui to formulate the 'two states' formula, however, does not endear her to Beijing.

Such appointments were typical of the Chen cabinet. By the time most of the positions had been filled in mid-April, the majority of ministers were non-party individuals drawn largely from academia, and there were even more KMT members than DPP. The appointments thus avoided the ringing of alarm bells in Washington and Beijing that would have been caused by the appointment of radical advocates of secession from DPP ranks. Friction with the personnel of the ancien régime was minimised and the KMT could hardly mobilise opposition in the legislature to a government led by one of its own members. Perhaps most important of all, these were impressive signs of moderation in the eyes of the majority of the electorate who had voted against Chen in the presidential election out of fear over DPP radicalism. Although Chen denied that he was forming a coalition government, his strategy of co-opting the KMT was, however, starting to look like a departure from his campaign appeal for a 'change of party' (*lunti zhengdan*).

The fourth party?

Rather than say that the future of politics in Taiwan will be shaped by three main parties, it might actually be more accurate to add a fourth, the Chinese Communist Party. Although, of course, the CCP does not exist in Taiwan, its policies and historical fate are intimately tied up with that of the DPP. The way in which Taiwanese identity will change during four years of a DPP presidency, and the implications of this for international perceptions of Taiwan, will have important repercussions for the party leadership in Beijing. This is because the coming to power of Chen Shui-bian in Taiwan represents not only a major failure for the PRC's policy of national unification, but also a challenge to the nationalist credentials upon which the CCP bases its legitimacy to rule as a one-party dictatorship.

Beijing's initial reaction to Chen Shui-bian's victory was to declare a stance of 'Listen to his words, watch his actions'. This meant that Chen's every word and action was to be scrutinised to see if he moves Taiwan further towards *de jure* independence. The most recent criteria that have been provided for this are laid down in the State Council's 2000 white paper *The One-China Principle and the Taiwan Issue*, and are as follows: the separation of Taiwan from China in any name; if Taiwan is invaded and occupied by foreign countries; if the Taiwan authorities refuse, *sine die*, the peaceful settlement of cross-Strait reunification through negotiations (Taiwan Affairs Office 2000: 17).

Regarding the issue of foreign intervention, Beijing has grounds for a degree of optimism due to the drift towards supporting Beijing's China policy that took place in Washington under the Clinton administration after the United States was nearly dragged into armed conflict with the PRC during the run-up to the island's 1996 presidential election. Since that time, the message that the United States is not bound to come to Taiwan's rescue if it provokes Beijing by declaring independence has been delivered to Chen Shui-bian and other political leaders in the island by a stream of recently retired or about-to-be-appointed State Department and Defence Department officials shuttling between Washington, Taipei and Beijing. The tone of the meetings these figures held with leading politicians in Taipei was one of firm pressure for a restarting of cross-strait dialogue, an optimistic assessment of Beijing's sincerity, and the importance of maintaining the one-China principle. With the PRC also having gained brownie points in Washington for the stabilising role it played during the Asian financial crisis and in promoting stability on the Korean peninsula, the need for Washington to build good relations with Beijing has been at a high price for Taiwan. This was indicated most clearly when President Clinton stated his policy of 'three noes' for Taiwan during his visit to the PRC in June 1998, namely: 'No one China, one Taiwan; no Taiwan independence; no Taiwan membership in international organizations requiring statehood.'

Although CCP leaders can take some comfort from the American stance, a more difficult problem is posed by the possible development of a strong form of Taiwanese nationalism inside Taiwan. If this were to be strong enough to positively support a referendum on independence, it would be difficult for the United States to maintain its 'three noes' policy. Short of this, a strengthening Taiwanese nationalism would certainly pressurise the Taipei government to promote a more ambitious foreign policy, as was shown when the KMT was forced by public pressure to launch the campaign for the ROC to rejoin the United Nations in the early 1990s.

To avoid such an outcome, the CCP has intensified the 'united front' strategy that it has applied to Taiwan since Washington normalised relations with Beijing and de-recognised Taipei on 1 January 1979. According to the contents of an allegedly leaked speech to a meeting in Shanghai on 29 March given by Wang Daohan, director of the mainland's Association for Relations Across the Taiwan Strait (*CT* 7 April 2000), a new effort is to be made to categorise key figures in Taiwan politics so that the propaganda war can be intensively focused on the most vociferous advocates of independence. Although the authenticity of this document is far from clear, it is significant that on 7 April Xinhua issued a strong attack on Annette Lu, who was one of the figures singled out by Wang Daohan.

Wang was also reported to have recommended that sanctions should be taken against business people from Taiwan in the mainland who supported Taiwan independence when they were at home. Again, authenticity is lent to this by the fact that, on 8 April, the Taiwan Affairs Office of the State Council of the PRC announced that in future the mainland would not welcome Taiwanese doing business in the mainland who supported independence when they were at home. Reports began to appear in the mainland media singling out Stan Shih, president of Acer Computers, as an example. This was the first time that the PRC had made such a threat against Taiwanese business people, and signalled a new willingness to use to the full the leverage that two decades of economic integration has put into the hands of the CCP. Its effectiveness was indicated when Shih attended a computer exhibition in Beijing on 27 April where he stated that he did not support Taiwan independence (*Yahoo! Taiwan*, 28 April 2000).

That the CCP has a lot of mileage in such tactics is due to the fact that two decades of united front policy have made the Chinese mainland the primary target for Taiwanese overseas investment. With Taiwanese firms eager to take part in opportunities in the mainland, such as the development of the western provinces and the opening of the telecommunications market, the pressure from inside Taiwan for some kind of direct links with the mainland is intense. Indeed, one of the reasons Chen was elected was that he seemed to promise a change from Lee Teng-hui's 'no haste – be patient' policy, that put a ceiling on the size and type of investments after the 1996 election. Many of the prominent business people who supported his campaign will expect to see him deliver. Their way of thinking was indicated when Chen Shui-bian announced to a meeting of business leaders that he envisaged Taiwan as a 'silicon island', only to be met with complaints that such visions would be impossible without opening up the Three Communications with the mainland.

Negotiating 'One China'

The most dramatic policy development signalled by Beijing's White Paper was the addition of a new condition that could lead to the use of force against Taiwan, namely the indefinite postponement of negotiations between the two sides. With pressure on Chen to work towards opening up the Three Communications growing inside Taiwan, Beijing has been able to take an uncompromising stance on the issue of Taiwan's identity by insisting that it will only talk to representatives of the new administration if Chen publicly states his acceptance of the 'one China principle' which holds that Taiwan is a part of China.

This demand would seem to present an insurmountable barrier to negotiations for a member of a party that is committed to Taiwan independence. However, aware that the CCP cannot drop its demands either, Chen's initial strategy has not been to reject the 'one-China principle'. Instead, he has interpreted it as a topic on which both sides could start negotiations, rather than a precondition for negotiations to begin, as he made clear on 20 March in a publicised conversation with the president of Eva Air, Chang Yung-fa.

This diplomatic move is perhaps a reflection of the fact that the DPP has in fact built up some experience of negotiating with the CCP already. Contacts between the opposition in Taiwan and the CCP began even before the DPP was formally established, when pro-opposition Taiwanese business people made contacts with the various united front agencies established by the CCP. Such links have at times been somewhat farcical, as when Annette Lu made an embarrassing point by leading a group of pro-independence activists to the mainland early in 1992, only to be turned away at Beijing airport because they did not have visas. They have also been highly sensitive, sometimes even leading to the dismissal of United Front Department personnel. Such was the case when, in March 1993, Zhang Yihong, the deputy convenor of the DPP Legislative Yuan caucus, announced that the CCP was ready to have party-to-party talks with the DPP after he secretly met with united front personnel.

Although developing channels of communication has been difficult for both sides, at least Zhang and leading figures of the less independence-minded DPP factions such as Hsu Hsin-liang and Chen Zhongxin began to make overtures to the mainland and started the work of developing a properly thought-out China policy for the DPP. More recently even leaders of somewhat more pro-independence-minded factions such as Chiu Yi-ren and Hong Inching have also gone to the mainland. Perhaps most important is that even Chen Shui-bian himself, during his time as a legislator, went to the mainland and spoke to think tanks there. One of his close advisers, Lou Wenches, also visited the mainland and met Wang Daohan and other ARATS personnel.

Some of these visits have been strategically well timed, such as the visit of a delegation of 16 DPP county and city committee members and the visit of the head of the DPP China policy unit Yen Wan-chin, in February 1998, just a few days after the DPP had held a conference to thrash out its China policy. And the flow has also been in the opposite direction with numerous mainland researchers and academics from Beijing and Shanghai visiting Taiwan before the presidential election. Some of these figures have had close links with the Shanghai faction in the CCP leadership and made contact with the DPP. After the election these visits continued, with the most significant being a visit by the deputy director of the Taiwan Research Institute of CASS, Yu Keli, who visited Taipei in late April and visited the DPP under the status of a private individual.

These contacts should help the DPP to understand Beijing's position and develop a more effective negotiating stance. The shape of this began to become clear when, on 22 March, Chen Chao-nan of the New Century Parliament Office faction of the DPP put forward a motion at the DPP Central Executive Committee to water down the commitment to independence in the party charter. What he wanted was to change the sentence 'establish a sovereign independent Taiwan Republic' to read 'consolidate the independent self-determination of national sovereignty'. He also suggested changing the sentence 'According to the original principle of civic rights, the establishment of a sovereign independent Taiwan Republic and advocating of the determination of a new constitution, should be decided by the means of a referendum of all the residents.' This would become 'Any change in the status quo of national sovereignty, should be decided by referendum of all the residents of Taiwan'.

Such a suggestion could actually be presented as a new step in the movement away from the DPP's independence platform that had been taking place since early 1999, and which had contributed to the electability of Chen Shui-bian. In April of that year Chen himself publicly stated that the DPP charter was not in fact a 'Taiwan independence charter', but was merely intended to stress the position that any declaration of independence would have to be approved by referendum. The following month this position was more formally stated when the second plenum of the eighth central committee of the DPP passed a resolution on 'The Future of

Taiwan', which stated for the first time in a party document an acceptance of the name 'Republic of China' for Taiwan. On the day before voting, the leader of the key Justice Alliance faction, Sheen Fu-suing, helped to steady public support for Chen following the issuing of Beijing's White Paper by airing his view that the party charter could be revised.

Chen Chao-nan claimed to have support from most of the party factions. However many leading members of the DPP expressed differences of opinion on the value of changing the charter. Some members of the committee felt that it would be a good gesture to make to Beijing and give Chen Shui-bian more room to manoeuvre. However, others felt it would lead to divisions in the DPP. Lin Cho-shui of the New Tide faction was against changing the charter because it would only weaken Chen Shui-bian's hand in any negotiations with Beijing. Standing Central Committee member Zhang Yihong for example was of the opinion that the charter should be changed only if Beijing made a gesture first, such as giving up the threat to use force. New Tide leader and Standing Central Committee member Wu Nai-jen was of the opinion that the Taiwan republic part of the charter had become a defensive measure and need not be changed at present. Another New Tide member and Standing Central Committee member, Liu Shih-fang, was of the opinion that no changes should be made until the attitudes of Beijing and Washington after the election became more clear (*CT* 22 March 2000). There were also fears that if a proposal to change the charter was defeated by the national congress, this would only stoke fears in the mind of the public and Beijing that the DPP was still bent on declaring independence.

Although Chen Shui-bian attended the central executive committee meeting, he did not express an opinion. This is particularly interesting if this is seen as one of the first tests of his ability to balance pressures from the mainland and from within factions in his own party. It has been suggested that what the whole exercise was about was in fact to fly a kite to see Beijing's reaction. It could be argued then that Chen actually achieved quite a lot by not expressing his own opinion but allowing Beijing in effect to make the decision. This is because a major concession such as changing the DPP charter could only be made if Beijing looked like giving some kind of positive sign to the incoming government.

Beijing's apparently uncompromising line began to waver when, in early April, the Taiwan media claimed that an authoritative figure concerned with Taiwan policy in Beijing had stated that the two sides should return to the consensus reached in 1992 that talks could proceed if both sides accepted that there is one China, with the rider that each has its own interpretation of what 'one China' means. Head of the DPP foreign affairs office, Hsiao Bi-khim, said that the DPP saw this as a positive response at last from Beijing to Chen's numerous overtures to Beijing. She stated that the DPP did not necessarily reject the idea of one China, but did insist that its implications have to be discussed. She claimed that there are people in the mainland who accept that one China can be interpreted with more flexibility (*CT* 4 April 2000).

Chen Shui-bian persisted throughout April in probing Beijing for signs of flexibility on the one China principle. One of his boldest initiatives was made on 21 April, when he declared that it might be possible to discuss the idea of a cross-straits confederation (*CEP* 21 April 2000). This was not a new idea. In fact the DPP had criticised Lien Chan when he proposed it during the presidential campaign. Now Chen was raising it himself, though. He even traced its origins to former premier Sun Yun-suan, the veteran KMT adviser to Lee Teng-hui who would have been Chiang Ching-kuo's successor had he not been severely handicapped by a stroke.

What Beijing was waiting for, however, was Chen's inauguration speech. On 27 March the importance of Chen returning towards the one-China principle on this occasion was made clear when Chen Yunlin, head of the Taiwan Office of the State Council, and deputy director Tang Shubei met the New Party's vice-presidential candidate Feng Hu-hsiang in Beijing. This, they pointed out, would be the precondition to be met before any contacts could be made with representatives from the new administration (*CT* 28 March 2000).

When Chen did make his inauguration speech, it contained as many concessions to Beijing as are possible without antagonising his own party. He repeated the Four Noes, and added a fifth, that he would not repeal the KMT's mainland policy, The Guidelines for National Unification, or the National Unification Council that was set up by Lee Teng-hui to advise on unification policy. He also waxed eloquently about the shared Chinese ethnicity of the people on the two sides of the Strait, and expressed his desire for cooperation. On the crucial issue of the one-China principle, though, Chen could only say that he hoped the two sides could come together under the right conditions to commonly deal with the issue.

Chen's speech was initially condemned by mainland sources as being too ambiguous on the one-China principle. However, despite the negative rhetoric, some signs of flexibility have begun to emerge that could point the way to a more positive relationship. The most important of these was contained in the official reaction from the Xinhua news agency, which for the first time stated in public an appeal for Taiwan to begin negotiations by returning to the 1992 consensus. This was a significant message from Beijing. The response from Taipei, however, was to try to reinterpret the 1992 consensus in a way more favourable to itself. This amounts to stating that the consensus does not include acceptance by both sides that there is only one China, but merely that talks can go ahead on the basis that each side has its own interpretation.

Conclusion

It has been argued above that the victory of Chen Shui-bian marks a significant advance along Taiwan's road to democracy. However, the nature of Taiwan's electoral and party systems and the nature of the ROC Constitution means that there is still some way to go before the island's democracy can be said to be truly consolidated. Despite this, one of the most interesting features of Taiwan's democratisation is the way in which it constrains Taipei's cross-Strait policy by encouraging policy-makers to maintain a status quo of 'no unification and no independence' that has become entrenched throughout the 1990s. The March 2000 presidential election has not upset this tendency. On the one hand, the Chen Shui-bian presidency has emerged from the election so weak that it would be difficult to take risks in encouraging the development of Taiwanese nationalism or provoking the mainland by taking bold steps towards *de jure* independence on the international stage. On the other hand, with public support for unification with the PRC increasingly weak, democratisation will also make it hard for any administration to stay in power while moving too far towards unification.

From this perspective, although democracy makes the CCP's goal of unifying Taiwan with mainland China more difficult, it will also require policy-makers in Taipei to exercise their imagination to find a way to peacefully co-exist with the PRC. The DPP has acknowledged this by moving a long way from radical secessionism and towards a willingness to consider whether the concept of 'China' can be interpreted in such a way as to satisfy all sides. Rather than being anti-Chinese, many leading figures in the party are willing to accept that they share common ethnicity with the people in the mainland, and that the relationship between the two sides of the Strait should be one with special characteristics.

While anti-China rhetoric used to be useful for undermining the authoritarian regime in Taiwan, it became an electoral liability when the KMT itself moved towards democratic legitimacy. These days, the DPP's insistence on Taiwan independence has become a defensive posture against being taken over by the PRC. So as to maintain international support and not provoke the PRC, the party has had to learn to live with the position developed by the KMT under Lee Teng-hui that the ROC on Taiwan is already a sovereign state and need not make a declaration of independence to prove the point. Leading members of the party even indicated, when interviewed by the author shortly after Chen's victory, that if mainland China becomes prosperous and democratic, there may come a time when popular will in Taiwan will lead the island towards unification.

It is important, therefore, that the CCP realises that democratisation in Taiwan is not necessarily bad news for its own ambitions of unification. Rather than leading the island towards *de jure* independence, it could actually open up opportunities for developing new formulas that will enable peaceful co-existence between the two sides. This will only be realised in Beijing, however, when mainland leaders come to understand that democracy is not just an ideal advocated by Western powers, but is the most viable way to achieve good governance by addressing the fundamental problems that give rise to chronic corruption and social and ethnic cleavage in societies, be they Chinese or otherwise.

Bibliography

CEP: *China Evening Post* (*Zhongshi Wanbao*), Taipei.

CT: *China Times* (*Zhongguo Shibao*), Taipei.

Hughes, C. (1998) *Taiwan's Political Changes and Challenges* (CAPS Paper No. 23), Taipei: Chinese Council of Advanced Policy Studies.

Taiwan Affairs Office (2000) *The One-China Principle and the Taiwan Issue*, Beijing: Taiwan Affairs Office and Information Office, State Council of the PRC.

Chapter 10

Rational Authoritarianism and Chinese Economic Reform

Zhao Chenggen

Introduction

Authoritarian regimes obviously have existed throughout history and have come in a variety of forms. Armies, parties, oligarchies, corporatist business elites – all can be the locus of those who inaugurate and maintain authoritarian rule. Clearly also, the political institutions of a society bear some relationship to the level of the development of that society. According to the classical view, modern industrialised societies have democratic politics. Authoritarian politics, in short, is thus incompatible with the modern society. This at least would appear to be the view of Samuel Huntington, who argued that authoritarian systems are only a short-term phenomenon in the transitional period of a state (Huntington 1970: 3–47).

In a modern complex industrialised society, traditional simple authoritarian polities surely cannot provide good governance. The reason for this is that the political institutions in a modern pluralist society have to satisfy contradictory needs. Hence, the political institutions have to form a complex equilibrium system comprising different institutional arrangements to execute various functions. During the third democratic wave from the 1970s to the 1990s, one-party authoritarian regimes in many developing countries, products of the convulsive processes of social, economic, and political change in the 20th century, could not live up to the democratic challenge inherent in the process of modernisation. Eventually, almost all of the authoritarian regimes in southern Europe, Latin America, Southeast Asia, and Africa, like the Communist totalitarian regimes in the former Soviet Union and Eastern Europe, collapsed and started their transition towards becoming democracies. So much so that one-party authoritarian regimes, mainly a phenomenon of the 20th century, appeared to have waned together with this century. However, the political and economic developments in China, one of the most important countries in the world, should lead us to rethink the inevitability of the fall of authoritarianism.

When the third wave of democratisation swept across the world and different kinds of authoritarian states collapsed and then embarked upon their respective transition to becoming democracies, China's totalitarian Communist state transformed itself into an authoritarian state while successfully embracing market-oriented economic reforms. When the Soviet Union and the Eastern European Communist states collapsed, the Chinese one-party authoritarian system cracked down on the 1989 democracy movement. From 1992 onwards, it took market-oriented reforms to a new historical stage. China's economic development and reform have led to great accomplishments in the past 20 years. The Chinese authoritarian regime itself has also been well sustained and there is no evidence that it faces collapse. Initially, many analysts believed that China's reforms could not succeed under the leadership of the Chinese Communist Party (CCP). However, anyone who is concerned about the fortunes of China and those of the Chinese people and who believes that the development of the country is crucial may have quite different views about many of the points that are often raised by the critics of authoritarianism.

After all, China's experiences, surely, are contributing some new things to the world. If the demise of the Communist Soviet Union took everyone by surprise because no one had predicted its sudden and peaceful collapse, China's successful transition to becoming an authoritarian state and the consolidated sustenance of the CCP similarly challenges existing political and economic theories (Przeworski 1991: 1). The modernisation model created by China's one-party authoritarian state tells us that we should perhaps re-evaluate and revise many of our views about democratisation and democracy. China's national authoritarian state, which is different from both the totalitarian communist state and the authoritarian states in the developing world, in my view, provides a new model of authoritarianism.

China's new rational authoritarian regime, which has been established for the past 20 years and is still in transition, has implanted many institutional arrangements from different kinds of political and economic systems. Authoritarian statesmen have always made efforts to find an equilibrium between authority and liberty, between power and political participation, between state and society, between party control and government performance, as well as between other institutional demands and the establishment of sustainable one-party authoritarian politics. Although it is still difficult to predict the future of Chinese authoritarian politics, there is clearly a new polity to be found in China that is restructuring China's economy and society and that has been creating a great economic miracle in an Eastern civilisation, while transforming itself. Anyone who wants to understand what has been happening in China in the past 20 years, as well as the dynamics of China's development, should not overlook the new authoritarianism in China.

Rational authoritarianism and economic reform

The political and economic reforms initiated in China in the late 1970s can be seen as the communist regime's response to the crises faced by the country after the Cultural Revolution. The Cultural Revolution left China with disastrous socio-political legacies: hundreds of thousands of people from almost all social strata had been persecuted mentally and physically, and the national economy was on the brink of bankruptcy. The people's living standard had failed to improve, had even declined, in many areas. The consequences of policies of the Radical Left had estranged a great number of the Chinese people from the Communist Party and led to serious scepticism about the merits of its official ideology. In short, the Cultural Revolution did irreparable damage to the party's image. The Chinese and totalitarian Communist regime thus found itself in a deep legitimacy crisis.

The reforms initiated under Deng sought to re-establish the party's popular image and save it from total political ruin. Deng's original political purpose was to tranquillise China's society and recreate a consensus among the people, which would reinforce one-party rule. However, the reforms had consequences that went beyond Deng's original intention and changed the nature of China's totalitarian regime, paving the way towards the transition to a rational authoritarian regime.

Chinese authoritarian politics, like all other forms of authoritarianism, shares indelible markings that denote an elite's domination of society through state control. In China's one-party authoritarian politics, the CCP has controlled sovereign power and played a dominant role in governance. Although a variety of actors from different parts of the state, the military, and associated socio-economic groups co-exist within the party, the CCP is the highest and most important actor in the political system. All the other actors are under the party's leadership and, as such, its subordinates. The party monopolises the locus of legitimacy, political recruitment, and the processes that determine the substance of policies. The dominant role played by the party, its control over the institutions and processes of governance, a charismatic leader, and its legitimacy without popular inclusive and competitive elections are the core characteristics of China's model of authoritarian politics.

When political analysts compare the reforms in China with those undertaken in the former Soviet Union, they attribute the success of China's reforms to the fact that Beijing focused on economic reforms and pursued political ones only incrementally. Gorbachev is seen as having focused on a political reforms first rather than on economic reforms. This approach is considered to have led to sharp socio-political conflicts which led to the failure of reforms in the Soviet Union and the collapse of the communist state. In my view, however, this point is not the major distinction between the reforms undertaken in the former Soviet Union and those in China. I believe that it is not that the reform strategies had a different focus but that China benefited from a charismatic leadership in her implementation of reform. Arguably, Gorbachev also began by concentrating on economic reforms and only later changed his priorities to political reforms. He only did so when the politically powerful radical Communist left opposed his economic reform policies. The most important reason, then, that led to Gorbachev's failure was the leftists' powerful position in the Soviet empire. As for Deng, he also encountered much obstruction both from the radical leftists and the radical rightists, who raised ambitious reform demands most of the time. Deng was successful in his reform policies, given the incrementalism with which he pursued the reform agenda and the compensation awarded to those who would suffer as a consequence of the reform process. Still, it was his charismatic personality and authority that proved the decisive factor in his successful political struggles during the first two decades of reform.

Reform means to change an existing system from top to bottom. It is very important to have a powerful leadership to start and proceed with reform. Since reforms are about the redistribution of powers and affect interests, some social interest groups will suffer from reform whereas other social strata will benefit. The social strata whose interests are damaged by the reforms implemented will very likely resist the reform policies. Meanwhile, vested interests embedded in the existing system will also oppose the reform agenda. The outcome of all reforms is decided by political struggles, especially between reformers and anti-reform forces. Without a powerful leadership centre, it is impossible to struggle successfully against anti-reform forces, especially when the reform process is in crisis. Historically, successful reform processes have originated with and were led by ironhanded statesmen. When Deng Xiaoping launched his reforms, he found himself in an enormous dilemma. Faced with rising social protests against economic stagnation that resulted essentially from the inefficiency of central planning, market-oriented reforms were necessary to generate renewed public support for the regime. But to the extent that these reforms could prove successful, they required a change in the system and hence had to hurt the interests of party bureaucrats who benefited from the status quo. Also, the reforms inevitably damaged at least in the short run many people's interests. As regards the Chinese reform process, sharp political struggles between the reformers, the Communist leftists and the radical rightists were the basic phenomenon. Deng's charismatic authority and his powerful leadership where the most important preconditions for the success of China's reforms. Only a powerful reformist leadership centre can provide a reliable guarantee for successful reforms.

Secondly, reform is about the peaceful transformation of the socio-political and economic order. The existence of a strong state and the latter's provision of stability is the precondition for such a transformation. One of the great advantages of authoritarian rule is that with it goes the capability to maintain stability and order. This is extremely important in a changing society like that of the People's Republic, because the transformation of a society may easily see the latter experience disorder (and chaos).

China's rational authoritarian leadership has always made stability its top priority (*wending yadao yiqie*) during the country's 20 years of reform. One further consideration was that the radical left might fill an emerging power vacuum if the reformers were unable to control the political and economic situation sufficiently well during China's economic reforms and the state's transition towards authoritarianism. If societies experience disorder, this might result in a dictatorship, military rule, or even a socio-political split and war. The failure of the former Soviet Union to reform can be attributed to the fact that there was no powerful reform leadership that could deal with crises associated with reform and various challenges emanating from different social forces. The government lost control and this ultimately led to the collapse of the Soviet state. To stress the point, liberty and peaceful political and economic transformation can only be achieved in the context of political stability. Furthermore, the rational authoritarian state's capability to maintain political and social order are preconditions to open up to the outside world and to absorb international capital.

If we look in global terms at how states have modernised, we can find that the transitional road to the modern economy and society, at least for the late developing state, is related to the authoritarian polity. This is true for the modernisation of Germany and Japan as it is for that of the Soviet Union and the 'four tiger economies' (Ding 1990). Two reasons in particular explain why this will also apply to the late developing countries. First, the late developing countries began their organisation in an international society in which developed capitalist countries existed. Without the strong state it is impossible to contend with transnational capital and to export one's own capital to other countries. Modern capital expansion is backed up by a strong state. British merchant ships travelled around the world accompanied by the Empire's gunboats at the beginning of modern capitalism. In today's interdependent global setting, only the strong state can make the corporations of that country enjoy equal opportunities with their competitors. Second, it is very important for the late developing countries to concentrate their resources on modernising their respective economies and societies in a short period of time.

The strong state and the free economy

While the strong state can maintain the stable order which is so important for liberty and development, it is the free economy alone, the market-oriented economy, that can provide the vigour and liberty that economic development needs. The main task of China's economic reforms in the late 1970s was to reform the economic system of centralised planning. There was to be a separation of the economy and society from the totalitarian state and the establishment of a 'state-free' economy and an 'economics-free' state. China's economic reforms have involved a process of marketisation, which has not led to radical privatisation of the 'socialist' state-owned enterprises, as happened in the former Soviet Union and Eastern Europe in the late 1980s. This radical reform of the public sector has led to the distribution of interest and aroused social and political conflicts. While radical reform is accompanied by high risks, the Chinese experience has been one of incrementalism. China chose the least controversial area as a starting point for economic reforms. Rather than seeking to privatise state-owned enterprises, Chinese economic reforms first focused on the establishment of small personal enterprises, village and town enterprises and joint ventures involving foreign capital.

Most of the market policies for which Deng Xiaoping is noted were not planned in detail in advance, but were improvised according to the particular circumstances and opportunities encountered by the reformers. The great attraction of the opportunities afforded soon caused increasing amounts of capital as well as human resources to move into the private sector. As the advantage of economic marketisation and liberalisation became clearer, more and more sectors, regions and enterprises became involved in the process, and increasing numbers of people supported it. The resistance of the radical-left to this process was defeated more and more easily. As the results of free and fair competition between non-state owned enterprises and the state-owned enterprises became clearer, the deficiencies of the latter in terms of ownership and management brought about an increasing number of state-owned enterprises to fall into decline or deficit. From 1984 China began the marketisation reform of its state-owned enterprises. After Deng Xiaoping's speech during his journey to southern China in the spring of 1992, the Communist party finally decided to establish a socialist market economy.

By implementing economic reforms in incremental fashion, great institutional change has been made possible and a socialist market economic system has gradually been established. The market economy is now dominant in today's economic life of the People's Republic. For example, as a result of market-oriented reforms, the value of industrial output by state-owned enterprises decreased from 59.2 per cent in 1978 to 56 per cent in 1996. It is estimated that the output of state-owned enterprises in relation to GDP reduced to 37.2 per cent by the year 2000 and would reduce yet further to 34.7 per cent by the year 2010. Consequently, China's employment structure changed profoundly. 112.44 million workers were employed by the state-owned enterprises in 1996, while those working for various non-state-owned enterprises reached 63.06 million, but the latter group was growing far more quickly than the former. The non-state sector of the economy is now bigger than the state sector and is fast becoming the mainstay of China's national economy. This means that the state can no longer interfere directly in large parts of the economy. For the one-party state, therefore, the reform of state-owned enterprises (SOEs) has entailed new relations with the state-owned sector of the economy. In today's China, SOEs are enhancing their standing and influence through autonomous business operations, becoming relatively independent economic organisations. A modern corporate system is being established in China's state-owned enterprises.

Privatisation and marketisation have led to improving political and economic results and changed the balance between state, economy, and society. First, as the above analysis makes clear, the fundamental distinction between China's new authoritarianism and totalitarianism is to be found in the relationship between the state and the economy. China's authoritarianism has been established under the premise that the state and the economy are separate. The retreat of the one-party-state from direct control of all economic sectors and the transformation of the state's role in economic management has greatly changed the character of the state.

Second, the free-market economy has provided a good channel for the latent capacity of individuals to be fully utilised. The latter had been stifled during the times of economic planning. The free market economy has facilitated high economic growth over the past 20 years. From 1978 to 1999 the average economic growth rate has been 9.6 per cent. The free market mechanism, once again, has created an economic miracle in an Eastern country.

Third, market-oriented reforms have provided new opportunities (*chulu*) for social vigour and aptitude. As the market sector has developed and expanded in China's national economy, more and more of the technical and management elite have left lifeless state-owned enterprises and Communist bureaucratic posts and thrown themselves into the free market economy. The process of marketisation has thus provided opportunities for everyone, namely the right to choose freely in a free economy in a politically dictated one-party authoritarian state. The people voted with their feet in relation to their economic activities, while having no right to vote with their hands in political affairs. In other words, they had that right to decide for themselves on the enterprise they owned and managed although they were still denied the right of democratic representation.

Many scholars argue that democracy is a precondition of liberty. Yet for the theorists of the New Right, marketisation and economic liberalisation is the most important foundation of liberty. According to Friedrich Hayek, a democratic state may protect liberty if it is properly organised, but it is not the only kind of state that is able to do so. Liberty is defined as 'that condition of man in which coercion of some by others is reduced as much as possible in society.' Coercion by individuals can be greatly reduced if one social agent, the state, is able to punish individuals who infringe laws governing individual exchange. The problem then becomes how to reduce coercion by the state itself; the answer lies in the construction of a private sphere free from public interference. Such a private sphere can only come into existence if there are certain protected activities and rights that cannot be infringed by the state or government (Gamble 1979: 7). In China, the case of China's marketisation and economic liberalisation indicate that the private sphere created by the existence of non-state enterprises has provided enormous social choices. The free-market mechanism has provided a place for the people to escape from state coercion and thus led to the unavoidable decline of the dictatorship of the state.

However, the destruction of political liberty is always regrettable. But clearly it does not compare to the far more serious loss of economic freedom for capital and labour. Economic liberalisation and liberty are very important and their role in national development and their social outcomes are quite different from those of political liberty. Economic liberty leads to good accumulation of resources and capital and will promote economic growth. It can also limit a political dictatorship by confining the scope in which this state can dictate and by influencing the operation of the state. If we further examine the political implications flowing from economic liberalisation, we find that the choices people make in relation to their economic activities are actually an important part of their political liberty. To be able to choose and change one's employers, or to decide in which of the different economic areas to invest one's capital, means that you have greater opportunities to decide your own future. One is then an autonomous person.

The rationalisation of the one-party state and its governance

In general terms, the response to the crisis of a totalitarian state is democratisation and political liberalisation. The first important reform undertaken by Deng following his rehabilitation was to transform the totalitarian state and its radical-leftist policies. However, Deng did not seek democratisation and political liberalisation in the Western sense, but instead thought to replace the totalitarian state with an authoritarian state. The political and administrative reforms by Deng and his followers gradually led to the establishment of a rationalised authoritarian state.

Marxist ideology

Marxism was the official ideology of the communist state. It provided legitimacy to one-party hegemonic rule. The CCP thus has had to maintain Marxist ideology. But, in today's China, Marxism is only a concept, one that reformers can freely define. The reform policies, especially reform policies in the economic field, are made not under the guidance of ideology but on the basis of social demands. Actually, Chinese authoritarian governance is on the verge of becoming non-ideological. Marxism, then, is no longer a 'holy' ideology but a tool for the rule of the one-party state. Indeed, the Communist Party is still in command, but its guiding ideology has decayed beyond repair. Even if it tried to revive its revolutionary ideology, the effect would be minimal since such philosophy and ethics have long ago lost any appeal to the people and only help to expose the gulf between the party's deeds and words. Indeed, China today 'is no longer a communist country in any meaningful sense' (Kristof 1993).

However, when the party fought its revolutionary war, it concluded that it had to find the right road ahead, not on the basis of abstract doctrine but on the basis of the situation in China at the time. Similarly, after his rehabilitation, Deng was to lead a 'thought liberation movement' contending that 'practice is the only standard that can evaluate what is the truth'. 'To seek truth from facts' became the basic line of thought for the Communist Party, as did the emphasis that the aims of the reform focused on establishing 'socialism with Chinese characteristics'. Although there were sharp ideological struggles between reformers and radical leftists during the past 20 years of reform, the processes of China's reform can be conceived as a 'thought liberation movement' to cast away the shackles of orthodox Marxism.

In today's China the legitimacy of the one-party state has shifted from classical Marxism to government performance. One of the goals of economic reform is to re-establish the party's popularity that had been severely shattered during the Cultural Revolution, hence to reinforce the ruling position of the party's new leadership. As Deng himself put it in early 1979, 'if the social productive forces are not developed and people's material life is not improved, then our socialist political system cannot be consolidated.' He repeatedly told the party both before and during his reforms that it was imperative for the one-party state to meet public demands by improving people's standard of living. For instance, during his travels to southern China in 1992, Deng told a group of high ranking provincial leaders that 'if we don't carry out reform and an open-door policy, develop the economy, and improve people's living standard, there is only a dead end' (Deng 1993: 370). For Deng and his supporters, therefore, economic reforms can also be seen as a means, a set of tools, to be used in the service of their fundamental political aim: a revitalisation of the party's popularity and the restoration of its legitimacy. With economic reform posting an average growth of 9.6 per cent during 1978–1999, the party's image was largely salvaged.

There is no doubt that the authority of the Communist Party is no longer based on any ideology but rather on its performance in government, and especially on its success in pushing forward economic reforms. The relationship between the one-party state and society is undergoing a profound transformation. The days when the state could control everything have gone and even the priorities of the state are now being challenged. The communist regime must respond to the needs of society, especially those in the economic sphere. The growing power of societal forces and regional actors, and the party's consequent dependence on economic progress, is an important characteristic of the Chinese authoritarian state.

The Chinese Communist Party

The Chinese Communist Party is the ruling party in the state, although there are many other parties that have good opportunities to participate in the governance of the state. The Party has an organizational system that corresponds to different levels of government; it also has representatives of the Party in every ministry of the State Council. The Party is the leading force in the legislature, executive and judiciary and is actually the highest state ruling organization. The Party also controls the nation's military forces. The Party makes all the important policies that become public policies. Laws are passed and then implemented by the government. The existence of the highly disciplined Communist Party, and its highly centralized leadership and control of all state agencies and activities, is also one of the most important characteristics of the Chinese authoritarian state.

In the past twenty years of reform, the party has transformed itself from a revolutionary party committed to class struggle to a rational ruling party, displaying a readiness to respond to the demands of various interest groups and the outside world. Although the name of the party is still the Communist Party, it is not the traditional revolutionary Communist Party, but a pragmatic ruling party, unfettered by radical-left communist ideology, which deals with the concrete concerns of the contemporary world. It is a ruling party that is flexible and open to the changing world. While the Communist Party changed China with its market economy policies, the ideas of the market economy have also changed the Party and created a new Communist Party. This is the core of the new rational authoritarian state.

The party and the state

In the Chinese authoritarian state, new relations have been established between the Communist Party and the state. Before 1982, there was no distinction of functions and institutions between the Party and the state. Especially during the Cultural Revolution, almost all of the state's institutions were destroyed and the Party directly controlled the People's Congress, the State Council, and the judiciary system and interfered with the daily administrative affairs. To ensure the separation of the Party and the various state organs, and to allow them to perform their functions, is thus a very important part of China's political reform.

The separation of the Party and government has made some important progress in the past twenty years. In 1980 and 1986, Deng repeatedly called for the separation of the Party from the government. In line with his requirements, the reform of separation of the Party from government has made considerable progress since the 1980s. This progress has manifested itself in the following ways. First, Party organizations at various levels have put an end to their overlapping institutions with government and thus ensured that the government and its departments perform their functions independently of one another. Second, a decision has been taken to establish an executive responsibility system for heads of governments at various levels as well as their departments and to make the party organizations at the same level subordinate to the former. Third, it was decided to make a distinction between decisions about important affairs and daily public administrative work. Party committees at various levels remain in control of the former. The daily administrative affairs are left for the relevant government to deal with. Fourth, the role of the People's Congress has been greatly enhanced. Fifth, the judicial system has become much more independent than before and plays an increasingly important role in law enforcement.

Administrative reform

The government has been reforming itself while it has reformed the economic system. There are three points to be made in this context. First, China's government has carried out public administrative reforms on four occasions since the 1980s. An administrative system appropriate to the market economy is being established. Second, in order to allow full play to the initiative of local governments in promoting economic reform and development, the national government has promoted decentralisation since the 1980s. Decentralisation has greatly changed centre–local relations and promoted the competence of local government. Third, a modern civil service system has been established since the 1990s. The professional bureaucrats, instead of party cadres, have become the main actors in Chinese governance, and administrative efficiency has greatly improved.

China's authoritarian state has become much more institutionalized in the past twenty years. The powers of and relations among various state organs as well as the procedures for public policy-making and its implementation have all been institutionalized. 'Rule by law' is becoming one of the priorities of the authoritarian state.

Public participation in rational authoritarian governance

As in all other societies undergoing change, demands for democratization emerge as soon as the rulers begin to reform the existing system. From the onset of Deng's rehabilitation and his reforms, there existed a strong demand for political liberalization and democratization. Deng responded unyieldingly with an iron hand. When many dissidents expressed their wish for democratic rights on the Xidan democratic wall in Beijing 1978 and the demonstration for democratic elections in Beijing 1980, Deng cracked down on them. In 1979 Deng put forward the 'four basic principles'. The most important of these was the insistence on the leadership of the Communist Party. On the basis of these principles China was transformed into an authoritarian state during the first years following Mao's death, providing stable political circumstances and the powerful leadership necessary for economic reform.

As economic reforms continued in the 1980s, the demands for democratisation and political liberalisation became stronger and stronger, both in the party and the wider society. Many people hoped that democratisation would encourage opposition against the political corruption that was so widespread and massive during the period of economic reform. When economic reforms ran into difficulties in 1986, demands for democratisation increased, with some of the Party's leaders also hoping that democratisation would put an end to the stagnation of economic reform. But when the democratic demonstrations happened in 1986 and 1989, Deng did not want to compromise with the dissidents and again dealt with them with an iron hand.

Meanwhile China's authoritarian state in transition promoted public participation and more avenues for allowing citizens to influence Chinese governance. The authoritarian state also institutionalised formal and legal channels for political participation. These efforts have greatly enhanced the authoritarian state's responsiveness and responsibility to the people's demands and made the regime more adaptable and flexible in today's complex, plural market society. Five points will be made in this regard.

First, the roles of the legislature have been enhanced greatly and the framework of the legal system has been developed. Since 1978 the enhancement and improvement of the People's Congress System has been the major task of socialist democratic construction and political reform. The Party committees and governments at different levels have encouraged and supported national and local People's Congresses to play their roles in law-making, the supervision of law enforcement, the inspection of the work of other state organs, and in examining and passing important decisions about state affairs. Previously, the Chinese People's Congress was regarded as a 'rubber stamp' parliament. Now the 'rubber stamp' is becoming harder and harder. Although the selection of representatives is still decided by the Party, more and more representatives from the new rising forces of the market society are coming into the People's Congress and their interests and opinions increasingly influence public policy-making. The days of the traditional 'unanimous adoption' of resolutions, etc., have passed, and more and more proposals are being adopted with many representatives abstaining or casting dissenting votes.

Second, the Political Consultative Conference, the democratic parties and other social political organizations are becoming more and more important for the elites from different fields to participate in their governance.

Third, the judicial system, including the courts and the procurators' offices, have been re-established and their roles and positions have been continuously enhanced.

Fourth, increasing the transparency of public administration and law enforcement is an important factor for promoting democracy in China. In the mid-1980s there were only a few government departments that made public their decision-making procedures and the results of the implementation of their work, so that the people could easily deal with and supervise these government officials. Since then more and more local governments and their departments have adopted similar practices. Some government departments have recently established web sites so that the citizens can obtain relevant information via the Internet. Meanwhile, since the 1990s, some local People's Congresses and their standing committees have allowed the citizens to be present at their sessions or meetings, and citizens can even voice opinions at these meetings. Today it has become a legal requirement to inform villagers about village and financial affairs, as outlined in the new 'Organizational Law of Village Committees'. The practice of increasing the transparency of public administration has also been taken on board by the judicial system. The Supreme People's Procuratorship has recently taken concrete measures to ensure 'the transparency of procuratorial affairs'. The Supreme People's Congress began to implement an 'open trial' system in 1999. Journalists are allowed to enter the courts for live broadcasts or to report on court proceedings; citizens are permitted to monitor trials.

Fifth, village democracy has undergone continuous development and has made great progress in the past twenty years.

Generally, the ability of the state to institutionalize formal and legal channels for political participation, especially for moderate opposition forces, is quite important for its performance and stability as well. If the political system allows the new social forces to participate in the policymaking process through institutionalized channels, it may avoid (or at least revise in time) unpopular policies, thereby preventing an explosion of popular grievances. The choice to further liberalize the political system will depend on the adaptability of the ruling party in the face of any future public demand for greater freedom. The efforts to build again on the political channels destroyed during the Cultural Revolution, and to create many new ones for the social elite and the ordinary people to make them participate in public governance, have greatly alleviated the pressures against the authoritarian state. Some scholars have thus even looked at the authoritarian state in terms of a consultative democracy (Wei 2000: 35–43).

The future of the rational authoritarian state

The success of China's economic reforms, the collapse of the Soviet Union after its failure to implement political and economic reform, and the decline of Russia have encouraged more and more Chinese scholars and statesmen to believe in a new conservatism. Even many famous political dissidents have now become believers in the new conservatism. Today, what many Chinese scholars are concerned about is how long the new authoritarian state can coexist with the liberalized economy. However, from the discussion above, we can see that it has been the successful transition from the totalitarian communist state to the rational authoritarian state that has provided the preconditions for China's economic reform. It was the political leadership headed by ironhanded reformers of the authoritarian state that initiated Chinese economic reform and attained great achievements both in changing China's economic and political structures and in promoting the country's economic growth. The Chinese authoritarian state is governing China very well now. However, the Chinese government's negative responses to democratic demands and pleas for economic and administrative reform have been impediments to Chinese economic development in the past twenty years, and in the future they will fly in the face of rational decision-making. They may well hinder the sustainable development of the Chinese economy as seen from a long-term perspective.

The rising new pluralist forces will also not tolerate being excluded from the political process for a long period, because exclusion from political power means removal from many economic interests. They will surely challenge the Communist Party's hegemonic rule and try to replace it with a competitive regime that will create equilibrium among pluralist interests. As with China's economic development, more and more people are unlikely to tolerate a political system without political liberties, such as a free press.

The rationalization of the Communist Party since 1979, in some senses, was the by-product of the political and economic disorder and calamity in the wake of Communist rule since 1949, especially the Cultural Revolution. If one likes, one can also say it is a revival of Chinese civilization after the political disorder and war of the past 100 years. As a statesman who deeply understood Chinese history, Mao once made a famous statement in which he generalized on the replacement of order and disorder in different dynasties in Chinese history. He said, 'great calamity is accompanied by great development' (*da luan da dao da zhi*). Mao is right. Chinese economic development since 1979, in some senses, is the by-product of a long spell of disorder. If we cannot have sustainable political stability and good governance, the economic achievements may be destroyed by future political disorder. To establish a consolidated democratic state is fundamentally important for China's continuing development.

Furthermore, an authoritarian state without free democratic elections and a competitive political party system is a polity without balance. In a liberal democratic state the ability to respond to new social and economic problems, and the expression of public opinion to influence governance, is the lifeblood of that system. The demands that drive the political system become the interests of the ruling party/ies and the government and these are interrelated with the interests and demands of the people. In an authoritarian state a response to the people's demands is not decided by the inner logic of the political system. Many special interests, especially the bureaucrats' interests, have greatly influenced the state's policy-making and have privileged their position in the state. Heavy political corruption is a structural problem in the governance of the Chinese authoritarian state.

China will surely develop into a democratic state in the future. But in the meantime we should understand that the new authoritarian state still plays a very positive role in terms of what it achieves by way of economic reform and development. China's democratization will take a long time before it succeeds. The best road for Chinese democratization to take is possibly that of gradual evolution, similar to China's experiences with economic reform.

Bibliography

Deng Xiaoping (1993) *Selected Works of Deng Xiaoping* (Beijing: People's Press).

Ding Xueling (1990) 'East Asia Model and New Authoritarianism', *Democratic China*, April 1990.

Gamble, A (1979) 'The Free Economy and the Strong State: The Rise of the Social Market Economy', *The Socialist Register* (London: Merlin Press).

Huntington, S (1970) 'Social and Institutional Dynamics of One-Party Systems' in Huntington, S and Moore, C H (eds) *Authoritarian Politics in Modern Society: The Dynamics of Established One-Party Systems* (New York: Basic Books).

Kristof, N D (1993) 'China Riddle: Life Improves though Repression Persists', *New York Times*, 7 September.

Przeworski, A (1991) *Democracy and Market* (Cambridge: Cambridge University Press).

Wei Pan (2000) 'Democratic Superstition and Consultative "Rule of Law" Polity' in *Chinese Social Sciences Quarterly*, Vol. 31 (Autumn).

Chapter 11

(Post-) Asian 'Crisis' and 'Greater China'

On the Bursting of the 'Bubbles' and Hi-Tech (Re-)Imaginations

Ngai-Ling Sum

Introduction

The Asian 'Crisis' has been explained from many viewpoints. Rather than engaging in a debate on the causes of the 'Crisis', this chapter focuses on two issues: the differential impact of the 'Crisis' on economies in the region; and its role in reorienting and restructuring accumulation regimes. The differential impact was largely related to the pre-existing strengths and embedded capacities of economies in the region, e.g., the relative levels of foreign currency reserves and external debts (see next section). During the early phase of the 'Crisis', the economies in the cross-border region of 'Greater China' (Hong Kong, southern China and Taiwan)[1] escaped the worst and most direct impact of the 'Crisis'. As the 'Crisis' continued, however, these economies began to experience secondary effects, such as the bursting of the 'stock/property and Itic bubbles'.[2] Thus governments in the region developed diverse stimulus packages covering new stabilization schemes in supporting the property markets and bailout measures. Such confidence-building projects were criticized for favouring vested interests, and it is certainly important to explore their connections with the politics of distribution (see page 193). Nonetheless, as we shall see, governmental resort to 'institutional quick fixes' such as increasing public spending, raising tax rebates and buying up some shares, failed to re-vitalize domestic demand and exports. Hence, since late 1999, these economies have also been actively engaged in promoting a politics of (Internet) optimism. There is a general adoption of the discourses of 'information technology', 'Silicon Valley' and 'e-commerce'. This suggests that one way in which economies in the region aim to remake themselves is through the strategy of siliconization in which private-public, and local-regional-global actors seek to develop new modes of techno-economic coordination that are derived from the

'Silicon Valley' metaphor. This strategy involves the reinvention of new objects of economic growth as well as subjectivities and practices that may create new opportunities as well as grounds for competition (see page 201). In this regard, the remaking of the 'Greater China' region is characterized by sometimes competing, sometimes complementary strategies and projects that may (or may not) be regularized into a new regional division of labour. Whilst it is too soon to say whether this will happen, it is important to be aware of the significant new trends and projects identified below.

The differential impact of the Asian 'Crisis'

There are a number of popular explanations of the 'Crisis'. They range from the case of failure of 'Asian state capitalism' (e.g., state intervention distorts the functioning of the market and gives rise to 'crony capitalism') (Fischer 1998; Krugman 1998) through the self-fulfilling 'panic story' (as rooted, for example, in the volatility of currency and speculative flows) (Radelet and Sachs 1998) to the vulnerability of the typically East Asian 'high household saving, high corporate debt' mechanisms (Wade and Veneroso 1998). Rather than engaging in a debate on the causes of the 'Crisis' (see Sum 2002), however, this chapter focuses on its differential impact upon the region and its role in restructuring the accumulation regimes in the region.

The differential impact of the 'Crisis' was largely related to the pre-existing strengths and embedded capacities of economies in the region. Data relevant to this period reveal a differential impact of the 'Crisis' on then 'stronger' economic formations, such as Singapore, Taiwan and Hong Kong, and 'weaker' formations, such as the Philippines, Malaysia, South Korea, Thailand, and Indonesia (Table 1). In this regard, it is perhaps more accurate

Table 1 Differential impact of the 'Crisis': Changes in stock prices and currency (%, measured in US$, Jan. 1 to Oct. 31, 1997)

	Stocks	Currency
A) 'Stronger' Economic Formations		
Singapore	−28.7	−12.3
Taiwan	6.9	−12.1
Hong Kong	−19.5	0.0
B) 'Weaker' Economic Formations		
Philippines	−42.4	−33.4
Malaysia	−46.0	−32.8
South Korea	−28.0	−14.3
Thailand	−45.4	−58.0
Indonesia	−21.6	−53.0

Source: Adapted from *Fortune*, Nov. 24, 1997: 32.

to refer to Asian *Crises* instead of the Asian 'Crisis'. Economies in the so-called 'Greater China' region, especially Taiwan, seem to have escaped the direct/worst effects of the contagion.

This differential impact of the 'Crisis' was largely related to the pre-existing strengths and embedded capacities of each economy. Relevant factors here include current account balances (Table 2), foreign debts and reserves (Table 3), degree of openness to global capital, state capacities (e.g., regulatory capacities over financial institutions) and, equally important, the balance of economic, political, and social forces with different interests.

Table 2 Current account balances (as % of GDP)

	1995–6	1998–9
A) 'Stronger' Economic Formations		
Singapore	16.1	16.4
Taiwan	3.0	2.2
China	0.6	0.7
Hong Kong	1.4	1.1
B) 'Weaker' Economic Formations		
Philippines	−3.7	0.3
Malaysia	−7.1	−1.4
South Korea	−3.3	7.0
Thailand	−8.0	5.6
Indonesia	−3.6	2.2

Source: Adapted from J.P. Morgan, *World Financial Markets*, First Quarter 1998.

Table 3 Asian foreign debt and reserves (US$ billion): end 1997 estimates

	Total Debt	Short-Term Debt	Reserves
A) 'Stronger' Economic Formations			
Singapore	–	–	88
Taiwan	46	29	81
China	152	42	141
Hong Kong	–	–	75
B) 'Weaker' Economic Formations			
Philippines	58	15	9
Malaysia	39	14	24
S. Korea	155	60	17
Thailand	102	32	20
Indonesia	131	27	28

Source: Adapted from J.P. Morgan, *World Financial Markets*, First Quarter 1998.

It is beyond the scope of this paper to deal with the specificities of individual economies and their diverse strategies of restructuring.

A substantial body of literature has addressed the cases of Indonesia, Malaysia, Thailand and South Korea, with the latter two economies showing signs of economic recovery since the end of 1998. Instead, the next section seeks to examine briefly some of the 'stronger' economic formations – especially those within the 'Greater China' region.

The Asian 'Crisis' and 'Greater China': the bursting of the property and Itic bubbles

The 'Greater China' economies seem to have escaped from the more direct and devastating impact of the contagion. However, none of these economies has been sheltered from its 'secondary' effects. Let us start with why these economies escaped from the worst of the contagion.

Escaping the worst of the contagion

Taiwan escaped from the direct and devastating impact of the contagion. This is attributable to its pre-existing strengths which include: a) its position as an exporter of capital, with large reserves; b) the associated low external debts of the government and corporations; c) a not yet fully financially de-regulated system, with exchange controls on foreign investment; d) a flexible exchange rate, in which Taiwan devalued the New Taiwan Dollar (NT$) earlier than other countries in August 1997; e) a flexible manufacturing sector dominated by small- and medium-sized firms; f) a flexible small- to medium-sized manufacturing system based on cost-effectiveness; and g) the demand for Taiwan's electronic products in US and European markets remained strong. Benefiting from this strong position, Taiwan's currency depreciated by less than 20% against the dollar during 1997. It was still expecting an official GDP growth rate of 4.7% in June 1999.

China also has escaped the direct impact of the contagion because of its: a) sizable trade surpluses; b) relatively large foreign currency reserves and saving deposits; c) limited financial liberalization in capital account and stock market – which prevented short-term capital flows; d) partial command economy with exchange and credit controls; e) non-convertible currency that is not a good target for speculators; f) large inflow of (long-term) foreign direct investment; and g) domestically-oriented economy with export assistance. Compared with Taiwan, there was frequent talk that the Chinese Yuan would devalue, especially when the Yen was weak against the dollar. China's justifications for not devaluing were: a) the high import content of China's trade would cancel out the possible benefits on exports after devaluation; b) a Yuan devaluation would mean greater debt-servicing and this would affect the values of H-share and Red Chip companies; c) devaluation would lower the inflow of foreign direct investment; d) China was unwilling to devalue on the fiftieth Anniversary of communist rule; and e) it would put severe pressure on Hong Kong's currency board system. Up to 1999, China still expected a growth rate of around 7%.

In contrast to the relative 'calm' in Taiwan and China, the Hong Kong dollar came under speculative pressure on several occasions in 1997 and 1998. However, the government was able to maintain the pegged system because of: a) its high foreign reserves; b) its long-established prudent fiscal policy, which meant there was no external debt; c) its in-built mechanism for interest rate adjustment; d) its tight supervision of financial institutions (e.g., the use of a gross simultaneous account system among these institutions); and e) its capacities derived from acting as an industrial, financial and commercial middleman between China and the rest of the world. Despite its struggle to maintain the pegged system, the Hong Kong dollar came under fresh attack in August 1998 when the Yen depreciated against the dollar. Speculative attacks propelled significant amounts of capital outflow, as some people believed this might also force a Yuan devaluation. This time the government reacted with two new measures (see below, pages 199–200) to maintain the pegged system: drawing on its reserves to buy US$ 15 billion worth of selected Hong Kong shares; and introducing a package of technical measures to strengthen the transparency and operation of the linked exchange rate system (e.g., a rediscount facility to reduce interest rate volatility). The pegged system was once again maintained but at the expense of high interest rates, weak domestic demand and rising unemployment.

Compared with most East Asian economies, Hong Kong and China emerged as the two non-devaluing economies. Their governments co-ordinated actions to maintain Hong Kong's pegged system and insulate the 'Greater China' region from currency decline. China provided its foreign exchange market expertise and stand-by funds to defend the Hong Kong dollar. It was worried that a devaluation of the Hong Kong dollar would affect the value of HK$-denominated investment and the prices of Chinese H-share and Red-Chip corporations. It would also have increased these companies' debt-burden in the Hong Kong currency, and, perhaps, have led to higher interest charges and the possibility of non-performing loans. Conversely, a Yuan devaluation might not benefit China and could trigger a devaluation of the Hong Kong dollar. Since they were not devalued, the Hong Kong dollar and Chinese Yuan become interesting crucial (sub)-regional nodes through which to observe the further development of the global-regional financial system. Hong Kong is in fact co-opted into the Interim Committee of the IMF.

The 'secondary effects' of the 'Crisis': the bursting of stock/property and Itic bubbles

Although their strengths offered them some shelter, economies in the 'Greater China' region still experienced several problems that occurred elsewhere in Asia. In particular, crisis-related 'secondary effects' began to appear in Taiwan and China in the middle of 1998.

(1) The bursting of Taiwan's 'stock bubble'

Despite its early devaluation, Taiwan's first symptom of 'Crisis' in what remains an export-led growth dynamic appeared in its trade sector. Exports declined by 9.4% in 1998 to US$ 111 billion while imports declined 8.5% to $ 105 billion, reducing its trade surplus to $ 5.9 billion, 18% lower than in 1997. This led the Council of Economic Planning and Development to revise down its provisionally reported growth rate of 6.7 for 1998 to 5%. This positive rate of growth was supported by private consumption and fixed capital investment. However, other symptoms began to appear first in the exchange and then the stock markets. The eruption of the Indonesian political crisis and the decline of the yen's position in May 1998 sent the Taiwan Securities Index (Taiex) from a peak of 9,338 in April to 7,000 in early June. The government imposed new controls on foreign exchange, cutting off speculators' access to the local dollar by restricting trade in non-delivery forward (NDF) contracts by domestic financial institutions and corporations. Continuous speculation by foreign banks with NDF operations and the illegal use of foreign currency accounts by domestic financial institutions sent the New Taiwan dollar near NT$ 35 to the US dollar. This dumping of the NT dollar was halted by the central bank supplying the market with over NT$ 50 billion in June 1998 (Engbarth 1998b: 5). The NT dollar then stabilized, but Taiwan cannot be fully sheltered from contagion in the stock market.

Given that private credit comprises 166% of GDP and public credit takes the total to 200%, problems began to surface in its stock market. According to the Central Bank of Taiwan, the average non-performing loan ratio for domestic financial institutions is 5.1% for a volume of NT$ 637.4 billion (Engbarth 1999a: 4). In the corporate sector, for example, there was financial trouble at the Central Bills Finance and the Taichung Medium Business Bank, both of which were temporarily taken over by government-linked institutions in November 1998. Together with a series of defaults on stock payments and debts by medium-sized firms (e.g., An Feng Steel, Kuoyang Construction Company), the stock index plunged by 40% between its August 1997 peak and January 1999. The squeezing of the stock and financial markets paved the way for further corporate loan and stock transaction payment defaults in the last quarter of 1998.[3]

Table 4 Foreign banks in Taiwan with pre-tax losses 1999 (in million NT$)

Australia National Bank	511
Canadian Imperial Bank of Commerce	224
Union Bank of California	206
Deutsche Bank	107

Source: *Business Asia*, Sept. 30, 1999, 7(1): 17.

With an eye on the forthcoming legislative elections on 5 December 1998, the KMT-led government intervened to halt the 'bursting of the stock bubble' with a series of measures. These included: a) setting up a Stock Stabilization Fund of US$ 8.7 billion to prop up share prices; b) introducing a $7 billion scheme to bail out the real estate market; c) offering NT$ 150 billion for low interest loans to home buyers; d) allowing banks to write bad debts off balance sheets before the process of confiscation and auctioning of collateral assets; and e) allocating NT$ 30 billion in postal saving funds for small businesses and production enterprises. These measures to support equity prices, housing prices and corporate liquidity have had mixed results. First, they failed to halt the spread of corporate distress in Taiwan. In particular, loan defaults in local banks also involved their foreign counterparts in 1999 (see Table 4). Second, on the domestic scene, these confidence-building measures have helped to cushion property and financial interests against the secondary effects of the 'Crisis'. Thus, given the local political context (especially the challenge of the DPP), the KMT's support packages were criticized for being short-term and for favouring certain capitalist interests at the expense of other fractions of capital, organized labour, and the general population. In response, the government offered a broader package of reforms in February 1999. These included steps to strengthen its financial institutions, to extend tax breaks for high-tech industries for another 10 years, to develop the capital markets, and to reform labour and land-development laws. These attempts to orchestrate a politics of confidence-building co-exist with the rise in unemployment rate to 3% at the beginning of 1999 as well as the implementation of a labour-protection law that required the spelling out detailed rules of the workplace. Thus confidence-building is closely linked to the politics of distribution.

(2) The bursting of China's 'Itic bubble'

As for China, the 'secondary effects' of the 'Crisis' can be seen in the frequent rumours concerning an imminent devaluation of the Yuan and in the actual slowdown of exports and investment inflows. This loss of exports and foreign investment cost China 2–3% of overall growth in 1998. The Chinese government sought to remedy this in three main ways. First, it deployed a Keynesian programme of fiscal stimulus by assembling a 200 billion renminbi (RMB) fund aimed at financing increased public works projects. It also increased tax rebates on exports of coal, cement, ships, textiles and steel by 2–8%. As a result, the economy accumulated a financial account deficit of US$ 6.28 billion in 1998 compared with a surplus of US$ 22.98 billion in 1997. Second, the government slowed down the pace of reform of the SOEs and has extended the deadline to 2010. It has been argued that the selling-off of SOEs would increase unemployment and threaten social stability. Third, the government also slowed down financial reform by making access to credit easier (e.g., interest rates have been cut seven times between 1997–9). In January 1998, the governor of People's Bank of China announced a programme of financial reform by ordering the breaking up of the cozy networks of officials, state bankers, managers of state enterprises, and mayors who fixed 70% of bank lending among their own networks. As the 'Crisis' began to affect enterprises, the government ordered banks to resume lending in July 1998 so as to reduce layoffs and finance the retraining of workers.

These fiscal and monetary measures could not halt the spread of the financial contagion to China through its least regulated sector – the International Trust and Investment Corporations (Itics). In total there are 242 Itics in China. Their business scope ranges from direct stakes in corporations and large investments in infrastructure to loans and financial derivatives. The first Itic that ran into trouble was the Guangdong Itic (Gitic). It had borrowed huge sums without proper authorization from the State Administration of Foreign Exchange. Similar to most Asian debts, Gitic's borrowing was short term against high rates, but for financing long-term projects. For repaying loans and interests on deposits, Gitic invested in speculative real estate, stocks and futures. When the property and stock markets collapsed, Gitic was left to repay debts amounting to an estimated US$ 4.3 billion. In October 1998, Gitic faced mounting difficulties and the People's Bank of China ordered its closure. This collapse sparked off the following: a) worries among the foreign lending community and the recall of loans to China; b) fears about a 'bursting of the Itic bubble', both in China and abroad;[4] c) tightening by the central government of the 'freewheeling' activities of the southern provinces; and d) intensification of the central–local conflict over how Beijing could regain control. More specifically, and in relation to the reassertion of central control over Guangdong, Beijing had sent northerners to the province to implement its controls since the early 1980s. But it now strengthened its controls. It transferred the province's long-serving Communist Party secretary, Xie Fei, up to a ceremonial post in Beijing and replaced him with Li Changchun, a native of China's northeastern Liaoning province. Beijing later appointed another northerner, Wang Qishan, as the province's executive vice-governor – answering directly to Beijing. A phalanx of northern cadres later arrived

Table 5 Gitic's failure and its outstanding debt

Creditor bank	Outstanding debt (US$ million)
UBS	205.0
Dresdner	60.8
Dai-Ichi Kangyo	61.3

Source: Kazuhiko Shimizu, *Institutional Investor*, Jan. 1999, 24 (1): 83.

to break up the local government's old-boy network. These changes have sparked off the local–central conflict over southern 'pragmatism' and northern 'dogmatism' as well as the rivalry between Guangdong and non-Guangdong cadres. The bursting of the Gitic bubble has intensified this conflict and, in January 1999, the central government decided not to bail out Gitic. This has obviously aroused considerable criticism from international and regional bankers, e.g., Switzerland's UBS, Germany's Dresdner Bank and Japan's Dai-Ichi Kangyo Bank (Table 5).

This non-bailout strategy was reversed when the Guangdong Enterprises (GDE) collapsed in May 1999. This reversal in policy can be explained in the following ways: a) there is the fear that this may trigger an Itic 'domino' effect as confidence collapses; b) China needs to establish a landmark precedent concerning the debt restructuring of bankrupted financial institutions; and c) GDE subsidiary Guangdong Investment is part of the Hang Seng Index and, if it collapsed without a subsequent bailout, this could have affected the Hong Kong stock market and the price of other Red Chips and H-shares. Hence a bailout plan was announced. It involved a debt-for-equity swap and injection by the Guangdong government of its wholly-owned Dongshen Water Project into GDE. The swap arrangement enabled creditors to recover 46% of their outstanding loans to GDE (Wong 1999: 1). The injection of state-owned assets to support the GDE seems, however, to be the exception rather than the rule. In most cases, provincial and municipal governments have neither the resources nor inclination to forfeit assets. This can be seen in the cases of other financially fragile Itics (e.g., Gzitic (Guangzhou Itic), Hitic (Hainan-based Huitong Itic) and Ditic (Dailan Itic)) which resorted to debt-to-equity swaps with other financial institutions (see Table 6). This means the setting up of joint-venture commercial banks to help pay off part of the debt.[5]

(3) The bursting of Hong Kong's 'stock and property bubbles'

As for Hong Kong, share prices peaked in early August 1997, with the Hang Seng Index setting an all-time high of 16 673 on August 7. However, from mid-August onward, the Hong Kong stock market fell along with others in East Asia and amidst concerns about speculative attacks on the Hong Kong

Table 6 The financially-fragile Itics and their plans for restructuring

Itic	Estimated size of debt (in US$)	Plan for debt restructuring
Gitic	4.37 billion	Closure/Non-bailout
GDE	2.94 billion	Swapping debt for equity with the injection of Dongshen Water Project with an annual revenue of 2.74 billion Yuan
Gzitic	35 million	Swapping 50% of debt into equity
Hitic	140 million	Swapping 40% of debt into equity
Ditic	3.56 billion (HK$)	Merging with four other Itics in the city

Sources: Author's compilation from various issues of *South China Morning Post.*

dollar. When the first currency attack came in October, the government maintained its pegged exchange rate (one US dollar to HK$ 7.78) by raising the interest rates as high as 300% on 23 October. This maintenance of high interest rates further pushed the local stock market index down to 8 775, the lowest for two-and-a-half years. As for the property market, high interest rates and reduced external demand pushed the residential property prices down by over 50% between October 1997 and June 1998. This 'bursting of the stock and property bubbles' cuts at the heart of Hong Kong's internal 'growth' dynamics as this had developed since the opening of China. For, while Hong Kong firms move their manufacturing industries to the mainland, the service and property sectors have been filling the gap created by this so-called 'hollowing-out' process. More specifically, the property sector became even more dominant. It comprised banks (in the form of credit), construction companies (in the form of property assets), the government (in the form of land and revenue), and middle classes (in the form of wealth). The bursting of the 'property bubble' has given rise to fear among this property-related bloc about further asset depreciation. In order to prevent the asset from further depreciating, the government adopted the following measures between October 1997 and August 1998. These were: a) to refund rates to local residents; b) to raise the overnight interest rate to over 200% for a short time and to keep long-term interest rates high for a prolonged period; and c) to freeze land sales until April 1999.

The Hong Kong dollar came under further attack in August 1998 when the yen depreciated against the dollar, with hedge funds selling the Hong Kong stock market short in the expectation that the index would fall as interest rates rose. Speculative attacks propelled significant capital outflow as some people believed that this might also force a Yuan devaluation. The government reacted with more short-term measures which included: a) drawing on its reserves to buy US$ 15 billion worth of selected Hong Kong shares (60% of these were property related – higher than this sector's weight in the stock market); and b) introducing a package of technical measures to strengthen the transparency of operation of the linked exchange rate system (e.g., a discount facility to reduce interest rate volatility). These measures provided some calming effects, with the pegged exchange rate intact and interest rates at relatively stable level. However, the Gitic debacle in October 1998 caused some financial ripples. Government officials announced that the exposure of local banks to mainland companies amounted to under HK$ 90 billion; but some banks have a larger share of non-performing loans. One such bank is the Bank of East Asia which revealed that its mainland-related loans accounted for 15% of its HK$ 82.6 billion loan portfolio and that it had already written off the HK$ 1.5 billion loan to Gitic. This unraveling of banks' exposure to non-performing loans further fueled economic pessimism in Hong Kong.

The Hong Kong authorities moved to revitalize the economy, which was based on real estate, tourism, and financial services. The Financial Secretary, in his 1999 budget speech and subsequent announcements, gave two 'kisses of life' for the economy. They relate to the building of a 'cyberport' (see Table 7 on page 208) and a Disneyland theme park, overwhelmingly property-related projects. In this regard, the Hong Kong government's support packages for the financial and real estate interests involved the making of a politics of confidence building. At the present time, imagined technology projects (e.g., cyberport, Chinese herbalport) are driving the stock market. This politics of optimism intersects with the politics of redistribution as the unemployment rate rose to 5.8% in the same period.

The 'Crisis' has burst the 'property and Itic bubbles' in the region. Yet its impact has still been uneven insofar as Taiwan and China still enjoyed positive growth rates. The former was at 6.8% in 1997 and 4.8% in 1998 and the latter's (official) growth rate was at 7.8 in 1998. Hong Kong is the only economy in the region with negative rate from 6.9% to 5.7% to 3.5%. In this regard, it can be said that Hong Kong's bubble burst with a 'bang', Taiwan's burst with a 'pop', and China's began to leak at its least regulated points. Economies in the region suffer from deflationary trends that stem from the intertwined problems of falling profit margins, high debt, rising bankruptcies, credit crunch, falling real estate prices, weak domestic demand, falling foreign direct investment, low increase/falling in average wages, and worker unrest. These strains accentuate the pre-existing problems of excess inventory and industrial capacity and declining profits facing private and state-owned enterprises in the region. Among these economies, Hong Kong is the most vulnerable because of: a) its over dependence on the property sector; b) the lack of hi-tech investment; c) its weakened entrepot services due to competition from ports in Shenzhen; and d) the rising 'tide' of the information revolution. As for Taiwan, revived exports (especially in electronic products) to North American and Asian markets have failed to avert the threat of deflation (evident in tight bank credit, sluggish stockmarket, falling corporate earnings, low increase in average wages and higher unemployment). As for China, deflationary conditions coincide with rising unemployment despite an expected growth rate of 7%. This 'deflationary boom' is largely the result of increased government expenditure/increased bank loans unmatched by consumer spending. The 100 million workers in the SOE sector are reluctant to spend because they worry about unemployment.

'Bubble avoidance' and the remaking of the 'Greater China' region: a strategy of siliconization

Given these problems and their associated challenges, regional actors have shown increased concern with the politics of confidence building. The resort to 'quick policy fixes' such as increasing public spending, cutting interest rates, improving the transparency of financial institutions and buying up some shares failed to win back foreign direct investment or revitalize domestic demand and/or exports. Thus, at the time of writing, leading forces in different economies within the region are now resorting not only to confidence-building measures, but are also promoting a new politics of (Internet) optimism. Most of them adopt the discourses of 'information technology', 'Silicon Valley' and 'dotcom'. In this regard, one way in which actors reorient the accumulation regimes is through the strategy of siliconization. This involves the privileging of 'Silicon Valley' discourses that construct new objects of 'future growth', and the use of these objects to reconfigure techno-economic subjectivities/identities in the hope of stabilizing an emerging 'regime of truth'. Actors attempt to win support for these discourses and to generate consensus on a wider scale. These identities and shared voices are re-ordering material practices and (re-)building networks across time, space and scales to enhance the coordination of the information age. However, as with all strategies, whilst they involve a continued search for ways to significantly remake identities and practices, this remaking of the region cannot be guaranteed.

Discourses of 'Information Technology' and 'Silicon Valley'

This politics of regional economic optimism in the post-'Crisis' period can be discerned, first of all, in official discourses. The discourse of 'high technology' is being reinvented and circulated among private-public actors to move beyond the old bubble mentality, expectations, and practices. By deploying the symbolism of 'information technology', 'Silicon Valley' and 'e-commerce', they are imagining a 'bright (post-Crisis) future' by riding on the next information wave. In the case of China, this can be seen from Premier Zhu's visit to Shenzhen in October 1999. Attending the first China Hi-Tech Fair there, he pledged in internal talks that:

> 'We must learn the lesson of the Asian Financial Crisis. Only when high technology is developed can we avoid the phenomenon of a "bubble economy".'
>
> (Source: *South China Morning Post*, 13 October 1999)

It is interesting to note the linkage here between 'high technology' and 'bubble avoidance'. Zhu's optimism concerning 'high technology' resonated with those of other Chinese leaders at various levels. At central level, it echoed President Jiang's earlier policy line of 'reinvigorating the nation through technology' (such as information technology, space science and new energy) under the 1988 Torch Plan promoted by the State Department of Science and Technology. At the provincial level, Guangdong sought to implement this plan by constructing its own 'Silicon Valley' in the Pearl River Delta. This project involved a total investment of US$ 11 billion concentrating on R&D, Training and Education, Trade and Industry and Hi-Tech Exhibitions. The location of the first state-level High-Tech Fair in Shenzhen and Zhu's visit symbolized the city's intended status as a hi-tech zone. This image was reinforced, more recently, by Shenzhen's mayor Li Zibin during his visit to the Guangdong Technological Innovation Symposium in March 2000. He announced that Shenzhen would focus on the 'high and new technology sector, especially information products based on Internet and digital Valley'. In addition, he also stressed during the Shenzhen Information Technology Working Conference that the information industry will form a solid foundation for Shenzhen to become 'China's Silicon Valley' with an IT output value expected to have reached US$ 16.9 billion by the end of 2000 (China Online 2000).

This kind of 'hi-tech' talk could also be found in post-1997 Hong Kong. In March 1998, Hong Kong's Chief Executive, Tung Chee Hwa, set up the Commission on Innovation and Technology to examine the possibility of turning Hong Kong into a centre of innovation and technology. The first report came out in September 1998 and it provided the background for Tung to link 'hi-tech' with the 'Asian Crisis' in his first policy speech in October 1998. In this speech, Tung remarked:

> 'To help our economy respond to the changes I have described (Asian Crisis), our strategy will be to focus on increasing the diversity of the economy by creating conditions for growth in sectors with a high value-added element, in particular in those industries which place importance on high technology and multi-media applications.'
>
> (Source: 'From Adversity to Opportunity', Address by the Chief Executive The Honorable Tung Chee Hwa at the Legislative Council meeting on 7 October 1998: 8, Hong Kong SAR)

The Hong Kong Financial Secretary in his 1999 budget speech translated this push for high technology into more concrete projects. In this document,

Donald Tsang remarked:

> 'There is no question that, for Hong Kong to meet the challenges of the 21st Century, it must adapt to the new forces of the Information Age. Technological advances such as digitalization and broadband networks are introducing new ways of doing business, transforming traditional markets and altering existing competitive advantages...
>
> To respond to these mega trends ... the Government proposes to develop a 'Cyberport' in Hong Kong. The Cyberport will provide the essential infrastructure for the formation of a strategic cluster of information services companies. These companies would specialize in the development of services and multi-media content to support businesses and industries...'
>
> (Source: 'Onward with New Strength', Speech by the Financial Secretary, 3 March 1999: 15, Hong Kong SAR)

These 'high-technology Silicon Valley' discourses resonated with those that emerged in Taiwan as early as the 1980s. A 'Silicon Valley' imagination motivated the Hsinchu Science-Based Industrial Park and government plans to attract Silicon-Valley 'returnees' through tax breaks and other economic incentives and through organizations such as Monte Jade. Almost half of the companies in the Park in 1997 had been started by US-educated engineers. It concentrated on OEM (Original Equipment Manufacturing) and its networks of producers came to produce almost 40% of notebook PCs sold in the world along with two-thirds of motherboards, keyboards and mice. Anticipating the growing importance of R&D, the National Science Council of Taiwan published its first-ever 'White Paper on Science and Technology' in December 1997. The paper outlined one major challenge facing Taiwan on the eve of the 21st century as:

> The arrival of the 'information society' is deeply affecting the way people live and work, changing the way companies and the government operate, and bringing about a new culture in a world that is fast becoming an even more closely-knit global village.
>
> (Source: 'White Paper on Science and Technology', December 1997: 2, National Science Council, Republic of Taiwan)

In order to realize this challenge, the National Science Council recommended that Taiwan should develop into a 'technologically advanced nation' during the first decade of the next century. Deploying the image of 'clustering', it envisioned the 'building of the "National Information Infrastructure" (NII)' – an economic objective that would be achieved in several steps. It would start by: a) establishing suitable 'core and satellite science-based industrial parks/clusters' throughout Taiwan; b) using these clusters as nuclei for building 'science cities'; and c) linking these cities by various major infrastructural networks in order to turn Taiwan into a 'science island' (White Paper 1997: 5–6). This scientific-technological construction of Taiwan's economic future was then translated into more concrete measures and specific timetables in the Action Plan for Building a Technologically Advanced Nation in April 1998. More specifically and in relation to the establishment of science-based industrial parks and high-tech campuses, the Plan recommended the building of satellite industrial parks at Chunan and Tungluo as well as Software Parks at Nankang and other locations (Executive Yuan 1998: 10). Taiwan's 'science island' imagination was reinforced and deepened by President Chen Shui-bian (then the opposition party leader of DPP) in his visit to London. In his London speech in December 1999, noting parallels with Blair's 'Third Way', he identified the 'New Middle Way' as Taiwan's future in the context of 'globalization'. One particular dimension of this 'New Middle Way' was the vision of Taiwan as a 'Green Silicon Island'. Chen remarked:

> 'I am both optimistic and worried as I look to Taiwan's future economic development under globalization. I am worried and concerned about Taiwan's lack of natural resources. Taiwan's economic accomplishments have been established on a low-cost labour force, and Taiwan has relied solely on imports for raw materials and energy. Taiwan thus confronts an urgent problem of potential energy shortage.
>
> At the same time, my cause of optimism arises from Taiwan's comparative advantage in information technology. The high-tech industry concentrated in Hsinchu and surrounding areas has become the base for the world's computer hardware, and Taiwan's software development is acquiring global stature. This is Taiwan's chief opportunity.
>
> Over the years, I have had a vision of developing Taiwan into a Green Valley. I believe that human beings are entitled to enjoy a beautiful natural environment as well as the convenience of advanced technology; I cannot imagine an essential conflict between the two. Therefore, the current rapid industrialization that has been accompanied by the destruction of the environment must be temporary. I believe it is time to transcend this conflict in order to achieve both environmental harmony and technological development.
>
> My blueprint for Green Valley must be extended to the entire island, based on the current successes and resources of Taiwan's silicon and computer high-tech industry. I hope that Taiwan in the next millennium will indeed become the Green Silicon Island.'
>
> (Source: 'The Third Way for Taiwan: A New Political Perspective', 6 December 1999, London, DPP Organization)

Chen's silicon imagination was reinforced in his inaugural speech in May 2000. This envisioned the development of Taiwan as a 'sustainable green silicon island' that provides a 'balance between ecological preservation and economic development' (Chen 2000: 4). These post-Crisis discourses and their imagined IT-futures are generating a new techno-economic subjectivity/identity in the 'Greater China' region. Most actors deploy the symbolisms of 'information technology' and 'Silicon Valley' and market themselves as new objects of 'future growth/development' that go beyond cheap production, e.g., 'multimedia hub', 'Green Silicon Island'.

New 'Shared Voices' on 'hi-tech' and 'Silicon Valley'

These official pronouncements created a space in which key corporate actors and their discourses mutually reinforced such internet 'optimisim' up to mid-2000. Some projects even emerged as 'hi-tech' icons. For example, Cyberport is presented as Hong Kong's 'e-hub', which is seeking to capture global 'information flows' and to manage these within the service-space of Hong Kong and its broader region. This project resonated within a global-regional-local epistemic community comprising local capital (e.g., Richard Li of the Pacific Century CyberWorks), the Hong Kong Government (e.g., the Chief Executive, the Financial Secretary, the Secretary for Information and Broadcasting), quasi-governmental organizations (e.g., Hong Kong Industrial Technology Centre), and global-regional capitalists (e.g., Microsoft's Bill Gates, Yahoo!'s Jerry Yang, and IBM's Craig Barrett). The latter group of 'cyber-gods' flew to Hong Kong, publicly endorsed the idea, and even highlighted their own role as future tenants of the Cyberport. In July 1999, Tung himself visited the original Silicon Valley. In a luncheon meeting attended by 800 IT industry leaders, he promoted the image of 'Hong Kong as a hub of innovation and technology in Asia, and particularly China'. His trip contributed to the building of new linkages with the diasporic Chinese communities in the Valley. The Hong Kong–Silicon Valley Association was set up and a new website (SV-Hong-Kong.com) came into operation in November 1999.

Concurrent with the hi-tech spectacle in Hong Kong, several Chinese cities in the Pearl River Delta region were also seeking to ride the information wave. Guangzhou's municipal government signed an agreement with Hong Kong to expand cooperation in new and hi-tech business in 1998. They agreed to enhance greater cooperation between the colleges and universities in the hi-tech field. They wanted to build a new 'hi-tech' corridor along the Guangzhou–Kowloon Railway which would include Shenzhen, Dongguan, Huizhou, Zengcheng and Guangzhou city. In pursuance of this goal, Shenzhen's hosting of the first state-level Hi-Tech Fair in October 1999 helped to boost the hi-tech imagination. Zhu's high-profile visit to the Fair helped to consolidate the city's 'hi-tech' identity. Apart from Zhu, the Fair was also attended by global-regional-local actors that included: a) Chinese senior officials (e.g., the Minister of Science and

Technology, Foreign Trade Minister and Minister of Information Industry); b) national leading firms (e.g., Huawei Technologies, Great Wall Computer); c) hi-tech icons and advocators (e.g., the 1997 Nobel prize-winner for physics Chinese-American Steven Chu, Hong Kong's Financial Secretary Donald Tsang, and former Japanese Prime Minister Kaifu Toshiki); d) delegates from universities on the mainland, Hong Kong and Taiwan; and e) multinational big-players (e.g., Microsoft, IBM, Epson). This group echoed the hi-tech 'shared voices' and helped reinvent Shenzhen as a 'gateway of information technology' in and through their exhibits, speeches, lectures, and on-site visits. Riding on Shenzhen's hi-tech spectacle/fanfare, Dongguan city also hosted the first Computer Information Product Exposition in October 1999. Among the 500 exhibitors, 75% came from Taiwan. Many were representatives from Hsinchu Science Park in Taiwan.

Fearful of being left out of the information race, Taiwan was stepping up its plans for other hi-tech clusters besides the Hsinchu Science Park. 'Hsinchu' and its founders (e.g., Li Kuo-ting) were frequently deployed as icons to highlight the successful transfer of the 'Silicon Valley model' to Taiwan. It symbolizes Taiwan as a 'high-flying graduate' from the Valley that specializes in semiconductor OEM production. Given its success in hardware, there are fears that its 'software is a little bit behind'. Appropriating the 'Silicon Valley–Hsinchu' metaphor, the 1998 Executive Yuan's Action Plan aimed to extend Taiwanese 'success' to cover the whole of Taiwan. Taiwan as a 'science island' was reinforced by Chen's vision of Taiwan as a dynamic 'Green Silicon Island' building on knowledge-based technologies. This economic identity is variously promoted by the DPP government, the Mayor of Taipei City (e.g., Taipei hosted the 2000 World Congress on Information Technology in June), some business leaders (e.g., Stan Shih of the Acer Group) as well as a community of Taiwan-Americans with close connections and personnel exchanges with California's Silicon Valley. The members of this trans-Pacific community are sometimes known as the 'astronauts' because they work as engineers, executives and 'angel' investors in both places and spend most of their time in aeroplanes. This group coordinates Taiwan's financial and manufacturing strengths with Silicon Valley's engineering and research skills through their hyperactive travels (e.g., twice every month) (Hsu and Saxenian 1999) and internet networks. The Acer Group actually runs a number of websites that link this community. One well-known one is called the *Silicon Valley Journal*, which is a Chinese-language portal. It deploys the 'new economy' discourses and profiles itself as the 'Chinese Wall Street Reports'. It links the Chinese-American community in the Valley with the Asia-Pacific region in and through the 'Silicon Valley' dream. The latter is 'a kind of metaphor of hi-tech culture' that symbolizes 'innovation', 'entrepreneurialism', 'networking', 'venture capital', 'clustering', 'risk taking', 'knowledge workers', and even an 'unprecedented gold rush'. This image of a new 'gold rush' is reinforced on the website by publishing the 'success stories' of notable internet 'whizzkids'. In December 1999, they used the wealth of Chinese-American infopreneurs (e.g., Yahoo!'s Jerry Yang was then worth US$ 4,889,033,295) to highlight the essence of the 'Internet dream'. These constructions of 'Silicon Gold' and the rich Chinese infopreneurs are powerful icons that resonate with other discourses of the region, e.g., Taiwan as a 'Green Silicon Island', Hong Kong as 'e-hub' and Shenzhen as 'China's Silicon Valley'.

Remaking of 'Greater China' for hi-tech accumulation: new discursive and material practices

At the time of writing, there is no lack of discourses or discursive practices concerned with reinventing economies in 'Greater China' around 'hi-tech' accumulation. Actors use the symbolism of 'hi-tech', 'e-commerce', 'Silicon Valley' and even 'Silicon Gold' in an effort to establish a new regime of techno-economic truth. This seemed to be gathering strength at least up to May 2000, when the stockmarket 'technology bubble' burst dramatically. Whether this drastic market correction will affect longer term enthusiasm for 'hi-tech' and 'information technology' remains to be seen. Nonetheless, this regime of techno-economic truth has begun to guide the reordering of certain material practices, albeit at a slower pace since the 'bubble'. These practices include: a) developing flagship 'incubators' that profile themselves as 'the next Silicon Valley' and are promoted by private–public partnerships; b) building new regional-global networks with Silicon Valley in California and elsewhere (for example, Singapore); c) forming alliances and interpenetration of old and new economies; d) rearticulating the global-regional-national-local scales of activities for hardware, software and internet delivery; e) developing new sources of networking (for example, industry–university cooperation and finances for hi-tech ventures); f) tapping of overseas/Chinese IT experts (for example, the Admission of Talent Scheme in Hong Kong) and visa wars; g) changing the identity of highly skilled workers, especially those who are being offered stock options; and h) changing the nature of work and the emergence of contingent employment (for example, temporary and part-time work). The rest of the chapter will provide a preliminary discussion of some of these emerging practices.

Let us start with the case of Hong Kong. The Financial Secretary of Hong Kong appropriated a private initiative suggested by Richard Li to spearhead hi-tech development in his 1999 Budget Speech. The flagship project is to build the 'Cyberport' that involves private–public partnerships in creating a critical mass of firms nurtured by the physical form of the environment that is to model on the 'Silicon Valley' (see Table 7). Hong Kong's Chief Executive even visited Silicon Valley in July 1999 to promote

Table 7 Hong Kong's Cyberport

Cost:	HK$ 13 billion (USD$ 1.68 billion)
Size:	64 hectares
Location:	Telegraph Bay, Pokfulam
Completion date:	2007 (commencing from 2003)
Partners:	Pacific Century CyberWorks (HK$ 7 billion worth of equity capital)
	Hong Kong Government (land worth HK$ 6 billion)
Cluster:	Home to global and local information companies
Signed-up tenants:	8 (Microsoft, IBM, Oracle, HP, Softbank, Yahoo!, Hua Wei, Sybase)
Job creation:	4,000 during construction
	12,000 professional jobs on completion
Metaphors	'Silicon Valley', 'clustering' and 'critical mass of firms'

Source: Author's compilation from various issues of *South China Morning Post*, 1999.

the project and to set up linkages with the Valley by starting the Hong Kong–Silicon Valley Association. Just before the bursting of the 'technology bubble', the 'Cyberport' and Richard Li became economic icons – especially when their activities kept making newspaper headlines. Apart from securing subsidized land worth HK$ 6 billion from the government, the project gained access to equity capital by buying up Tricom, which was a listed company on the Hong Kong Stock Exchange. Tricom later turned itself into an Internet-related company with a new name: Pacific Century CyberWorks. Riding on the Nasdaq boom and the surplus of regional and local funds searching for new investment objects after the 'property/Itic bubbles', its share prices rose by 2258% from 1 January to 30 December 1999. Pacific Century CyberWorks continued to make headlines by its other activities in capturing fast cybertime and localized it in the regional space of 'Greater China' and Asia-Pacific. These include: a) forming a joint venture with Intel – a global partner – to develop high-speed broadband Internet connectivity that can deliver complex applications and enriched contents; b) joining forces with China's Legend Holdings to co-develop broadband services in China and co-brand PCs with built-in cable modems giving exclusive Internet access; c) merging with the 'old economy' in the form of Cable and Wireless HKT to strengthen CyberWorks' broadband infrastructure and enhance its Internet service delivery; and d) using broadband services to develop B2C and B2B e-commerce and to speed up the relatively lengthy supply chains and fragmented markets.

These high-profile activities undertaken by Pacific Century CyberWorks and Richard Li have affected the wider society. Large property/commercial conglomerates in Hong Kong began to diversify from the so-called 'old economy'. For example, in August 1999, Sun Hung Kai Properties (SHKP) transformed its empty properties in Tsuen Wan to establish a 'Cyber-incubator' project. Under this scheme, SHKP planned to provide rent-free space for new 'infopreneurs' for three years in return for 10% stakes in their respective businesses. Apart from this innovative use of its old property assets, the property developer also stretched into the 'new economy' by developing an internet arm called SUNeVision. The latter has expanded the temporal-spatial reach of the conglomerate by developing its information technology infrastructure and Internet services (e.g., selling property and insurance on the net). According to its chairman, Raymond Kwok, he sees SUNeVision as:

> ... the first company in China and Asia to integrate and leverage the entire Internet value chain to achieve critical mass with significant economies of scales.
>
> (Source: http://www.sunevision.com/about_overview.htm)

Preparing for China's entry into the WTO and the opening of its hi-tech sectors, SUNeVision and SmarTone announced a US$ 20 million 'C Tech Fund' that would focus on venture capital investments in IT, healthcare and biotechnology, the environment, telecommunications and other technology-related fields on the mainland. In addition, SHKP obtained its capital through listing on Hong Kong's new Growth Enterprise Market.

Apart from large conglomerates announcing their new hi-tech ventures, small start-up firms are beginning to form clusters. New urban IT clusters are emerging in different tower blocks in Central Hong Kong. One building in the central district even changed its name to 'Dotcom House' and, after negotiations with its hi-tech tenants, transformed the block into a smart building by installing new facilities such as fibre-optic cable, more phone lines, 24-hour air-conditioning and a back-up power generator. These new start-ups also network among themselves and with 'angel investors' through intermediary organizations such as Internet & Information Asia (I&I). The latter organizes informal gatherings every Wednesday night by bringing start-up firms to venture capital. Apart from these networkings with 'angel investors', the Hong Kong Stock Exchange launched the Growth Enterprise Market (GEM)[6] in 1999, which is Hong Kong's version of Nasdaq, to offer an alternative listing choice for incubating start-up technology companies and venture capital firms in the 'Greater China' region. As of June 2000, 12 firms were listed with 7 from Hong Kong, 4 from China and 1 from Taiwan. The bursting of the 'technology bubble' has slowed down company listing on the GEM; but with China joining the WTO, Hong Kong will profile itself as a 'logistic, financial and digital centre of intermediation between [the] Mainland and the rest of the world' (Yam 2000: 2).

As for Taiwan, it is advantageously positioned in terms of its hardware electronic industries. Although the earthquake in September 1999 caused some delay, no real damage occurred to its production capacity. Hsinchu Science Park is still a manufacturing powerhouse with good connections to California's Silicon Valley. The mantra has been 'Silicon Valley creates it, Taiwan makes it'. In accordance with the 1997 White Paper and its Action Plan, Taiwan is upgrading its research capacity by developing other clusters in Tainan, Chunan and Tungluo. Apart from building industrial parks, then President Lee Teng-hui inaugurated the opening of a 'milestone-type' software park in October 1999 in Taipei county – the Nankang Software Park. This flagship (software) project was commissioned by the Ministry of Economic Affairs and was developed by Century Development Company, a joint venture of 19 domestic and foreign companies (see Table 8). The Ministry of Economic Affairs purchased floor space of 2,000 pings (1 ping = 36 sq. ft.) to develop an international R&D cooperation centre. In addition, it spent NT$ 995 million to procure 3,100 pings of floor space to set up a software incubator centre available for use by 80–100 local software companies. Similar to the Cyberport project in Hong Kong, the Ministry sent a task force to the US and Japan to lure software firms to set up laboratories in the park. This launching of a new incubator to pursue Taiwan's software 'ambition' coexists with its continuing hardware success.

On a corporate level, the Acer Group is a good illustration of how conglomerates are seeking to reposition themselves. The Acer Group is expanding its computer-manufacturing business into Southern China. It invested in a US$ 50 million plant in Zhongshan in Guangdong Province in late 1999 to produce computers and DVD players. It also diversifed into the 'new economy' in 1999 by establishing the Acer Digital Services Corporation. This has embarked on the following activities: a) establishing a global-regional alliance with Cisco Systems and General Electric Information Services; b) operating an Internet shopping mall under the AcerNet; c) developing X-media for media display to be used in convenience chain stores under Web Point; d) developing and marketing children's software services; and e) entering the venture capital business by funding start-ups in the US and Asia-Pacific under Acer SoftCapital Group.

As for the Pearl River Delta and Guangdong Province, there are numerous attempts to build hi-tech industrial development zones in Shenzhen, Zhuhai, Huizhou, Zhongshan and Foshan under the auspices of government ministries (e.g., Ministry of Science and Technology) and municipal authorities. Most attempts include the offer of tax exemptions and/or the opportunities of domestic sales for multinational and national firms to enter the zones. For example, the Guangzhou Economic and Technological Development District (which merged with Guangzhou Hi-Tech Industrial Development Zone in 1998) is one of the first state-level development districts. One of its recent flagship projects is to develop the Guangzhou Science City, which profiles itself as 'the Rising Silicon Valley in Guangzhou'. As a state-run project, it offers tax exemptions for investors

Table 8 Nankang Software Park

Cost:	NT$ 12.8 billion (US$ 402.5 million)
Size:	8.2 hectares
Location:	Nankang, Taipei County
Completion date:	2003
Partners:	Century Development Corp.
Cluster:	Home to global and local software companies
	Proximity to the Academia Sinica's Institute of Information Sciences
Signed-up tenants:	15 (e.g., IBM, HP, Compaq, Intel)
Terms:	Foreign companies have to sign cooperative agreements with Taiwan companies
Expected return:	US$ 14 billion by 2005

Source: Author's compilation from various publications of the Central News Agency, 1999.

for the initial two years and unlimited sales in Guangdong for products in electronics, computer communication, and aerospace engineering.

Similar zones/parks can be found in the Pearl River Delta. Shenzhen's Hi-Tech Industrial Park has attracted a host of multinational and national technology firms, such as IBM and Great Wall. These firms produce electronic and IT products (such as computer component parts, mobile telecommunication products and computer software) with an output value of 29.69 billion yuan in 1999. Apart from the state-run park, the Shenzhen Municipal Government is encouraging enterprises to develop R&D centres and private–public partnerships. In 1999, there were 271 R&D centres in Shenzhen with some having connections with Silicon Valley in California as well as with similar milieux in Beijing, Shanghai and Nanjing. The government is also encouraging overseas and national universities to cooperate with local concerns. For example, the government granted Qinghua University 10 000 square metres of land to build an R&D centre; and 60 million RMB to finance research projects. Beijing University, along with the Hong Kong University of Science and Technology and the Shenzhen Municipal Government, have together invested 80 million RMB in an education and research centre. This public–private partnership runs an MBA programme, conducts biotech research and is home to iSilk.com, a firm that is developing simultaneous translation software for the Internet (Saywell 1999: 52–54; Li 2000: 4–5).

Private–public partnerships have been further developed in a new flagship project approved by the Ministry of Science and Technology and the Shenzhen Municipal Government. This involved the establishment of the mainland's first venture capital fund to build a hi-tech park – CyberCity Shenzhen (see Table 9). This scheme was spearheaded by Simon Jiang (the

Table 9 CyberCity Shenzhen

Venture capital:	US $ 250 million private-equity fund (Memorandum of Understanding regarding US$ 100 million with DynaFund Venture)
Land:	80% below market price from Shenzhen Municipal Government
Size:	36,000 square meters (40.5 hectares)
Completion date:	2004
Partners:	Hong Kong-based Cyber City International
Cluster:	Home to 100 international and local software and information companies
Signed-up tenants:	60 global and local firms
Listing:	Selling 80% stake to Hing Kong Holdings (a company listed on the Hong Kong Stock Exchange)
Network:	Cooperation agreement with 10 mainland software parks (e.g., Kunming, Tianjin, Pudong, Xian)

Sources: Author's compilation from various issues of *South China Morning Post*, 1999.

son of former National People's Congress chairman Qiao Shi) in conjunction with Hong Kong investment company Cyber City Holdings and US venture capital company Dynamic Technology Inc. Based on the symbolism associated with 'Silicon Valley's high-risk, high-return promise', its aim is 'to nurture software and Internet firms to market' (CyberCity Shenzhen website) by connecting them with overseas firms and investors. Since its inception, this experimental private–public partnership has managed to extend in two spatial directions. First, it managed to extend its network into the Hong Kong financial sector by arranging a backdoor listing on the Hong Kong Stock Exchange. It sold 80% of its stake to a China-owned Hong Kong-listed company – Hing Kong Holdings. Second, it further extended its network to the 'Intelligent Island' of Singapore by selling 13.3% of its stake to Temasek Holding (an investment arm of the Singapore government) and Fraser and Neave (a Singapore consortium) in April 2000. CyberCity Shenzhen planned to set up a Singapore office that 'will bring (its) regional strengths in Chinese Internet content and infrastructure to Singapore' (Jiang 2000). Such emerging transborder Hong Kong–Shenzhen–Singapore linkages may mark new modes of coordination that stretch beyond Hong Kong, Taiwan and southern China.

These emerging economic activities/practices undertaken by private-public and local-national-regional-global actors may well contribute toward the building of new modes of economic coordination around hi-tech accumulation. Such rebuilding processes are often mediated by struggles that cut across different scales of activities. On the national scale, for example, Taiwan, which has a longer history of pursuing the siliconization strategy, has consolidated a silicon coalition of powerful capitalists (for example, Stan Shih of Acer, Morris Chang of Taiwan Semiconductor). With the entry of China into the WTO and hi-tech industries clamouring for gateways to China, Taiwan's silicon capitalists are worrying about being left behind because of current investment limits of NT$ 50 billion to China. At present, they are adopting three strategies: a) persuading the government to abandon investment restrictions on hi-tech industries (for example, notebook computer production, semiconductor manufacturing, removing the ban on the 'three links' with China), and pushing for the development of R&D and 'information/knowledge-based economy' in Taiwan; b) bypassing government policy by investing in notebook computer production in China (nine out of ten notebook makers have already done so); and c) planning and making contacts to expand into the Chinese Internet and telecommunications markets (for example, Acer Inc. – the Internet company under the Acer group – is considering going public in China and not on Nasdaq). Taiwan's Ministry of Economy announced in June 2000 that Taiwanese investment in the mainland had increased by 1.4 times during January to May compared to the same period in 1999. All new changes re-ignite the 'hollowing out' debate in Taiwan and the related fear of unemployment, technological upgrading and the nationalist independence project of the Democratic Progressive Party.

On a regional level, there is the question of whether the strategy of siliconization will deepen the geoeconomic (sub-)regional division of labour and intensify the scope of competition within the 'Greater China' region. With the upgrading of technology, Taiwan may concentrate more on R&D. Its computer/IT companies and component parts would continue to move into southern China. This deepening of export-oriented cross-border production would also be enhanced with the development of B2B e-commerce in the region. In the case of Hong Kong, its role as a traditional entrepot/gateway city is declining with the emergence of other ports in the Pearl River delta (for example, Yantian, Shekou and Chiwan).

The Asian 'Crisis' has also exposed Hong Kong's overdependence on property and financial markets. Hong Kong is thus repositioning itself as a 'logistical, financial and digital centre' with hard and soft infrastructure for Internet services (broadband networks, e-commerce, business consultancy, data centres, content distribution and marketing skills, venture capital, GEM) and project finance. Given that Taiwan is relaxing restrictions on investments in China (e.g., small- and medium-sized enterprises are allowed to increase their investment from NT$ 60 to NT$ 80 billion) while China's demand for investment and venture capital is likely to increase with its entry into the WTO, Hong Kong is strategically positioned to act as a net gateway and fund-raising centre for the 'Greater China' region. Likewise, Shenzhen and the Pearl River Delta could continue their concentration on electronics and IT products as well as offshore software sites for Chinese-language and multi-lingual products.

Despite the possibility of a new regional division of labour along this long silicon supply chain, competition can also be found among incubators such as science/software parks. The number of software parks is growing in the region (e.g., Cyberport, Nankang Software Park, CyberCity Shenzhen, Guangzhou Science City). These similarly conceived projects may well compete when: a) seeking to provide facilities to house software companies specializing in, for example, Chinese-language software applications; b) incubating smaller local start-up firms for joint ventures and market listings; and c) attempting to attract global big players (e.g., Microsoft, IBM, Oracle) to locate in their complexes.[7]

Conclusion

This chapter has focused on the differential impact of the 'Crisis' upon the 'Greater China' region and its role in reorienting and restructuring accumulation regimes. Largely due to their pre-existing strengths and embedded capacities, economies in the region (with the exception of Hong Kong) escaped the most direct and severe impact of the financial contagion in 1997. However, crisis-related 'secondary effects' began to emerge in Taiwan and China in the middle of 1998 in the form of the 'bursting of the stock/property and Itic bubbles'. Quick fixes carried out by these governments failed to revitalize the economies and leading forces in the different economies began to promote a new politics of (Internet) optimism. They deploy the symbolism of 'hi-tech' and 'Silicon Valley' to redefine their economic futures. This strategy of siliconization, in which actors seek to develop new modes of coordination around new accumulation regimes, is by no means bound to succeed in establishing and regularizing a new regional division of labour. Indeed, judging from the recent activities of these private-public and global-regional-local actors, there is scope for intensified competition as well as cooperation within the region. For example, with the upgrading of its technology, Taiwan may concentrate more on R&D at home and move the manufacture of its more sophisticated components and notebook computers into southern China. This strategy of deepening the regional division of production co-exists with other strategies or emerging practices that often point in other directions. Among these strategies and practices, as we have seen, are: a) the repositioning of Hong Kong as a 'logistic, financial and digital centre'; b) the introduction of the GEM as a fund-raising avenue; c) the emergence of a number of science/software parks in the region providing IT/incubation facilities for global and new start-up firms; d) the pursuit by leading 'old-economy' firms in the region to form strategic alliances or joint ventures to map 'Greater China' as an e-production and e-service space; and e) the competition among various global and regional capitalists to redefine and consolidate their IT stakes within these e-production and e-service spaces. It is too soon to predict how this complex field of sometimes competing, sometimes complementary, strategies and practices pursued by private-public actors on different scales will remake post-'Crisis' 'Greater China'. However, it is clear that their attempts to redefine their IT stakes in the region are contributing to changing identities and governance mechanisms. These processes cannot be fully understood without more work on the identity/interest struggles involved in the strategy of siliconization.

Notes

1 'Greater China' denotes the so-called 'growth triangle' which includes Taiwan, (southern) China, and Hong Kong. For a theoretical and empirical account of pre-Crisis 'Greater China', see Sum (1999: 129–146).
2 'Itic' is the conventional abbreviation in China for International Trust and Investment Corporations. For further details, see page 197.
3 Taiwan's property sector 'bubble' had already burst in the early 1990s. So an excessively overvalued, speculative real estate market does not plague it.
4 China's Itics had a total external debt in 1998 of US$ 8.1 billion. Investors and government officials alike feared that the collapse of Gitic and GDE would cause a 'domino effect'.
5 The impact of the 'Crisis' on Itics has been uneven. The Fujian, Shandong, Shanghai, Shenzhen and Tianjin Itics have managed to repay their maturing debt operations.
6 The Growth Enterprise Market (GEM) came into operation on October 25 1999 in Hong Kong. It was created to develop Hong Kong's information technology industry and is one of several Asian attempts to emulate the USA's Nasdaq. The GEM is expected to serve the 'Greater China' market, whereas Singapore's Sesdaq and Malaysia's Mesdaq are to serve the south Asian markets while Kosdaq serves the Korean market. Some competition could come from China, where Shanghai and Shenzhen are reported to want second boards to compete with Hong Kong and Nasdaq. However, Beijing currently prefers mainland non-state enterprises to seek flotation in Shenzhen and the GEM. The biggest competitor is Nasdaq, which has drawn a number of initial public offerings from the region. Many venture capitalists are far more comfortable with the 28-year-old Nasdaq, given its liquidity and stable regulatory environment. Fearful of losing its edge, Hong Kong Stock Exchange has eased its requirement for a lock-in period, during which management were unable to sell their shares, from two years to six months.
7 These tendencies for competition within the 'Greater China' region are further fuelled by similar projects elsewhere in Asia, e.g., Malaysia's 'Multimedia Supercorridor', and Singapore's 'intelligent island'.

Bibliography

Business Asia (1999) 'NAB Registers Biggest Loss of Foreign Banks in Taiwan', 30 September 7(1): 17.

Chen, S.-B. (2000) 'Taiwan Stands Up: Toward the Dawn of a Rising Era', http://www.chinatopnews.com/Politics/Sat_May_20_18_19_32_2000.html

China Online (2000) 'Shenzhen Plans to Become "China's Silicon Valley"', http://www.chinaonline.com/industry/infotech/newsarchive/secure/2000/april/b200033411.asp, accessed on 5 June 2000.

CyberCity Shenzhen website, http://www.szcci.com/szcci/english/

Cyberport website, http://www.cyber-port.com/

Engbarth, D. (1999a) 'Bank Task Forces Faces Uphill Struggle', *South China Morning Post*, 19 May, Business Section: 4.

Engbarth, D. (1999b) 'Strong in the Face of Crisis', *The Banker*, July, 148 (869): 5.

Fischer, S. (1998) 'The Asian Crisis: A View from the IMF', *Journal of International Financial Management and Accounting*, 9 (2): 167–176.

Hong Kong SAR Government (1998) 'From Adversity to Opportunity', Address by the Chief Executive The Honorable Tung Chee Hwa at the Legislative Council Meeting.

Hong Kong SAR Government (1999) 'Onward with New Strength', Speech by the Financial Secretary.

Jiang, S. (2000) 'Cybercity Announces the Opening of Singapore Office', http://www.cybercityhk.com, accessed on 3 January 2001.

Krugman, P. (1998) 'Saving Asia: It's Time to Get Radical', *Fortune*, 7 September, http://mypage.channeli.net/huntkim/saving%20Asia.htm., accessed on 5 September 2000.

Li, N. (2000) 'Hi-Tech Industrial Zones: New Impetus Pushing Economy Up', http://www.china.org.cn/Beijing-Review/2000Apr/bjr2000–17e–6.htm, accessed on 5 June 2000.

National Science Council (1997) 'White Paper on Science and Technology', Republic of Taiwan.

Radelet, S. and Sachs, J. (1998) 'The Onset of the East Asian Financial Crisis', http://www.stern.nyn.edu/nroubini/asia/AsiaHomepage.html, accessed on 5 June 2000.

Saywell, T. (1999) 'Watch Your Back', *Far Eastern Economic Review*, 16 September: 42–55.

Shimizu, K. (1999) 'Gitics Galore', *Institutional Investor*, 24 January (1): 83.

Silicon Valley Journal website, http://www.svjournal.com/bingif/ and http://www.svjournal.com/about/index.asp/, accesed on 5 June 2000.

Smith, G. (1999) 'China Scrambles to Overcome History of Economic Blunders', *Asian Wall Street Journal*, 24 February.

Straits Times (1999) 'Taiwanese Firms Shifting Technology to China', 6 December.

Sum, N.-L. (1999) 'Rethinking Globalization: Rearticulating the Spatial Scale and Temporal Horizons of Trans-border Spaces' in K. Olds et al. (eds) *Globalization and the Asia-Pacific*, London: Routledge, pp. 29–146.

Sum, N.-L. (2002) 'A Material-Discursive Approach to the Asian "Crisis": The Breaking and Re-making of the Production and Financial Orders' in P. Masina (ed.) *Rethinking Development in East Asia: from Illusory Miracle to Economic Crisis*, London: Curzon and New York: St. Martins, pp. 53–78.

Wade, R. and Veneroso, F. (1998) 'The Asian Crisis: The High Debt Model Versus the Wall-Street-IMF Complex', *New Left Review*, 228: 3–23.

Wong, L. (1999) 'GDE Creditors Brave for Drawn-out Flight over Debt', *South China Morning Post*, 26 May.

Yan, J. (2000) 'Hong Kong: The Hub of Asia', Speech delivered at the 7th Annual Hong Kong General Chamber of Commerce Business Summit, 13 December, http://www.chamber.org.hk/bus, accessed on 28 February 2001.

China:
Developments in External Relations

Chapter 12

China and the United States

An Uneasy and Unstable Relationship

Jürgen Haacke

Introduction

Chinese analysts and policy-makers generally refer to Sino-U.S. relations as China's 'most important bilateral relationship.' And yet, in the last few years, the nature of Sino-U.S. relations has variously been described as 'precarious' (Bernkopf Tucker 1998), 'fragile' (Gurtov 1999) and 'uncertain' (Harding 1999). This chapter discusses what would appear to be the core issues and dynamics underlying bilateral co-operation and conflict. It is divided into five sections. The first section reviews recent developments into 2000, including those that brought the relationship to a nadir in 1999. Sections two to four discuss three interrelated and highly contentious issues in Sino-U.S. relations: approaches to regional and international security, the Taiwan issue, and the anticipated U.S. deployment of National Missile Defence (NMD)/Theatre Missile Defence (TMD) systems. The fifth section briefly explores to what extent tensions in Sino-American relations are likely to be mitigated by commercial and economic interests.

Sino-U.S. relations in the late 1990s: in search of stability

As China sought to implement its ambitious long-term reform programme, Deng Xiaoping formulated a 16-character guideline on relations with the United States, which has also been attributed to Jiang Zemin: *zengjia xinren, jianshao mafan, fazhan hezuo, bugao duikang* (to increase confidence, reduce trouble, enhance co-operation and avoid confrontation). When 'trouble' emerged at the end of the Cold War, particularly over the violent suppression of the widespread street protests in China in 1989, Chinese leaders had little choice but to wait until the worst part of the political storm had passed. As soon as that happened, Beijing again endeavoured to further develop co-operative relations with Washington. However, post-Cold War bilateral relations have in many ways proved more complicated than those in the days of the strategic alignment of the two countries in the face of the common Soviet threat. Then, human rights issues, trade problems and diverging security interests did not constitute major spanners in bilateral relations. By contrast, the initial post-Cold War ties were complicated by angry exchanges over the annual renewal by the U.S. Congress of Beijing's MFN status, the Clinton administration's criticisms of human rights practices in the PRC, and disagreements arising over China's export of nuclear and missile technology, to name but some issues. Taiwan became the most sensitive topic in bilateral relations.

While the Chinese government is in many ways impressed by the structural power of the lone superpower in the post-Cold War period, the rapid re-emergence of China as a regional power has raised a multitude of questions for U.S. analysts and policy-makers. These questions have, among others, revolved around how best to: (a) ensure the long-term continuation of a U.S.-led regional order in East Asia, (b) manage changes in the regional balance of power, and (c) promote U.S. security, political and economic interests in the future. The PRC's rapid economic development and its future role in particular prompted debates among American academics and policy-makers about the merits of 'engaging or containing' Beijing.

In the second half of the 1990s, Sino-U.S. relations experienced two particularly bad patches. One developed in the wake of the decision of the Clinton administration to issue a visa to Taiwanese leader Lee Teng-hui, despite prior assurances to the contrary, which subsequently saw Beijing's resort to coercive diplomacy – including missile exercises just off Taiwan – between the autumn of 1995 and March 1996.[1] The other followed the bombing of the Chinese Embassy in Belgrade in May 1999.

Notably, in both instances, Sino-U.S. relations improved again within a relatively short period of time. Following the Taiwan crisis of 1995/96, concerns about possibly devastating consequences of mutual misperceptions as well as the prospects of a further deterioration in ties despite shared interests prompted the exploration and discussion of the establishment of a 'constructive strategic partnership'. Such a partnership was subsequently announced during President Jiang Zemin's first state visit to the United States in October 1997. In the event, President Clinton's official return visit to the PRC in the summer of 1998 raised further the prospect of improved ties and enhanced co-operation between the two sides, even though in the end it led to little in terms of new substantive developments.

Indeed, by March 1999 bilateral ties had reached a new low as NATO started to bombard the Federal Republic of Yugoslavia in order to coerce Slobodan Milosevic to withdraw his forces from the province of Kosovo where ethnic Albanians were exposed to a 'humanitarian catastrophe'. Washington's decision to bomb without the authorisation of the UN

Security Council and, more pertinently, Clinton's failure to consult Jiang prior to the bombing illustrated the limitations of the 'strategic partnership' with Beijing. Washington's lack of flexibility to reach agreement on a bilateral accord on the terms of the PRC's entry into the World Trade Organisation (WTO) only a few days later, unexpected concessions from the Chinese side notwithstanding, constituted a second slap in the face for the Chinese side. Not surprisingly, the subsequent mistaken bombing of the Chinese Embassy in Belgrade in May constituted for many Chinese leaders the last straw.[2] In riposte, apart from not preventing, but even encouraging, violence against American and other Western diplomatic and consular missions in China, the leadership also suspended military-to-military co-operation with Washington as well as the bilateral human rights dialogue and discussions on arms control and non-proliferation. Even after Beijing had finally accepted and publicly aired President Clinton's formal apology over the embassy blunder, the Chinese authorities insisted that a complete and thorough investigation of the incident be undertaken and those responsible be severely punished. Beijing's initial seemingly uncompromising attitude and attendant diplomatic rhetoric in turn provoked a negative response within the Clinton administration, which warned China against seeking to exploit the bombing to win political concessions from Washington in areas of disagreement.

At the time of writing, relations between the two sides have again improved significantly. Summit level contacts started to resume with a meeting between Presidents Clinton and Jiang Zemin on the sidelines of the APEC summit in Auckland in September 1999. Other high-level visits soon followed. In February 2000, for instance, Deputy Secretary of State Strobe Talbott, Under-Secretary of Defence Walter Slocombe, and Joseph Ralston, Vice Chairman of the Joint Chiefs of Staff visited Beijing to resume a strategic dialogue with China. Then, Admiral Dennis Blair, commander of U.S. Pacific forces, and National Security Adviser Samuel Berger, informed Chinese leaders that Washington remained committed to building a 'strategic partnership' with Beijing. In June, Secretary of State Madeleine Albright visited Beijing, as did the Secretary of Defence in mid-July. Further exchanges took place on the sidelines of the 2000 APEC Leaders' Meeting in Brunei Darussalam, involving Madeleine Albright, Samuel Berger, Chinese Vice-Premier Qian Qichen and Foreign Minister Tang Jiaxuan. Clinton and Jiang also still met twice before the end of 2000, first on the sidelines of the UN Millennium Summit in New York and then, for a final summit, on the fringes of the November APEC meeting.

While not all of these exchanges necessarily yielded significant outcomes, progress in restoring normalcy in bilateral ties was made, as will be further discussed below. The accelerating frequency of high-level contacts in itself reflects again a turn toward a more positive development in bilateral ties. As regards the substantive progress that was achieved, Washington and Beijing reached agreement on the compensation settlement for those injured in the Belgrade embassy bombing as well as for the families of those who were killed. Senior officials also successfully concluded negotiations on compensation for damage to the Chinese embassy and American diplomatic and consular missions in China, attacked in reprisal in the aftermath of NATO's embassy bombing. To be sure, the agreement has not implied that Chinese officials have accepted Washington's contention that the bombing was indeed 'accidental' (Glaser 1999).

In November 1999, Beijing and Washington finally signed an agreement on China's terms of accession to the WTO. Following intensive lobbying on this issue by President Clinton, the House of Representatives and the Senate in May and September 2000 respectively, voted in favour of granting the PRC permanent normal trading relations (PNTR) status. Notably, President Jiang made a personal call to President Clinton to express his gratitude for the outcome of the House vote.

Military-to-military contacts resumed at the end of 1999 when the PLA (Hong Kong) and American forces conducted joint search and rescue manoeuvres, which were repeated the following year. China has also again relaxed its position on allowing U.S. ships to conduct port-calls in Hong Kong (Bernkopf Tucker 2000). In January 2000, high-level military contacts were restored with a visit to Washington by the People's Liberation Army (PLA) deputy chief of staff, Lt. General Xiong Guangkai for the bilateral Defence Consultative Talks. These had started in late 1997 following Jiang's visit to the United States. In the event, Lt. General Xiong and Under-Secretary of Defence Slocombe agreed on a programme for military-to-military contacts for 2000 that, among others, included a series of visits and various confidence building measures (Glaser 2000a). In April, Admiral Shi Yunsheng, commander in chief of the PLA navy, headed a high-ranking delegation to the United States for discussion with Secretary of Defence William Cohen.[3] Then, the Chairman of the Joint Chiefs of Staff, General Henry Stelton, was hosted by the PLA Chief of General Staff, Fu Quanyou, in October 2000, followed by a visit by the director to the United States of the PLA General Political Department, General Yu Yongbo. This visit was in turn followed by the fourth round of US–China Defence Consultative Talks.

Washington has sought to constructively involve itself in the Taiwan conflict. When former Taiwan leader Lee Teng-hui described the relationship between Taipei and Beijing as one of 'state-to-state' or at least 'special state-to-state' relations in July 1999, the Clinton administration rejected endorsing the statement. While warning Beijing to act with restraint *vis-à-vis* Taipei, Washington reiterated its 'One-China' policy and urged both parties to resume the unofficial dialogue between the two sides.

Washington and Beijing themselves resumed the official dialogue on arms control and non-proliferation when John Holum, the State Department's

Under Secretary for international security affairs, visited Beijing in July 2000. In mid-September, Assistant Secretary of State Robert Einhorn and Sha Zukang, head of the PRC Foreign Ministry's arms control department had consultations on the non-proliferation of weapons of mass destruction (Glaser 2000c). During their last summit meeting in November 2000, Clinton and Jiang moreover struck a deal whereby China is not to export nuclear-capable missiles or their technologies and is to reinforce export controls on missiles. In return, China will benefit from a waiver of economic sanctions that Washington was about to impose for past Chinese proliferation to Pakistan and Iran (Glaser 2000d). Clinton and Jiang at the time also agreed in principle to restart the bilateral human rights dialogue.

Co-operation in other areas has also been initiated or strengthened since the Belgrade bombing. For instance, in June 2000, the two sides announced an agreement to share information and evidence in relation to drug smuggling (Glaser 2000b).

Notwithstanding recent improvements in bilateral ties, the relationship still faces enormous challenges in the coming years. To appreciate these challenges, the next section will focus on three issues that can be expected to have significant impact on future Sino-American relations: differences over the future security architecture in East Asia, the Taiwan issue and the likely deployment of National Missile Defence/Theatre Missile Defence systems.

Sino-American differences over the future of regional security

Leaders of the People's Republic of China and the United States for years privately if not publicly agreed on the importance of the role as a balancing power that Washington has played in East Asia. Apart from welcoming the containment of the Soviet threat in the Cold War, CCP leaders also were glad to see that the alliance between Tokyo and Washington limited Japan to playing a very circumscribed regional political-military role. In the post-Cold War period, Beijing and Washington have continued to share some strategic interests. For example, as testified by their co-operation in the 1990s, the United States and the PRC have sought to prevent (a) the collapse of North Korea, (b) the emergence of a unified Korea as a nuclear power, and (c) an armed conflict on the Korean Peninsula. Another pertinent example was Beijing's preparedness to accept a neutral stance adopted by Washington in relation to the South China Sea dispute and the U.S. interest in maintaining open sea lines of communication.

In the second half of the 1990s, however, this measure of shared strategic interest was increasingly in doubt. Having consistently regarded its alliance system as the cornerstone for the maintenance of regional peace and security in East Asia, but then found that in particular the U.S.–Japan security relationship to be going adrift (Funabashi 1999), Washington sought to revitalise its bilateral alliances. Notably, in its 1998 East Asia Strategy

Washington not only focuses on retaining U.S. primacy in the region, but also embraces both military security and 'comprehensive security', with the latter implying a willingness to engage and co-operate with states on an array of regional and transnational security issues. By contrast, China is increasingly questioning the legitimacy and usefulness of the United States as the chief security guarantor in East Asia if that, inter alia, implies a possible loosening of restraints on Japan to play a 'normal' diplomatic and security role. Equally, China has, for example, little, if any, strategic interest in seeing the continued deployment of American forces on the Korean Peninsula following an eventual reunification of the two Koreas.

To Beijing, Washington's efforts to strengthen bilateral alliances and military security co-operation with countries neighbouring the PRC arise from a 'Cold War' mentality that it regards as outdated. It has made this clear on several occasions, be it during meetings linked to the ASEAN Regional Forum or in its official publications (e.g. *China's National Defence in 2000*). As an alternative to the U.S. model of security co-operation, Chinese policy-makers have advocated the embrace of the five principles of peaceful co-existence as the basis for international security, and promoted a system of strategic dialogues with regional powers as well as a focus on co-operative security. As regards the latter, Beijing has pointed not merely to the workings of the ASEAN Regional Forum, but also to the statements on joint co-operation that the PRC has signed or issued with all of the member states of the Association of Southeast Asian Nations.[4] Meanwhile, American officials and analysts would like Chinese recognition of the legitimate and indefinite presence of the United States in the western Pacific. It is in this sense that bilateral relations have increasingly been characterised by strategic competition following prior strategic drift (Shambaugh 2000). We shall now explore in more detail the concerns that underpin Beijing's reaction to U.S. security policy *vis-à-vis* East Asia.

Beijing's security concerns

The Chinese leadership has a number of security concerns that arise as a consequence of Washington's national security strategy, which, in declaratory and practical terms, seeks to promote military security, democracy and prosperity, and is spelled out with regard to the region in its 1998 East Asia Strategy. First, Chinese leaders are genuinely worried about the depth of U.S. structural power, particularly its lead in technology and knowledge production and its dominant influence in international organisations including its power projection capabilities. U.S. comprehensive national strength surpasses that of China by a considerable margin, not least owing to enormous advances made in information technology and the revolution in military affairs, on the back of greatly enhanced productivity and strong economic growth in the U.S. of around 3–6% throughout the

Clinton era. Chinese leaders also realise that the disparity in military power between the two countries is set to widen if current U.S. spending patterns are not reversed. America's defence spending stood at US$ 305.4 billion for fiscal year 2001, compared to the official figure of the PRC military budget of US$ 14.6 billion. Significantly, even credible unofficial estimates of China's defence expenditure do not suggest that Beijing's overall military spending surpasses that of Tokyo, which is far less than that of Washington. PRC policy-analysts and -makers thus 'perceive China to be vulnerable to coercion in a way that ought not be possible in a relationship between major powers' (Montaperto and Roberts 2000: 29).

PRC analysts and policy-makers worry in particular about a trend in Washington toward ever more sophisticated defensive weapons systems. This striving towards absolute security – as some Chinese America-watchers believe – is likely to add to the degree of recklessness that characterises the United States behaviour in international relations. The CCP leadership, meanwhile, has to balance security concerns associated with a developing country with those that demand the further modernisation of the PLA (Karmel 2000a). Not surprisingly, therefore, Chinese leaders have voiced concern about the possibility of an intensifying international arms race as the United States is developing new generations of weapons.

Third, CCP leaders also worry that China's representation as a threat in the United States might in some way impair the PRC's prospects for economic development, national security and international standing. Although Beijing had some success in the mid-1990s in questioning the persuasiveness of the notion of the 'China threat' in the context of relations with other East Asian states, Chinese leaders are not keen to see the U.S. Congress and the governing administration espouse the notion more openly. A recent case in point is the 'Cox Committee Report', which basically concluded that China had conducted long-term espionage against American nuclear weapons laboratories, and that it possessed both the capability and the intention to build a nuclear arsenal equal to that of the United States. The Cox Report also suggested that Beijing had been using Hong Kong as a trans-shipment point for high-technology products and weaponry. Seemingly as a consequence, the National Defense Authorisation Act for Fiscal Year 2000 prevented the Pentagon from pursuing confidence building measures that might give China access to sensitive national security information. Washington also exerted significant pressure on Israel to abrogate the sale of a Phalcon Airborne Warning and Control System (AWACS) in the summer of 2000. More recently, in this context, given the improving political situation on the Korean Peninsula, Chinese analysts have become increasingly sceptical that 'rogue states' can for long continue to serve as the official justification for NMD/TMD. And some are to some extent concerned about the implications of the 'rogue-state' argument losing plausibility.

As mentioned already, Beijing is also wary of the revitalisation of the U.S.–Japan alliance undertaken since 1996 which has led to the subsequent revision of the 1978 Guidelines for U.S.–Japan Security Co-operation. The new guidelines give Tokyo a potential auxiliary role in meeting regional crises in 'areas surrounding Japan'.[5] Related defence laws were passed in May 1999. Japan's enhanced regional role has led to considerable anxiety among Chinese analysts. First, as they see it, the possibility that both the United States and Japan might intervene in a conflict in the Taiwan Strait on behalf of Taipei cannot be discounted. Second, Chinese security planners suggest that the new defence guidelines may only be the first major step by Japan to shed existing political restraints that may ultimately lead the country to again become a 'normal' rather than remain a 'civilian' power. Meanwhile, Reinhard Drifte (2000: 455) has argued that American moves to strengthen the alliance make Japan 'run the risk of entrapment', in the sense that Japan's ability to reach and take independent decisions on China is increasingly circumscribed.

Chinese analysts and policy-makers clearly are also concerned about Washington's efforts to upgrade existing forms of security co-operation with a number of countries in Southeast Asia and other areas along China's periphery. China has, for example, loudly protested against recent military exercises between the navies of the Philippines and the U.S. that have again become possible in the wake of the ratification of the Visiting Forces Agreement by the Philippine Senate. From Beijing's perspective, these manoeuvres imply that Washington is no longer acting in a manner of passive neutrality as it did in the past. Accordingly, Chinese officials have attempted to restrict such exercises, by including a relevant formulation in a regional code of conduct that ASEAN member states, and particularly the Philippines, have sought to agree with the PRC. Apart from following with suspicion the strengthening by Washington of its existing network of alliances, Chinese analysts and policy makers have also watched with some apprehension the increasing influence of the United States in Central Asia, mediated through the NATO Partnership for Peace programme. Chinese analysts also took note of the strategic intent underlying President Clinton's South Asia initiative of rebuilding and enhancing relationships, especially with India (Yang 2000).

Washington also poses a challenge to Chinese leaders in so far as successive U.S. administrations have pursued a policy of 'peaceful evolution' and in this context sought to undermine the legitimacy of CCP rule, not least by sustained attacks on China's human rights record.[6] For Beijing the embedded challenge of such castigation is twofold: first, external criticism may lead to a possible loss of international standing of the PRC even when the allegations are publicly repudiated. Second, it is also seen as encouraging dissidence within the country. Not surprisingly, therefore, Chinese leaders were adamant to avoid in March 2000 a verbal censuring by the United

Nations Human Rights Commission in Geneva. For similar reasons, Chinese authorities have also gone to considerable length in 'justifying' the repression of the Falungong movement to both domestic and international audiences.[7] Beyond the annoyance that stems from verbal interference, Beijing has also been worried about the mutually reinforcing propositions that NATO should be considering out of area operations and that strict interpretations of the principle of non-interference are untenable in a modern globalised world. These propositions pose a security challenge to Beijing in so far as they herald further erosion of the principle of sovereignty, a principle that has served Beijing as a normative shield. There is moreover a fear that international discourse on the issues at stake could be redirected to embolden advocates of Taiwan independence as well as those bent on ethnic unrest in some of China's border areas, especially in Xinjiang and Tibet (Karmel 2000b).

From an analytical point of view, security concerns do not appear to be the only determinant underlying the uncertainty and instability of Sino-U.S. relations. Arguably, there is also a psychological dimension to this instability. The context here is the antagonism between Washington's prescriptions for regional order and Beijing's struggle for recognition as a major power.

Chinese resentment at U.S. power and policy

Chinese policy-makers and analysts generally believe that the United States is seeking to deny Beijing its core ambitions. First, Washington is seen as playing a major part in preventing the mainland's reunification with Taiwan (see next section). Maintaining the status quo is seen to be in the interest of the United States because reunification would lead to a significant strengthening of China's position in the world economy and international politics. Similarly, the Chinese leadership is intensely dissatisfied with what it perceives as efforts by the United States to circumscribe its role in East Asia and beyond. While perhaps not aspiring to the restoration of the Middle Kingdom, Chinese leaders continue to struggle for recognition as the premier regional power in East Asia. Third, Chinese decision-makers resent that Washington ignores what the former believe to be important concessions favouring U.S. security interests, particularly in the area of non-proliferation, while being purposefully oblivious of Beijing's legitimate if not vital security interests. Accusing Washington of a 'double standard', PRC leaders in particular do not see the United States as having adequately reciprocated for Beijing's termination or suspension of supply of nuclear and missile technologies to the Middle East and South Asia (Bullard 2000).

This section has argued that the instability and uneasiness underlying Sino-U.S. bilateral relationship not only arises from different strategic perspectives, but also from Chinese perceptions that Washington disregards

China's vital interests, while simultaneously seeking to enhance its own security,[8] and to make permanent U.S. regional primacy. Taiwan is of particular significance in this regard. The next section therefore explores in greater detail the Sino-American conflict over the Taiwan issue.

The Taiwan issue

PRC leaders are adamant that Taiwan is an inalienable part of China and that ultimately Beijing must exercise full sovereignty over the island. The preamble to the 1993 Constitution of the People's Republic identifies 'the great task' of reunification as the 'inviolable duty of all Chinese people'. This is significant in so far as nationalism has for some years served Beijing as the major replacement ideology for socialism to the extent that the pursuit of nationalist objectives has accorded the CCP a measure of legitimacy in the eyes of the wider Chinese public. Notably, while Chinese leaders are committed to peaceful reunification, they have under certain circumstances reserved the right to use force against Taiwan. These include a grave turn of events leading to the separation of Taiwan from China in any name, the invasion and occupation of Taiwan by foreign countries, and the refusal of the Taiwan authorities, *sine die*, to pursue the peaceful settlement of cross-Strait reunification through negotiation (Taiwan Affairs Office 2000). The PRC has also indicated its preparedness to use force should Taiwan acquire nuclear weapons. Most observers and analysts believe that China would resort to war even if the leadership thought it would lose this war on the battlefield. As Philip Saunders (2000b: 9) put it, 'Losing a war but maintaining domestic legitimacy [is] better than not fighting and losing legitimacy.'

By contrast, the United States considers 'any effort to determine the future of Taiwan by other than peaceful means, including by boycotts or embargoes, a threat to the peace and security of the Western Pacific area and of grave concern to the United States' (*Taiwan Relations Act* 1979). While encouraging peaceful reunification, Washington is committed to provide Taiwan with defensive arms. This commitment builds on several motivations including Taiwan's strategic value, the island's former status as a U.S. ally, and its process of democratisation since the 1980s. Linked to these are also considerations about the perceived need to demonstrate credibility in defending democracy, not least with a view to relations with Japan and South Korea.

Identifying prolonged procrastination to enter into negotiations over reunification as a reason to use force against Taipei, as Beijing did in its White Paper on the 'One-China' principle and the Taiwan issue, produced a firm reaction in Washington, with warnings of 'incalculable consequences' (Glaser 2000a).[9] This reaffirmed the stance of strategic ambiguity adopted by the United States in relation to the possible defence of Taiwan. As the

Pentagon Report on the Implementation of the Taiwan Relations Act (2000) makes clear, Washington is very seriously considering the role of U.S. forces in deterring the use of force or in assisting Taiwan if deterrence fails (U.S. Department of Defence 2000).[10] This was of course also already clearly illustrated by the dispatching of two U.S. aircraft carrier battle groups in March 1996 in response to missile exercises by the PLA Navy off the Taiwanese coast.

U.S. arms sales

A key issue regarding Taiwan in Sino-U.S. relations is Washington's arms sales to Taipei and Beijing's view of how such sales might influence the prospects of reunification. As noted, Washington's continued commitment to make available to Taiwan such defence articles and services in such quantity as may be necessary to enable Taiwan to maintain a sufficient self-defence capability is beyond doubt. Significantly, the United States has also stated that it takes its obligation to assist Taiwan in maintaining a sufficient self-defence capability very seriously not only because it is so mandated by U.S. law, but also because 'it is in our own national interest' (U.S. Department of Defence 2000). In practical terms, this stance has been translated into the sale of sophisticated weaponry, including the 150 F-16s sold to Taipei by the administration under George Bush, the sale of Knox-class frigates and that of the Modified Air Defence System. Since 1994, the U.S. has, inter alia, also provided Taiwan with 'non-hardware' programmes in defence planning, C4I, anti-submarine warfare, and air defences. Meanwhile, Beijing has charged that these weapons sales contravene the 1982 communiqué in which Washington agreed that arms sales would 'not exceed, either in qualitative and quantitative terms,' the level of those supplied to Taiwan between 1979 and 1982.

Beijing's apprehensions

Beijing feels that Washington's arms sales to Taipei are feeding the latter's 'creeping independence'. At worst, the decision-makers in Beijing seem to believe that they are a factor in making Taipei more indisposed to seek a political compromise on Taiwan's future than might otherwise be expected. In other words, U.S. arms sales to Taiwan have at least as much if not more of a political than a strictly military dimension. The significance accorded to Taipei's arms purchases from the United States thus depends on Beijing's dual assessment of the domestic political context in Taiwan and Washington's interpretation in practice of the 'One-China' principle.

As regards the former, many Chinese analysts and decision-makers continue to perceive in Taiwan a trend toward independence. Many also feel a sense of impotence in reversing the rise of a Taiwanese identity separate from China, let alone in arresting the development of competing visions of national identity in Taiwan (Hughes 1997). Given its starting point of 'One China', Beijing vilified former Taiwan leader Lee Teng-hui for arguing that relations between Taipei and Beijing were those of 'state-to-state' or 'special state-to-state' relations. The defeat of the Kuomintang (KMT) incumbent, Lee Teng-hui, by Chen Shui-bian, candidate of the Democratic Progressive Party (DPP), in Taiwan's presidential elections in March 2000 initially raised further concerns about the possibility that Taipei might formally declare the island's independence. However, these concerns were to some extent allayed when the newly incoming Taiwan leader opted for a conciliatory line and tone, as evidenced by his inaugural address (Chen 2000). Chen declared that as long as the CCP had no intention of using military force against Taiwan, he would not declare independence, not change the national title, not push for the inclusion of the 'state-to-state description' in the Constitution, and not promote a referendum to change the status quo. Nevertheless, Beijing has since complained about Chen's 'obscure and evasive attitude' in addressing the Taiwan issue. This is above all a reference to the reluctance of Chen to reaffirm the consensus that Beijing claims was reached on the meaning of the 'One-China' principle during the 1992 Wang–Koo dialogue. Meanwhile, PRC leaders fret about the stance of the DPP, whose members have shifted their position on independence to one that leads them to assert that Taiwan is already an independent sovereign country (Wu 2000). Chen Shui-bian has added that Taiwanese public opinion is contrary to unification with the PRC. Hence, although Beijing may relish the thought of the DPP moving away from its platform favouring a formal declaration of independence, it remained opposed to any notion of Taiwan being a separate state and worried about the further evolution of the DPP stance on cross-Strait relations.

Significantly, Chinese analysts and decision-makers have also worried that Washington's strategic ambiguity might be abandoned in favour of overt political support for Taiwanese independence. In February 2000, in a marked demonstration of bipartisan political support for Taiwan, an overwhelming majority in the U.S. House of Representatives (341–70) passed the Taiwan Security Enhancement Act (TSEA) (1999) against Beijing's protestations. Although not immediately signed into law, the TSEA poses a significant challenge to the reunification of Mainland China and Taiwan. For instance, the legislation states that the determination of the ultimate status of Taiwan must have the express consent of the people of Taiwan. The Act moreover affirms that 'it is in the national interest of the US to eliminate ambiguity and convey with clarity continued US support for Taiwan.' The TSEA also supports the provision of additional defence articles, including missile defence equipment, satellite early warning data, air defence equipment, diesel-powered submarines, and Aegis combat systems. Notably, the TSEA furthermore stresses that the determination of the nature or quantity of defence articles or defence services to be made available to Taiwan is not be made on any basis other than the defence needs of Taiwan. The TSEA thus effectively affirms the Taiwan Relations Act as superseding the 1982 communiqué.

President Clinton did vow to prevent the TSEA from becoming law in the event of Senate approval. Chinese leaders welcomed this as they have regarded the potential political implications of the TSEA as highly destabilising in so far as they hold that the supply of military hardware expressly mentioned in the Act might embolden Taiwan's leadership to declare independence or to conduct a referendum on independence. Yet, for the reasons expounded above, the Clinton administration has nevertheless sought to uphold a military balance in the Taiwan Strait. Significantly, U.S. analysts have begun to suggest that the military balance across the Taiwan Strait is shifting in Beijing's favour, not least in view of the 250–300 short-range missiles that Beijing has stationed opposite Taiwan. In April 2000, the White House therefore approved the sale of a long-distance radar system that can detect missile launches within 3000 miles. The Clinton administration moreover approved the sale of medium-range air-to-air missiles and upgraded infrared-guided Maverick anti-ship missiles (Pan and Chang 2000). However, the administration postponed selling P-3 Orion anti-submarine aircraft, diesel submarines and Aegis destroyers, which can monitor, track and engage up to 100 targets simultaneously at ranges up to around 450 km.

To thwart a possible declaration of independence by Taiwan and to gain leverage over the United States on the issue of arms sales to Taipei, Beijing's decision-makers have decided on a two-pronged approach: first, Beijing is rapidly further increasing its short-range ballistic missiles in areas facing Taiwan across the Strait. The PRC's arsenal of short-range ballistic missiles is expected to number 650 by 2005 (Shambaugh 2000: 104). For Beijing, the deployment of missiles offers one of the few credible options that conceivably might impede Taiwan from declaring independence. Significantly, whether or not the deployment of these missiles or the conduct of military exercises off Taiwan's coast actually prove counterproductive, because they harden the resolve of Taiwanese to postpone unification as long as possible, does not seem to disturb decision-makers in the PRC.

Second, the Chinese leadership has also been trying to link U.S. weapons sales to Taipei to PRC–U.S. negotiations and discussions on arms control and non-proliferation. In the meantime, Chinese civilian and military officials are seeking further assurances from Washington in relation to Taiwan beyond the reaffirmation of its 'One-China' policy and the so-called 'three noes' expressed by President Clinton when on a state visit to China in 1998. Indeed, from the Chinese perspective, this is all the more urgent as President Clinton supported Taiwan's participation in the World Health Organization in December 1999. Moreover, Beijing has warned Washington against the sale of Aegis destroyers and further anti-missile systems.

However, the United States government has not given the assurances sought, leaving the overall confidence building process between the two sides strained and Beijing suspicious of American intentions. U.S. policy-makers claim that they find it difficult to respond to China's concerns as the more exercises China conducts in the Taiwan Strait, the more pressure there is on American politicians and policy-makers to provide Taiwan with adequate defence, leading to yet further sales of weapons. The same logic is seen to apply to the deployment of Chinese missiles that might hit Taiwan. Congress in particular has been responsive to the Taiwan lobby and the growing number of studies that debate the question whether China would be able to invade and conquer Taiwan and whether the United States would intervene (e.g. O'Hanlon 2000). Not surprisingly, the United States has repeatedly urged Beijing to reduce the missile threat to Taiwan. As we shall see in the next section, the missile threat against Taiwan also provides the link for a discussion of the third of the highly contentious issues between Washington and Beijing that has further accentuated the instability of the relationship: plans for the deployment of higher-tier missile defence systems.

NMD/TMD deployment

According to the Clinton administration, National Missile Defence was designed to protect the United States against 'rogue states' that possess both a weapons of mass destruction capability as well as the requisite delivery systems to hit North America. Theatre Missile Defence was meant to offer protection from offensive missiles that might target forward-deployed American forces or U.S. allies.

Beijing opposes the deployment of both a national missile defence and a theatre missile defence system by the United States. There are military and political reasons for this. First and foremost, the deployment of NMD is seen as having the potential to undermine China's nuclear deterrence. At present China would appear to have only deployed about 20 DF-5 ICBMs (*China Nuclear Forces Guide* website). Apparently, the number of sea-launched ballistic missiles available to Beijing is also only 12–14 (Centre for Defence and International Security Studies website). Depending on how many missiles the NMD may ultimately be capable of dealing with – under the Clinton administration talk had been of up to a hundred – China can no longer take its effective second-strike capability for granted.[11] To be sure, in August 1999, Beijing test-fired the DF-31 with a range of approximately 8000km and is currently developing the DF-41. However, given the uncertainty as to what kind of NMD system the United States may ultimately choose to deploy, it is unclear in what number all of these missiles would need to be deployed to ensure the PRC's nuclear deterrence capability even if the missiles were equipped with multiple warheads. In any case, the modernisation of its strategic arsenal notwithstanding, at least some Chinese leaders would appear to prefer to spend scarce resources on economic development, not least to maintain domestic stability, than to undertake potentially massive investment to compete in a nuclear arms race. Without a credible nuclear deterrence capability, however, Beijing is open to nuclear blackmail and may be even less able to prevent American intervention in the event of a war across the Taiwan Strait.

A second reason for opposing the deployment of NMD systems concerns Russia. Chinese policy-makers have thus far been annoyed that while Washington arms control specialists under the Clinton administration had remained sensitive to Russian protests about the development of NMD, significantly less sensitivity had been demonstrated *vis-à-vis* China. Significantly, Russia's deterrence capability, unlike that of the PRC, is not put into serious question by the NMD project as planned at the time of writing. Moreover, the changes proposed by the United States to the Anti-Ballistic Missile (ABM) Treaty would allow for a limited NMD deployment, while preserving the ban against strategically significant missile defences.

For the moment, the implications of such a development for the triangular Sino-U.S.-Russian strategic relationship remains, as American analysts have argued, 'intellectual terra incognita' (Montaperto and Roberts 2000: 7, 50–53). Still, it seems safe to assume that Chinese decision-makers, against the backdrop of Beijing's self-perception as the rising regional power in East Asia, would not relish the thought of seeing their minimum deterrence eclipsed, while a perceived declining power like Russia would, as a consequence, see its prestige relatively enhanced. Beyond the political symbolism, the development of the triangular strategic relationship may also affect the quality of the Sino-Russian partnership. In military terms, for instance, there would already appear to be worries that Moscow might adapt its strategy to a first-use doctrine from its hitherto avowed no-first-use policy. It has also been argued that should Washington proceed with NMD and unilaterally abrogate the ABM Treaty, the possibility of a new arms race at the strategic level among the United States, Russia and China would only be one element of further conflict. Another might for example concern the possibility of Moscow making available existing technology to India that could result in a substantial improvement of New Delhi's deterrence posture (Montaperto and Roberts 2000: 42–43). Furthermore, China's moves toward upgrading its nuclear and missile arsenals as a result of a decision to deploy NMD is bound to effect Beijing's relations with Tokyo. Already, China's implicit admission that it is targeting Japan with nuclear weapons has significantly heightened Japan's sense of insecurity in the post-Cold War period.[12]

As regards TMD, Beijing may be prepared to generally accept its deployment to protect troops at the local theatre, but seems reluctant to endorse it at the level of countries (May 2000). Beijing has certainly vehemently rejected plans for the inclusion of Taiwan in any upper-tier missile defence architecture. The reasons for this rejection are again both military and political but the latter would seem to outweigh in importance the former. Above all, the required integration of Taiwanese command and control systems with American ones in the event of Taiwan's inclusion in any upper-tier system would amount to a *de facto* revival of the military alliance between Washington and Taipei abrogated in 1978. The point here is again that Chinese analysts fear that the formation of such a quasi-alliance might strengthen Taipei's perceived drift toward political independence.

There is another point that makes plain why political rather than military considerations are paramount in Beijing's rejection of Taiwan's participation or inclusion in an upper-tier missile defence system. This is that Taiwan already possesses lower-tier theatre missile defences. A related point is that both lower- and higher-tier missile defence systems are vulnerable to cruise missiles. As Christensen (2000: 85) has pointed out,

> even if a system of limited effect is developed, it is not at all clear that comparatively cheap countermeasures cannot defeat such a system through saturation, decoys, elusive maneuvers by ballistic missiles, or exclusive use of cruise missiles that fly below the TMD system's umbrella.

Meanwhile, to the extent that China's ballistic missile defence programme and its development of cruise missiles are continuing apace, Taiwan's assumed ability to maintain air superiority in the Taiwan Strait in the event of war and its defensive capabilities are put in doubt. Consequently, U.S. domestic pressure on the governing administration to restore the military balance by accelerating and upgrading the quality of arms sales to Taipei is likely to increase. A possible arms race across the Taiwan Strait of course has the potential to lead to war. However, any decision to engage in armed conflict, although possible, is not going to be taken lightly, not least given the stakes involved. For the PRC, an armed encounter in the Taiwan Strait is bound to have disastrous effects on the further prospects of its economic development and international trade. The last section of this chapter therefore briefly reviews the significance of Sino-U.S. economic relations.

Economic interests

China–U.S. economic relations have not been without conflict: over Chinese protectionism and the PRC's relative reluctance to liberalise, China's inadequate protection of intellectual property rights and the country's trade surplus with the United States. However, from Beijing's perspective, ever since the adoption of economic reforms, access to the huge American market has been extremely important. At the end of the 20th century, approximately thirty per cent of PRC exports were destined for the United States, making for more than just a measure of economic dependence and attendant political vulnerability (Saunders 2000a: 67–74). Also, China has sought to diversify its export markets. Its leaders have been prepared to pay the costs associated with accession to the World Trade Organisation to have permanent access to the U.S. market, including the possibility of seeking redress at the WTO dispute settlement mechanism. Indeed, it is not an overstatement to suggest that China's exports to the United States help preserve domestic stability in the PRC as exports guarantee literally millions of jobs. In a sense, therefore, the legitimacy of the CCP, which is based in large part on economic performance, depends on the continuation and further development of a strong economic relationship with the United States. Also, the current pattern of an economic asymmetrical relationship with the U.S. is meant to give way to a more prosperous and powerful Chinese state in the future. To achieve this objective, CCP leaders hope, inter alia, to continue to draw on U.S. foreign direct investment and the transfer of technology, while recognising that China's economic and technological power is hostage to the goodwill of Western regimes, markets, and suppliers (Swaine and Tellis 2000: 103). In short, without considerable investment from foreigners and trade with the outside world, China will find it difficult to further restructure its economy and make its companies competitive on a global scale. Therefore, as Robert Ross (1999: 190) put it,

> to the extent that the Chinese economy becomes dependent on the US market and US capital, the greater interest China has in maintaining cooperative relations with the United States, and thus accommodating bilateral and global US interests.

As such, the economic dimension, perhaps more than any other, provides a context for Sino-U.S. bilateral relations. Indeed, none of the other major powers with which the Chinese leadership has agreed to forge a 'strategic partnership' quite offers the PRC similar advantages stemming from economic engagement, not even Japan. For example, notwithstanding the rhetoric exchanged between Russian and Chinese leaders, Moscow remains for the time being in Chinese eyes something akin to a sick economic man, the transfer of high-tech weaponry to the PRC notwithstanding.

None of the above implies that Sino-American economic ties are, or will be, problem-free. For example, it is possible that economic friction will increase when China's WTO accession starts to bite. Even so, to Beijing, economic relations with the United States will not lose their significance. Indeed, we may assume that Chinese leaders will be highly reluctant to sacrifice the objectives that opening up its markets and the integration into the world economy are designed to achieve. That implies that the economic dimension can play an extremely important role in helping the two sides weather many storms, albeit perhaps not all.

Conclusion

This chapter has argued that Sino-U.S. relations remain uneasy and unstable at the beginning of the new millennium. Chinese leaders regard Washington's policies as the biggest obstacles to the realisation of their core nationalist objective, the unification of China, as well as to the success of Beijing's struggle for China's restoration of geopolitical centrality in Asia. Other dimensions of conflict are clearly discernible, stemming for instance from Washington's encouragement of a more assertive regional role for Japan. The political and military competition imbuing Sino-U.S. ties poses very real challenges for regional security in East Asia. Nevertheless, CCP leaders have by and large pursued a pragmatic foreign policy *vis-à-vis* Washington, in line with the PRC's broad interest in peace and economic development, and in recognition of Beijing's dependence on access to U.S. technology, capital and markets.

The question is whether the new Chinese leadership, likely to emerge from the Sixteenth Party Congress in 2002 and the National People's Congress in 2003, will want to or is able to follow the 16-character guidelines quoted at the beginning of this chapter. In particular, it is not yet clear how they would react to future crises between Beijing and Washington. And crises of course could be numerous.

It is, for example, possible that the incoming Bush presidency could unilaterally abrogate the ABM Treaty and opt for a grander version of NMD than contemplated by the Clinton administration. This might accentuate Chinese worries that Beijing's deterrence capability will be eroded or undermined and spur an arms race. Likewise, it is possible that the Bush administration could proceed to sell more highly sophisticated weapons to Taiwan or offer the latter protection against missile attack by including the island in a possible ship-based upper-tier missile defence system deployed by Washington and Tokyo. This would remove (further) the ambiguity so far demonstrated by Washington and could increase the likelihood of armed conflict. Also, it is possible that Taipei could attempt to take advantage of Sino-U.S. conflict and rivalry by becoming more assertive in arguing the case of Taiwan's independence. Pressure on Chen Shui-bian to do so could for instance arise if the Democratic Progressive Party succeeded in reversing the current KMT majority in the Legislative Yuan in its favour. This could lead to new rounds of coercive diplomacy, the outcomes of which are open to speculation. It is also possible that the socio-economic effects of China's WTO accession, as foreign business competition translates into further redundancies and workers' disillusionment, are so severe that they will induce the new leadership to play much more on nationalist outrage against the West (Miles 2000: 56–59).

Whether or not the underlying economic fundamentals of Sino-American relations prove sufficiently strong to prevent a serious fall-out in bilateral ties is an empirical question. Arguably, however, prospects for the future of Sino-US relations are not necessarily bleak if the proven resilience of ties is anything to go by. We might also, especially in the case of positive movement toward the resolution of the Taiwan conflict, expect significantly fewer strains in bilateral ties.[13] That said, great power rivalry between Washington and Beijing will probably make for an unstable and uneasy relationship in the years ahead.

Notes

1 For details on the Taiwan Strait Crisis of 1995/6, see Garver (1997) and Zhao (1999).
2 See Yahuda (1999) for an assessment of the Embassy bombing on Sino-U.S. relations.
3 See Glaser (2000b) for details of other military exchanges.
4 See Chapter 14 in this volume.
5 The term 'areas surrounding Japan' has been clarified to refer to 'situations which, if remained untouched, may bring about direct armed attack against Japan'. For this point, and a wider discussion, see Wang (2000: 340).
6 In the Foreign Operations, Export Financing and Related Programs Appropriation Act of 2001 the United States has recently made available funds for non-governmental organisations that seek to promote democracy in the PRC.
7 On the Falungong, see the website managed by Haar.
8 The following draws on Wu Xinbo (2000).
9 China's insistence that a timetable be drawn up for unification talks was widely interpreted as an ultimatum. However, since, discussions at 'track-two' level have helped to clarify that neither analysts in Beijing nor Taipei understood the term in this way. As some analysts clarified, the term merely implies an objective which everyone involved should strive to attain. The notion of a timetable served the purpose of building domestic support. On this point, see Saunders (2000b: 13).
10 According to the Pentagon Report on the Implementation of the Taiwan Relations Act, U.S. 'goals include that the PRC be persuaded against or deterred from attacking or threatening attack, that if a threat is made it is unavailing, and that if an attack is made it is unsuccessful.'
11 The number of warheads the NMD system is designed to defeat is classified. For a further discussion, see Daalder, Goldgeier and Lindsay (2000: 10).
12 For a further discussion, see Green and Furukawa (2000).
13 See Steve Tsang (2000) for an interesting proposal.

Bibliography

Bernkopf Tucker, Nancy (1998) 'A Precarious Balance: Clinton and China', *Current History*, no. 620, September 1998: 243–249.

——. (2000) 'Security Challenges for the United States, China, and Taiwan at the Dawn of the New Millennium', http://taiwansecurity.org/IS/Tucker-032400.htm.

Bullard, Monte R. (2000) 'Undiscussed Linkages: Implications of Taiwan Straits Security Activity on Global Arms Control and Nonproliferation', Center for Nonproliferation Studies, Monterey Institute of International Studies, http://cns.miis.edu/pubs/reports/illinois.htm.

Centre for Defence and International Security Studies (CDISS), Lancaster University, http://www.cdiss.org/chinabms.htm.

Chen Shui-bian (2000) Inaugural Speech, http://www.fas.org/news/taiwan/2000/e–5–20–00–8.htm.

China's National Defence in 2000, http://www.china.org.cn/e-white/2000/index.htm.

China Nuclear Forces Guide, http://www.fas.org/nuke/guide/china/index.html.

Christensen, Thomas J. (2000) 'Theater Missile Defense and Taiwan's Security', *Orbis: A Journal of World Affairs*, 44 (1): 79–90.

Daalder, Ivo H., James M. Goldgeier and James M. Lindsay (2000) 'Deploying NMD: Not Whether, But How', *Survival*, 42 (1): 6–28.

Drifte, Reinhard (2000) 'US Impact on Japanese–Chinese Security Relations', *Security Dialogue*, 31 (4): 449–462.

Funabashi, Yoichi (1999) *Alliance Adrift* (New York: Council on Foreign Relations Press).

Garver, John W. (1997) *Face Off: China, the United States, and Taiwan's Democratisation* (Seattle: University of Washington Press).

Glaser, Bonnie (1999) 'Progress Amidst Persisting Deep Suspicions', *Comparative Connections,* 1 (4), http://www.csis.org/pacfor/cc/994Qus_china.html.

——. (2000a) 'Taiwan Tops the Bilateral Agenda', *Comparative Connections*, 2 (1), http://www.csis.org/pacfor/cc/001Qus_china.html.

——. (2000b) 'Progress in PNTR Boosts Relations, But Only Slightly', *Comparative Connections*, 2 (2), http://www.csis.org/pacfor/cc/002Qus_china.html.

——. (2000c) 'Clinton and Jiang Hail PNTR Passage, but Agree on Little Else', *Comparative Connections*, 2 (3), http://www.csis.org/pacfor/cc/003Qus_china.html.

——. (2000d) 'Bilateral Relations on Reasonably Sound Footing as 2000 and the Clinton Administration Come to a Close', *Comparative Connections*, 2 (4), http://www.csis.org/pacfor/cc/004Qus_china.html.

Green, Michael J. and Katsuhisa Furukawa (2000) 'New Ambitions, Old Obstacles: Japan and Its Search For an Arms Control Strategy', *Arms Control Today*, July/August 2000, also available at http://www.foreignrelations.org/public/pubs/green_japanarms_article.html.

Gurtov, Melvin (1999) 'Fragile Partnership: The United States and China', *Asian Perspective*, 23 (2): 111–141.

Haar, Barend ter (updated 2001) 'Falun Gong: Evaluation and Further References', http://www.let.leidenuniv.nl/bth/falun.htm.

Harding, Harry (1999) 'The Uncertain Future of US–China Relations', *Asia-PacificReview*, 6 (1): 7–24.

Hughes, Christopher (1997) *Taiwan and Chinese Nationalism: National Identity and Status in International Society* (London: Routledge).

Karmel, Solomon M. (2000a) *China and the People's Liberation Army: Great Power or Struggling Developing State?* (Basingstoke and London: Macmillan).

——. (2000b) 'Ethnic Nationalism in Mainland China', in Michael Leifer (ed.) *Asian Nationalism* (London: Routledge), pp. 38–62.

Manning, Robert A., Ronald Montaperto and Brad Roberts (2000) *China, Nuclear Weapons, and Arms Control* (New York: Council on Foreign Relations).

May, Greg (2000) 'China's Opposition to TMD is More About Politics Than Missiles', *Foresight*, February 2000, at http://www.nixoncenter.org/publications/articles/2_00ChinaTMD.htm.

Miles, James (2000) 'Chinese Nationalism, US Policy and Asian Security', *Survival*, 42 (4): 51–71.

O'Hanlon, Michael (2000) 'Can China Conquer Taiwan', *International Security*, 25 (2): 51–86.

Pan, Herman and Maubo Chang (2000) 'US Agrees Sale of Arms But No Destroyers to Taiwan', CAN, 18 April 2000, http://www.fas.org/news/taiwan/2000/e-04–18-00–26.htm.

Ross, Robert S. (1999) 'Engagement in US China Policy', in Alastair Iain Johnston and Robert S. Ross (eds) *Engaging China: the Management of an Emerging Power* (London and New York: Routledge), pp. 176–206.

Saunders, Philipp C. (2000a) 'Supping with a Long Spoon: Dependence and Interdependence in Sino-American Relations', *The China Journal*, no. 43 (January 2000): 55–84.

——. (2000b) *Project Strait Talk: Security and Stability in the Taiwan Strait* (Monterey: Center for Nonproliferation Studies).

Shambaugh, David (2000) 'Sino-American Strategic Relations: From Partners to Competitors', *Survival*, 42 (1) (Spring 2000): 97–115.

Swaine, Michael D. and Ashley J. Tellis (2000) *Interpreting China's Grand Strategy: Past, Present, and Future* (Santa Monica, CA: RAND).

The One-China Principle and the Taiwan Issue (White Paper) (Beijing: Taiwan Affairs Office and the Information Office of the State Council, 21 February 2000), http://www.china-embassy.org/eng/7128.html.

Taiwan Relations Act, Public Law 96–8 96th U.S. Congress, http://ait.org.tw/ait/tra.html.

Taiwan Security Enhancement Act, http://taiwansecurity.org/IS/IS–991026-TSEA.htm.

Tsang, Steve (2000) 'China and Taiwan: A Proposal for Peace', *Security Dialogue*, 31 (3): 327–336.

U.S. Department of Defence (1998) *East Asia Strategy Report*, http://www.defenselink.mil/pubs/easr98/index.html.

——. (2000) *Pentagon Report on the Implementation of the Taiwan Relations Act for the fiscal year ending 30 September 2000*, http://www.fas.org/news/taiwan/2000/taiwan-001219.htm.

Wang Qing Xin Ken (2000) 'Japan's Balancing Act in the Taiwan Strait', *Security Dialogue*, 31 (3): 337–342.

Wu, Sofia (2000) 'DPP Does Not Rule Out 'Unification' as Option for Taiwan's Future', Central News Agency, 6 September 2000, htpp://www.fas.org/news/taiwan/2000/roc-00906-prc2.htm.

Wu Xinbo (2000) 'U.S. Security Policy in Asia: Implications for China–U.S. Relations', http://www.brook.edu/fp/cnaps/papers/2000_wu.htm.

Yahuda, Michael (1999) 'After the Embassy Bombing', *China Review*, no. 14, http://www.gbc.org.uk/yahuda14.htm.

Yang Haisheng (2000) 'An Attention-Getting Readjustment of U.S. Policy Towards South Asia', *International Strategic Studies* (Beijing), no. 3 (July 2000): 31–35.

Zhao Suisheng (ed.) (1999) *Across the Taiwan Strait: Mainland China, Taiwan, and the 1995–96 Crisis* (London and New York: Routledge).

Chapter 13

Re-assessing the Sino-Japanese Axis in the New Strategic Triangle

A Case for Peaceful Co-existence?

Caroline Rose

Introduction

The China–Japan relationship is often viewed as prone to history-related problems and to potential conflict given disputes over territory. In particular it is often considered to be the weak link in the US–Japan–China triangle. This chapter offers a different perspective and suggests that Sino-Japanese relations are fairly robust and able to cope with the challenges posed by history, territory and security issues.

Overview: the new strategic triangle and Sino-Japanese relations

By the mid-1990s, the strategic triangle (comprising the USSR, United States and PRC) which had dominated during the Cold War gave way to the emergence of a new strategic triangle in which Japan moved into position in place of the defunct USSR. The nature of interaction within this new triangle has attracted a growing amount of attention amongst academics, analysts and policy makers, and a consensus has emerged that the US–China–Japan relationship is the key to security and stability of the Asia Pacific region (Rozman 1999: 393; Christensen 1999; Hughes 2000; Kokubun 1997; Zhang 1997).

Many Western, and a number of Japanese, analysts tend to agree on the roles that Japan, China and the US play in the triangle. For example, much has been written about the US' *primary role* in the 'management' of China's rise, and the US is often seen as playing the key role of stabiliser (or sometimes de-stabiliser) in the three-way relationship. Zhang and Montaperto argue, for example, that US policy toward Japan and China could determine peace or war between Japan and China, and therefore, between the three major powers (Zhang and Montaperto 1999: 118). Japan is often viewed as a bridge between the US and China, acting as mediator or facilitator (for example in bringing China back onto the international stage after the Tiananmen Square incident, or facilitating its entry into the WTO). But Japan is also seen as China's chief rival for power in East Asia, and therefore the role of the US in balancing potential conflict between the two regional hegemons is seen as crucial. China's role in the triangle is often viewed as 'problematic', and the task of managing the rise of a superpower is seen to fall to the US, with Japan playing a secondary role.

There is further agreement on the nature of the bilateral relationships within the triangle. Often seen as a 'two-against-one,' hostile triangle, the relationships and power distribution between the three sides are unequal. As far as the dynamics of the triangle are concerned, the US–Japan link is often considered to be the strongest, whereas the links between the US and China on the one hand, and Japan and China on the other, are seen as the weaker sides of the triangle. In some cases the US–China side of the triad is perceived as the most fragile relationship of the three, but more often the Sino-Japanese axis is viewed as the weakest.[1]

The 'weak link' hypothesis is, of course, supported by historical precedent. It is further strengthened by a widely-held assumption that Sino-Japanese relations have yet to evolve beyond Cold War style face-offs, and that historical experience has created mutual perceptions (or misperceptions) of each other's capabilities and intentions which continue to dominate, and disrupt, bilateral interaction. China and Japan have no security alliance, but do have ongoing territorial disputes. China's Japan-watchers tend to see the US–Japan alliance as one aimed at containing China, a two-against-one scenario. This view was strengthened by the revision of the US–Japan defence guidelines in the mid-1990s and US–Japanese joint research and development on Theatre Missile Defence (TMD) in the late 1990s. Some Japanese academics and politicians, on the other hand, see China's rapid economic growth, military modernisation and 'creeping assertiveness' in the South China Sea as potentially threatening to regional stability.

Such arguments are frequently cited as the sources of potential tension between China and Japan, but they tend to overlook an underlying stability in the relationship. The aim of this chapter is to temporarily divorce Sino-Japanese relations from the strategic triangle and question the notion that the China–Japan link is the 'weak link'. The argument starts from the assumption that *continuities* in post-World War II Sino-Japanese political and economic relations provided a stable foundation for the relationship in the late 20th and early 21st century. In the nearly 30 years since the signing of the 1972 Joint Statement, Sino-Japanese relations have strengthened and deepened. Despite periodic problems and crises, governments on both sides have been able to avert serious, long-term disruption to the relationship. Although the end of the Cold War provided the bilateral relationship with a different international environment in which to operate, the manner in which issues emerged and were resolved between the two governments did not appear to undergo fundamental change. Those thorny history-related issues, which continued to trouble the relationship in the 1990s, were not remarkably different from those of the 1980s – either in terms of the way they manifested themselves, or in the ways in which they were resolved. Moreover, new problems (e.g. security), which presented themselves in the 1990s as a result of the new international environment and domestic developments within China and Japan, still appeared to be very much bound up in 'old' issues of history and/or perceptions based on historical experience. But again, old, 'learned' patterns of behaviour facilitated a relaxation of tension and (albeit) temporary resolution of such issues.

To these continuities we must add key *changes* in Chinese and Japanese foreign policy since the end of the Cold War which contributed to positive developments in bilateral relations. Both Chinese and Japanese foreign policy in the 1990s was marked by a more pro-active stance in terms of the development of other bilateral relations and engagement in regional multilateral organisations. Such shifts in foreign policy were prone to be construed as evidence of more independent, assertive or even aggressive, and therefore potentially threatening stances (and spawned much literature on the China and Japan 'threats'). But they were also associated with positive steps towards improved bilateral links, regional confidence-building and the opportunity for greater dialogue at a number of levels.

The sum of these continuities and changes is, I argue, a stability which has allowed China–Japan relations to become increasingly intertwined at the political and social/cultural levels and increasingly interdependent in terms of trade, aid and investment. This deepening and widening of the relationship evolved in the 1990s into what I would describe as a robust relationship, able to cope with intermittent bilateral 'mini'-crises such as the history problem or security issues (which often have less to do with history, security and/or perceptions than is generally thought). This perspective is at odds with much recent literature on Sino-Japanese relations which tends to focus on the potential for conflict and the security dilemmas faced by China and Japan within the strategic triangle. The chapter therefore begins by reviewing some of the common themes in recent writing on the state of Sino-Japanese relations, and finds that in many cases the major impediment to Sino-Japanese relations is seen to be the legacy of the past, and mutual suspicions based on history. The extent to which these mutual suspicions actually affected Sino-Japanese relations in the late 1990s is considered in the next section, which offers a 'balance sheet' of the state of the relationship. It focuses on the ways in which Chinese and Japanese governments coped with or overcame problems which *seemed* to have their roots in history, but which in many cases can be explained by considering more mundane domestic political issues. The main aim of the chapter is to question the idea that Sino-Japanese interaction is a 'slave to history' by illustrating that explanations which emphasise the 'psychological' level (i.e., that the relationship is dominated by perceptions) overlook other important determinants of the relationship.

China–Japan relations: the 'weak link'?

The main starting point for the 'weak link' argument is that China and Japan continue to experience 'fundamental' problems in most facets of the relationship, and that these produce tension, instability and unpredictability. Zhao Quansheng's view of the relationship as having deteriorated throughout the 1980s and 1990s, casting 'a shadow over regional and global affairs in the post-cold war era' (despite the valiant efforts of Chinese and Japanese leadership to the contrary), is not untypical as far as assessments of Sino-Japanese relations are concerned (Zhao 2000: 25). Zhao identifies the 'usual suspects' in terms of China–Japan problems: Taiwan, territory (Senkaku islands) and 'the potential resurgence of Japanese militarism, memories of which stem from past Japanese aggression' – in other words, the legacy of history (Zhao 2000: 18). The latter point is considered particularly important in recent studies of East Asian security, which, in their application of the security dilemma or balance of threat theories, place much emphasis on the role of Chinese and Japanese mutual images and perceptions.

It all comes down to history?

The potential for conflict between China and Japan has become a predominant theme in the literature. In particular, the joint research programme undertaken by the US and Japan on Theatre Missile Defence (TMD) in the wake of the North Korea missile threat in the late 1990s spurred a great deal of academic analysis of the implications of TMD for China, Japan and the US. A common thread running through many of these studies appears to be the impact of history and the accumulation of certain fixed perceptions. For example, the Chinese 'belief' that Japan has not yet faced up to its war responsibility and is prone to revert to 1930s-style militarism is frequently cited as one of the main obstacles to an improvement in Sino-Japanese relations. Japanese perceptions of a rising, threatening China are seen to be key determinants in Japan's China policy in the 1990s. A lack of transparency and fundamental misunderstanding of each other's systems represents another common theme in the literature. The idea that a lack of mutual understanding stems from a lack of in-depth discussion and multi-layered exchange is put forward by Zhao who is not the only observer to suggest that 'neither country has a clear understanding of the nature of the other's domestic politics and foreign policy decisions' (2000: 26).[2]

The 'balance of threat' theory, which has been taken up by a number of scholars, is seen to apply not only to the way Japan responds to China, but vice versa too. The balance of threat theory posits that states balance against threats (i.e., political and military power) *plus perceived intentions* (Midford 2000: 2).[3] Midford argues that China's reaction to the US–Japan decision to revise their defence guidelines showed a tendency to balance against the threat of Japan's expanding power within the alliance and the perception based on 'robust cognitive roots' that Japan possessed malevolent intentions regarding regional security (Midford 2000: 21). Based on these assumptions then, the PRC responded with alarm to the threat of a Japan potentially free from, or at least enjoying greater autonomy within, the US alliance. In this context, the balance of threat theory relies on the idea that Chinese perceptions and beliefs about the Japan threat, themselves based on the events of history (i.e., Japan's capacity for militarism) impact upon Chinese behaviour towards Japan. Only by showing good behaviour does Japan stand a chance of reassuring its neighbours that it no longer harbours militaristic intentions and will it be able to convince its former victims of its peaceful intentions.[4] Looking at Japan's China policy in the 1990s, Michael Green (1999) argues that a balance of threat behaviour is discernible. Green suggests that Japan's foreign policy, adapted during the 1990s to cope with a changing China, is shifting away from a 'commercial liberalism' to a 'reluctant realism'. Thus Japan hedged against China's growing military and political power and the threat of China as regional hegemon by strengthening the alliance with the US, but at the same time attempted to bring China into multilateral economic organisations to avoid isolating China (Green 1999: 159–165).

The role of psychological factors (which in the context of China and Japan, Christensen describes as 'historically based mistrust and animosity') is often considered to be particularly important to an understanding of the security dilemma[5] facing Northeast Asia in the 1990s. China's 'historically rooted and visceral distrust of Japan', 'Tokyo's refusal to respond satisfactorily to Chinese requests that Tokyo recognize and apologize for its imperial past', are, according to Christensen, at the heart of the problem, and will prevent China and Japan from forming close ties in the near future (Christensen 1999). A similar view is expressed by Kim Taeho who argues that rivalry and distrust are linked to 'deeply ingrained cultural, historical and perceptual factors' rather than shared economic or strategic interests, and are therefore more difficult to control (Kim 1998: 361). Wu Xinbo also accounts for the strong mutual suspicions between China and Japan in terms of history, memory and lingering negative perceptions – China's memory of Japan's aggression and perception of Japan's national character as 'exclusivist and resistant to external pressure', and Japanese suspicions that China still 'embraces the traditional "Middle Kingdom mentality"' (Wu 2000: 308).

This small sample of recent literature suggests a common view that China and Japan are heading inexorably towards conflict or, at least, rivalry due to unchanging attitudes based on history and perceptions of history. While it is difficult to deny that developments in the mid-1990s did seem to suggest an increasing tension, relatively little attention has been paid to positive progress made in various aspects of the relationship. For this we need to consider continuities in the way Chinese and Japanese governments have come to deal with one another. Understanding patterns of behaviour is crucial to an understanding of the way the relationship is likely to evolve in the future. The aim of this chapter is certainly not to deny the possibility that tension may develop in the future, but merely to address the widely held belief that Sino-Japanese relations are particularly vulnerable to history given the problem of fixed beliefs and perceptions of the other side's power capabilities and intentions. Indeed one question missing from recent analyses is that *despite* problems associated with history and lingering mutual suspicions, Sino-Japanese relations have not been seriously harmed. The remainder of the chapter suggests two possible reasons for this: first that history is not really the crux of the matter, and second that both sides have developed a set of 'coping' behaviours to avert a downward spiral of tension.

Issues in Sino-Japanese relations in the late 1990s – a balance sheet

Contrary to appearances, in many ways the post-Cold War Sino-Japanese relationship, though not without its problems, has been far more stable than it is often portrayed, and it has also often been more predictable than Sino-US relations. Though acknowledging Chinese continued resentment of Japanese reluctance to face up to the past, Wang Jisi notes that, compared with Beijing–Washington relations, 'the atmosphere of Sino-Japanese official relations in the last few years has been markedly better' (Wang 1998: 28). The economic aspect is without doubt the strongest, most stable aspect of the relationship, the political and security aspects less so, although in recent years trade and aid have emerged as potentially divisive issues. The next section considers some of the strengths and weaknesses of various aspects of the relationship in the late 1990s.

Economic relations: trade, aid and investment

This is perhaps the strongest and least problematic aspect of the relationship. The volume of trade reached its highest level in 1999 of over 66 billion dollars (up 16% on the previous year). Japan's aid and direct investment continue to be an essential, and increasingly valued, source of funding for China's modernisation programme (Jetro 2000: 21). One aim of Zhu Rongji's visit to Japan in October 2000 was to encourage further economic co-operation, and secure greater Japanese investment in the Chinese hinterland by pledging to improve the investment environment in China. Prior to his visit the Japanese government agreed to a 17.2 billion yen loan, the latest tranche of the ongoing special yen loan packages first implemented under Prime Minister Massayoshi Ohira in the 1970s.[6]

On the downside though, the economic relationship is not without its problems. Japanese investors have been reluctant to become involved in what they regard as a relatively unstable investment environment in China, and fingers have been burned on a number of occasions. During his Japan trip in October 2000, Zhu made reference to the problem of the default by Hainan International Trust and Investment Corporation on its 'samurai yen-dominated bonds' which he attributed to China's economic bubble of 1993.[7] Similarly during Kono Yohei's trip to China earlier in the year (May 2000), the Foreign Minister alluded to the damaged caused to Japanese investors as a result of the failure of the Guangdong International Trust and Investment Corporation (Przystup 2000b: 90). Losses incurred by Japanese banks through collapse of these and several other International Trade and Investment Corporations is estimated to have amounted to over 4 billion yen, and continues to be a source of concern for existing and potential investors (Przystup 2000a: 78). To that end, Prime Minister Mori Yoshiro urged Zhu Rongji to ensure reliable debt repayment (from investment trust firms), in addition to easing restrictions on steel imports and allowing Japanese insurance companies into China.

Another potential problem is related to Japan's aid provision to China. Deng Xiaoping explicitly linked Chinese demands for – or rather expectations of – Japanese economic assistance in the early 1980s by raising the spectre of 'historical debt'. Japan soon became, and continues to be, China's largest aid donor. But it seems that there is a growing sense of 'aid fatigue' among LDP diet men who are increasingly unhappy with the high levels of ODA going to China. Their frustration seems to be concerned with the lack of appreciation from the Chinese side, especially when the aid continues to be supplied despite the poor health of the Japanese economy. In addition, concerns have been voiced about growing Chinese military expenditure. The ODA 'debate' within the LDP continued into late 2000, with some diet men discussing the possibility of attaching conditions to aid for China. If Japan did want to get tough on aid to China it could do so by invoking the 1992 ODA charter which makes aid conditional upon recipients' military expenditure and democratic credentials. Indeed, Foreign Minister Kono raised the issue with a surprised Tang Jiaxuan in May 2000, observing that China's increased military spending and high economic growth was cause for Japan to reconsider its aid provision.[8] In addition, ODA is being linked with China's handling of the 'history problem' inasmuch as 'China's handling of the history issue is used to strengthen the argument for reducing ODA to China, as some 1.8 trillion yen of Japanese taxpayers' money since 1978 seems to have done little to cultivate the Chinese goodwill, let alone forgiveness for Japan's past wrongs' (Yang 2000: 8–9).[9]

The history problem

Whereas the economic sphere presents relatively few controversies in Sino-Japanese relations, the same cannot be said for the 'history problem'.[10]

Many of the key controversies in Sino-Japanese relations in the 1990s related in some way to history. References to 'the history problem' (*lishi wenti; rekishi mondai*) or 'history awareness' (*lishi yishi; rekishi ishiki*) began to appear more frequently in official statements and documents, in the media and in Chinese and Japanese academic accounts of the 'state of the relationship'. To be sure, there appeared to be sufficient indication that Chinese and Japanese perceptions of the past remained as far apart as ever. But history-related problems were by no means new, and were not necessarily any more threatening to the stability of the relationship in the 1990s than in previous decades. Indeed, it is possible to argue that regular occurrence of such issues enabled both sides to develop a means of 'coping' and of avoiding escalation. In many respects this was due to the fact that these recurring problems actually had far less to do with history than with internal domestic dynamics on both sides in addition to external, international stimuli.

The 'history problem' concerns the perennial issue of the legacy of history and its almost constant presence at the top of the diplomatic agenda since the 1980s. The 1980s saw almost annual instalments of wrangles over textbooks, apologies, LDP Diet members' gaffes and so on. These continued into the 1990s. The wording of apologies by Japanese Prime Ministers (since 1993) or the Emperor (1992) remained a bone of contention at summit meetings. The interpretation of China–Japan history in Japanese school textbooks (in the 1990s this concerned the plight of 'comfort women')[11] or historical revisionism in the Japanese intellectual community,[12] in addition to (Prime) Ministerial visits to the Yasukuni Shrine and so on, also continued to upset diplomatic relations.[13] Some new problems also came to the fore (or, perhaps more accurately) new expressions of old problems in the 1990s. The resurgence of nationalism in both China and Japan produced a greater focus on and sensitivity to issues related to national identity and sovereignty and these were easily inflamed either by the government or at the popular level. In addition, compensation cases (for example of former comfort women and forced labourers) and 'new' research (for example on Unit 731, biological/chemical warfare and the Nanjing Massacre) were brought into the international arena, marking a new trend.[14]

Such issues were rarely out of the press in the 1990s, but progress on the matter of history was, nonetheless, discernible. Yang Daqing argues that 'Since Jiang's visit in late 1998, the history issue has taken a back seat, as the Chinese government seems to have undergone a policy shift toward Japan' (2000: 33). Johnston also argues that, largely due to generational change, history is losing its power in terms of Beijing being able to play the 'history card' and Japan giving in to its guilt complex.

There are a growing number of instances which point to an increase in co-operation on history matters at the elite/diplomatic level and a willingness on both sides to reach a compromise. Examples could include chemical weapons negotiations, which have been lengthy but nonetheless 'successful', without the issue having been transformed into a symbolic reminder of the nature of Japan's warfare in China. Yang Daqing points to further positive steps towards some sort of reconciliation at the political level, for example former Prime Minister Murayama's visit to the Marco Polo Bridge Memorial, Hashimoto's visit to Northeast China (the first Prime Minister to do so since the war) and former LDP Secretary General Nonaka Hiromu's visit to the Nanjing Massacre Museum in May 1998 (Yang 1998).

Other positive signs in the 1990s were the more restrained reactions of the Chinese government to normally sensitive issues (for example during the 1996 instalment of the Senkaku issue). In particular, the reluctance of the Chinese government to allow anti-Japan protests to get out of hand was noticeable. Of course, one could account for this by looking at the Chinese leadership's domestic reasons (to prevent such actions from turning into anti-governmental protest) rather than viewing it merely as a good public relations exercise, but it did have the effect of maintaining stability in the relationship, and perhaps even building some goodwill.

Further research is still required, but it seems that restraint is also being shown in the Chinese press which in recent years has tended *not* to play up significant anniversaries (such as the September 18th Incident taken by the Chinese as the start of the Japanese invasion in 1931). One such example can be seen in the *China Daily* edition of 19 September 2000, in which a story on page 2 entitled 'Japanese prisoners of war rue misdeeds' told of a ceremony held at a former prisoner of war prison in Fushun at which Japanese delegates expressed remorse for Japan's invasion. This represents a fairly positive Chinese take on the war issue, illustrating that even ex-military are now willing and able to acknowledge Japan's history. It should be noted that this was juxtaposed with the inclusion of a brief report (on the same page) referring to a recently discovered map commemorating the enthronement of the 'emperor' of Manchuria state – thus providing 'evidence of Japan's invasion'.

Chinese official and press response to Prime Minister Mori's 'gaffes'[15] was also restrained, and the visit of key Japan-watcher Zeng Qinghong in April 2000 underlined a willingness not to dwell on the matter of history (Przystup, 2000b: 94–5). Zhu Rongji's visit to Japan in mid-October 2000 provided further indication that the Chinese leadership was willing to move on as far the history issue is concerned and focus, instead, on economic matters. That said, Zhu Rongji did manage to send mixed signals on the question of apology. In a television interview Zhu stated that 'Japan has never apologised to the Chinese people in any of the official documents' and that former Prime Minister Murayama's 1995 statement (made prior to the announcement of the Diet resolution) did not qualify as an apology to the Chinese people (since it was directed to Asian people at large).[16] He was later reported to have toned down that comment, stating rather that 'China has always highly valued the 1995 statement. Our goal is not to demand an apology. Our goal is to deepen our friendship by learning from history'.[17] Such ambivalence on the apology issue is not new, but the history issue did not dominate Zhu's visit as it had Jiang's visit two years earlier (see below). Instead Zhu Rongji came to Japan, the Japanese press reported, 'hoping to improve China's standing in the eyes of the Japanese people' – in other words to make amends for Jiang's public relations disaster of 1998.

In many respects then, evidence of progress on the history issue can be seen in the Chinese government's mild reaction, or even 'non-action', on the sorts of issues which have previously been prone to protest and demands. Perhaps this is not surprising – the extent to which history was allowed to disrupt China–Japan relations in the 1980s and 1990s depended largely on domestic political issues and/or external stimuli. The history 'problem' came in cycles and was very often used as a tool for domestic political manipulation (in both China and Japan) or leverage on another foreign policy issue. A few examples should help to illustrate this.

The textbook issue of 1982, for example, should be analysed within domestic political contexts of the time. Both the Chinese and Japanese governments were in the throes of 'patriotic education campaigns' (themselves designed to shore up legitimacy of the respective incumbent governments), and the topic of school history textbooks became a highly symbolic issue which struck at the heart of national identity. The issue was sparked off by erroneous reporting in the Japanese press, which alleged that the phrase 'invasion of China' had been changed by the Japanese Ministry of Education to 'advance into China'. These reports were eventually picked up by the Chinese government which lodged a diplomatic protest and launched a rigorous anti-Japanese media campaign. The Japanese response was to send various delegations to China to explain the workings of the Japanese education system and apart from a minor amendment to the guidelines on curriculum content, no major alterations were made to history textbooks as a result of China's protests.

One other history-related issue concerns Jiang Zemin's state visit to Japan in November 1998 and the debacle over the apology issue. Jiang's visit took place one month after the highly successful visit of President Kim Dae-Jung during which the Korean and Japanese governments had agreed to 'settle the past' and place Japan–Korea relations on a new footing. In the immediate run-up to Jiang's visit the Japanese and Chinese speculated on whether the history problem between Japan and China could be resolved in the same way. This was not to be the case, however, and Jiang's visit provided a stark contrast to Kim's with the wording of the Japanese apology becoming the main sticking point of the trip.[18] There are a number of explanations for the reluctance of both sides to 'give in'. Obuchi was faced by pressure from the LDP who are not inclined to apologise yet again to China, especially when the issue has been settled in the 1972 Joint Statement and the 1978 Peace and Friendship Treaty. This sentiment was echoed in both public opinion and the media which questioned the number of times the Japanese were expected to apologise to China. Having pulled off a diplomatic coup with President Kim in October, Obuchi was not keen to lose the support of the public on China by engaging in a grovelling diplomacy with China.

As far as the Chinese side goes, it could be that Jiang Zemin was genuinely interested in persuading his Japanese counterparts to adopt the correct view of history and apologise. But there are more convincing arguments for his stance. It is likely that Jiang Zemin used the 'history card' because it was politically useful for him to do so, and it enabled him to achieve a number of domestic political objectives. Nakamura, for example, suggests that Jiang's nitpicking on the apology/aggression issues (as well as his insistence on the inclusion of Taiwan 'clauses') related more to problems at home than to fundamental problems of 'history consciousness' in the China–Japan relationship (for example, Jiang's need to consolidate his authority and support from certain sections of the PLA and conservative factions by 'being tough' on Japan (*Asahi Shimbun*, 24 November 1998, p. 2)). So both Obuchi's and Jiang's positions are probably better understood within a domestic context: Jiang was able to score valuable points at home by being tough on Japan, and Obuchi was able to buoy his popularity by not giving in to Chinese demands.

Media reporting on the issue described the Jiang–Obuchi summit as a total embarrassment for the Japanese government, but it should be stressed that the issue did not in fact cause irreparable damage to Sino-Japanese relations. In fact, Jiang was heavily criticised in some Western and Japanese media for dwelling too much on the history issue. Nonetheless, in diplomatic-speak, the relationship achieved its 'upgrade' to a friendly co-operative partnership. The history problem did not impede the more than satisfactory economic and cultural ties furthered during the 1998 summit, and Obuchi's return visit to China in the following year was marked by the complete avoidance of the history problem. It should also be noted that the history problem is not guaranteed to flare up when a reckless remark is made or an apology not given. Note for example Jiang Zemin's relatively muted response to the remarks made by Ministers Sakurai and Nagano in 1994 at which time he merely stressed that 'the bonds of friendship between China and Japan must be developed while keeping in mind the past as an admonishment for the future' (*Japan Times Weekly*, 16–22 May 1994, pp. 1–5).

What these examples illustrate is that often seemingly unrelated domestic or external factors impact upon issues in Sino-Japanese relations, which are then played out in an almost routine manner.[19] On the history problem at least, Harris's argument that 'the two countries' current foreign policies and postures owe at least as much to other factors as to concerns about each other' (Harris 1997: 130) is convincing.

The security issues

It is difficult to argue against the burgeoning consensus that security represents the weakest aspect of Sino-Japanese relations. Since the end of the Cold War, a series of security-related issues do seem to have strengthened the case for, rather than against this argument. To name but a few, Chinese increases in arms expenditure and its military modernisation programme, the strengthening of the US–Japan alliance, the expansion of Japan's role within the alliance, mutual threat perceptions (the China/Japan threat discussions), Chinese suspicions about the US–Japan TMD programme, Japanese concerns about China's nuclear weapons programme and its stance on Taiwan, the regular flare-ups of the Senkaku Islands dispute, and so on, have contributed to the potential for a spiralling of tension in the region. Nonetheless, signs of 'coping' strategies and of 'regularised' patterns of behaviour *are* discernible. In addition, progress towards an albeit fledgling security dialogue can be identified.

One example of a form of 'coping strategy' can be found in the Japanese response to China's vocal concerns regarding the revision of the US–Japan Defense Guidelines – specifically the provisions for US–Japan cooperation in case of an armed attack against Japan and 'areas surrounding Japan'. China's adverse reaction to the ambiguity concerning Taiwan's inclusion in the Japan–US security sphere was persistent and prolonged, but tension was defused by what Hughes describes as Japan's policy of 'managing' the issue in such a way as to provide room for 'strategic manoeuvre' and to 'avoid final conflict scenarios' (2000: 8). This, Hughes argues, was achieved by a 'hedging strategy', whereby Japanese officials, whose job it was to appease their Chinese counterparts, left the definition of 'areas surrounding Japan' highly ambiguous (referring to it as a situational rather than a geographical referent). The outcome of the hedging strategy was successful inasmuch as Chinese policy makers were (fairly) convinced that 'Japan may still not align itself too closely with the US' and China 'retained some room for manoeuvre in order to protect its national interests' (Hughes 2000: 33). In a manner reminiscent of the handling of history-related disputes, it would seem that Japanese officials adopted a similar strategy in the security sphere (that is, ambiguously-worded explanations) when high levels of tension appeared to demand it.

There are other similarities between the history issues noted above, and security-related issues – specifically the Senkaku Islands dispute (Diaoyu-tai).

In particular the regular appearance of such issues and the almost ritualised manner in which they are handled by both sides is notable. The Senkaku island issue flared up in the mid-1990s and continues to be a 'potential' flashpoint in the 21st century, but analyses of the various disputes (from the 1970s through to the 1990s) suggest that the reasons behind each flare-up and the manner in which they are resolved have become 'ritualised', symbolic, and, very often, have little to do with territorial concerns.[20]

As noted in regard to the ODA debate above, the activities of Chinese maritime research vessels and PLA warships in Japan's international waters were of increasing concern to Japanese politicians in 2000. In reply to Japanese governmental protestations, the Chinese official responses were, variously, that the ships were within their rights to be there (i.e. there was no violation of international law), and that the central government was not aware of PLA navy activities (and has no jurisdiction over PLAN anyway). The Japanese view was that the activities were 'openly provocative', particularly because prior notification by the Chinese side had not been provided. The issue escalated through 2000, spilling over into the economic sphere as the LDP delayed agreement on the loan package. In addition, the issue made it into the Defence White Paper 2000, indicating the seriousness with which it was viewed by the military in Japan (Przystup 2000b: 93).

This is not to say, however, that the issue will necessarily escalate, and it is wise to put this and previous instalments of the Senkaku island dispute into a broader context. Valencia provides a succinct summary of the various maritime disputes in Northeast Asia which threaten the stability of the region, and outlines the underlying causes of the disputes. He points to the potential resources (fish, oil, gas) contained in Exclusive Economic Zones but, more importantly perhaps, also refers to 'unassuaged historical grievances and the politics of national identity' bound up in these disputes (2000: 5). The Diaoyu-tai have become a powerful symbolic reminder to the Chinese of Japan's militarist past. This was particularly the case in 1996 when the Japanese government was seen to take an intransigent stance on the lighthouse problem, thereby strengthening 'widespread resentment ... of what is perceived as Japan's ongoing failure to confront and deal satisfactorily with its militarist past'. In addition, Valencia argues that these disputes originate from '*unrelated domestic political agendas*' (italics added), whereby politicians seek to achieve domestic political goals through manipulation of what is often very genuine popular sentiment (Valencia 2000: 5). In the 2000 'instalment' of the issue, then, it could be argued that certain LDP legislators played up the activities of Chinese vessels not out of concern for national sovereignty *per se*, but to enable them to pursue their domestic goals of, for example, reducing aid levels to China overall or appealing to anti-China sentiment amongst the public. Clearly, these domestic political agendas differ according to the situation, but they do help to explain the extent to which either side appears willing to pursue the issue (and play it up in the media). Importantly, these agendas suggest that this issue is not likely to lead to hostilities in the near future.[21]

There is also room for optimism in the form of an emerging security dialogue between China and Japan. Starting in 1993, both sides agreed to hold regular high-level security meetings. Separate meetings of Foreign and Defence Ministry personnel took place in the early years of the dialogue, but in 1996 joint sessions were instituted and became a useful forum for explaining defense policies and discussion of such sensitive issues as the Senkaku islands (Ross 1996: 7–8). Although these meetings were suspended between 1997 and 1999, they have since resumed and visits of key military personnel took place in mid-2000. There has been some movement towards expanding the Japan–China Security Dialogue to a US–Japan–China trialogue (Wu Xinbo 2000, Funabashi 1999), and indeed some US analysts see the potential for joint exercises. The latter is no doubt some way off. Nonetheless, increasing cooperation between China and Japan on regional issues (such as Korea) and participation by both parties in regional organisations (both Track One and Two) can only help to build mutual confidence and increase the opportunities for further discussion and transparency (Asano 1998 and Wada 1998).

Conclusion

The main arguments used to substantiate the 'weak link' hypothesis can be reduced in many cases to one factor: history. This could be the history problem *per se* or security issues which originate from mutual images and perceptions – themselves often based on historical experience. Nonetheless, despite the existence of issues which have the potential to cause tension between China and Japan, the relationship has in fact evolved considerably since the 1980s to the extent that a network of relations at all levels has served to strengthen the relationship. International and domestic developments that took place after the Cold War forced Chinese and Japanese politicians and analysts to re-assess the way in which they viewed their own and each other's economic, political and strategic future. Despite the existence of mutual threat perceptions, issues in Sino-Japanese relations in the 1990s did not deteriorate to the point of diplomatic rupture, and the underlying stability of the relationship nurtured since the 1970s was not seriously threatened.

Drifte sums up Japan's China policy neatly stating that 'in contrast to the US, engagement as a policy is hardly contested in Japan. No mainstream politician or academic suggests that there may be irreconcilable conflicts of interest between Japan and China, as seems to be the case in US–Chinese relations on the Taiwan issue or on human rights' (Drifte 2000: 3). Major changes in China's foreign policy such as a shift in favour of regionalism, or the, albeit reluctant, move towards multilateral dialogue have been encouraged and facilitated by Japanese politicians and diplomats whose long-term strategic aims are to engage and integrate China into the regional and international community.

Cooperation between the two countries has progressed in all aspects despite sporadic disputes over history and sovereignty. Referring to a combination of bilateral economic cooperation, political summitry, security dialogue and a restrained Chinese media, Robert S. Ross argues that 'the two sides have developed foreign policies and a bilateral relationship that suggests a long-term ability to maintain and constrain the inevitable competition that will develop between two great powers in close proximity' (Ross 1996: 5).

To be sure, highly sensitive issues do remain on the agenda – Taiwan is key – and may result in greater volatility in the future. But one interesting development in Japan–China diplomacy of late 1999/early 2000 is the apparent switch in positions, with China on the defensive (for example on history and trade) and Japan on the offensive (for example on investment, ODA, maritime activities). Continued bad press in Japan after Jiang Zemin's 1998 trip produced an increasing amount of anti-China sentiment, which the Chinese have fought hard to correct in 2000. Zhu's obvious need to maintain strong economic links with Japan (to execute his Western Development Plan) have enabled Japanese policy makers to apply more pressure on Beijing than was the case a few years ago (Przystup 2000b: 91). At the same time, longer-term trends towards greater bilateral cooperation at various levels could just be coming to fruition, enabling both sides to move forward and leave history firmly in the past, thereby necessitating a re-assessment of the Sino-Japanese axis within the new strategic triangle.[22]

Notes

1 Zhang and Montaperto view the US–China side of the triad as 'the most fragile and vulnerable' (1999: 116). Also note Funabashi's contention about the frail intellectual and political underpinnings of the US–Japan relationship, and the worries shared by both partners that each threatens to get too close to Beijing thereby shifting away from the US–Japan alliance (cited in Zhao 2000 and Drifte 2000).

2 Osaki (1998) makes a similar argument, considering generational change a key factor in the current lack of mutual understanding between Chinese and Japanese.

3 See Midford (2000). Walt refined the balance of power theory (which maintains that states balance against other states' power) arguing that the balance of threat theory provides greater explanatory power. Specifically, 'whereas balance of power theory predicts that states will react to imbalances of power, balance of threat theory predicts that when there is an imbalance of threat (i.e., when one state or coalition appears especially dangerous), states will form alliances or increase internal efforts in order to reduce their vulnerability' (Walt 1987: 263).

4 Midford goes on to argue that in this respect Japan's strategy of engagement since the early 1990s has begun to pay off gradually and achieved a certain amount of success in terms of confidence building.
5 The security dilemma states that 'in an uncertain or anarchic international system, mistrust between two or more potential adversaries can lead each side to take precautionary and defensively motivated measures that are perceived as offensive threats. This can lead to countermeasures in kind, thus ratcheting up regional tensions, reducing security, and creating self-fulfilling prophecies about the danger of one's security environment' (Christensen 1999: 49–50).
6 *Japan Times Online* 'Mori, Zhu vow to build a better future' 14 October 2000 http://www.japantimes.co.jp/cgi-bin/getarticle.pl5?nn20001014a1.htm (accessed 23/10/2000). Note that this most recent tranche had been put on hold in response to deliberations within the LDP about China's maritime activities in the seas around the Senkaku islands.
7 *Japan Times Online* 'Zhu tones down stance on wartime atonement', 17 October, hhtp://www.japantimes.co.jp/cgi-bin/getarticles 15 2nn 20001017a1. htm (accessed 23 October 2000).
8 See Przystup (2000b: 89).
9 Other sources of concern in Sino-Japanese economic relations relate to the potential for trade friction. For example, in April 2000 the Chinese Ministry of Foreign Trade and Economic Cooperation judged that the ROK and Japan were guilty of dumping (stainless steel rods). In Japan, the textile industry is threatened by imports of Chinese poplin and broadcloth, despite China's promises to impose self-restraint (Przystup 2000b: 89)
10 Rozman (1999: 393) summarises Chinese thoughts on which issues are the most contentious. The 'two Ts' and the 'two Hs', for example, refer to Taiwan and the US–Japan treaty, and history and human rights.
11 See Muzi.com News 'New Japanese textbooks drafts say less about sex slaves' 1 July 2000, http://latelinenews.com/II/english/75452.shtm/ (accessed 20 October 2000).
12 Note for example Chinese reaction to the Osaka conference on the Nanjing Massacre in January 2000, and Zhu's reference to it in March at the National People's Congress (Przystup 2000a: 75).
13 One recent example is Transport Minister Morita's visit to the Yasukuni Shrine on 15 August 2000 which, according to the Japanese press, led to 'rescheduling' by Beijing of Morita's impending visit to Beijing. The Chinese side did not mention the shrine visit as a reason for cancellation for obvious reasons, but Zhu Rongji did later mention the Yasukuni Shrine issue in general in a 12 September meeting with a group of Japanese polticians (Przystup 2000c: 92–101).
14 Recent examples include the filing of a 'class-action' lawsuit in the United States against the Japanese government in August 2000 by 15 former comfort women (4 of whom are Chinese) who are seeking compensation and an apology. This is the first case of former sex slaves filing a lawsuit *in the US*, and the first time that the Japanese *government* has been named as defendant. Previous compensation cases have been filed against Japanese *companies*. Such lawsuits have been filed under the 18th century 'Alien Torts Claims Act' which enables foreign citizens to sue other foreign citizens and entities for abuses of international law. The claim here is that the comfort women system violated *jus cogens* norms of international law and are not covered by sovereign immunity (see *Japan Times Online*, 'Ex-sex slaves file suit in US' 20 September 2000 http://www.japantimes.co.jp/cgi-bin/getarticle.pl5?nn20000920a6.htm (accessed 23 October 2000).

15 For example, his comment (later rescinded) of 26 April 2000 regarding the question of whether the war was one of aggression and his 15 May 2000 remark about Japan being a 'divine nation'.

16 *Japan Times Online* 'Japan has never "apologized": Zhu' 15 October 2000 http://www.japantimes.co.jp/cgi-bin/getarticle.pl5?nn20001015a5.htm (accessed 23 October 2000).

17 *Japan Times Online* 'Zhu tones down stance on war atonement' 17 October 2000 http://www.japantimes.co.jp/cgi-bin/getarticle.pl5?nn20001017a1.htm (accessed 23 October 2000). In fact, during a visit to China by Murayama in September 2000, Zhu Rongji was reported to have praised the 1995 statement as the 'first public apology to victims'. See Muzi.com News 18 September 2000 http://dailynews.muziws.cgi?=english&a=express&p+89813

18 Specifically the problem concerned the wording of the joint declaration due to be signed by Jiang and Obuchi. The Chinese side requested inclusion of the words invasion and apology. After numerous rounds of negotiation between Foreign Ministers and their staff, it was finally agreed that while the word *invasion* be incorporated into the joint declaration, *apology* would not. Instead Prime Minister Obuchi would issue a verbal 'apology' (using *owabi*) during his talks with Jiang Zemin, but Jiang Zemin refused to sign the joint declaration as a sign of his dissatisfaction (*Asahi Shimbun*, 25 November 1998, p. 1; 27 November 1998, p. 3; and 29 November 1998, p. 3).

19 'Routinisation' is discussed in Rose (1998). There are many other examples of influencing factors, such as succession politics (for example Deng Xiaoping in the early 1980s, Jiang Zemin in the 1990s), factional disputes in the LDP, domestic differences of opinion on foreign policy matters (for example between certain factions of the PLA and top Chinese decision makers), Chinese dissatisfaction with Japan's Taiwan policy, etc. External factors such as the nature of shifting alliances or 'partnerships' (for example between Russia and China, Russia and Japan, China and the US, etc.) are also likely to have an impact on Sino-Japanese relations if they are considered potentially worrisome.

20 The Senkaku Islands dispute, and the domestic political reasons behind the various 'instalments', is now well-covered. See for example Downs and Saunders (1998), and Suganuma (2000).

21 This is not the view taken by certain Japanese analysts, for example Edo (1998), Chugoku Josei Kenkyukai (1998).

22 Acknowledgment: Research for this chapter was made possible by generous funding from the EU–China Academic Network, the Japan Foundation Endowment Committee and the Universities' China Committee, to whom the author expresses her gratitude.

References

Asano Ryo (1998) 'China and Japan: Improving Direct Communication', in Nishihara Masashi, (ed.) *Old Issues, New Responses: Japan's Foreign and Security Policy Options*, Tokyo: Japan Centre for International Exchange, pp. 1–29.

Christensen, T.J. (1999) 'China, the US–Japan Alliance and the Security Dilemma in East Asia', *International Security* 23(4): 49–80.

Chugoku Josei Kenkyukai (1998) *Nitchu Shototsu (Sino-Japanese Clash)*, Tokyo: JitsugyonoNihonsha.

Downs, Erica Strecker and Phillip C. Saunders (1998) 'Legitimacy and the Limits of Nationalism: China and the Diaoyu Islands', *International Security* 23(3): 114–146.

Drifte, Reinhard (2000) 'The Impact of the US on Japanese–Chinese Security Relations', Unpublished manuscript. Sino-Japanese Relations – Beyond Bilateral Statist Approaches, Warwick/RIIA Workshop, September 4–5, 2000.

Edo Yuusuke (1998) *Kitarubeki Chugoku to no senso (The coming war with China)*, Tokyo: Kenyukan.

Funabashi, Y. (1999) *Alliance Adrift*, Washington DC: Council on Foreign Relations.

Green, Michael J. (1999) 'Managing Chinese Power: the View from Japan', in Alastair Johnston and Robert S. Ross (eds) *Engaging China*, London, New York: Routledge, pp. 152–175.

Harris, Stuart (1997) 'The China Japan Relationship and Asia Pacific Regional Security', *Journal of East Asian Affairs* XI(1): 121–148.

Hughes, Christopher W. (2000) 'Ballistic Missile Defence and Sino-Japanese Relations: Japan's inescapable security dilemma?', Unpublished paper. Workshop on the Chinese–Japanese Relationship, Swedish Institute for International Affairs, Stockholm, August 17–19, 2000.

Jetro (2000) 'Japan-China Trade', *China Newsletter 144*, Tokyo: Japan External Trade Organisation.

Kim Taeho (1998) 'A Reality Check. The "Rise of China" and its Military Capability towards 2010', *Journal of East Asian Affairs* XII(2): 321–63.

Kokubun Ryosei (1997) *Nihon, Amerika, Chugoku: kyocho e no shinario (Japan, America, China: moving towards co-operation)*, Tokyo: TBS Britannica.

Midford, Paul (2000) 'Chinese Perceptions of Japan as a Military Power: Balance of Power, Balance of Threat and the Psychological Dynamics of Reputation', Unpublished paper. Workshop on the Chinese–Japanese Relationship, Swedish Institute for International Affairs, Stockholm, August 17–19, 2000.

Osaki Yuji (1998) 'China and Japan in Asia Pacific: Looking Ahead', in Kokubun Ryosei (ed.) *Challenges for China–Japan–US Cooperation*, Tokyo: Japan Centre for International Exchange, pp. 90–113.

Przystup, James J. (2000a) 'Japan–China Relations: No Escaping History – or the Future', *Comparative Connections* 2/1, http://www.csis.org/pacfor/ccejournal. html.

Przystup, James J. (2000b) 'Japan–China Relations: Old Issues ... and New Approaches?', *Comparative Connections* 2/2, http://www.csis.org/pacfor/ccejournal.html.

Przystup, James J. (2000c) 'Japan–China Relations: Waiting for Zhu', *Comparative Connections* 2/3, http://www.csis.org/pacfor/ccejournal.html.

Rose, Caroline (1998) *Interpreting History in Sino-Japanese Relations*, London and New York: Routledge.

Ross, Robert S. (1996) 'Managing a Changing Relationship: China's Japan Policy in the 1990s', http://carlisle-www.army.mil/usassi/ssipubs/pubs96/manag/manag.pdf.

Rozman, G. (1999) 'China's Quest for Great Power Identity,' *Orbis* 43(3): 383–402.

Suganuma Unryu (1999) *Sovereign Rights and Territorial Space in Sino-Japanese Relations: Irredentism and the Diaoyu/Senkaku Islands*, Honolulu, University of Hawaii Press.

Valencia, Mark J. (2000) 'Domestic Politics Fuels Northeast Asian Maritime Disputes', *Asia Pacific Issues* No. 43, http://EastWestCenter.org/stored/pdfs/api043.pdf. [Accessed 10–10–2000].

Wada Jun (1998) 'Applying Track Two to China–Japan–US Relations', in Kokubun Ryosei (ed.) *Challenges for China–Japan–US Cooperation*, Tokyo: Japan Centre for International Exchange, pp. 154–183.

Walt, S.M. (1987) *The Origins of Alliances*, Ithaca and London: Cornell University Press.

Wang Jisi (2000) 'Building a Constructive Relationship', in M.I. Abramowitz, Funabashi Yoichi and Wang Jisi (eds) *China–Japan–US: Managing the Trilateral Relationship*, Tokyo: Japan Centre for International Exchange, pp. 21–36.

Wu Xinbo (2000) 'The Security Dimensions of Sino-Japanese Relations: Warily Watching One Another', *Asian Survey* 40(2): 296–310.

Yang Daqing (2000) 'Mirror for the Future or the History Card? Understanding the "History Problem" in Japan–China Relations', Unpublished paper. Workshop on the Chinese–Japanese Relationship, Swedish Institute for International Affairs, Stockholm, August 17–19, 2000.

Zhang Ming and Ronald Montaperto (1999) *A Triad of Another Kind: The United States, China and Japan*, Basingstoke and London: Macmillan.

Zhang Yunling (1997) *Hezuo haishi duikang: lengzhanhou de Zhongguo, Meiguo he Riben (Cooperation or Conflict? China–US–Japan Relations after the Cold War)*, Beijing: Zhongguo shehui kexue chubanshe.

Zhao Quansheng (2000) 'Sino-Japanese Relations in the Context of the Beijing–Tokyo–Washington Triangle', Unpublished paper. Workshop on the Chinese–Japanese Relationship, Swedish Institute for International Affairs, Stockholm, August 17–19, 2000.

Chapter 14

China and ASEAN

Setting Parameters for Future Co-operation

Jürgen Haacke

Introduction

Much scholarly attention has focused on how member countries of the Association of Southeast Asian Nations (ASEAN) have pursued different policies of engagement toward the People's Republic of China (PRC) in the post-Cold War period (see contributions in Johnston and Ross 1999). This chapter will primarily attempt the reverse, namely to explore Beijing's perceptions and policy initiatives *vis-à-vis* ASEAN member states. It examines in particular the development of China–ASEAN relations since the height of the financial and economic crisis in late 1997. However, to the extent that it is useful to understand the evolving nature of China–ASEAN relations by also analysing ASEAN member states' perspective of their ties with the PRC, such analysis will complement the main account. The chapter is divided into three sections. The first section seeks to locate PRC–ASEAN relations in East Asia's dynamic politico-strategic environment and examines why and how Beijing has reassessed ties with governments in Southeast Asia in the aftermath of the Asian Financial Crisis (AFC). The second section highlights major points of the joint statements on future co-operation that China signed or issued with all ASEAN member states between early 1999 and late 2000. The significance of these framework agreements is then assessed by analysing the substance of the Sino-Thai and Sino-Indonesian joint statements in more detail in the context of developments in the respective bilateral relationship. The final section examines China–ASEAN relations in the context of the emerging monetary and economic regionalism involving ASEAN and Northeast Asian countries (ASEAN plus Three).

Conceptualising China–ASEAN relations

Since the end of the Cold War, Chinese analysts and decision-makers have argued that the continued existence of conflict, limited wars and civil strife notwithstanding, the current era of peace and development will see the emergence of a multipolar world following the ongoing transitional period. Beijing has attempted to consolidate bilateral ties with the core global powers, not least by forging with them so-called 'partnerships' for the 21st century. This form of relationship is meant to convey a measure of significance superseding that of ordinary diplomatic relations. One feature of such 'partnerships', constant consultation, is designed to reinvigorate personal relationships which, together with intensive economic co-operation, are in turn designed to create an important foundation for a stable relationship. As of the mid-1990s, the PRC entered into several such partnerships. For instance, Beijing and Moscow agreed, in April 1996, to develop a 'strategic co-operative partnership' of equality, mutual confidence and mutual co-ordination in the attempt to establish a new international order characterised by multipolarity and the rejection of hegemonism (Garver 1998). In May 1997, the PRC and France issued a joint declaration in which both purported to build a 'comprehensive co-operative partnership'. And in October of the same year, China and the United States agreed to forge a 'constructive strategic partnership oriented toward the 21st century' (Chen 1998).[1]

Notably, at the end of 1997, China also signed a Joint Statement with ASEAN that emphasised the promotion of 'partnership of good neighbourliness and mutual trust' between the two sides (*Joint Statement of the Meeting of Heads of State/Government* 1997). However, while the China–ASEAN relationship was designated as a 'partnership', this 'partnership' was clearly one of a lesser kind, not least given that the descriptive labels 'strategic' or 'comprehensive' had not been applied. From ASEAN's perspective, the label of 'strategic partnership' probably was in any case politically undesirable if not unacceptable in view of its members' concerns *vis-à-vis* China and their reliance on the United States for external security. The qualifying words chosen, 'neighbourliness and mutual trust', clearly reflected ASEAN's lingering concerns as regards the prospects of China becoming a good citizen in regional international society.

From a Chinese perspective, addressing these concerns was important, but the invoked label also suggests that Beijing may have considered ASEAN to lack strong comprehensive power, especially economic and military power. This raises the question how PRC–ASEAN relations were conceptualised at the time in the broader context of Chinese analysts' thinking on the 'international pattern' (*guoji geju*), by which is understood the structure formed by the interactions among the major powers.

In the post-Cold War era, Chinese scholars and practitioners have generally identified and continue to identify four power triangles in world politics. In all cases, the focal point is the United States (Chan 1996: 96–112, Dittmer 1997: 17). The other four core powers in international politics are identified as Russia, Japan, the European Union countries, and the PRC. In other words, most Chinese analysts have not regarded ASEAN as constituting a pole in international politics, neither globally nor regionally. The Association is merely viewed as a 'potential pole' (Weggel 2000: 109).

In spite of ASEAN's perceived lack of 'comprehensive power', Chinese policy-makers and analysts have found themselves re-evaluating the significance of ASEAN and the ASEAN Regional Forum (ARF) since at least 1996. This re-assessment occurred in response to the stand-off in the Taiwan Strait in 1995/96 and the subsequent revitalisation of the Japan–U.S. alliance. Both developments to some extent also demonstrated to the Chinese leadership that their assumptions and arguments in relation to multipolarity were highly questionable and that the politically unwelcome scenario of monopolarity was beginning to take on ever more substantive and visible form. Further evidence of the overwhelming global U.S. structural power was provided by the role Washington played in the eventual relief extended by international financial institutions to East Asian countries caught up in the storms of the regional financial and economic crisis of 1997/98.

Beijing followed the decline of ASEAN members' economies and their collective loss of international standing with a measure of disquiet. There were several reasons for this. First, ASEAN's economic and financial dependency on Washington opened up possibilities that Southeast Asia would be unable to withstand U.S. pressure on an array of issues over which ASEAN governments and the United States had registered divergent views or the former had even defied the latter in preceding years. In this context, China's regional analysts expressed doubts whether ASEAN would be able to continue to practise equidistance *vis-à-vis* East Asia's major powers. Second, ASEAN's loss of standing in international society undermined international receptivity to its claim to want to remain the driving force of the ARF. To Chinese leaders, this point was particularly relevant in so far as Western powers had repeatedly brought significant pressure to bear on ASEAN as regards the future agenda, character and control of the ARF. Any increase in such pressure was an unwelcome scenario for Beijing, not least because the ARF had become the testing ground for the application of China's 'new security concept' that has been contrasted against U.S. 'power politics', 'hegemony' and 'Cold War mentality' (Finkelstein and McDevitt 1999). Third, the loss of influence and standing of the Association also raised questions to what extent basic principles of international society, as had generally been applied in Southeast Asia, particularly the principle of non-interference, could maintain their regional validity.[2] Having relied on the hitherto unswerving attitude of Southeast Asian governments that these basic principles should not be tampered with, Chinese analysts and decision-makers were to some extent surprised at the intramural debate among ASEAN countries on 'flexible engagement'.[3] However, even now principles at the core of ASEAN's diplomatic and security culture remain salient to the People's Republic: to defend Beijing's position on Taiwan, Tibet, Xinjiang, or other matters deemed to fall into China's jurisdiction.

While recognising that ASEAN was likely to remain inward looking for some time to come, with their bilateral relations remaining exposed to increasing strain, Chinese analysts have nevertheless held that ASEAN should be strengthened. This view was justified given the latter's continued significance in East Asian international politics by virtue of the Association's role in the ARF, Asia Pacific Economic Co-operation (APEC) and Asia–Europe Meeting (ASEM) processes. Consequently, Chinese decision-makers have since the Asian financial and economic crisis gone to significant lengths to reaffirm the PRC's diplomatic support for the Association.

China's at times emphatic endorsement of ASEAN's regional role and importance since 1997 should be seen in the context of attempts to counterbalance American and Japanese influence in Southeast Asia and East Asia more generally. As noted in Chapter 12 of this volume, bilateral ties between the United States and the PRC had improved somewhat in the aftermath of the 1996 Taiwan Strait crisis but deteriorated again sharply in 1999. Tokyo and Beijing too have increasingly found themselves to be competing for regional influence in Southeast Asia. China has moreover been intent on fostering a regional foreign policy mood in which the 1997 revision of the 1978 guidelines for U.S.–Japanese defence co-operation will not lead to a significantly more assertive security role by Japan in East Asia. Against this background China's defence of basic principles of international society has proved an important dimension of Beijing's political strategy.[4] The minimalist objective has been to prevent ASEAN leaderships from siding against Beijing when pursuing their various national interests. The more ambitious goal has been to deepen as much as possible political and economic ties with Southeast Asian countries, including those with which Beijing has had problematic relations in the past. This is illustrated by the three policy objectives identified by Chinese Premier Zhu Rongji: first, to enhance its own stability and development; second, to maintain peace and tranquillity in the region; and third, to conduct dialogues and build up co-operation with regional countries (*Asian Defence Journal*, March 2000: 20).

In practice, China has attempted to inspire confidence in ASEAN leaders by promoting 'a united, stable and prosperous ASEAN'. Testifying to ongoing Chinese concerns in this respect, Premier Zhu (1999a) recently stated that

> We believe that ASEAN will maintain its characteristic self-respect, self-improvement and independence, strengthen its internal unity and

> cooperation in accordance with such effective principles as equality and mutual benefit and decision by consensus, and play a more active and constructive role in promoting regional multipolarity and peace and development.[5]

China has also continued to endorse ASEAN's prerogative role in the ARF, as the latter is seen as an expedient venue for China's foreign minister to build up moral pressure or counter-pressure on issues of particular significance to Beijing. As was noted above, Beijing has advocated the adoption of a 'new security concept' that emphasises respect for sovereignty, mutual trust, solving disputes through dialogue and seeking co-operation through co-operation. For the Chinese leadership, enlarging military blocs and strengthening military alliances run counter to the tide of the times (*China's National Defense* 1998, *China's National Defence in 2000*). Moreover, rather than seeking to guarantee security by an increase in arms or by military alliances, Chinese officials argue that security should be based on mutual trust and common interests.

With the effects of Asia's economic and financial crisis still breathing down the neck of regional decision-makers, Chinese officials have further calculated that ASEAN's interest in averting a recurrence of the crisis might also help promote China's economic security. Not surprisingly, the issue of economic security has recently gained in significance in the ARF. Similar to many of their Southeast Asian counterparts, Chinese analysts have considered the achievements thus far attained by the ARF to have been the product of greater economic interdependence and a benign regional security environment based on the greater prosperity of its members.

Having discussed how Beijing has perceived ASEAN in the final years of the 20th century in the broader context of contemporary East Asian international politics, we shall now turn our attention to China's bilateral relations with individual member states of the Association. As we shall see, Beijing has recently gone to quite significant lengths to improve ties with ASEAN member states. The key expression of this undertaking has been the signing or issuance of joint statements with all ASEAN countries on future co-operation in the 21st century.

The joint statements

Between February 1999 and December 2000 the People's Republic of China signed or issued joint statements with all ASEAN countries on their respective future bilateral co-operation. As the following list illustrates, Thailand was the first Southeast Asian country to do so, and except for the first and the last two statements, signed with Thailand, Laos and Cambodia respectively, all others were signed in Beijing:

(1) China–Thailand Joint Statement on a Plan of Action for the 21st Century, signed in Bangkok, 5 February 1999.
(2) China–Vietnam Joint Statement signed in Beijing, 27 February 1999. During President Tran's visit to Beijing in December 2000, the two sides subsequently also signed a Joint Statement on All-round Cooperation in the New Century, Beijing, 25 December 2000.
(3) Joint Statement by the People's Republic of China and the Republic of Indonesia on the Future Directions of Bilateral Cooperation, signed in Beijing, 8 May 2000.
(4) Joint Statement between the Government of the People's Republic of China and the Government of the Republic of the Philippines on the Framework of Bilateral Cooperation in the Twenty-First Century, signed in Beijing, 16 May 2000.
(5) Joint Statement by the Government of Malaysia and the People's Republic of China on the Framework for Future Bilateral Relations signed in Beijing, 31 May 1999.
(6) China and Brunei Joint Communiqué on the Orientation of Future Bilateral Relations, issued in Beijing, 24 August 1999.
(7) China–Singapore Joint Statement on Bilateral Cooperation, issued on 11 April 2000 in Beijing.
(8) Joint Statement of the People's Republic of China and the Union of Myanmar on the Framework of Future Bilateral Relations and Cooperation, signed in Beijing, 6 June 2000.
(9) Joint Statement by the People's Republic of China and the Kingdom of Cambodia on the Framework of Their Bilateral Cooperation, Phnom Penh, 13 November 2000.
(10) Joint Statement by the People's Republic of China and the Lao People's Democratic Republic on the Framework of Their Bilateral Cooperation, Vientiane, 12 November 2000.

Substance of joint statements

Details of the joint statements vary, but it is possible to identify several parallels. First, all statements set out the basic principles that are to guide bilateral relations between the People's Republic and individual ASEAN member states. As one would expect, most statements make reference to the principles of the UN Charter, the Five Principles of Peaceful Co-existence (FPPC), the principles of the Treaty of Amity and Co-operation (TAC) and other recognised principles of international law. Without reading too much into deviations or omissions from this list, it is nevertheless interesting to note that the TAC was not mentioned in the China–Singapore statement, while the China–Brunei statement lists the TAC prior to the FPPC, contrary to the order in other statements. The China–Indonesia Statement also invokes the Ten Principles of the Bandung Declaration.

Secondly, the statements identify the areas in which bilateral co-operation is to be explored or enhanced. While the future relationships between China and ASEAN member states are meant to be 'all-directional', the emphasis on trade and investment is conspicuous. The focus on enhanced trade and foreign direct investment evidently serves the dual purpose of satisfying material needs and offering security-boosting effects, not least at the regional level. The importance of underlying considerations about economic security is also discernible, in the professed intention to jointly promote changes to the international financial regulatory regime as noted, for example, in the statements agreed between China and Indonesia and China and Malaysia.

Another commonly stated objective is the advancement of political co-operation by developing close and frequent contacts between leaders. Moreover, agreement exists that China and ASEAN members, where feasible and desirable, are to fine-tune diplomatic positions in various international forums such as the ARF, APEC, ASEM, ASEAN plus Three, and the United Nations, etc. Some framework agreements also explicitly mention co-operation in security and defence. For example, the China–Malaysia statement notes, inter alia, the possibility of bilateral co-operation in the defence industry sector. Another example is the envisaged security co-operation between Bangkok and Beijing by way of confidence building measures as well as military diplomacy. The Indonesia–China statement also contains a vague reference to co-operation in defence and political and regional security. Statements signed with Cambodia, Laos and Myanmar stress security co-operation against cross-border crime, particularly smuggling, drug and aliens trafficking, as well as military exchanges.

Significantly, despite winning the assent of all Southeast Asian countries to sign or issue a respective bilateral framework agreement, the texts illustrate that Beijing did not succeed in winning unambiguous or comprehensive declaratory support from regional governments for China's diplomatic rhetoric. For instance, the China–Singapore statement bears no reference to 'multi-polarity' or the establishment of a 'new just and equitable international political and economic order',[6] whereas Malaysia and the Philippines agreed to the formulation of a new 'equitable and rational' political and economic/world order respectively. The Indonesia–China statement is by far the most assertive in tone, by calling for a 'just and more balanced new international political, economic *and security* order'.[7] Interestingly, only two of the framework agreements refer explicitly to the South China Sea dispute (China–Philippines, China–Malaysia).

All the statements/communiqués commit individual ASEAN states to a One-China policy. However, the formulations on the issue of Taiwan do vary, with some describing Taiwan as simply 'part of China' (Singapore), an 'integral part of Chinese territory' (for instance, Thailand, Philippines), or an 'inalienable' part of China. In return for their respective One-China policy, Beijing has vowed to observe basic principles of international society *vis-à-vis* all Southeast Asian countries. Among other things, China has, for instance, reiterated its respect for the independence, sovereignty and integrity of the Kingdom of Cambodia, the sovereign equality of Brunei Darussalam, as well as the stability, integrity and prosperity of Indonesia.

Significance of joint statements

From China's perspective, the signing of the statements on bilateral co-operation with the ten ASEAN countries possesses symbolic and practical value. The symbolism of plans to initiate, deepen and expand 'all-directional' co-operation, including security and military co-operation, with all ASEAN countries is self-evident. In practical terms, the above framework agreements are likely to prove useful as a building block for a coherent foreign policy toward Southeast Asia that is sustainable in the long-term and makes it less likely that the members of the Association will collectively side against Beijing. Moreover, some of the joint statements may well represent a major step toward reshaping in a fundamental way relations with core Southeast Asian states.

Not surprisingly, the United States has already sought to counter the PRC's diplomatic initiatives toward Southeast Asian countries. Beijing's rhetoric on a 'new security concept' is now being matched by Washington's advocacy of an 'Asia-Pacific Regional Initiative' (APRI).[8] The purpose of APRI is to involve ASEAN states in joint planning, training and exercises with U.S. forces with a view to possible multilaterally conducted humanitarian operations, peacekeeping and other missions that entail the deployment of armed forces by regional states to UN-mandated operations. The ultimate objective is to develop so-called 'security communities'.[9]

While China's signing of joint statements with all ten ASEAN member states marks a significant development, it seems premature to argue that diverse strategic, political and economic interests have been bridged as a consequence. Indeed, some statements are notable for their cautious and non-committal tone, as is for instance the case with the China–Singapore Joint Statement or the communiqué issued by the PRC and Brunei Darussalam. As noted, it is above all the Indonesia–China framework agreement that is considerably more assertive in tone, suggesting similar grievances that to some extent are related to the character of their respective ties with the United States. However, it is China's official perspective that relations with all ASEAN countries have upside potential. As China's Foreign Minister put it:

> Facts have proven, and will continue to prove, that China–ASEAN friendly relations and cooperation based on the Five Principles of Peaceful Coexistence are firmly founded and widely endorsed, and

> promise tremendous potentials and broad prospects. There are big and small countries in the world. And they may vary from one another in historical background, social systems, level of development, cultural traditions, and values. However, so long as they respect each other, treat each other as equals, seek common ground while shelving differences and conduct mutually beneficial cooperation, they will be able to coexist in harmony and achieve common development. This is useful experience gained in the ever-growing China–ASEAN relations, and it serves the fundamental interests of people of all countries, contributes to regional peace and stability, and can facilitate the establishment of a new, just and rational order of peace and cooperation. Observance of the Five Principles of Peaceful Coexistence, the purposes and spirit of the UN Charter as well as the principles enshrined in the Treaty of Amity and Cooperation in Southeast Asia is the soul of China–ASEAN relations. It is also of vital significance to the international relations and international order in the 21st century.
>
> (Tang 1999)

To assess whether China's bilateral statements with ASEAN countries on the contours of future bilateral ties already reflect or are giving way to actual improvements in diplomatic, political and economic relations, the following section will explore in more detail the Sino-Thai and Sino-Indonesian statements and relate both to respective developments in China–Thailand and China–Indonesia relations. Both Thailand and Indonesia are core states of the Association of Southeast Asian Nations. Until recently Indonesia was regarded without hesitation as ASEAN's *primus inter pares*. Thailand has for some time sought sub-regional leadership in continental Southeast Asia. Notably, China and Thailand had entered a *de facto* military coalition against Vietnam to reverse the latter's 1978 occupation of Cambodia, but China's relations with Indonesia were only normalised in 1990. If we find evidence that both the Joint Statements reflect substantive changes in relations, or at least indicate significant upside potential for bilateral ties, China's influence in Southeast Asia may be seen as having improved markedly.

China–Thailand relations

China has had a longstanding strategic interest in continental Southeast Asia. In the Cold War period, when Vietnam seemed to Beijing to aspire to sub-regional hegemony, the PRC's pragmatic relationship with Thailand was highly valued by Chinese leaders. Sino-Thai relations have remained friendly in the post-Cold War period, although some within the Kingdom may have been somewhat uneasy at the increasing Chinese influence in neighbouring Myanmar. Significantly, recent Thai governments have been adept at furthering the relationship with Beijing by generally engaging in prior consultations on decisions and initiatives that might affect China's interests. Some friction has nevertheless remained, not least in the field of trade. In the context of the financial and economic crisis of 1997/98 the relationship received a new boost when Bangkok initiated moves that ultimately led to the decision to formulate a mutually acceptable agenda for further co-operation. This took the form of the Joint Statement on a Plan for Action in the 21st Century.

To understand Thailand's economic motives, it is useful to recall that by early 1998 the Thai government was desperately exploring options to reverse the country's economic contraction which, inter alia, had found expression in depreciated asset markets, formidable bad loan problems and rising unemployment. Having experienced American reluctance to extend financial assistance in the early months of the crisis, the then incoming administration headed by Chuan Leekpai focused on strengthening all existing export markets as well as considering available options to forestall a collapse of Thailand's financial institutions. Those options included proposals to invite Taiwanese investors, which were explored with a senior Taiwanese official, the chairman of the Council of Economic Development and Planning, who visited Bangkok in January 1998.

Concerned about Taipei's efforts to exploit the economic crisis for political purposes, China's then Vice-Foreign Minister Tang Jiaxuan visited Thailand in early February, warning his Thai guests that its surplus foreign reserves notwithstanding, Taiwan was unlikely to make a major contribution toward helping Bangkok overcome the crisis. Indeed, Tang probably added that whereas China and Hong Kong had each contributed 1 billion US$ to the bailout package for Thailand (17.2bn US$), making Thailand the first ASEAN recipient of China's first-ever financial package, Taiwan had not provided meaningful financial assistance. Tang also assured the Chuan government that China would not devalue the Chinese yuan in response to the depreciation of Southeast Asian currencies. This pledge stood in direct contrast to the devaluation of the Taiwanese currency in the early stages of the financial crisis. He also pledged to help maintain the peg of the Hong Kong dollar despite attacks on that currency and promised to increase bilateral trade and investment to enable Thailand to get its economy back on track. Tang's promises apparently had the effect of making Thai officials propose a framework for bilateral co-operation to face the challenges of the 21st century, which was then worked out in subsequent months.

Although the vague formulations on security co-operation in the Joint Statement seem to have attracted most media and scholarly attention so far, other passages on co-operation in the development of the Mekong River sub-region through existing forums are no less interesting. China had not been keen to participate in multilateral Mekong development schemes until recently, especially if these involved Japan. For Bangkok, however, China's participation is highly desirable because the purpose is to promote Thailand as a gateway for Chinese products to other ASEAN countries, the Middle East, Europe and the United States. Thailand also hopes to be able to export significantly more to the 290 million people who populate China's land-locked south-western provinces of Yunnan, Sichuan, Guizhou and the Guangxi autonomous region than has been the case in the past.

Notwithstanding the emphasis on economic co-operation in the Joint Statement, political considerations clearly also did enter into the process of its drafting, namely on how to develop relations with China and the latter's regional role in the future. In this regard, some Thais initially tended to interpret the U.S. response to Thailand's financial troubles in 1997, especially Washington's reluctance to support Thailand in the same way as Mexico in 1994, as an indication that Washington was no longer fully committed to continental Southeast Asia. At the same time, China's economic weight and leverage is expected to grow considerably. Secondly, Thailand will require substantial financial support to promote its further economic development, which includes major infrastructure projects. Also, the Thai political elite believes that the success of such projects depends on China's active support. The markets of 'Greater China' are viewed as an alternative to that of 'Japan', not least because the Chinese markets are bigger and increasingly less protectionist. Thirdly, Thailand's influence in Indochina is considered more likely to increase if Bangkok forges a partnership with China in developing sub-regional economic co-operation in the Mekong basin rather than by pursuing such plans individually.

The state of Sino-Thai relations

The Joint Statement would not appear to be a dead letter. For instance, the rate of state visits and official exchanges between Bangkok and Beijing has reached impressive levels. Among others, former Premier and current NPC-Chairman Li Peng visited Thailand in April 1999. In September 1999, China's President Jiang Zemin paid a state visit to Thailand. And Vice-President Hu Jintao travelled to Thailand in July 2000 on the occasion of the 25th anniversary of the establishment of diplomatic relations between Bangkok and Beijing. Conversely, Thai Premier Chuan Leekpai visited China in late April/early May 1999, to urge Chinese leaders to play a more active role in helping Asia recover from the crisis. Her Majesty Queen Sirikit visited China in the autumn of 2000.

On the economic front, Bangkok won several concessions from Beijing in recent negotiations on the terms of Beijing's WTO accession that are likely to increase Thai exports to China and, potentially, to raise the level of mutual investment. In the past few years Thailand has had a relatively small trade deficit with China, with two-way trade totalling around US$ 3.2 billion (*The Nation* 2000a). Chinese interest in investments in Thailand, which had decreased up to 1998 because Chinese investors no longer necessarily saw a technological skills advantage favouring the Thai over the Chinese workforce, is again forthcoming. For example, Beijing has pursued discussions on investing in a pulp and paper project for which the Thai cabinet approved the reservation of large tracts of denuded forest.[10] Moreover, China's state shipping line is involved in a project to open a container terminal on Thailand's eastern seaboard. Thirdly, China and Thailand have expressed interest in developing a joint merchant navy.

Co-operation in other areas, such as combating the trafficking of drugs, has increased, but does appear to have involved some hitches. At issue is the enormous inflow of illegal drugs into Thailand in the aftermath of the Asian financial crisis, especially of methamphetamine tablets (known as crazy medicine or 'ya-baa'). The Thai government has become seriously concerned about the social and economic problems associated with 'ya-baa'. These problems are apparently considered so serious that the Thai military on occasion has been considering cross-border strikes to knock out drug factories in Myanmar (East 2000).

While production sites of these drugs would appear to be mostly located within Myanmar, the drug problem is associated with and caused in significant measure by the United Wa State Army (UWSA). Myanmar's State Peace and Development Council (SPDC) argues that it cannot do much about the drug trade of the UWSA because the latter is signatory to a cease-fire agreement with the military regime in Yangon. During the July 2000 visit by Vice-President Hu Jintao, Thai Premier Chuan Leekpai therefore requested Chinese assistance in combating the drug problem in Myanmar. The request appears to have been made because the UWSA has been close to SPDC's Lt. General Khin Nyunt who is deemed to be 'pro-Chinese' (Lintner, Chanda and Dhume 2000). However, Beijing initially was not very forthcoming on this point as it considered the issue to be a matter of Myanmar's internal affairs (Khumrungroji 2000).[11] Interestingly, however, Beijing had reportedly asked the Burmese authorities to relocate Wa villagers living close to the border with the PRC. From Thailand's perspective, it has been unfortunate that the Wa shifted bases and refineries from near the Chinese border to areas close to the Thai border *(Far Eastern Economic Review*, hereafter *FEER*, 7 December 2000, p. 10). That said, by purchasing sugar from Myanmar China has also been encouraging poppy farmers to substitute growing drugs with planting sugar cane (*Bangkok Post*, 20 July 2000, p. 4). As regards another area of bilateral PRC–Thailand security co-operation, Beijing has been interested in winning Bangkok's co-operation on the issue of the Falun Gong. Thai Foreign Minister Surin Pitsuwan raised the possibility that its leader might be extradited to the PRC if he again visited Thailand and Beijing requested his extradition (Winn 1999).

Longstanding institutionalised bilateral military-to-military exchanges have continued after the signing of the Joint Statement. Between May and early July 1999, for instance, Thai Army Commander-in-Chief Surayut Chulanont and General Mongkhon Amphonphisit, Supreme Commander of the Thai Armed Forces, visited Beijing. General Surayut Chulanot again visited China in May 2000, meeting with Chinese Chief of the General Staff of the PLA Fu Qianyou and Zhang Wannian, Vice Chairman of the Central Military Commission, to discuss, inter alia, China's possible use of force against Taiwan (Thayer 2000). Later that month, General Mongkun Ampornpisit again visited Beijing and met with Fu Qianyou and Defence Minister Chi Haotian to discuss bilateral military exchanges and the Taiwan issue (Thayer 2000). China became a donor of military assistance (US$ 3 million) to Thailand in May 1996 (Chongkittavorn 1997).

However, as a speech by Chinese President Jiang Zemin in Bangkok in September 1999 made clear, Chinese leaders have also hoped that their Thai counterparts would endorse if not support PRC foreign policy positions. This applies to basic principles that are to guide interstate relations, but goes beyond this. In the wake of NATO's intervention in the Kosovo conflict, for example, China also sought to rekindle and promote a sense of Asian nationalism that would promote China's regional interests in Southeast and East Asia to the possible detriment of Western interests. As Jiang (1999) put it,

> Having suffered enormously from imperialist invasion and bullying, and from the disintegration of their countries and families, the Asian people have cherished dearly the hard-won national independence and unity. It is the sacred right of the Asian peoples to safeguard national dignity and State sovereignty, choose independently their own social system, the road to development and way of life and reject external intervention in their internal affairs. It is also the basic guarantee of the prosperity of Asian countries.

Significantly, Thai foreign policy makers have resisted joining Beijing in denouncing 'economic neo-colonialism' and a 'new gunboat diplomacy'. Ascribing to the Joint Statement the trappings of a quasi-alliance may thus be premature if not inappropriate. Bangkok has consciously sought to avoid, albeit not necessarily with much success, causing suspicions among its ASEAN neighbours that Thailand is becoming a conduit for Chinese influence into Southeast Asia. This is testified by Bangkok having been uncomfortable with the idea of labelling bilateral ties with China as a 'strategic partnership' to describe the future level of co-operation, in contrast to Beijing. Importantly, Thai leaders have not only been cautious in their description of Sino-Thai relations, but also promoted a stable regional balance of power in Southeast and East Asia.

Bangkok's search for a stable balance of power is illustrated in part by the language used when Thailand reacted to NATO's intervention in Kosovo.

Then, Prime Minister Chuan Leekpai merely said that Thailand would abide by the principles of the United Nations and follow any solution on which the United Nations would agree. When the shelling of the Chinese Embassy in Belgrade occurred, the Foreign Ministry was circumspect in so far as its spokesman said Washington owed the Chinese people and government a thorough explanation and compensation regardless of whether the bombing was accidental or otherwise (*The Nation* 1999). Notably, these comments were made at a very low point in U.S.–Thai relations due to Washington's lack of diplomatic support for Thailand's candidate for the post of WTO-chief, Deputy Prime Minister Supachai Panitekpakdi.

Thailand's efforts to balance great power influence in continental Southeast Asia, and beyond, are further illustrated by the steps taken to subsequently consolidate its relationship with the United States.[12] For instance, the annual Cobra Gold exercise has not only been continued, but – as of 2000 – also been opened to third parties, in line with Washington's recent emphasis on multilateralising specific forms of possible security co-operation, primarily peacekeeping and peace enforcement. Moreover, relying on U.S. logistical support, Thailand assumed a major role in contributing to the UN-sponsored International Force in East Timor (Interfet). In the autumn of 2000, around 700 Thai peacekeepers stationed in East Timor's Sector East were among the troops supporting the United Nations Transitional Administration in East Timor (UNTAET) mission, with a Thai general serving as the overall commander (*FEER*, 19 October 2000, p. 12). Additionally, Bangkok proposed setting up a regional centre to train troops for UN peacekeeping missions (*FEER*, 7 December 2000, p. 10). Meanwhile, Thailand and the United States also agreed on substantially deepening co-operation in anti-drug-trafficking operations. Washington is to train Thai counter-narcotics forces and to provide helicopters. The Chuan government has also re-ordered aircraft that could not be purchased during the AFC, thus responding positively to American urgings that interoperability between the Thai and U.S. forces should be a concern for Bangkok.

In short, although Thai–China relations are expanding and deepening in line with the perception that both sides can benefit by cultivating the bilateral relationship, the Joint Statement does not, as yet, signal a change to Thailand's traditional balance of power orientation in foreign policy. Indeed, while we may assume that Thailand will probably continue to pay attention to Chinese sensitivities and interests, Bangkok will also pursue its own interests, some of which are not necessarily fully compatible with those of Beijing. We shall now briefly explore Sino-Indonesian ties.

Sino-Indonesian relations

It took more than two decades to normalise relations between Beijing and Jakarta after the suspension of diplomatic relation on 30 October 1967 in the wake of China's alleged involvement in the 1965 Gestapu affair. In the event, the resumption of diplomatic ties, agreed with effect from 8 August 1990, coincided with the end of the Cold War.[13] An initial series of high-level visits followed but these did not give a decisive boost to bilateral ties, although during President Jiang Zemin's visit to Indonesia in November 1994, for instance, an agreement on the promotion as well as protection of investments was signed. So was a memorandum of understanding on co-operation in science and technology. By 1997, bilateral trade had increased to 4.51 billion US$ from 1.18 billion US$ in 1990 (Chinese Foreign Ministry, undated). The increase did not imply that Indonesian suspicions about Chinese intentions in Southeast Asia had been allayed, especially in view of China's persistently ambiguous rhetoric and behaviour in the South China Sea. Indeed, in 1995, irrespective of Jakarta's longstanding emphasis on non-alignment, concern about China appears to have prompted then Indonesian President Suharto and Australia's Prime Minister Paul Keating to sign a security agreement.[14]

The Asian financial and economic crisis opened up new challenges for the leaderships of both countries as well as opportunities to further develop bilateral ties. In the aftermath of the May 1998 riots in Jakarta, relations dipped as PRC officials joined officials from other countries in expressing concern about the violence perpetrated against ethnic Chinese Indonesians. Despite some ensuing resentment in Jakarta, and in contrast to 1994, when Beijing had last been perceived to interfere in Indonesia's domestic politics (Sukma 1994), relations with Beijing were not damaged, however. The administration of B.J. Habibie responded positively to widespread international concerns by promising effective measures to protect the legitimate rights and interests of ethnic Chinese in Indonesia in future. It did so not least with a view to attempting to invite the return of urgently required Chinese capital.

Following the election of Abdurrahman Wahid as President in October 1999, Sino-Indonesian relations were transformed, at least at the level of diplomatic rhetoric. Announcing a 'Look Toward Asia' policy, Wahid's visit to China in December 1999 marked the president's first official trip abroad, although he had previously visited other ASEAN countries and the United States.[15] The reason for visiting the PRC was explained with reference to China's 'consistent support' for Indonesia's diplomacy. Such support included China's challenge to the outcome of a special meeting by the UN Commission on Human Rights, which voted to set up an inquiry to establish responsibility for post-referendum atrocities committed in East Timor (Office of the United Nations High Commissioner for Human Rights 1999). In the event, Wahid's visit to China led the two sides to issue a joint press communiqué, considered 'of great significance to the joint efforts to deepen China–Indonesia relations in the future' (PRC–Indonesia Joint Press Communiqué 1999).

Significantly, the December communiqué already spelled out many of the core aspects that were subsequently laid down in the co-operative framework agreement mentioned in the preceding section. Parallels are, for instance, the emphasis on frequent exchange of high-level visits and contacts, or the identification of trade, investments, science and technology, industry, agriculture, forestry and plantation, fishery, energy, mining, telecommunication and finance as areas of co-operation. Moreover, both documents insist on the validity of and respect for basic international principles such as sovereignty and non-interference. They also express a willingness to seek universal and effective compliance with the implementation of the provisions of bilateral as well as multilateral agreements on disarmament, in particular with respect to weapons of mass destruction. On the latter point, the December communiqué highlighted the significance of the Anti-Ballistic Missiles (ABM) Treaty in maintaining international peace, security and strategic stability as well as the Treaty on the Southeast Asia Nuclear-Weapon-Free Zone (SEANWFZ) as an important contribution to regional and global peace and stability. This reflected Beijing's fears that the United States will disregard and 'violate' the ABM Treaty and Indonesia's disappointment at Washington's adamant refusal to sign the protocol of the latter treaty. Implicit in the communiqué, as in the later joint statement, is the suggestion that the power and influence of the United States should be balanced. According to the communiqué,

> [t]he two sides were of the view that profound changes are taking place in the international situation and that multipolarization is a general trend in international relations. The two sides emphasized that the United Nations Charter, the Five Principles of Peaceful Co-existence, the Ten Principles of the Bandung Conference and the universally recognized basic norms governing international relations should continue to be the basis of a new international political, economic and security order which is more just and balanced, and should therefore be observed by all nations. No country has the right to interfere in the internal affairs of other sovereign states under whatever pretext.[16]

The communiqué and joint statement represent a re-description of sorts of the China policy pursued under the New Order as well as Indonesia's longstanding approach to playing an active and independent role in international relations. The rapprochement clearly suits Beijing's economic, political and strategic interests. First, China is interested in realising the potential of trade and investment ties with the most populous country in Southeast Asia. Second, Beijing is fully supportive of Jakarta's attempt to maintain full territorial integrity and to reduce perceived foreign interference because the PRC is itself a multi-ethnic and multi-religious country. Consequently, Chinese leaders thus backed President Abdurrahman Wahid in rejecting foreign intervention in restoring law and order in the riot-hit Maluku islands. Meanwhile, Indonesia has reiterated its adherence to the One-China policy and restated its recognition that the government in Beijing is the sole legal government of the entire Chinese people. Third, Beijing seeks to exploit disenchantment between Jakarta and Washington to increase China's regional influence while countering that of the United States. China's Vice-President Hu Jintao spelled out this triple objective clearly during his visit to Indonesia on the occasion of the 50th anniversary of establishment of diplomatic relations, in July 2000. Indeed, Hu Jintao emphasised four areas of co-operation: economic development, regional economic co-operation, fostering a 'new security concept', and the establishment of a new equitable international political and economic order.

As regards co-operation in the economic and military fields, Indonesia has publicly welcomed China's WTO-accession in spite of the related fears on the part of some of its ASEAN counterparts (see next section). Given the suspension of military assistance to Indonesia by U.S. Congress in 1999, some within the TNI have even suggested turning to Beijing for arms purchases to meet minimum standards for defence equipment (*Asian Defence Journal* 3/2000: 50–52).[17] In July 2000, Chief of Staff of the Indonesian Navy, Achmad Sutjipto, reportedly held talks with Fu Quanyou to discuss co-operation between the two navies. Meanwhile, Jakarta's displeasure with the United States reached new heights in the second half of 2000, in view of the perceived interference by U.S. Ambassador Robert Gelbard in Indonesia's domestic political process, including such matters as the selection of new army chief Wirahadikusamah (McBeth 2000: 34).

In a symbolic move, Abdurrahman Wahid has furthermore sought to remove other remaining obstacles impeding improvement in Sino-Indonesian relations by, for example, allowing public debate about the legalisation of the Indonesian Communist Party. The easing of apprehension towards the representatives of contemporary communism was further testified by visits to Beijing by members of GOLKAR and the Indonesian Democratic Party of Struggle under Vice-President Megawati Sukarnoputri in order to build relations with the Chinese Communist Party.

While Sino-Indonesian relations have thus enjoyed significant improvement during Abdurrahman Wahid's accession to the Indonesian Presidency, two qualifications seem in order. First, rapprochement between Beijing and Jakarta does not signal a return to the days, under Sukarno, when the two countries represented in part the camp of the 'New Emerging Forces' in international politics, in the sense of an anti-Western coalition. Second, the extent of Indonesian resentment at the United States and Western financial institutions and bitterness over pressure on West Timor may be significant, but Jakarta remains dependent, for the foreseeable future, on Western sources of finance and technology as well as access to the U.S. market (Smith 2000).

Although the Sino-Indonesian relationship has evolved quickly against the background of shared deep-seated resentment at the success of U.S. power politics and interference, it moreover seems premature to suggest that the deepening of bilateral co-operation is irreversible. Several issues could yet obstruct a sustained improvement in ties, and raise questions about the extent and depth of co-operation between Beijing and Jakarta. One possible stumbling block is Jakarta's treatment of ethnic Chinese Indonesians. As the Chinese side officially affirms (Chinese Foreign Ministry b, undated), the 'issue of Chinese Indonesians and overseas Chinese in Indonesia remains sensitive in bilateral relations due to various reasons'. A second stumbling block could well be the as yet unresolved nature of Chinese claims in the South China Sea, including the Natunas (He Kai 2000). Third, a deepening of Sino-Indonesian relations is of course also likely to be accompanied by Jakarta's attempts to seek improvements in ties with other major regional powers in order to maintain a working balance of power in East Asia.

Having found Chinese foreign policy makers to have made headway in institutionalising and ameliorating ties with two core Southeast Asian countries, we shall now explore China–ASEAN relations in the context of the 'ASEAN plus Three' process. The purpose is to establish whether the efforts undertaken by the PRC to strengthen bilateral ties with ASEAN members have also been accompanied by efforts to upgrade China–ASEAN co-operation against the background of accelerating East Asian regionalism.

China–ASEAN ties in the context of an emerging regionalism

This section begins by providing a brief summary of the rise and development of East Asian regionalism since the Asian crisis, before examining the roles that the PRC and ASEAN have played in it. While East Asian regionalism is of course no longer a new phenomenon, its scope and depth have arguably attained new levels. These levels have in part been attained because the more recent East Asian monetary and economic regionalism has built on a grammar of resentment and frustration as well as on a struggle for international relevance by Southeast Asian countries. As regards the first of these points, some East Asian leaders have, for instance, resented the delay of assistance provision to countries in need. Many have also been bitter at the imposition of unwelcome political and structural economic change in return for the assistance provided. Moreover, all have showed some degree of frustration at tenacious efforts by European countries to block a realignment of voting power in the IMF in accordance with present economic indicators which would give Asian countries greater representation and thus more institutional influence.[18] As regards the second point, the struggle for international relevance, it is noteworthy that ASEAN has been in considerable disarray since 1997. Individual member states have also faced considerable domestic political strife that has dented investor confidence in Southeast Asian markets. The resentment and frustration as well as negative extra-regional perceptions have provoked converging nationalist and regionalist sentiments and led to moves intended to shift – if only a little – the balance of power in the politics of international finance.

Development of East Asian regionalism since the Asian crisis

Tokyo's 1997 proposal for an Asian Monetary Fund (AMF), in the form of a permanent facility with committed funds and a secretariat, constituted the first attempt at forging an emerging East Asian regionalism in the politico-financial realm that appeared possible. However the AMF was opposed, if not *de facto* vetoed, by the United States, officially on the grounds of possible duplication of IMF tasks and the likelihood of it causing a moral hazard problem. In reality, Washington essentially repudiated the proposal as the creation of an AMF might have undermined its leadership role in the Asia-Pacific (Godement 1999).

In order not to draw the ire of the United States, the AMF proposal has formally been put to rest for the time being, although arguably its underlying intentions and objectives have informed recent advances in monetary and economic regionalism. Indeed, East Asian regionalism has gathered considerable momentum since September 1997. Initially, it found expression in four informal summits that ASEAN hosted at the sidelines of the ASEAN's thirteeth anniversary in Kuala Lumpur in late 1997. The format of the meeting between ASEAN, China, Japan, and South Korea and the summits ASEAN holds with these countries individually are respectively labelled as 'ASEAN + 3' and 'ASEAN + 1' processes.

To a significant extent the regionalism in the form of the 'ASEAN + 3' process has built on deepening sub-regional co-operation in Southeast Asia. The starting point, in a sense, was in October 1998, when the ASEAN Surveillance Process (ASP) was formally established at the Special Meeting of the ASEAN Finance Ministers.[19] The process encompassed two aspects: first, monitoring global, regional as well as national economic and financial developments in a surveillance report to avert a relapse into major economic difficulty.[20] The second aspect of the ASP has been the peer review process conducted by the ASEAN Finance Ministers. To achieve economic recovery, ASEAN subsequently adopted the Hanoi Plan of Action (HPA) in December 1998. The second informal ASEAN + 3 summit meeting in November 1998 in Hanoi saw a show of support by Japan, China and South Korea for the HPA and the accompanying Bold Measures.[21] Also, an initiative led by the late Japanese Premier Keizo Obuchi paved the way to Japan–ASEAN Consultations and the announcement of a US$ 5 billion Special Yen Loan facility in addition to elements of the New

Miyazawa Initiative decided between October and November.[22] In April 1999, following the first ministerial peer review of the ASEAN Surveillance Report (ASEAN 1999a), ASEAN agreed on a common position on reforming the international financial architecture (ASEAN 1999b). Having done so, ASEAN member countries exchanged views with China, Japan and the Republic of Korea on monitoring short-term capital flows and international financial reforms.

At their Third Informal summit in Manila in November 1999, ASEAN plus Three resolved to enhance this dialogue process and strengthen co-operation with a view to advancing East Asian collaboration in priority areas of shared interest and concern (*Joint Statement on East Asia Co-operation* 1999). East Asian leaders agreed on relatively broad areas of economic as well as monetary and financial co-operation. Interestingly, East Asian political leaders raised negative if not false reporting on the region as a problem, thus advocating projection of an Asian point of view to the rest of the world. Meanwhile their formulations on political and security co-operation remained vague. Still, they committed their countries to an ASEAN + 3 Foreign Ministers' Meeting on the margins of the Post-Ministerial Conference in Bangkok in 2000, to review the progress of the implementation of the 1999 Joint Statement. Notably, still in 1999, Japan increased its financial assistance to ASEAN by proposing to make available loans for human resource development ('Obuchi fund'), while ASEAN countries sought to make permanent the funds available under the New Miyzawa Initiative.[23] In the event, leaders at the ASEAN + 3 summit decided to 'institutionalise' and 'expand the availability of the loans' (Richardson 1999). The leaders agreed that regional co-operation should span trade, investment, monetary and financial co-ordination, technology transfer, scientific exchange and training. The ASEAN Finance Ministers (ASEAN 1999c) at the time also decided to explore with their Northeast Asian counterparts ways of co-operation by strengthening the institutional capacity for consultation and collaboration on monetary, fiscal and financial issues, including policy dialogue.

Highlighted as a milestone in regional monetary integration (Dieter 2000), the ASEAN + 3 countries announced the Chiang Mai Initiative on the sidelines of an ADB annual meeting in May 2000. The initiative, which built on the outcome of a meeting of Finance Ministers and Central Bank deputies in Bandar Seri Begawan two months earlier, has two core elements. First, it was decided to expand in scope and amount the existing but limited ASEAN Swap Arrangement under which early members have until recently been able to draw US$ 80 million to meet temporary liquidity problems. The ASEAN Swap Arrangement (ASA) has since increased to 1 billion US$ and been extended beyond the founding members of the Association to the new entrants. Second, leaders resolved to establish a network of bilateral swap arrangements between individual ASEAN countries, China, Japan and

South Korea. Significantly, neither details of how the swap-arrangement would work in practice were discussed, nor the size of any bilateral swap-arrangements that might be made available, nor the latter's likely conditionality. That said, Japan already has separate swap-arrangements with Malaysia and with South Korea at the value of US$ 2.5 billion and US$ 5 billion respectively.

Significantly, the wording of the agreement has left open the possibility of further institutionalisation beyond consultation and exchanges on issues such as short-term capital flows (ASEAN 2000). Also in May 2000, trade ministers from the 13 countries met for the first time to confer on the strengthening of co-operation in trade, investment and e-commerce in Yangon. The first ever meeting of the foreign ministers of the ten ASEAN countries and China, Japan, and South Korea, chaired by Surin Pitsuwan in Bangkok, was soon followed by the fourth ASEAN + 3 summit in Singapore in November 2000.

A number of proposals surfaced concerning the creation of free trade zones and a free investment area. The meeting also resolved that a study group explore, as Singapore's Prime Minister (Goh 2000) put it, 'the feasibility, the implications, the complications, the benefits and negative implications, if any, of the ASEAN plus three organisation evolving into an East Asia summit'. On the sidelines of the fourth ASEAN + 3 informal summit Chinese Premier Zhu Rongji, Japanese Prime Minister Yoshiro Mori and South Korean President Kim Dae-Jung agreed on regular trilateral summits during their second private meeting outside the formal sessions of the Singapore summit.

Having briefly outlined the contours and development of East Asian regionalism since the crisis, we shall now focus on China's perspective on the emerging regionalism, the issues that the ASEAN plus Three process poses for China–ASEAN relations and any China–ASEAN initiatives that arose before the end of 2000.

China's position

Interestingly, similar to Washington, Beijing had also not reacted enthusiastically to the AMF proposal, for at least two reasons. First, China then had little desire to antagonise the Clinton administration given that Beijing was – at the time – keen on building a strategic partnership with Washington and planning for reciprocal presidential visits. Second, the establishment of such a fund would at least have considerably enhanced Japan's regional political and financial clout, a development that Beijing considers not to be in its interest. In the event, Chinese leaders preferred to raise Beijing's own regional stature by making and delivering on the promise not to devalue the Chinese yuan, a step that at the time was regarded as a likely trigger for a possible second round of devaluation of regional currencies. Furthermore, Beijing and the Special Administrative Region of Hong Kong also provided US$ 1 billion each to the US$ 17.2 billion package offered to Thailand. The central role of the IMF in addressing the regional crisis was reaffirmed not least by China in the so-called Manila Framework, endorsed by APEC leaders in November 1997.

For the time being, Beijing's participating in and supporting of regionalism at the level of ASEAN + 3 would appear to serve at least four objectives. First, Chinese leaders see regionalism as strengthening the PRC's own hand in meeting future crises and addressing economic vulnerabilities. Indeed, they do not regard China's economic security as a given.[24] Second, Chinese leaders seek to reinforce their credentials for long-term regional leadership. Notably, Beijing has joined the consensus of the other East Asian states even when no practical benefits were apparent. For instance, given the considerable foreign currency reserves accumulated on the mainland and Hong Kong, the establishment of a network of bilateral swap-arrangements as agreed at Chiang Mai promises to be of but limited practical significance to the PRC. Nevertheless, Beijing appears to have assented to the arrangements in part for fear of otherwise being characterised as a spoiler of monetary regionalism. A pro-active stance on the issue promises political gain even if the agreements are ultimately not actualised.

That said, Premier Zhu Rongji recently called on his counterparts to proceed with the clarification of how in practice the initiative could be implemented. This would indicate the salience of the third objective of participating in regionalism, the pursuit of China's economic and financial interests in the region and beyond. Advocating a six-point proposal on advancing co-operation between China and ASEAN, Premier Zhu has up to the time of writing identified political co-operation, human resources development, infrastructure building in the Mekong River Basin, hi-tech co-operation, agriculture and agricultural machinery, trade (including barter trade, countertrade) and two-way investment links as priority areas of co-operation (Zhu 2000). In relation to the last point, Zhu recently also proposed the creation of a China–ASEAN free trade zone. Already, China–ASEAN trade has increased to US $32 billion for the period from January to October 2000, an increase of 48% on the same period in 1999.

The fourth objective is political-strategic in so far as Chinese leaders seem to regard the PRC's participation in regionalist endeavours as a counter-balance to American and Japanese efforts to achieve regional influence in East Asia in general, Southeast Asia and the Mekong River sub-region.

China's economic challenge to ASEAN

This is not the place to discuss how in detail China's economy would benefit from the conclusion of a free-trade zone with ASEAN. Given that the PRC is heavily dependent on the major markets as export destinations, especially the United States and Japan, it is understandable that the Chinese leadership is interested in further diversifying its export markets. It may also well be that China's proposal was a response to the various bilateral FTA proposals currently being examined in policy-making circles, not least in Japan.[25] Significantly, China's proposal for a free trade zone with Southeast Asia comes with WTO-accession of the People's Republic being relevant. It also comes at a time when discussion within ASEAN has grown as to what extent Beijing's WTO-membership presents an economic challenge to its member states, even if some trade problems, especially in the agricultural sector, may feature less in the wake of successfully concluded bilateral WTO negotiations (Crampton 2000). China has of course argued that its accession to the WTO constitutes not a threat but an opportunity for the Association. As Zhu Rongji (1999b) put it: 'China cannot develop without East Asia, neither can East Asia prosper without China'.

However, many within ASEAN fear that China will suck in even more foreign direct investment from extra-regional countries than has already been the case since the Asian financial crisis. In 1999, FDI into China amounted to approximately US$ 39 billion, whereas Southeast Asia received merely US$ 7 billion. Some within ASEAN expect to lose a further 10% in foreign investment as a result of China's entry into the WTO (Manibhandu and Krongboonying 2000). It is further feared that China will eat into ASEAN's market share in developed markets (such as the United States). Interestingly, Thailand's Commerce Minister Supachai Panitchpakdi, who is due to become WTO-chief, has suggested that the free-trade area could also eventually include South Korea and Japan (Manibhandu and Krongboonying 2000).

Singapore's leaders, meanwhile, are fretting about the slackening pace of regional and global liberalisation in trade and services. To Singapore, there is an increasing prosperity gap between North and Southeast Asia, which makes it necessary for the city-state to 'leapfrog' out of Southeast Asia (Tang 2000, also see Bowring 2000). Singapore has thus sought to expand the range of bilateral free trade areas.[26] For their part, Chinese leaders seem keen to take advantage of Singapore to promote the development of China's export and securities market (Jin 2000).

The idea of a free trade zone between ASEAN and China is however not equally attractive to all ASEAN members. Indeed, implementation of AFTA has not significantly increased ASEAN's overall attractiveness for inward investment activity. There is also a question about the extent to which ASEAN members are prepared to commit themselves to face increasingly stiffer competition by reducing tariffs as prescribed by AFTA.[27] Indeed, rules have recently been formulated which allow members 'experiencing difficulties to temporarily withdraw' from sensitive sectors (Richardson 2000b).

Despite the ongoing attempts at deepening regionalism it is thus clear that ASEAN and China will need more time to agree on the details of the free-trade initiative. Also, while ASEAN member states would clearly like to see Southeast and Northeast Asia speak with a single voice, as this would improve their economic position and international relevance, in doing so ASEAN states will have to take account of rivalry between China and Japan and thus avoid falling prey to the influence of just one of the great powers. Not surprisingly, ASEAN has indicated an interest in the suggestion of Korean President Kim to also study the feasibility of an East Asia Free Trade zone, yet remains very much interested in engaging the United States, strategically and economically. Indeed, beyond the uncertaintities of the extent of future cooperation, there also remain areas in which China–ASEAN relations have not yet moved beyond disagreement and stalemate.

ASEAN–China differences over the envisaged regional code of conduct for the South China Sea are of particular importance in this regard. These differences reflect intramural ASEAN disagreements as to whether the code of conduct should also apply to the Paracels. Vietnam has insisted on this with a certain degree of intransigence, to some dismay of other ASEAN member countries. Not surprisingly, Chinese officials have been equally adamant that the Paracels, disputed only between Vietnam and the PRC, should not be covered in any agreement on a code of conduct valid between ASEAN and Beijing. The ASEAN–China Senior Officials Meeting on 15 March 2000 saw both sides present drafts that bore considerable similarity on safety of navigation, search and rescue and the advocacy of self-restraint and the undertaking not to resort to the use or threat of force to decide competing claims. However, differences over the geographic spread of the proposed code remained. The Philippines, seeking to bridge the gap by introducing into the draft a formulation whereby the code would cover 'disputed areas claimed in the South China Sea by more than two claimant states', was unsuccessful (*Philippine Daily Inquirer*, 16 March 2000, p. 2.). Although broad agreement pertains that the proposed code should cover how to handle disputes in the South China Sea, how to build trust and confidence, to promote co-operation on marine issues and environmental protection, and modes of consultation, the finalisation of the draft has continued to elude officials.[28]

Conclusion

This chapter has argued that China has refocused its attention on ASEAN member states in the aftermath of the Asian financial crisis for politico-strategic and economic reasons. I showed that significant improvement in bilateral relations notwithstanding, and encapsulated in the signing of co-operation framework agreements, Thailand and Indonesia were upgrading ties with Beijing to promote not only their own narrower economic interest but also a stable regional balance of power. At the same time I noted the obstacles to a further major short-term enhancement of Sino-Thai and Sino-Indonesian relations. Focusing on ties between China and ASEAN as a grouping, the chapter moreover demonstrated what is – at least for the moment – a considerable overlap of policy preferences in relation, for instance, to the politics of reform of the international financial architecture. On the other hand, the disparity in economic development within ASEAN has, as yet, provoked diverse responses by member states to Beijing's proposal for a free trade agreement between the PRC and Southeast Asia. Nevertheless, China–ASEAN ties are developing relatively quickly, both at the level of relations between Beijing and individual ASEAN governments and at that of China–ASEAN ties. The precise implications of this for the international politics of Southeast Asia will require further research.

Notes

1 The substance of the so-called 'partnerships' varies. Also, some partnerships have less substance than the diplomatic rhetoric suggests. See Anderson (1997) for a discussion of the Sino-Russian strategic partnership.
2 On the significance of sovereignty at the threshold to the 21st century, see Jackson (1999).
3 Interviews by the author with Chinese interlocutors in July 1998. See Haacke (1999) on the concept, origins and fate of the proposal for 'flexible engagement'.
4 For recent works suggesting that China is quite pragmatic in the practice of the principles that it espouses as the basis of its foreign policy, see Yahuda (2000) and Gill and Reilly (2000).
5 See Ganesan (1999) for a discussion of the intramural difficulties within ASEAN.
6 For details see 'China's Proposition on the Establishment of a New International Political and Economic Order' (undated) and 'China's View on the Development of Multi-Polarity' (undated).
7 My emphasis.
8 For details, see transcripts of interviews with U.S. Secretary of Defence William Cohen (2000a, 2000b).
9 See Blair (2000) for a recent statement on the establishment of 'security communities'.
10 According to press reports (*The Nation* 2000b) the reservation is meant to sustain a Baht 38 billion joint venture paper mill project. The government estimates the paper mill will contribute Baht 11.4 billion worth of exports. The Cabinet has also lifted the law prohibiting private entities to acquire over 500 rai of forest land for business activities.
11 The same message was re-articulated to a Thai delegation visiting Beijing which was headed by Thailand's Deputy Foreign Minister M.R. Sukhumbhand Paribatra, Secretary General of the National Security Council (Khachatphai Buruphat), and the Deputy Secretary of the Office of the Narcotics Control Board. The delegation was tasked to discuss the issue of narcotics suppression in the Golden Triangle with Chinese officials from the Ministry of Public Security in late August 2000; also involved were State Councillor Luo Gan, Deputy

Minister of Internal Security Bai Jingfu and Deputy Foreign Minister, Yang Jiechi.

12 The attempts to balance the major regional powers have also led Bangkok to explore the relationship with India. Prime Minister, Atal Bechari Vajpayee, was scheduled to visit Thailand in early 2001.

13 On the development of Sino-Indonesia ties, see Sukma (1999).

14 The agreement was cancelled in the wake of the East Timor crisis in September 1999.

15 When meeting Chinese students in Beijing, Wahid apparently won spontaneous applause when he noted that his daughter was learning Mandarin at university in Indonesia. He apparently got even louder applause when he added that he hoped that 'one day she will be here, learning Chinese more fully from you, because I come from Chinese stock.' Wahid claims that his ancestors originated from China's Xinjiang Autonomous Region some 500 years ago.

16 Notable is the absence in the communiqué of any reference to the principles enshrined in the Treaty of Amity and Co-operation. Mention of the TAC was however made in the joint statement of May 2000.

17 The lifting of the suspension has been tied to senior Indonesian military officers being made accountable to the atrocities in East Timor as well as the return of refugees from West Timor.

18 In this context, it is worth noting that ASEAN supported Japan's bid to nominate its former vice finance minister, Eisuke 'Mr. Yen' Sakakibara, as the new head of the International Monetary Fund. In 2000, regional countries largely supported Thai Deputy Prime Minister and Commerce Minister Supachai Panithpakdi as World Trade Organisation chief.

19 See ASEAN (1998) for further details.

20 The forum of ASEAN Finance and Central Bank Deputies and its working group, the ASEAN Select Committee for the ASEAN Surveillance Process, have institutionally supported the ASP. It has been further assisted by the ASEAN Surveillance Co-ordinating Unit (ASCU) based at the ASEAN Secretariat and the ASEAN Surveillance Technical Support Unit (ASTSU) based at the Asian Development Bank in Manila.

21 The Statement of Bold Measures focused on an acceleration of the establishment of the ASEAN Free Trade Area, or AFTA, and ASEAN Investment Area, or AIA, including the provision of special incentives and privileges to qualified foreign investors for a limited period. To further encourage investment, the leaders agreed to waive the 30% national equity requirement for firms wishing to take advantage of the ASEAN Industrial Cooperation Scheme. Finally, they agreed on a new round of negotiation in services beginning in the year 1999 and ending in 2001, in all services sectors and all modes of supply. On AFTA, the six original members agreed to achieve a minimum of 90% of their total tariff lines with tariffs of 0–5% by the year 2000 and bring forward the implementation of AFTA from 2003 to 2002.

22 For details on the New Miyazawa Initiative, see Japanese Ministry of Foreign Affairs (1998).

23 For a recent overview of Japanese financial assistance to Asian countries, see Japanese Ministry of Foreign Affairs (2000).

24 Accordingly, Zhu Rongji has proposed, first, to institutionalise the meeting of finance and central bank deputies; second, to share information on financial reforms and to set up an ad hoc committee for an in-depth study of the supervision and regulation of international capital flow, the improvement of capabilities of guarding against and forecasting financial risks, the restructuring

of the international financial system and other questions; and third, to co-ordinate the positions of East Asian countries on major financial and economic issues through this mechanism. See Zhu Rongji (1999b).

25 Japan has taken up negotiations with Singapore. Malaysia has also been interested in a bilateral free trade area with Japan. See *Südostasien aktuell*, November 2000, p. 488.

26 Singapore has initiated negotiations to conclude bilateral free trade agreements with New Zealand, Australia, Japan and the United States. See Richardson (2000a).

27 Malaysia recently asked to withdraw automobile products from the AFTA tariff-cutting scheme. Tempted by the move from Kuala Lumpur, Manila said it would opt out of the petrochemical and automobile sectors. See Severino (2000) for a response to this development.

28 While Malaysia and Vietnam continued to differ over the geographic extension of the code, other contentious points were settled. The Philippines and China agreed on a compromise wording to ensure no new occupation or structures will be built in the disputed areas. Malaysia's concerns about the interpretation of disputes as questions of territorial integrity or sovereignty were settled by an agreement that these be decided on a case-by-case basis.

Bibliography

ASEAN (1998) Terms of Understanding on the Establishment of the ASEAN Surveillance Process, Washington, D.C., 4 October 1998 at http://www.asean.or.id/economic/term-fin.htm.

——. (1999a) Joint Ministerial Statement of 3rd ASEAN Finance Ministers' Meeting, Hanoi, 20 March 1999 at http://www.asean.or.id/news/afmin_3.htm.

——. (1999b) Common ASEAN Position on Reforming the International Financial Architecture, adopted at Special ASEAN Finance Ministers' Meeting, Manila, 30 April 1999, at http://www.asean.or.id/general/publication/comm.htm.

——. (1999c) Joint Ministerial Statement of the Special ASEAN Finance Ministers' Meeting, Manila, 25 November 1999, http://www.aseansec.org/economic/jps_sfin.htm.

——. (2000) Joint Press Statement at Third Meeting of the ASEAN Investment Area (AIA) Council, 4 October 2000, Chiang Mai, http://www.asean.or.id/ecnomic/invest/3thaia.htm.

Asian Defence Journal, 3/2000, pp. 50–52.

——. (2000) 'Interview with Zhu Rongji of the People's Republic of China', 3/2000: 18–20.

Anderson, Jennifer (1997) *The Limits of Sino-Russian Strategic Partnership*, Adelphi Paper 315 (Oxford: Oxford University Press for The International Institute for Strategic Studies).

Bangkok Post, 20 July 2000.

Blair, Dennis (2000) Commander in Chief, U.S. Pacific Command, at the Carnegie International Non-Proliferation Conference, 16 March 2000, http://www.ceip.org/programs/npp/blair2000.htm.

Bowring, Philip (2000) 'Southeast Asians Have a Big Stake in Northeastern Stability', *IHT*, 25 July 2000, http://www.iht.com/IHT/PB/00/pb072500.html.

Chan, Gerald (1999) *Chinese Perspectives on International Relations: A Framework for Analysis* (Basingstoke and London: Macmillan).

Chen Peiyao (1998) 'Grand Adjustment of Sino-U.S. Relations: On a constructive strategic partnership', *IISS Journal* (Shanghai), 5 (2): 1–8.

China's National Defense (1998) (Beijing: Information Office of the State Council of the People's Republic of China).

China's National Defence in 2000 (Beijing: Information Office of the State Council of the People's Republic of China).

China's Ministry of Foreign Affairs (undated a) 'China and Indonesia' at http://www.fmprc.gov.cn/eng/4360.html.

——. (undated b) 'China's Proposition on the Establishment of a New International Political and Economic Order', http://www.fmprc.gov.cn/eng/4493.

——. (undated c) 'China's View on the Development of Multi-Polarity', http://www.fmprc.gov.cn/eng/4499.html.

Chongkittavorn, Kavi (1997) 'A New Stage Prepared for Thai-Sino Relations', *The Nation*, 22 February 1997, http://www.202.44.251.4/nationnews/1997/199702/19970222/2049.html.

Cohen, William (2000a) Transcript of interview with Secretary of Defense William Cohen at http://www.defenselink.mil/news/Sep2000/t019182000_t0917sda.html.

——. (2000b) Transcript of interview with Secretary of Defense William Cohen at http://www.defenselink.mil/news/Sep2000/t09202000_t0919sec.html.

Crampton, Thomas (2000) 'Thai Calls for Concessions to Protect Less Developed Economies', *IHT*, 9 October 2000, http://www.iht.com/IHT/TC/00/tc100900.html.

Dieter, Heribert (2000) 'Asia's Monetary Regionalism', *FEER*, 6 July 2000, http://www.feer.com/_0007_06/p30.html.

Dittmer, Lowell (1997) 'Unstable Outlook: China's quest for a coherent foreign policy', *Harvard Asia Pacific Review*, 2 (1): 14–17.

East, James (2000) 'Drug Armies Using Thailand as Base: Yangon', *The Straits Times*, 31 July 2000, http://www.straitstimes.asia1.com.sg/asia/sea5_0731.html.

Far Eastern Economic Review 19 October 2000, 7 December 2000.

Finkelstein, David and Michael McDevitt (1999) 'Competition and Consensus: China's "New Concept of Security" and the United States Security Strategy for the East Asia-Pacific Region', *PacNet Newsletter*, http://www.csis.org/pacfor/pac0199.html.

Ganesan, N. (1999) *Bilateral Tensions in Post-Cold War ASEAN* (Singapore: ISEAS).

Garver, John W. (1998) 'Sino-Russian Relations', in Samuel S. Kim (ed.) *China and the World: Chinese Foreign Policy Faces the New Millennium*, 4th edition (Boulder, CO: Westview Press), pp. 114–132.

Gill, Bates and James Reilly (2000) 'Sovereign Intervention and Peacekeeping: The View from Beijing', *Survival*, 42 (3): 41–59.

Godement, François (1999) *The Downsizing of Asia* (London and New York: Routledge).

Goh Chok Tong (2000) 'Transcript of Remarks to the Media by PM Goh on the Discussion of the ASEAN + 3 Summit', 4th AIS, 24 November 2000, http://www.mfa.gov.sg/speeches/index.htm.

Haacke, Jürgen (1999) 'The Concept of Flexible Engagement and the Practice of Enhanced Interaction: Intramural Challenges to the "ASEAN way"', *The Pacific Review*, 12 (4): 581–611.

He Kai (2000) *Interpreting China–Indonesia Relations: 'Good Neighbourliness', 'Mutual Trust' and 'All-Round Cooperation'*, Working Paper 349 (Canberra: Australia National University).

Jackson, Robert (ed.) (1999) *Sovereignty at the Millennium* (Oxford: Blackwell).

Japanese Ministry of Foreign Affairs (1998) On the Record Briefing by Mr Sadaaki Numata, 17 November 1998, http://www.mofa.go.jp/policy/economy/apec/1998/brief17.html.

——. (2000) 'Asian Economic Crisis and Japan's Contribution', October 2000, at http://www.mofa.go.jp/policy/economy/asia/crisis0010.html.

Jiang Zemin (1999) 'Enhance Good Neighbourliness and Friendship: Build a Better Future Together', Speech at National Cultural Center, Bangkok, 3 September 1999, http://www.bjr99–38e–3.html.

Jin Zeqing (2000) 'China should rethink export policy', *China Daily*, 25 March 2000, http://www.chinadaily.com.cn/cndydb/2000/03/d4_1trad.325html.

Johnston, Alastair Iain and Robert S. Ross (eds) (1999) *Engaging China: The Management of an Emerging Power* (London: Routledge, 1999).

Joint Statement of the Meeting of Heads of State/Government of the Member States of ASEAN and the President of the People's Republic of China (1997), Kuala Lumpur, 16 December 1997.

Joint Statement on East Asia Co-operation (1999) Manila, 28 November, http://www.aseansec.org/summit/inf3rd/js_eac.htm.

Khumrungroji, Sa-Nguan (2000) 'China Urged to Put Heat on Burma', *The Nation*, 20 July 2000, pp. A1, A6.

Lintner, Bertil, Nayan Chanda and Sadamand Dhume (2000) 'Troubled Junta', *FEER*, 29 June 2000, p. 24.

Manibhandu, Anuraj and Woranant Krongboonying (2000) 'China trade ties welcome, says Supachai', *Bangkok Post*, November 24, http://www.bangkokpost.net/241100_News16.html.

McBeth, John (2000) 'Military Manoeuvres', *FEER*, 9 November, pp. 32–34.

Office of the United Nations High Commissioner for Human Rights (1999), Report of the Commission on Human Rights on Its Fourth Special Session, http://www.unhchr.ch/huridocda/huridoca.nsf/(Symbol)/E.CN4.1999.167.ADD.1, E.1999.23.ADD.1.En?OpenDocument.

Owada, Hisashi (2000) 'Japan–ASEAN Relations in East Asia', Singapore, 16 October 2000, http://www.jiia.or.jp/report/owada/singapore.html.

Philippine Daily Inquirer, 16 March 2000.

PRC–Indonesia Joint Press Communiqué, Beijing, 3 December 1999, http://www.deplu.go.id/china–3des99.htm.

Richardson, Michael (1999) 'Japan Endorses Standby Funds to Stabilize Southeast Asia', *IHT*, 27 November 1999, http://www.iht.com/IHT/MR/99/mr112799.html.

——. (2000a) 'Development Grows from Stalemate in World Trade Organization', *IHT*, 17 April 2000, http://www.iht.com/IHT/MR/mr041700html.

——. (2000b) 'ASEAN Tinkers with Free-Trade Agreement', *IHT*, 26 July 2000, http://www.iht.com/IHT/MR/00/mr072600.html.

Severino, Rudolfo C. (2000) 'The ASEAN Free Trade Area: Moving ahead on Regional Integration', 21 November 2000, http://www.asean.or.id/secgen/sg_mari.html.

Smith, Anthony L. (2000) 'Indonesia's Foreign Policy under Abdurrahman Wahid', *Contemporary Southeast Asia*, December 2000, 22 (3): 498–526.

Sukma, Rizal (1994) 'Recent Developments in Sino-Indonesian Relations: An Indonesian View', *Contemporary Southeast Asia*, 16 (1): 35–45.

——. (1999) *Indonesia and China: The Politics of a Troubled Relationship* (London and New York: Routledge).

Südostasien aktuell, November 2000.

Tang Jiaxuan (1998) Statement of the People's Republic of China at the Post-Ministerial Conference, Manila, 28 July at http://www.aseansec.org/amm/pmc31osh.htm.

——. (1999) Address at China–ASEAN Dialogue, Singapore, 27 July, http://www.aseansec.org/amm/pmc32osh.htm.

——. (2000) Statement at 7th ARF Foreign Minister Meeting, Bangkok, 27 July 2000, http://www.dfat.gov.au/arf/st_proc.html.

Tang, Edward (2000) 'BG Lee in Thailand: ASEAN Must Close Ranks, Press on', *Straits Times*, 1 December 2000, http://www.straitstimes.asia1.g/primenews/story/0,1870,7113,00.html.

Thayer, Carlyle A. (2000) 'China Consolidates Its Long-term Bilateral Relations with Southeast Asia', *Comparative Connections*, 2nd Quarter 2000, China–ASEAN Relations, http://www.csis.org/pacfor/cc/002Qchina_asean.html.

The Nation (1999) 'Compensate China for Nato Attack, US Urged', 11 May, http://202.44.251.4/nationnews/1999/199905/19990511/43134.htm.

——. (2000a) 'Supachai to Discuss Trade with China', 18 January 2000, http://202.44.251.4/nationnews/2000/200001/20000118/779.html.

——. (2000b) 'Plantation Secured for Joint Paper Mill Project', 2 February 2000, http://202.44.251.4/nationnews/2000/200001/20000202/1399.html.

Weggel, Oskar (2000) 'Multipolarisierung: eine Konkretisierung des Konzepts', *China aktuell*, February 2000, pp. 109–110.

Winn, Howard (1999) 'Avoiding Thailand May Be Sage Advice for Falun Gong Guru', *South China Morning Post*, 4 August 1999, http://www.FullText_asp_ArticleID_19990804.

Yahuda, Michael (2000) 'The Changing Faces of Chinese Nationalism: the Dimensions of Statehood', in Michael Leifer (ed.) *Asian Nationalism* (London: Routledge), pp. 21–37.

Zhu Rongji (1999a) Statement at the ASEAN+1 Informal Summit, 28 November, http://www.aseansec.org/summit/inf3rd/pr/prg_ch1.htm.

——. (1999b) Statement at the ASEAN+3 Informal Summit, 28 November, http://www.aseansec.org/summit/inf3rd/prg_ch3.htm.

——. (2000) Premier Zhu Rongji Attends 4th China–ASEAN Summit, *People's Daily*, 26 November 2000, http://www.english.peopledaily.com.cn/200011/26/eng20001126_56185html

Chapter 15

The Politics of the European Union's Relations with China

Paul Lim

Introduction

European Union (EU)–China relations have been highlighted by two issues: China's admission into the World Trade Organisation (WTO) and human rights – the former in a multilateral forum and the latter in a bilateral political dialogue. However, EU–China relations are more than these. We also have to consider the various forms and fields of cooperation and trade governed by the bilateral 1985 European Economic Communities (EEC)-China Trade and Economic Cooperation Agreement.[1] In addition we have to consider the bilateral political dialogue. In the most general terms, the EU's relations with China could be described as pushing it towards a market economy, opening it up further to the world, especially to EU investors and traders.

The background to the relationship

Christopher Dent has recently argued that in the context of the Cold War, Beijing promoted multipolarity and welcomed the EC's enlargement of 1973 as constituting a new bloc. As Dent sees it, the Chinese interpreted this development as challenging the bipolar status quo. Still, Beijing was aware that that the EC would wield more economic power but not necessarily political power on the world stage. Dent quoted Kapur on 'commmunicative diplomacy' between Beijing and Brussels, which was followed by 'exploratory diplomacy' (Dent 1999: 131–2). This led to the EEC establishing a relationship with China in 1973 when the External Relations Commissioner of the Commission, Sir Christopher Soames, met with Chinese Premier, Zhou Enlai. This was followed by the accreditation of China's first Ambassador to the EEC soon after.[2] The EC Council of

Ministers agreed in 1974 that future trade negotiations with China should be led by the European Commission, given that the latter had competence over trade matters. The trade-off was not to pursue formal relations with Taiwan in the future, which was accepted with some hesitancy (Dent 1999: 132). The first trade agreement with China was signed in 1978. Seven years later, a Trade and Economic Cooperation Agreement[3] was signed in 1985. This agreement was to be valid for five years with the possibility of renewing it each year provided neither side decided to terminate it. The agreement is still in force and can still be amended to take account of new situations. In October 1988, the Commission opened a Delegation in Beijing.[4] As a consequence of the Tiananmen incident in June 1989 relations were suspended. Relations were revived through higher level contacts following the General Affairs Committee (GAC) decision in October 1990[5] and, since January 1992, the Joint Committee (JC) meets under the Agreement. The revival of relations in 1992 excluded cooperation projects in the military field. The EC lifted its sanctions in November 1990 (Dent 1999: 137). June 1994 saw the establishment of a new arrangement for political dialogue, consisting of additional meetings at high level. In the same year a broad EU–China political dialogue was formally established through an exchange of letters.[6] On 5 July 1995, the Commission released its Communication on 'A Long-Term Policy for China–Europe Relations' (COM (95)–279 Final). This was adopted in the Council's Conclusions of the same year (C4-0288/95). In 1996, an informal China Experts Group was established to coordinate the Commission's activities with those undertaken by the Member States, complementing the existing consultative groups with the Member States (Asia Working Group, etc.). On 13–19 November 1996, Sir Leon Brittan made a trip to Beijing accompanied by European business leaders. A document was published on this trip. 1996 also saw the start of the EU–China human rights dialogue. On 25 March 1998, the Commission published another Communication, 'Building a Comprehensive Partnership with China' (COM (1998) 181 final). Soon after, the EU–China summit took place on the margins of ASEM in London on 2 April 1998. The next major event was the first official presidential visit to China by President Santer accompanied by two Commissioners, Leon Brittan and Yves de Silguy in October 1998. The major events of 1999 (visits and meetings) were very much tied up to WTO negotiations and the human rights dialogue. The second EU–China Summit took place on 13 May 1999. It should be noted that these recent years have also seen the signing of sectoral agreements, in the areas of energy, science and technology. The year 2000 saw the EU–China agreement on China's accession to the WTO. The third summit took place in October 2000.

What came with the 1985 agreement

Analysis will first focus on the 1985 Agreement as it is the legal basis of EU–China relations.

The Joint Commission

The 1985 Agreement institutionalised a Joint Commission (JC). The JC monitors and examines the functioning of the Trade and Economic Cooperation Agreement, reviews the various cooperation schemes, examines questions related to the implementation of the agreement, examines problems hindering the development of trade and economic cooperation, examines means and new opportunities of developing trade and economic cooperation and makes recommendations to achieve the objectives of the Agreement. It is one key institution where both sides meet regularly.

Areas of cooperation

It must be said that projects on the ground are the tangible nuts and bolts of the EU's relations with China. It is here that the EU actually deploys its resources. There are at least fifty-one cooperation projects or programmes.[7]

The EC first provided financial and technical assistance in 1984. Between 1991 and 1994, under the basic budget lines for development aid and economic cooperation in Asia, less than 20 million ECU were set aside each year for China.[8] The EU's budgetary resources since 1995 have tripled to around 70 million ECU per year up to 1999.[9] Since 1995 there has been a shift in emphasis.[10] Rural development projects continue, but must reflect the environmental dimension, centre on economic cooperation and feed the Chinese population. Poverty alleviation activities will be expanded to urban areas. The shift of emphasis has opened up four new areas: human resources development; promotion of economic and social reform; business cooperation and environment; and sustainable development. In these areas the rule of law and business cooperation are top priorities. Projects which are not central to these objectives will be phased out or not renewed.[11] Cooperation projects can be seen as the 'carrot' to promote market reforms and greater access to the Chinese market.

The following is a selection of recent cooperation projects and programmes in China.

(1) Rural/agricultural development cooperation

In this area, the projects include the China–Europe Cooperation in Agriculture Programme (CECA) (1997–2001), the Water Buffalo Development Project (1996–2002), the Land Reclamation Project (1992–1999), the Potato Development Project in Qinghai (1994–2001), livestock development in Qinghai (1994–2000), 'technical and commercial cooperation within the dairy and food processing sector' (1994–2000), and so on.

(2) Human resources development

In this category we find projects such as the China–Europe International Business School (CEIBS) (1994–); the EU–China Basic Education Project (1999–2003) in Gansu Province, the EU–China Higher Education Programme (1996–2000); the EU–China Academic Network (ECAN) (1997–2000); the EU–China Junior Managers Programme (1998–2003); EU–China 2000 Scholarship Programme (2000–2004); and so on.

(3) Economic and social reform[12]

This category includes the following projects: the China–Europe Public Administration (CEPA) Programme (1999–2003); the EU–China Intellectual Property Rights (IPR) Cooperation Programme (1997–1999–2001); a three-year programme called 'Framework Programme for EU support to China's accession to the WTO' (1998–); the EU–China Village Governance Programme (1997–2001); the EU–China Norms and Standards Programme (1997–2000); Statistics (February 1998-2001); a pilot public procurement programme (1999–2000); a financial services cooperation project (1999–2002); a legal cooperation programme (1999–2003); and so on. Such projects promote the rule of law since investors and traders would want a system in place which can guarantee the protection of foreign investments, create a climate of transparency, predictability and certainty.

(4) Cooperation in the field of the environment

In this category we find the following programmes: the Natural Forestry Development Programme (2000–2004); a programme looking at urban industrial pollution in Liaoning province (1999–2004); the EC–China Environmental Management Cooperation Programme (EMCP) (1997–1999–2000–); an environmental protection and poverty alleviation programme in Yunnan Province; a Municipal Solid Waste Management Programme (1999–2001); an Environmental Education Television Project (1999–2000); and so on.

(5) Energy

In this category a series of feasibility studies have been completed: biomass gasification for power generation in rural areas; energy efficiency in building; exploitation of marine currents for power generation; and low cost gas desulphurisation for coal-fired power plants. Other projects included co-generation (COGEN), an energy-efficient technology and a natural gas project, and the creation of a EU–China Natural Gas Centre in 2000.

(6) Scientific and technological cooperation

In this category the press (Agence Europe, 19 December 1998: 10) anticipated the signing of a Scientific and Technical Cooperation Agreement on 22 December 1998 for joint research programmes in the framework of the 5th Research Framework Programme (1998–2002).

(7) Health and education

In this important category we find an HIV/AIDS programme agreed in 1994, ending 1998, which funded training facilities in Beijing, Shanghai and Nanjing as well as 25 provincial training centres. This programme had a follow-up (1998–2001). A further example is the 980,000 euro grant to support the Disabled Persons' Federation for two years.

(8) Humanitarian aid

In emergencies, humanitarian assistance can be provided in the event of heavy snowstorms, earthquakes, floods, etc. The assistance takes the form of provision of food, clean water and so on.

(9) Business and industrial cooperation

In 1995 it was noted that European investment in China still lagged behind Hong Kong, the USA, Japan and Taiwan in terms of number of joint ventures and capital invested, but the average size of EU projects tended to be larger.[13] There was a clear perception that EU companies were less dynamic than their competitors in the Chinese market – and hence missing opportunities.[14] However, Dent has stated that the stock of EU direct investment in China rose in absolute terms from US$6,430 in 1993 to US$22,634 million by 1996. However, in relative terms, the EU's share of total inward foreign direct investment (FDI) into China declined further to 4.8% over this period, with both Japan (5.6%) and the USA's share (7.5%) ahead (Dent 1999: 135).[15] In 1998, the EU FDI was 3.7 billion euro.[16] In 1999, the EU recorded the highest FDI levels in China, excluding Hong Kong, as European companies again invested US$4.5 billion. However, the EU's share of FDI in China (9%) has remained disappointingly low (with a level of FDI only half of US or Japanese investments levels).[17]

(10) Trade

Bilateral trade flows are continuing to grow rapidly. Total two-way trade increased more than twentyfold since reforms began in China in 1978 and was worth 54 billion euro in 1998.[18] In 1999, the overall two-way trade stood at 69 million euro.[19]

Between 1990 and 1997, the EU's trade deficit quadrupled from 5.3 billion ECU to 20.9 billion ECU, a deficit only second to that with Japan of 23.3 billion ECU. In 1998, the EU's trade deficit with China reached 24.4 billion euro.[20] In 1999, the deficit reached 30 billion euro.[21] The EEC enjoyed a positive trade balance between 1983 and 1987, reaching a peak in 1985 with a 3.2 billion ECU trade surplus *vis-à-vis* China. Since 1988, however, the situation has changed dramatically. The EU's trade deficit is attributed to market access obstacles in China.[22]

Trade activities

During the 1980s the EC was losing market share of China's import market, but it was said that this slight reduction compared favourably with the collapse of the US (which declined from 19% in 1980 to 8% in 1990) and Japanese (from 26% in 1980 to 10% in 1990) shares in the same period. The EU managed to retain its relative position much more successfully than its competitors.[23] In 1992, there was an increase in market share to 12–13%.[24] In 1995, the EU had almost 15% of China's imports which made it the second largest supplier on the Chinese market after Japan and before Taiwan and the US.[25] The EU took pride in its market share of around 15% in the 1990s even though this was less impressive than that of Japan, but more impressive than the stagnant US share.[26] In 1997, the EU's share of China's imports fell from 20% to 13.1%. Nevertheless, the EU maintained its position as China's third most important source of imports (Dent 1999: 137). In 1998, the EU was again the second trading partner (14.8%) after Japan (20.2%).[27]

Conversely, China's exports to the EU have risen steadily since the 1980s. In 1980, China's share of EU imports was just 0.7%.[28] Between 1990 and 1997, EU imports from China tripled in value from 10.6 billion ECU to 37.3 billion ECU. In the same period, China's share of extra-EU15 imports rose from 2.6% to 5.6%. The EU nevertheless fell from third to fourth place in China's export market rankings, with the USA overtaking the EU in the early 1990s. By 1997, China had become the EU's fourth largest source of imports and the EU's share of China's exports rose from 10% to 13% (Dent 1999: 137). This figure reached 18% in 1998, making the EU China's second largest export market, replacing Japan. China is the EU's third largest non-European trading partner overall after the US and Japan.[29] In 1999, as regards EU imports, China was the fourth most important trading partner (6.4%), in a list of 20 countries exporting to the EU.[30]

The China–EU trade flow is affected by three interconnected mechanisms: quotas, anti-dumping and the Generalised System of Preferences (GSP). In respect of quotas, under the trade provisions of both the 1978 and the 1985 Agreements, the basis of EEC–China trade relations is the Most Favoured Nation (MFN) treatment. Dent (1999) spoke of a modified MFN as China was not a member of GATT. It was also decided to consider China a non-market economy. In practice, therefore, China did not receive the same range of benefits as GATT members (Dent 1999: 132). As long as China's economy was said not to be a full market economy, where prices were determined by market forces, the EC member states continued to have quantitative restrictions (QRs) on China's imports. China's exports sold below world market prices threatened domestic industries in the EC. When the single market was completed in 1992, a review of these QRs covering some 4,700 quotas on Chinese goods took place.[31]

In March 1994, these national QRs were replaced by EU-wide QRs reflecting the need for a common import regime in the internal EU market. These QRs accounted then for about 13% of EU non-textile imports from China. This was in the wake of the conclusion of the Uruguay Round. This new QR regime only put seven product categories under quota. Other products were to be subjected to a surveillance regime with no quantitative limitations. In addition, the quota levels had been raised substantially in 1995, to take account of EU enlargement and of specific problems in certain sectors.[32]

It is not our intention to trace the products under QRs and follow their history of liberalisation or abolition; but by the mid-1990s China was the only trading partner of the EU that faced such restrictions (Dent 1999: 134). However, China did not take full advantage of its quotas. For example, it was reported that China did not use up its quotas for toys, footwear and dishes into the EU in 1997 and the Commission redistributed the unused portion for 1998 (Agence Europe, 18 April 1998: 8). In 1999, quotas for Chinese porcelain, ceramic dishes and footwear were maintained, but rules were modified for the assignment of quotas for 'non-traditional' imports because individual quantities were sometimes insufficient to be profitable.

Anti-dumping investigations against Chinese producers has involved a long list of products. Dent (1999: 134–40) traced anti-dumping duties on China to 1979 when saccharin and its salts were first subjected to anti-dumping duty. Dent reports that between 1979 and 1986 China attracted an average of two anti-dumping duties per annum from the EC, a relatively high figure for any of the latter's trading partners. In the period 1990–1997 China was subjected to 45 anti-dumping investigations, with an annual average figure of just under six. These annual figures were far higher than those for any other EU trading partner, constituting 16.8% of all investigations undertaken by the European Commission for the period and around a third of those directed at East Asian countries.

The Chinese government did not give into anti-dumping quietly. The PRC Ambassador to the EU stated that it was a serious problem and risked turning into an 'important obstacle' for the future development of EU–China bilateral relations. Between 1979 and 1997, 71 cases were opened by the Commission, much more, proportionally speaking, compared to all countries of South East Asia. In the Chinese official view, anti-dumping was wholly unjustified. The PRC Ambassador, pointing to the EU's consideration of China as a state economy, protested that China was now a socialist market economy (Agence Europe, 26 November 1997: 9).

In the Commission's 1998 Communication entitled 'Building a Comprehensive Partnership with China', amendments to the EC anti-dumping legislation *vis-à-vis* China were proposed, in view of China's progressive market reforms. The amendments included the removal of the label 'non-market' economy which had previously applied to China, and proposed instituting a new case-by-case approach in anti-dumping proceedings, whereby Chinese exporters, who operated within clearly defined market economy conditions, would be granted market economy treatment.[33] China had criticised the former system whereby the EU had calculated its anti-dumping duties basing price and cost decisions on comparable third country producers of the good in question. Beijing claimed that the Commission was selecting third countries' criteria to suit the EU's desired outcomes: namely relatively high anti-dumping duties (Dent 1999: 143). This modification was a clear political gesture as the two countries were negotiating on Beijing's accession to the WTO (Agence Europe, 18 December 1997: 10).

Anti-dumping has proved an irritating issue between the EU and Asian countries. Asian countries see anti-dumping, along with import quotas of the EU and textile agreements, as manifestations of EU protectionism and, as such, of 'fortress Europe'. The EU argues that anti-dumping measures serve to end unfair competition practices, not to impose protectionist barriers (Agence Europe, 30 July 1998: 6). Dent stated that China's competitive threat to European manufacturers has been and will continue to be considerable. The sectors affected were textiles, clothing and footwear, metal manufactures and various low-tech manufactures. The EU also sustained deficits in higher-tech sectors such as office machines, computers and electrical machinery (Dent 1999: 139). EU importers and consumer organisations have been protesting on the same side, demanding action from the Commission against Asian exporters.[34]

On the other hand, China has been included amongst the beneficiaries of the EEC's GSP since 1980. Total exports from China to the EC increased by 167.1% over the 1988–92 period, whilst the increase was 176.5% for products covered by GSP. The proportion of China's exports enjoying GSP benefits jumped from 2.1 billion ECU in 1988 to 6.6 billion ECU in 1992 and the Chinese share in the total benefits of the EC system went up from 13.7% to 22.2%, three times as much as the second greatest beneficiary. In 1992, 13.85 billion ECU worth of imports to the EC from China were eligible to be covered by GSP and out of this 6.59 billion ECU worth was received, representing 47.6% of the possible total. The highest percentage was achieved in agricultural products at 79.4%, whilst the largest amount of GSP received in real terms was in industrial products at around 5.63 billion ECU. In 1997, China was by far the biggest GSP beneficiary, with more than 30% of the value of all beneficiaries' imports. However, the implementation of the GSP's graduation mechanism (by which GSP advantages for certain sectors would be withdrawn due to the high level of industrial development of those sectors) would over time necessarily reduce the advantages previously enjoyed by China.[35] One could conclude that the products that graduated out of the GSP often became subject to anti-dumping duties.

Cooperation activities (in summary)

The EU is committed to developing its relations with China. The Commission's Communication 'Building a Comprehensive Partnership with China'[36] states that:

> The five traditional pillars of EU–China cooperation set out in the 1995 Communication – human resources development, administrative and social reforms, business and industrial cooperation, environmental cooperation, rural and urban poverty alleviation – have stood the test of time through the successful implementation of a range of projects, and the principles behind the 1995 long-term strategy will continue to underpin the EU's approach to its cooperation programme. This approach was further developed in the EC–China Memorandum of Understanding (MOU) on the programming of EC–China cooperation projects signed in October 1997 between the Commission and the Chinese authorities.

The crucial question in regard to the implementation of projects is: success for whom and how? From the experience on the ground it is not always clear that the recipient or the target group is satisfied with the execution of projects affecting them. One issue often noted is their involvement in the decision-making and -taking process. Parliamentarians sometimes get negative feedback from those working on the ground or from NGOs, a point which they raise with the Commission. There was, for instance, the case of the Pa Nam integrated rural development project in Tibet which was the subject of a query to the Commission by parliamentarians.[37]

These kinds of cooperation programmes apply to all developing countries with which the EU has an agreement. What is specific to China is that the cooperation programme is directed towards moving China towards becoming a fully developed market economy in the expectation that there will be a consequent movement towards becoming a liberal-democratic political system.

Bilateral political dialogue

The status of political dialogue

As stated earlier, political dialogue is not within the scope of the 1985 Agreement, as is the case with other third country agreements which the EU signs. However, as also stated previously, in 1994, through an exchange of letters, a broad political dialogue was formally established.

The institutions of political dialogue with China

The instruments or mechanisms for political dialogue[38] include the following:

(i) ad-hoc Foreign Ministers' Meetings, since 1994;
(ii) twice yearly meetings between the Chinese Foreign Minister and EU Ambassadors in Beijing, as well as the EU Presidency's Foreign Minister and the Chinese Ambassador, since 1994;
(iii) meeting of Political Directors at the Senior Officials Meeting (SOM) on policy areas, since 1994;
(iv) biannual meeting on human rights between the EU Troika and the Chinese government, since 1996; and
(v) annual EU–China Summit, at Heads of Government level, the first of which took place on 2 April 1998.

Rationale, significance and scope of political dialogue

The EU–China political dialogue was established in recognition of China's status as an emerging power.[39] Sir Leon Brittan was reported as saying that the EU needed to do more to recognise China as a global power and make the level of dialogue commensurate with this status (Agence Europe, 4 February 1998: 4). The Commission consequently proposed the institutionalisation of contacts with China, including at Head of State level in the form of annual summits as organised in relations with the USA, Russia and Japan.

Sir Leon Brittan is reported as having said at the time that the Commission would also argue in its Communication for the extension of Euro-Chinese dialogue to subjects of global and universal importance, such as reform of the UN and the ban on land mines (Agence Europe, 4 February 1998: 4). Other issues tabled for political dialogue include drug trafficking, money-laundering, organised crime and illegal immigration. These are all areas where the European Commission was granted new responsibilities under the Amsterdam Treaty.[40] The future of the UN, disarmament, arms reduction and human rights were noted as issues in the Council's Conclusions to the 1998 Commission's Communication (Agence Europe, 25 June 1998: 8). In 'EU Foreign Ministers approve Commission's strategy for partnership with China', on the EU–China website, the environment and regional security in Asia are added.[41]

The goals and objectives of political dialogue with China

The 1995 Communication on 'A Long-Term Policy for China–Europe Relations'[42] proposed the following as goals:

(i) to promote a dialogue on regional and global security issues which encourages full Chinese engagement in the international community through accession to all the key international instruments governing non-proliferation and arms control;
(ii) to give practical support to the trend in China towards creating a reformed public management system based on civil society and the rule of law;
(iii) to develop a programme of effective and coordinated cooperation in the legal and judicial fields; and
(iv) to support the principles of the Joint Declarations governing the transfer of sovereignty of Hong Kong and Macau.

The European Parliament (EP), in response to this 1995 Communication, came out with a Resolution,[43] which recommended a focus on cooperation, international issues, human rights and Hong Kong, Macao and Taiwan.

The Foreign Affairs Committee of the National People's Congress (NPC) on the 13th June 1997 immediately replied to the adoption of this 1995 Communication by the Parliament on 12 June 1997 by a two-page solemn statement. The statement argued that the EP resolution unjustifiably accused and vilified China at great length in terms of its judicial system, its policies towards minorities and religion, its domestic economic policies and foreign relations. In addition, its wording on the issues of human rights, Tibet, Taiwan, Hong Kong and Macao constituted a gross interference in China's internal affairs. According to the Foreign Affairs Committee, the 1995 EP Communication had poisoned the atmosphere of China–European relations and disrupted development of bilateral ties.

The 1998 Communication on 'Building a Comprehensive Partnership with China' has as aims the following:

(i) engaging China further, through an upgraded political dialogue, in the international community;

(ii) supporting China's transition to an open society based upon the rule of law and the respect for human rights;
(iii) integrating China further in the world economy by bringing it more fully into the world trading system and by supporting the process of economic and social reform underway in the country;
(iv) making Europe's funding go further; and
(v) raising the EU's profile in China.

The reason given for this new Communication was that several developments of such significance had occurred since 1995 that the EU should respond by upgrading and intensifying that policy further.[44] Sir Leon Brittan spelled out the rationale for this 1998 Communication (Agence Europe, 4 February 1998: 4). The 1995 Communication (built essentially on three pillars: political dialogue, Chinese accession to WTO and the extension of sectoral cooperation) had stood the test of time and would remain the backbone of the EU's policy. But much had changed even over that brief period. China's long march to a market economy was now irreversible. China had become a factor of stability seen from the way Hong Kong was transferred to Chinese authority, the smooth political transition after the death of Deng Xiaoping and the active and constructive Chinese intervention in several international political issues. Moreover, the EU was itself undergoing a period of change. Hence, there were changes in China and in Europe and there were changes in the EU's relationship with China. All that confirmed the need for further improvements to Europe's China policy. There was a need to set out the agenda for a more active relationship with China in the final years of the century.

When the Council adopted the Commission's 1998 Communication, Sir Leon Brittan declared that China had embarked on a remarkable programme of reform and was increasingly influential on the world stage. China had played a notably responsible role in resisting devaluation during the Asian financial crisis. This new policy document thus sent an important further signal to the Chinese leadership. The realisation of China's potential as a leading power in Asia over the long term would hinge on its ability to match its domestic reforms with a commitment to open markets on a world scale. Europe must work now to strengthen its economic partnership with China, coupling these developments with an active commitment to encourage the creation of a strong and open civil society (Agence Europe, 29/30 June 1998: 7).

The EP's response to the 1998 Communication came in the form of a report, then converted into a resolution approving the guidelines proposed by the Commission but calling for a clause on human rights in the renewal of the 1985 Trade and Cooperation Agreement with China.[45] The resolution also raised points like improving prison conditions, allowing human rights organisations to make regular and confidential visits to detainees, China's WTO accession and Taiwan (Agence Europe, 12 February 1999: 3).

The EU–China summits

Fulfilling the intention of upgrading political dialogue with China, the first EU–China Summit was held in London on 2 April 1998, on the margins of the Asia-Europe Meeting (ASEM). For China the summit amounted to recognition by the EU as a world power in world politics. Its admittance into the WTO would further enhance its position in the world. Perhaps its further intention would be to be part of G8, which included Russia although it is still developing country. Chancellor Schröder stated that it was hard to justify the view that Russia had its place in this group for political and economic reasons, while China did not. He said that serious thought should be given to including China in a future G9, in spite of the resistance certain to be made to such a suggestion (Agence Europe, 6 November 1999: 5).

The second EU–China Summit scheduled for 13 May 1999 in Beijing was cancelled as a result of the air strikes which destroyed parts of the Chinese embassy in Belgrade. Chancellor Schröder, as President-in-Council, went to China for informal talks on the war in Kosovo and presented unreserved apologies on behalf of NATO for the bombing (Agence Europe, 13 May 1999: 4). The summit was re-scheduled for December 1999, to include negotiations on the conditions for China's membership to the WTO (Agence Europe, 10 December 1999: 3).

Human rights in political dialogue and civil society's reactions

Until the 1995 Communication, the consistency of the EU institutions towards China at the UN Commission on Human Rights (UNCHR)[46] was unquestionable, although Beijing managed to block resolutions critical of China put forward by the EU (Agence Europe, 20 February 1997: 9). The 1995 Communication stated that, as regards the UNCHR, '[t]he level of international support attracted for the resolution criticising the situation in China in February 1995 suggests that this approach is bearing fruit'.[47] But in 1996 the relationship turned confrontational. In 1996, the specific human rights dialogue[48] was interrupted after the EU tabled a critical motion at the UNCHR.[49] The Italian Foreign Minister Lamberto Dini proposed to the Chinese side the idea of sending an EU Troika mission to Tibet (Agence Europe, 15 October 1996: 3). If the visit could lead to 'identifiable' progress in human rights in Tibet,[50] this could open the way to adjusting the draft resolution.[51] Then, in a 1997 meeting between the EU Troika and China focused on human rights, the atmosphere of the exchanges was 'particularly tense'.[52] In 1997, EU member states could not reach agreement on the sponsorship of a resolution criticising China at the UNCHR.[53] The resolution was opposed by France, Germany, Italy and Spain (Agence Europe, 5 April 1997: 4).

In the light of this, Denmark submitted a resolution to the UNCHR co-sponsored by the majority of EU member states, the US, Norway, Iceland and Liechtenstein (Agence Europe, 12 April 1997: 2). China's response was to suspend exchange visits with Denmark and dialogue on human rights. Beijing also postponed a visit by a Dutch trade mission to China (Agence Europe, 16 April 1997: 3). Agence Europe quoted the Commission saying to the Chinese authorities that no third countries could discriminate against the member states regarding economic and commercial matters (Agence Europe, 22 May 1997: 11).

It was reported in 1997 that the EU Troika was trying to re-launch a dialogue on human rights with China by proposing to finance concrete cooperation projects like the training of lawyers and prison guards. The Chinese were ready to re-start the human rights dialogue conditional on the EU renouncing presenting a resolution on human rights to the UN. October 1997 was the date set for the dialogue in Brussels, without pre-conditions, replacing confrontation by cooperation, as the Chinese said, and based on equality and mutual respect. The EU qualified the dialogue as 'constructive' based on concrete cooperation projects (Agence Europe, 26 September 1997: 3). The Presidency in Council stated that the EU 'promised nothing in exchange' for the resumption of the dialogue and added that the tabling of another resolution in 1998 remained a possibility (Agence Europe, 26 September 1997: 3). China agreed to normalise relations with Denmark in October 1997 (Agence Europe, 16 October 1997: 6). In this field of human rights, the balance of power, in a neo-realist perspective, was more favourable to the Chinese. From then on, the EU, as the record shows, no longer co-sponsored or co-tabled any human rights resolutions at the UNCHR that were critical of China, using progress in EU–China human rights dialogue as an excuse – even when there was little, if any, progress.

In 1997, Human Rights Watch (HRW) stated that by going for a dialogue, it would prevent the EU from publicly criticising human rights practices in China (Agence Europe, 26 September 1997: 3). Earlier, HRW urged working towards tabling a resolution in 1998 saying that the threat of tabling a resolution had proved effective to pressure China, as demonstrated by some 'positive initiatives' (the release of dissidents and the 1994 invitation to the UN's Special Reporter on Religious Intolerance) (Agence Europe, 8/9 September 1997: 7). This seemed to be a damage control exercise.

It was reported in 1998 that a great majority of the EU Member States did not seem too keen on the idea that the EU should table a resolution on the human rights situation in China for the March 1998 session of the

UNCHR on the basis of initial results of the October 1997 dialogue (Agence Europe, 28 January 1998: 4). The French Minister for European Affairs stated that France regarded the Euro-Chinese dialogue to be preferable to the adoption of a resolution that made the EU look both aggressive and ineffective. The Danish Foreign Minister spoke of progress that China had made since 1997: she had signed the UN Covenant on Social and Economic Rights, agreed to the visit of the UN High Representative for Human Rights, resumed dialogue with the EU on human rights and agreed to EU ambassadors visiting Tibet. To table a resolution without a follow-up, it was argued, would be counter-productive for the human rights situation in China. In 1998, not surprisingly, the EU did not table or co-sponsor a resolution. The EU had completely caved in to China's demand. Behind all this one cannot help thinking that overriding interests, economic ones in particular, determined the decision.

In 1998, reacting against the GAC's decision not to table or co-sponsor a China resolution at the UNCHR, Amnesty International (AI) stated that the UNCHR was the main forum to address the human rights situation in UN Member States which could not be replaced simply by discussions in other fora. The GAC's decision was a disappointing message. The few improvements recorded in 1997 in respect of human rights in China did not warrant 'relaxing' scrutiny of China's human rights situation. HRW spoke of the EU–China dialogue as 'fundamentally flawed'. Laying out four 'benchmarks'[54] to measure progress, the EU set a low threshold with the most minimal requirements. By so doing, it virtually guaranteed that China could avoid any further debate in Geneva without substantially improving its human rights practices (Agence Europe, 4 March 1998: 5). The representative of the Tibetan Government-in-exile regretted that the EU decided not to back any resolution at the UNCHR. He said that they were in favour of dialogue if it led to results and he went on to speak of the worsening situation in Tibet (Agence Europe, 12 March 1998: 3).

A second meeting about human rights in Beijing was deemed 'encouraging', judged representatives of the Council Troika (Agence Europe of 26/27 October 1998: 12). But the third EU–China human rights dialogue scheduled for 8–9 February 1999 in Berlin[55] was reported in Agence Europe as: '[D]ialogue on human rights seems to be making progress, but stuck on issues of penal law and minorities' (Agence Europe, 15/16 February 1999: 5).

In 1999, the HRW stated that it was time to go back to Geneva, as China was carrying out one of the worst crackdowns against political dissidents since 1989. AI expressed disenchantment with the dialogue process as it lacked transparency, a satisfactory level of participation, as well as concrete results. Per Gahrton, President of the Parliament's Delegation to China stated that the dialogue had failed. It was necessary to have a pragmatic approach and to stay in contact with China. But it was not necessary to fear putting pressure on China which could not isolate itself from the rest of the world and which wanted to be recognised as a great international power, allowing her to save face (Agence Europe, 6 February 1999: 9). Dissident Wei Jingsheng urged a resolution for the 1999 session, saying that a strategy of 'closed door' dialogue would have the consequence of China being able to evade UN censure and return with renewed vigour to its repressive and brutal practices. The dialogue had not strengthened the pacificist faction of the government but, given the simultaneous easing of pressure by the USA and EU, the hard faction – boosting repression. Reforms that would make it possible to avoid social implosion in China could only be undertaken by the reform-minded members of government if international pressure was maintained (Agence Europe, 19 March 1999: 8). This assessment by Wei is helpful in understanding the internal balance of power in the Chinese Government.

On 20 March 1999, the GAC decided not to table a resolution in Geneva (Agence Europe, 24 March 1999: 8). It must have been a relief for China. Instead, the GAC proposed that the EU would pursue the tabling of a thematic resolution placing special emphasis on the rights of democratic oppositions. This was an indirect approach. The GAC welcomed progress in cooperation between China and the UN, as well as Beijing's signing of the UN Covenants, but regretted that this progress was unmatched by corresponding improvements on the ground. It offered technical assistance to the ratification of the UN Covenants. It did not support the resolution tabled by the USA (Agence Europe, 13 January 2000: 5).

Subsequently, six NGOs came together for the first time to put pressure on the EU to re-impose sanctions on China since 'constructive dialogue' had produced only 'symbolic' measures. Not only had international pressure led only to one-off results, such as the release of a few dissidents, but repression had since increased. Signing the UN Covenants and allowing the visit of the UN High Commissioner for Human Rights were just symbolic undertakings without real change in China, it was held. Discussions with member states had always focused not on the real human rights situation in China but on the wrong reasons not to table a resolution. The situation was different this year because it was clear that dialogue on human rights had achieved no results (Agence Europe, 12 February 2000: 6).

Chris Patten, in Parliament, concurred that up to this point results of the EU–China human rights dialogue had been rather meagre: 'If we count on this dialogue alone, we must demonstrate that we were getting somewhere'. As regards an EU resolution in Geneva, he observed that Chinese advocates for democratic freedom were convinced that tabling a resolution would be a 'valuable move' and that they should not be ignored (Agence Europe, 17 February 2000: 4). The Portuguese Presidency at this same parliamentary session admitted that pressure was put on the EU not to support the American proposal, but stated that defining a common position by the

Fifteen was not easy. He also admitted being dissatisfied with the results of the dialogue. He stated that, at the next EU–China dialogue seession, the EU would tell China that it expected progress on the ground and that Geneva was the legitimate forum for raising such questions. The European Parliament called on the EU to co-sign with the USA a resolution on human rights in China and to discourage countries represented in Geneva from voting for a resolution on China that did not make provision for action, which would prevent the UNCHR from engaging in a review of the human rights situation in that country (Agence Europe, 18 February 2000: 4).

Chris Patten declared that the EU–China dialogue in Lisbon on 25 February 2000 would be a 'test' as to whether the dialogue was successful or not. The EU would determine its position at the UNCHR from the results of the dialogue. Room was left for doubt, to retain pressure on Beijing. The mood among the Member States was described as more sensitive to public pressure (Agence Europe, 24 February 2000: 4).

It was reported that, after a marathon eleventh-hour session of the EU–China human rights dialogue, it concluded that there were no concrete results. The results were described as 'difficult'. The Chinese did not make any commitments concerning improving the human rights situation on the ground and did not announce the release of any prisoners. They rather proposed strengthening the dialogue by organising specific meetings on specific issues such as the death penalty. The European Commission would propose options ranging from simply pursuing discussions to the suspension of dialogue or presenting a resolution at the UNCHR. Most Member States, it was reported, were reticent about putting more pressure on China (Agence Europe, 1 March 2000: 3).

The GAC reportedly (Agence Europe, 22 March 2000: 4) decided that the EU reserved the right to make its position known at the very last moment, should a resolution denouncing the human rights situation in China be voted on during the UNCHR meeting. In Geneva, the Portuguese Presidency gave a robust speech but did not comment on the EU position on the US draft resolution. This position was left 'voluntarily in suspense'. Why? To avoid breaking the European front between Member States that want to support a resolution against China at the UNCHR and, on the other hand, to prevent unnecessarily laying themselves open to Chinese retaliation. The GAC welcomed China's stated willingness to cooperate with the UN Human Rights mechanisms, and encouraged China to ratify the UN Covenants as soon as possible and to sign the relevant Memorandum of Understanding with the Office of the High Commissioner for Human Rights. It regretted that the EU–China dialogue had not been followed up with concrete results on the ground. The Council would review the human rights dialogue with China with the aim of a more focused and result-oriented approach. Discussions over these three years had lacked 'vertical' effectiveness in the field.

'China blocks vote of resolution on human rights in Geneva, so EU does not have to give its stance' was the headline in Agence Europe (Agence Europe, 19 April 2000: 6). Given the vote of 22 to 18 on a 'non-action' motion, the resolution on China presented by the USA would not be put to the vote. The EU Member States voted alongside the USA against the non-action motion. The Portuguese Presidency deplored Beijing's use of a procedural tactic to block the USA's resolution: 'No country, small or large, can use procedural tactics to escape criticism and judgement of the international community.' HRW criticised the EU, Australia, Canada and Japan for refusing to 'co-sponsor' the American draft and for making no effort to lobby for a majority against the non-action motion (Agence Europe, 20 April 2000: 4).

One could probably conclude on human rights by quoting Sir Leon Brittan (Agence Europe, 4 February 1998: 5) who said that the question was simple – whether to discuss the issues which were of concern to the EU, or whether to take actions which registered criticisms and even condemnation to the point where dialogue was no longer possible. His feeling was that, in the longer term, an approach based on exerting as much pressure as possible by keeping the dialogue alive, but not necessarily at all costs, was the only realistic way of making progress towards a civil society in China based on the rule of law.

His successor, Commissioner Chris Patten, after the Dublin conference on the 'Protection of Human Rights in the 21st Century', spoke about the weaknesses of the EU, pointing out that it was difficult to reach agreement among the Fifteen on issues where political or commercial stakes are deemed to be high. He alluded to the Member States' inability to agree on a resolution on China and admitted that there were also many other examples of unanimous action on human rights issues, as in the case of the abolition of the death penalty (Agence Europe, 6/7 March 2000: 7). Here we have an honest explanation of the indecision over tabling a human rights resolution on China.

These political and commercial stakes determine the constitution of a balance of power. The balance of power is there if there is a common position of the Fifteen *vis-à-vis* China, as we find in WTO negotiations. When it is there, it is a negative platform: we do not allow any of us to be attacked by China and we do not want to table or co-sponsor a human rights resolution against China. We learnt the lesson of the Chinese threat of economic and trade sanctions in the face of US insistence on criticising Beijing on human rights. By taking a softer or gentler line on human rights with China, perhaps we will obtain economic rewards from China which the Americans will not. Persuasion is the way forward, not confrontation. Be positive through human rights programmes in China. On the other hand, if one believes in a western conspiracy against China, one could think along the lines of the carrot and stick. The EU uses the carrot and the USA the stick. But it does not seem as simple as that, as the EU wants to be a global player in its own right. One wonders, too, how much would be made of human rights without the pressures of the NGOs?

China's accession to the WTO

What was needed for China's accession to the WTO

China's admission into the WTO constituted the other key issue between the EU and China. In a Council document dated 27 November 1995 concerning the Commission's Communication, 'A Long-Term Policy for China–Europe Relations', it was argued that China's adherence to the WTO would be facilitated by the establishment of market economy mechanisms and by the convertibility of the Chinese currency (Agence Europe, 6/7 March 2000: 5).

Setting the stage

It is to be noted that China applied for General Agreement of Tariffs and Trade (GATT) membership in July 1986[56] and had wished to become one of the founder members of the WTO in 1995. This did not happen. China had acquired observer status in GATT in 1982 and special observer status in 1984, which allowed it to take part in GATT meetings as a non-voting member. 1989 saw work in the GATT Working Group suspended for two years following Tiananmen. China attempted to conclude its GATT negotiations in 1994.[57] The delay in getting into GATT/WTO was explained by Dent in two ways: the non-market principles of its economy and its large and rapidly expanding gross domestic product (GDP). Its burgeoning trade surpluses with the EU and USA raised the stakes further for both the powers to get the accession formula right (Dent 1999: 145). Apparently there is the fear of China as an economic threat in a balance of power. On the other hand, Sir Leon Brittan insisted on the security that would be created with China's admission to the WTO, as it would ensure that it respected international legal, administrative and institutional standards (Agence Europe, 10 June 1998: 14).

An area of agreement

The 1998 Communication accepted the concept of transitional periods as part of a final package for sectors which China needs to phase in its WTO obligations while adjusting its laws and practices. The EU has respected China's own policy of implementing reforms gradually.[58] It was reported that China would benefit from the transitional periods to implement provisions regarded as more difficult to respect for a developing country. At the same time, this phasing-in concept included reasonable tariffs and the elimination of the state monopoly on external trade (Agence Europe, 25 November 1996: 8). Commissioner Brittan stated that achieving these principles could take time and one could foresee phasing-in periods only if, in the meantime, European enterprises were not discriminated against as far as the granting of licences was concerned (Dent 1999: 147). The EU acknowledged the dualistic nature of the Chinese economy in that some aspects were reasonably advanced while others remained significantly underdeveloped (Dent 1999: 147). The proposal of transitional periods was to inject a new momentum to the negotiations.[59] The idea of transitional periods was first proposed by Sir Leon Brittan in 1994, a proposal then not acceptable to the USA, although the latter's stance softened after Clinton's re-election in 1996 (Dent 1999: 147). Transitional periods were described as a crucial innovation by which China would benefit fully from market access and other WTO rights from the day of accession while being allowed to maintain derogations from certain requirements (Agence Europe, 6 March 1999: 7). Agence Europe, reported (15/16 February 1999) Sir Leon Brittan even invoking the possibility of granting longer transitional periods. This was on condition that countries like Ukraine, Russia and China integrated the experience of 50 years' trade negotiations and came to Geneva with a new mandate and more ambitious market opening offers. Then existing WTO members would match such efforts by demonstrating renewed flexibility and creativity with respect to the implementation of commitments (Agence Europe, 15/16 February 1999: 8). China could indicate what areas it wished transitional periods to be applied (Agence Europe, 6 March 1999: 7). Transitional periods are a carrot, a reward for better offers. The EU would undertake to provide technical assistance to China to allow it to adjust to the obligations imposed by the WTO (Agence Europe, 26 June 1998: 8).

The WTO negotiations

In the last few years of China–EU negotiations on Beijing's accession to the WTO, progress was achieved.[60] The following was agreed:

(i) China pledged to respect the principles of national treatment and non-discrimination;
(ii) China agreed to phase out QRs on imports;
(iii) China pledged to reduce tariffs on all imported goods and limit 'peak tariffs'; and
(iv) China would improve its commitment so as to offer a real perspective of its market opening process.

In February 1998, in Beijing, Sir Leon Brittan pointed to the necessity of China presenting as soon as possible its offer on lowering its average tariff and eliminating most tariff peaks. He hoped to reach agreement on a set of fundamental principles setting out the objectives of market openness and flexibility in the services sectors so that China could present a detailed offer in services too. The Chinese confirmed a new formal and complete offer on tariff reductions to meet WTO admission criteria by early March 1998. When Beijing's offer on tariffs was presented, the EU considered that the tariff peaks above 15% remained too high with average top tariffs standing at 20% and automobiles and photographic film still at 50% duty.[61] In June 1998, in Brussels, on the occasion of the JC meeting, a Joint Press Release spoke of concluding WTO negotiations by the end of 1999 as a goal. China would shortly be putting forward new proposals in a number of areas, including tariffs, quotas and services. Negotiations would not make headway unless the new Minister of Foreign Trade managed to convince his colleagues that China had an interest in accession to the WTO (Agence Europe, 12 June 1998: 8).

The GAC of July 1999 invited China to continue negotiations with the EU as soon as possible. It stressed the need for China to implement WTO rules and to take into account the EU's specific priorities concerning market access (Agence Europe, 21 July 1999: 10). The EU had sent a document containing detailed requests which had so far received no response. That said, a response was not a pre-condition for the resumption of discussions in which the EU insisted that it would not accept a bilateral agreement on the basis of the US–China agreement (Agence Europe, 22 September 1999: 7). The October 1999 meeting did not make any solid progress, but brought about a better understanding of the respective positions (Agence Europe, 28 October 1999: 14). The new European Commissioner for Trade, Mr Pascal Lamy, was reported as having stated that no date had been set for the resumption of negotiations with China (Agence Europe, 20 November 1999: 9). At Seattle, it was agreed that Commissioner Lamy would go to China for further negotiations (Agence Europe, 3 December 1999: 9).

Agence Europe (12 January 2000: 6) announced the resumption of WTO talks. The EU wanted to broaden the twenty or so points on Chinese *erga omnes* concessions secured by the USA. Later, Agence Europe (26 January 2000: 13) announced the arrival of Chinese officials in Brussels. They were bringing with them Beijing's answers to the concessions requested by the EU to improve access to the Chinese market. The negotiations were described as 'constructive'. The Joint Declaration (Agence Europe, 27 January 2000: 8) stressed that negotiations covered all aspects. The atmosphere was defined as 'positive' and progress 'substantial'. However, less than half the EU's objectives were achieved.

In Beijing, on 21 February 2000, after four days of intensive talks, the negotiations broke off without having been able to agree on the conditions for China's accession to the WTO. Enormous progress was achieved but not enough to conclude the negotiations. The meeting was not a failure and the negotiating team did not leave Beijing immediately, to allow the Chinese to make last minute concessions. The Chinese side's assessment was more positive, negotiations were close to agreement and they invited Commissioner Lamy to come to Beijing to conclude the negotiations (Agence Europe, 25 February 2000: 25). Commissioner Lamy stated that the previous negotiations were 'disappointing' because too many issues remained to clinch a deal (Agence Europe, 2 March 2000: 8).

Commissioner Lamy was to leave for Beijing on 27 March 2000 in the hope of finalising negotiations (Agence Europe, 10 March 2000: 6). The Commissioner left Beijing for Brussels without a final agreement on the conditions of China's accession to the WTO. He considered that he showed considerable flexibility but the balance of the package was not satisfactory (Agence Europe, 1 April 2000: 8).

Commissioner Lamy left again for Beijing on 15 May 2000 with 'realistic' hope to resume negotiations. The Union was seeking to have its own and specific interests recognised in so far as Chinese market barriers continued to add to the European trade deficit of 23 billion Euro already reached in 1998 (Agence Europe, 27 April 2000: 11; Agence Europe, 12 May 2000: 10). But negotiations progressed very slowly (Agence Europe, 19 May 2000: 8).

WTO negotiations are a long-drawn-out bargaining game with mounting pressures and related ups-and-downs. The conclusion of the China–USA agreement in November 1999 obviously added pressure to conclude the EU–China agreement.

Then, on 19 May 2000, the Sino-EU Agreement on China's accession to the WTO was concluded in the morning and signed several hours later. The agreement covered tariffs, telecommunications, insurance, state monopoly on marketing, industrial products, motor vehicles, distribution, agriculture, horizontal measures (such as the suspension of trade-distorting measures and more transparent and non-discriminatory public procurement for foreign bids) and other liberalisation measures (touching on banking, tourism, legal services, accountancy, architecture and research) (Agence Europe, 20 May 2000: 10).

The *Financial Times*[62] reported the deal as including a Chinese promise to dismantle its state procurement monopolies on imports of oil, fertilisers and oil products.[63] This was expected to provide a boost for exporters like BP Amoco, Royal Dutch/Shell and BASF. More than 150 tariffs on EU-priority goods such as cosmetics, spirits, footwear, leather goods and machinery were to be cut by an average of 40% more than agreed between Beijing and Wahington.[64] Seven life insurance company licences would be granted to European firms.[65] The Chinese agreed to bring forward the dates by which foreign firms would be allowed to form telecoms and insurance joint ventures. The concession that clinched the deal was the Chinese promise to lift equity share restrictions on foreign retailers, allowing them to establish wholly-owned networks throughout the country. Limits on floor space were also abolished, presenting unprecedented opportunities for department and chain stores.

Commissioner Lamy told the press of 'real openings' achieved. 'A first-class agreement, the best possible'. It vastly improved market access via 'significant and permanent' reductions in customs duties and the abolition of non-tariff import barriers. It also offered a 'safer, more attractive and predictable commercial environment for foreign investors'. It sealed China's acceptance of the legally binding WTO dispute settlement mechanism (Agence Europe, 22/23 May 2000: 9).

The few shortcomings were due to the fact that Commissioner Lamy 'gave preference to the present rather than the future', opting for a balanced agreement rather than no agreement at all. For example, the level of ownership in joint ventures would still be lower than the target of 51% in telecommunications (here it would increase from 25% to 49% over three years),[66] but in return this level would be available immediately upon China's admission to the WTO. Rather than leaving European exporters confronted with 100% Chinese operators, he opted for other concessions, 'less "general public", in sectors related to telecommunication services, where profits were greater'. The same held true for the motor vehicle sector, where Europeans were largely compensated[67] for not obtaining tariff reductions above the 25% already conceded to the Americans, and in the distribution sector, where 'the Chinese kept a number of exceptions on books, newspapers, fertilisers, petrol, etc., which were particularly important to them'. 'A good deal of what we obtained was offered by the Chinese in compensation for what they could not concede', he summarised, explaining, 'In fact, we obtained a better agreement for a wider range of European industries than if we had focused solely on China's most politically sensitive interests' (Agence Europe, 22/23 May 2000: 9). The EU were not going to try to go into their political no-go zone, he said at the press conference following the agreement.[68] The *Financial Times* mentioned that the EU failed also to raise the 50% limits for life insurance joint ventures which the US side won.[69] The *International Herald Tribune* (*IHT*) reported that Premier Zhu, having already been severely criticised for giving away too much to the USA, was able to hold his ground. He refused to broaden provisions for foreign ownership of Chinese telephone networks and content-focused Internet services beyond limits fixed in the deal with the USA. China promised to shorten the timetable for implementing a number of concessions already granted to Washington. Most market-opening commitments will be implemented by the year 2005.[70]

Technical assistance would obviously play its role and the EU had a number of projects in place or in the planning stages for the implementation in the next few months (Agence Europe, 22/23 May 2000: 9). Five projects with a budget totalling around 22 million euro had already been devised. Some were underway and others were due to come on stream in the near future. A framework programme in support of WTO accession would begin in autumn 2000 regarding the training of Chinese officials for the implementation of WTO commitments. Assistance designed to bring about the reform and restructuring of the financial services sector would begin at the end of 2000. Other projects touched statistics, a framework for transparent and non-discriminatory public procurement and a modern and effective system for the protection of intellectual property rights.[71]

Technical assistance is one thing, but the Trade Commissioner also made clear that the Beijing central government would need to garner 'the necessary political strength at home to manage this change' and warned that, even after China joined the global trade group, a long period of transition would be needed. 'This will not be a one-shot market opening, and there will be transitions so that the Chinese system has time to adjust'.[72] The central government in Beijing will still have to explain, convince and even compel provincial governments down to the village to comply with WTO obligations.

The EU–China deal on China's accession to the WTO does not require ratification by EU national parliaments nor even an assent by the EP. In the June 2000 parliamentary session, the Portuguese Presidency nevertheless stated that Parliament would have a say on the WTO deal with China. Chris Patten noted that it is a case of a 'trade agreement of major importance' of the kind that would, in the future, be submitted for the Parliament's assent, if the Commission proposals for the Intergovernmental Conference (IGC) is accepted. However, the results of this IGC could not be anticipated, he added. In the event, the EP debated the issue of its assenting role, with some welcoming the deal and others being critical of it (Agence Europe, 16 June 2000).

Some afterthoughts of the negotiations

(1) The *rapport des forces*

The failure of China to get into GATT/WTO meant that it was obliged to negotiate its accession to the WTO with existing members on the basis of separate bilateral talks. This consequently gave more leverage to WTO members to acquire market access gains from China, which in turn were multilateralised to all members through the MFN principle. Existing members were not compelled to offer market access deals to China above those already conferred upon other members. Moreover, any leniency granted by WTO members regarding China's conformity to WTO rules was accompanied by the demand for reciprocal concessions which could include special safeguard measures to protect against 'injurious' competition (Dent 1999: 145–6). One wonders how China calculated that it will benefit more by joining the WTO than staying out of it. It was negotiating from a weaker position. It is not a level playing field. It is about the *rapport des forces*. But since China opened up and tasted the fruits of the market, it is logical that it would move towards WTO membership.

Within this unfavourable *rapport des forces* for China, the EU is competing with the USA in getting market access in China. Sir Leon Brittan was reported as expecting to tell his Chinese counterpart, Mr Shi Guang Sheng, that concessions made to the USA must also be made to the EU (Agence Europe, 10 June 1998: 14). In this *rapport des forces*, could China play the 'divide and rule' game? We see that while the EU and USA shared similar objectives, their interests do diverge – for example in the communications sector.[73] The Commission reacted positively but cautiously to the US–China WTO bilateral agreement, stating that 80% of European demands on China corresponded to American demands, but there remained to be negotiated with China 20% of specific European demands (Agence Europe, 15/16 November 1999: 8). Sir Leon Brittan was reported as stating that, while results obtained by the USA in their negotiations with China would be extended *erga omnes*, he specified that Europe had specific priorities and Europe wanted to go further than the USA (Agence Europe, 4/5 May: 13).[74] 'Divide and rule' does not go far with the multilateralisation of market access gains individually negotiated with China. Whatever the EU could obtain more from China would also benefit the USA and all other WTO members. In another speech he spoke of seeing what extra commitments are required to ensure that the EU's legitimate commercial interests were properly safeguarded in commenting on US–China negotiations (Agence Europe, 10 April 1999: 9). The EU wants to establish itself as another global player like a European State in its own right. He stated that no bilateral agreement between China and a third country could be imposed on other members of the WTO as a basis for a final accession deal (Agence Europe, 6 March 1999: 7). China was reported to have stood firm on its position, refusing to go beyond the concessions granted to the USA (Agence Europe, 22 December 1999: 5). The Chinese Trade Minister declared that China could only make offers proportionate to its economic weight (Agence Europe, 8 May 1999: 10). There was some resistance – but how far? Successive failures to complete an accession agreement led to Beijing accusing both the EU and the USA of delaying tactics to serve their respective market access objectives (Dent 1999: 146). Divide and rule does not work. This is the state of the *rapport des forces* between China on one side with the EU and the USA on the other.

It could have been different for China if the EU member states had negotiated individually with China. The *rapport des forces* would be in China's favour in the case of certain EU States. But as the European Commission negotiates on behalf of the member states, the Union is in a stronger negotiating position *vis-à-vis* China, a potential economic threat.

(2) The agreement

We could ask whether the WTO Agreement with China is fair. In the Opening Statement of Commissioner Lamy at a press conference given after the deal was done, it was said that the deal was good for China. Quite beyond the overall commercial opportunities stemming from WTO membership, the agreement on a package fostered gradual but lasting reform and sustainable development in China. A step-by-step market opening in many areas is underway with implementation within a three- to five-year timeframe, leading UK policymakers to say that we 'have not sought to expose China's firms and service providers overnight to the rigours of foreign competition'. The deal and WTO membership provide China an unrivalled anchor for reform. Lamy and others have said nothing was mentioned about China's market access to the EU in the different product and services sectors.

Little seems to have been said by the Chinese as to what they gained from the deal. In Xinhua, on 19 May 2000, the Chinese Minister of Trade and Economic Cooperation stated: '[T]his agreement, after five days of equal and friendly consultations and negotiations, shows the spirit of equality, friendship and mutual benefit, and has demonstrated the friendly ties between China and the EU.' He believed that the implementation of the agreement would inject vitality into Sino-EU relations and bring great opportunities to Sino-EU trade ties. He stressed that China would play a positive and constructive role in promoting the development of the global economy and trade, and the establishment of a new international economic order.

Conclusion: The future

With a bilateral agreement between the EU and China on its accession to the WTO, a question which one can ask is whether the EU now feels freer to pursue the human rights agenda? The EU did not want to jeopardise its WTO negotiations by censuring China in the human rights area. Having got in its bag its economic and trade gains, will it in future be willing to sponsor or table human rights resolutions in Geneva? With WTO-accession Beijing will be bound by WTO rules and this should give a freer hand to the EU to act on human rights in China. What is hypothesized here is that the EU strategy all along was a tie between the two, between China's WTO accession and human rights. Perhaps in this way the EU has a better strategy than the USA. The coming years will provide the answer.

I venture to say that human rights will remain a burning issue between the EU and China in the future. The EP will keep the issue alive. The other potential area of friction could be the EU's attempt to ensure that China does not make many exceptions if and when ratifying UN Covenants.

One could expect that trade frictions will lessen as quotas and anti-dumping are removed. Disputes submitted to the WTO for settlement may raise temperatures between the two sides but will be contained. Possible contentions may emerge about the length of transitional periods for China and its failure to execute its WTO obligations on the ground. The EU may have to offer more carrots to soften the blows of WTO compliance.

While EU investors and traders in China are likely to see their interests advance, it will be a different story for China. The Chinese will be able to ship their goods to the EU, but they are not about to invest there yet. Meanwhile China's accession to the WTO is also political, in that it signals Western acceptance of China in the world community. Perhaps China has the confidence that it can play the capitalist game to its advantage. Nothing is static. The *rapport des forces* could in the future turn to its advantage as it acquires economic muscle. This could lead it to play a dominant role, at least in Asia, challenging the USA or Europe. Finally, in the Commission's 1994 Communication *Towards a New Asia Strategy*, it is stated that EU–ASEAN relations were 'the cornerstone of the EU's relations with Asia'. We may ask whether it will be replaced by China in the years to come?

Notes

1 When speaking of agreements, we are speaking of the EEC or the EC, the first pillar of the Treaty of Maastricht which established the European Union (EU). In day-to-day usage, EU is used without reference to these legalistic distinctions.

2 'EU–China Relations – Background Note' and 'The EU and China', two unsigned and undated draft papers originating from the European Commission, p. 1, unless otherwise noted. Dent, Christopher, *The European Union and East Asia*, p. 132.

3 It must be clear from the very title of the agreement that it does not include political dialogue.

4 For the rest of this paragraph, the historical data are from 'EU–China Relations – Background Note', p. 1 and 'The EU and China', p. 1, unless otherwise noted.

5 From European Commission, 'Background Note for Macau Conference', 2–3 March 1995', p. 2, dated 23 Feburary 1995.

6 European Commission, 'The EU's relations with China: an overview', p. 1.

7 European Commission (draft) document, 'China: An Outline of Future EU–China Cooperation Activities', p. 3; 'EU–China Relations – Background Note', p. 3 and 'A Long-Term Policy for China–Europe Relations', pp. 17–18.

8 European Commission, 'A Long-Term Policy for China–Europe Relations', pp. 13, 38.

9 European Commission, 'Building a Comprehensive Partnership with China', p. 22; Agence Europe, 29/30 June 1998, p. 7.

10 This shift in emphasis was evident in the draft Commission document, 'China: An Outline of Future EU–China Cooperation Activities', pp. 2–3.

11 European Commission, 'A Long-Term Policy for China–Europe Relations', p. 16; 'EU/China: Visit of Sir Leon Brittan to Beijing, 13–19 November 1996', p. 9.

12 It must be noted that in the 1985 Trade and Economic Cooperation Agreement with China, economic cooperation is defined to include the following: industry and mining, agriculture, including agro-industry, science and technology, energy, transport and communication, environmental protection and cooperation in third countries. The last is not covered in this chapter. Development cooperation is referred to in Article 13 of the Agreement.
13 European Commission, 'A Long-Term Policy for China–Europe Relations', p. 25.
14 European Commission, 'The EU and China', pp. 5, 8; 'EU–China Relations: Background Note', p. 3; 'A Long-Term Policy for China–Europe Relations', p. 9.
15 Dent, *The European Union and East Asia*, p. 137.
16 European Commission, 'Bilateral Trade Relations: China', p. 2.
17 European Commission, 'The EU's Relations with China: an Overview' (recently updated), pp. 2–3.
18 European Commission, 'The EU and China', p. 2.
19 Calculated from the European Commission table, 'EU Trade with the World and China'.
20 European Commission, 'The EU's Relations with China: an Overview', p. 2.
21 European Commission, 'EU Trade with the World and China'.
22 European Commission, 'The EU's Relations with China: an Overview', p. 2.
23 European Commission, 'A Long-Term Policy for China–Europe Relations', p. 24.
24 European Commission, 'The EU and China', pp. 1, 4.
25 European Commission, 'EU–China Relations', pp. 2, 3.
26 European Commission, 'A Long-Term Policy for China–Europe Relations', p. 24.
27 European Commission, 'China's Trade with Main Partners 1998 (in Mio euro)'.
28 European Commission, 'China Economic Indicators 1980'.
29 European Commission, 'The EU's relations with China – an overview', p. 2, Agence Europe, 30 October 1998, p. 5. The figure of 18% contradicts that of the table on 'China Trade with Main Partners 1998 (Mio euro)' which gives the figure of 15.3% which puts the EU in third place after Japan with the USA first in that order. The table actually puts Hong Kong as the first partner which will put the EU as fourth.
30 European Commission, 'EU Trade with Main Partners 1999 (Mio euro)'.
31 Regulation 3420/83, Agence Europe, 3 March 1999, p. 11.
32 European Commission, 'The EU and China', p. 2; 'A Long-Term Policy for China–Europe Relations', pp. 36–37.
33 European Commission, 'Building a Comprehensive Partnership with China', p. 15.
34 A case in point concerned unbleached cotton.
35 European Commission, 'The EU and China', pp. 5–6; 'A Long-Term Policy for China–Europe Relations', p. 18; 'Building a Comprehensive Partnership with China', p. 15.
36 European Commission, 'Building a Comprehensive Partnership with China', p. 15.
37 In a meeting with the External Economic Relations Committee of the EP drawing on the speaking points of the 15th EC–China JC Meeting of 10–11 June 1998, Sir Leon Brittan mentioned that a financing agreement was signed at this meeting and gave information on the project. It aims to enhance the agricultural self-sufficiency and improve the education, health and sanitation of ethnic

Tibetan people in Pa Nam county. China guaranteed that only local Tibetan people will benefit from the project. Ethnic Tibetans will receive exclusive rights to the use of the land, and are to enjoy priority access to all management, engineering and training posts related to the project. The EU Troika of Ambassadors in Beijing visited Tibet and received further confirmation of these assurances by the Chinese authorities. It was further reported that the work of NGOs would not be hampered. However, the UK-based Save the Children Fund, the European partner, reported that China refused to grant a visa to one Fund member (Agence Europe, 10 June 1998). The EP queried as to who benefited from the project, fearing that it would facilitate China's colonisation of Tibet.

38 European Commission, 'A Long-Term Policy for China–Europe Relations' pp. 4, 6; 'The EU's Relations with China: an Overview', p. 1.

39 European Commission, 'The EU's Relations with China: an Overview', p. 1.

40 European Commission, 'The EU's Relations with China: an Overview', p. 1.

41 European Commission, 'The EU's Relations with China: an Overview', p. 2.

42 European Commission, 'A Long-Term Policy for China–Europe Relations', p. 7.

43 A4-0198/97 dated 29 May 1997 or PE 221.588/fin.

44 European Commission, 'Building a Comprehensive Partnership with China', p. 3.

45 This is the so-called 'third generation' agreement which has as Article One a reference to respect for human rights, democracy and the rule of law as the basis of the EU's relations with a third country. With China no formal bilateral agreement was envisaged (Agence Europe, 26 June 1998, p. 8). The 1998 Communication did not make provision for a formal cooperation agreement. Further, with a preference for a human rights dialogue, a new agreement looks more and more unlikely. China too can always say that if Australia rejected a binding third generation agreement why should it agree to one? Australia has consented to a declaration with the EU which refers to human rights, democracy and rule of law, but this was not acceptable to the Chinese side. Sectoral agreements for scientific and technological cooperation are the way out and have the added advantage of not requiring parliamentary assent as is the case for agreements with 'third generation' clauses. This means avoiding formal parliamentary scrutiny.

46 The EU had been co-sponsoring the US human rights resolutions in the UNCHR since 1990. A 1995 text was rejected by a single vote (Agence Europe, 13 January 2000, p. 5).

47 European Commission, 'A Long-Term Policy for China–Europe Relations', p. 6.

48 This dialogue took place in May. 1996. The preceding one was in February 1995 (Agence Europe, 26 September 1997, p. 3). China must have proposed the EU–China human rights dialogue as a way to draw away the EU from further co-sponsoring or tabling human rights resolutions in Geneva. The rejection of the 1995 resolution by a single vote must have shaken China.

49 European Commission, 'EU–China Relations: Background Note', p. 2.

50 In an undated Speaking Note, probably dated 1995, Tibet was mentioned when EU concerns about the human rights situation in China were expressed. It spoke of the importance of the Chinese government and the representative of the Tibetan people jointly finding a political solution

51 Agence Europe, 11 March 1998, p. 4.

52 Agence Europe, 17 February 1997, headlined it as a dialogue of the deaf, p. 8.

53 European Commission, 'EU–China Relations: Background Note', p. 2.

54 Sir Leon Brittan spoke of benchmarks identified by the EU on which progress made by China along the lines hoped for by Europe would be judged (Agence Europe, 29 January 1999, p. 13).

55 Agence Europe, 15 January 1999, p. 9. Agence Europe, 6 February 1999, reported that this was the fourth dialogue.

56 European Commission, 'The EU and China', p. 6; 'A Long-Term Policy for China–Europe Relations', p. 10; Dent, *The European Union and East Asia*, p. 145; European Commission, 'Overview of China's economic reforms and WTO negotiations', p. 1. Also see European Parliament 'Admission of China and Taiwan to GATT', 28 May 1993. This latter resolution stated that the PRC was formally resuming its status as a Contracting Party of GATT but that this would necessitate extraordinary transitional arrangements. There would be a substantially new accession and the Contracting Parties would remain entitled to invoke the non-application clause if they were not satisfied with the concessions offered for its accession. During the transitional period, neither the PRC nor other Contracting Parties would be obliged to mutually apply MFN. Contracting Parties were entitled to take specific safeguard measures against Chinese exports if these created or threaten to create a serious injury for their economies (A3-0092/93 or PE 203.426 final).

57 European Commission, 'Overview of China's economic reforms and WTO negotiations', p. 1.

58 European Commission, 'Building a Comprehensive Partnership with China', pp. 12–14.

59 European Commission, 'Overview of China's Economic Reforms and WTO Negotiations', p. 2.

60 European Commission, 'Overview of China's Economic Reforms and WTO Negotiations', p. 2.

61 Agence Europe, 16/17 February 1998, p. 6; 18 February 1998, p. 9; 19 Feburary 1998, p. 10 and 9 April 1998, p. 10; European Commission, 'Overview of China's Economic Reforms and WTO Negotiations', p. 2.

62 *Financial Times*, 20/21 May 2000.

63 The item under state monopoly is silk exporting which will be completely removed by 2005. China accounts for 70% of the world silk production.

64 Tariffs were cut to around 8–10% on over 150 leading European exports such as machinery, ceramics and glass, textiles, clothing, footwear and leather goods, cosmetics and spirits.

65 In both the life and non-life sectors.

66 This refers to mobile telephony and its market opening accelerated by 2 years. The leasing market, to rent capacity from Chinese operators and resell it, opening up in three years (European Commission, 'Highlights of the EU–China Agreement on WTO', p. 1). Mr Lamy in his 'Opening Statement at the press conference', page 5, stated that they wanted 50% or 100% ownership for mobile telecoms (European Commission).

67 The compensation took the form of i) the greater flexibility of European carmakers in China to choose which types of vehicles they build; ii) approval thresholds of Chinese provincial authorities will be raised from US$30 million to US$150 million; and iii) an agreement was obtained to eliminate the joint-venture restrictions for engine production upon accession. (See European Commission, 'Highlights of the EU–China Agreement on WTO', p. 2.) Mr. Lamy in his 'Opening Statement at the press conference', p. 5, stated that they had wanted to lift the 50%–50% joint-venture requirement for foreign car manufacturers (European Commission).

68 European Commission, 'European Trade Commissioner Pascal Lamy's Declaration on China's WTO accession: Opening Statement at the press conference', p. 5.
69 But insurance business will be opened to foreign companies two years sooner than foreseen in the Sino-US Agreement. Further, foreign brokers will be able to operate in China, free of any joint-venture requirement, five years after accession.
70 European Commission, 'Overview of China's Economic Reforms and WTO Negotiations', p. 2.
71 European Commission, 'China as a WTO Member – Implementation through Partnership', pp. 1–2.
72 Quoted in *IHT*, 29 May 2000.
73 Agence Europe (10 April 1999, p. 9), reported that China was moving away from the GSM standard towards the American CDMA standard.
74 The areas outlined were automobiles, mentioned already, along with spirits, cosmetics, leather goods and crockery in the area of custom duties. The EU wanted to go beyond the reduction of 'tariff peaks' obtained by the USA. In the spirits sector, the EU wanted reductions in duties for gin and cognac. In banking and services, foreign investors wanted to be able to own their joint ventures after five years as in the USA, and to have the right to manage accounts of Chinese clients, as well as access to investors in the life insurance sector, and to enlarge the the geographical coverage. In telecommunications, the EU won the right to hold 49% of an enterprise.

Bibliography

Agence Europe bulletins 1997–2000.

Belgian–Chinese Economic and Commercial Council, Belgian–Chinese Chamber of Commerce, 'China News Flash'.

Dent, Christopher, 1999, *The European Union and East Asia*, London, Routledge.

European Commission, 'EU/China: Visit of Sir Leon Brittan to Beijing, 13–19 November 1996'.

European Commission, 'Les Relations entre l'Union Européenne et la Chine: Background Note', 1995.

European Commission, 'Note for the File', 1 December 1999.

European Commission, undated, 'Thermie Summary of Activities in the PRC'.

European Commission, EU–China website on 'Bilateral Trade Relations: China', http:www.europa.eu.int/comm/trade/bilateral/china/china.htm.

European Commission, EU–China website, 'European Trade Commissioner Pascal Lamy's Declaration on China's WTO accession: Opening Statement at the press conference', http:www.europa.eu.int/comm/trade/bilateral/china/prc.htm.

European Commission, EU–China website, 'Highlights of the EU–China Agreement on WTO', http:www.europa.eu.int/comm/trade/bilateral/china/high.htm.

European Commission, EU–China website, 'The EU's Relations with China: an Overview', http:www.europa.eu.int/comm/external_relations/bilateral/china/intro/index.htm.

European Commission, EU–China website, 'China as a WTO Member – Implementation through Partnership', http:www.europa.eu.int/comm/trade/bilateral/china/imp.htm.

European Commission, EU–China website, 'Overview of China's economic reforms and WTO negotiations', http:www.europa.eu.int/comm/trade/bilateral/china/chr.htm.

European Commission, undated draft document, 'China: An Outline of Future EU–China Cooperation Activities'.

European Commission, undated draft on 'EU–China Relations – Background Note'.
European Commission, undated draft on 'The EU and China'.
European Commission, 'Background Note for Macau Conference, 2–3 March 1995'.
European Commission's Communication, 'A Long-Term Policy for China–Europe Relations' (COM (95)–279 Final), 1995.
European Commission's Communication, 'Building a Comprehensive Partnership with China' (COM (1998) 181 final), 1998.
European Parliament, Resolution on 'Admission of China and Taiwan to GATT', 28 May 1993.
European Parliament, Resolution on the Commission's Communication, 'A Long-Term Policy for China–Europe Relations', A4-0198/97 dated 29 May 1997 or PE 221.588/fin.
European Parliament, Resolution on the Commission's Communication, 'Building a Comprehensive Partnership with China', June 1998.

China: Conclusions

Chapter 16

China at the Start of the New Millennium

Jürgen Haacke and P.W. Preston

Introduction

The analysis of change is central to an understanding of contemporary China. A series of detailed analyses have been presented in this volume with respect to the economy, society and the politics of the country and some of Beijing's core bilateral ties in the evolving international politics of East Asia. As we noted in our introduction, the analysis of change is not intellectually straightforward. Having embarked upon a strategy of considering different approaches to the study of social relations as not standing in the way of a dialogue across disciplines and theoretical orientations, the contributions to this volume have illuminated various interrelated aspects of change in China. In doing so, the contributors have looked both at the intermediate and the more immediate events associated with change.

The manner in which China entered the modern world has proved disordered in many ways. This was the case under the Qing dynasty, in the aftermath of China's 1911 revolution and following the establishment of the People's Republic of China in 1949. Marxist-Leninism and nationalism – both distinctively modern ideologies – informed the thinking and political practice of China's revolutionary elite, even if both, but especially the former, were clearly adapted to China's specific historical circumstances. While the official discourse still emphasises socialism, it has been nationalism that has strongly, albeit not exclusively, informed the adoption of a variant of the East Asian model of state-sponsored communitarian development that has been widely commented upon.

As the contributors to this volume have noted, the economic reforms undertaken during the reign of Deng Xiaoping have been relatively successful. Broadly speaking, China has moved away from one imported and domesticated model of organising social relations of production and is in the process of importing and domesticating another. This has entailed the abandonment of the state-directed pursuit of egalitarian socialist development project in favour of economic efficiency. However one characterises the change, it is clear that China's historical development trajectory has shifted significantly as a consequence of the economic reform programme associated with Deng.

In the economic sphere, the reforms have involved moves in the establishment of a recognisably 'modern' financial system with a hierarchy of functional units (central banks, commercial banks, development banks, non-bank institutions, and so on). These reforms are also gradually leading to new patterns of economic control and power (as entailed in the shift from central planning towards an increasingly decentralised open and dispersed market system). The increasing stress placed on developing 'new' policy areas is accompanied by attendant institutional evolution. Examples discussed in this volume include monetary and foreign exchange policy and the development of the foreign trade regime. Alongside these moves towards a market-oriented system there have been extensive reforms in the area of state regulation, as well as already quite significant law-making processes that are designed to lead to China becoming a law-based state, a necessary condition of economic advance.

In the productive sphere of the economy, China's reorientation has involved massive change in the rural areas and, increasingly, also in the urban areas. The encouragement of the pursuit of private economic activity was followed by efforts to reform the key feature of the old centrally planned economy: state-owned enterprises. The nature of these enterprises has been distinctive in so far as they have embraced both productive activities and routine social and welfare provision. It is in this particular area that great problems have been found in implementing reforms that have had the aims of raising the level of economic efficiency of firms and of making them profitable. Still, as the state increasingly moves into the background in terms of its economic role, the need for its provision of social networks and support systems increasingly moves into the foreground.

In the political sphere, change has been rather modest. The hope by some that China's economic reform would soon be accompanied by more significant political reform has thus far been proved premature. Still, the unfolding process of marketisation has generated new challenges, both institutional and ideological. As regards institutional challenges, the embrace of market reforms has had implications for the politics informing the relations between the centre and the provinces. The reorientation of the economy has also thrown up problems of regional inequalities, as coastal areas have advanced more quickly than the central and western areas of the PRC. Such issues between centre and periphery represent of course an old theme within Chinese political life, but one that is taken seriously by state leaders. As economic decentralisation proceeded in the early and mid-1990s

– with increasingly powerful economic regions forming around the coastal zones from Guandong to Shanghai – numerous analysts and commentators speculated about the possibility of China's 'deconstruction' (Goodman and Segal 1994). However, notwithstanding regional disparities and the resultant grievances, the politics between the centre and the provinces have not yet become prone to unmanageable instability. The CCP leadership moreover routinely reshuffles the top political and military leadership of the provinces to prevent the emergence of regional power bases.

China's turn toward market reforms, justified and captured by Deng Xiaoping in a series of well-known aphorisms, has led the Chinese population to redirect their personal ambitions and qualify their judgement of the political establishment. Increasingly, state and party leaders seek to win legitimacy on the basis of economic performance, political and social stability and a growing popular nationalism.

As China integrates further into the regional and global economic system, CCP leaders have both high expectations and an array of concerns about the possible impact of the former on China. The development of novel technologies in telecommunications, such as the Internet or the mobile phone, poses opportunities and challenges and remains a double-edged sword for Chinese leaders. On the one hand, these technologies are helpful in assisting in China's drive for development. On the other hand, the same technologies possess a subversive potential. Given that it is not in the power of authorities to ban new technologies in any case, the party-state seeks to control their usage. More broadly, questions of economic development may well overlap with concerns about political stability and security. How the logic informing the search for security and the push for economic growth intermingle will do much to determine the shape of political developments over the upcoming period.

With the contributors having extensively explored in the earlier chapters the nature and extent of change in more detail, we now propose to briefly map out the trajectory of further change as we see it. Apart from the adage that 'history does not stand still', there are several reasons to expect China to undergo further change. Economic interdependence with the advanced industrial countries and in particular Beijing's commitment to international financial and economic institutions and regimes will further transform China's domestic economy. External linkages will thus reinforce the momentum for further economic reform measures adopted by the Chinese leadership. Moreover, the Chinese leadership is not immune from being influenced by events and developments in other areas. For instance, changes in the balance of power or the foreign policy of other major powers towards the PRC and Taiwan are bound to affect Chinese leaders' decision- and policy-making. Equally, new developments in military and other technology may influence them. Consequently, it is extremely difficult, if not impossible to say, even if one demonstrates the requisite modesty, how precisely domestic and international factors will influence the nature and extent of future change of China's domestic and international policies, and, indeed, its politics. Also, it is crucial to recognise the difficulties one can face in fully appreciating structural constraints, the diversity of actors and the variety of issues as well as their respective interlinkages at and across multiple levels in China.

With these caveats in mind, the final section of this concluding chapter explores four widely posed questions in relation to a China undergoing further change: First, will China find it easy to become an economic superpower? Second, will China remain stable in the foreseeable future? Third, what kind of political liberalisation, if any, should we expect in China in the near-term? And, fourth, is China likely to destabilise the East Asian region, as the country becomes more powerful militarily?

An easy transition to becoming an economic superpower?

China has achieved high growth rates throughout the period of economic reform. Indeed, over a number of years, China's growth exceeded that of any other country. Preliminary figures for 2000 suggest that China's economy was again growing by more than 8%. While this growth rate remains impressive, not least in view of the size of the economy, this does not per se make an economic superpower. Indeed, some China analysts believe that the label of a struggling developmental state is best suited to depict the country's overall economic circumstances. Even by its own estimates, the PRC will only become an 'intermediate developed' country by the third decade of this century.

The reasons are many why China cannot expect to become an economic superpower just yet. The notion of economic superpower may be contested but arguably one tends to associate with that concept an economy that not only is capable of allocating resources efficiently and creating prosperity for most, but also boasts companies that are dominant or at the cutting edge in their industries. An economic superpower probably also has a convertible currency and makes other countries trade in its own currency. Economic superpowers moreover probably also exert major influence on the world economy, by dint of their trade volume, market size and the dependency of other countries on access to their markets. Finally, economic superpowers exercise significant if not dominant influence in global economic regimes and organisations and possess the structural power to engage in political arm-twisting when pushing their economic interests internationally.

Arguably, if measured against these yardsticks China is a long way from becoming an economic superpower. China made up but 3 per cent of total world trade in 1997 and still only accounts for 11 per cent of total Asian trade, and less than 20 per cent of FDI into China originates from non-ethnic Chinese sources (Segal 1999). China's actual market size has been exaggerated as many international companies have found out in the past. Its influence in the IMF is a function of its voting power, which is almost minimal in comparison to that of other great powers. Moreover, China's economy remains beset by a host of problems.

For instance, China's current economic growth figure is unlikely to be sufficient to address successfully the challenge posed by the huge numbers of citizens seeking employment. Second, as repeatedly indicated in this volume, high overall economic growth rates disguise the differential impact of development thus far achieved. It is also not clear that regional inequalities have thus far been overcome though re-distributive tax reform, inter-regional co-operation schemes and revamped poverty-relief programmes. Moreover, further economic development will necessitate huge improvements in China's infrastructure, the costs for which will be staggering. Banks, facing serious problems with non-performing loans, still find it difficult to provide the capital for urgently needed investment, leaving the government to run massive budget deficits to spur the economy.

As regards the reform of the more sizeable state-owned enterprises, for instance, objectives such as higher efficiency, more accountability and greater profitability are likely to continue to clash with the need to maintain social stability. The introduction of modern management methods on a comprehensive scale will take time. So will overcoming the debt problems of many state-owned enterprises. On the issue of 'privatising' public and collective enterprises, questions as to who actually owns them, and, therefore, who possesses the right to sell them, remain complicated in the face of a lack of relevant national guidelines. Numerous issues, requiring time and sensitivity, often need to be addressed on the ground: will labour support management buy-outs? Are assets correctly priced?

Reforming China's economy, then, will continue to be no easy task. The success of such reform is also hostage to rampant corruption at all levels. For instance, corruption that has allowed smuggling to proceed unhindered has been a major source of lost revenue for the state. According to Ding (2000: 670) China's police registered more than 50,000 economic crimes in 1999, involving more than RMB 80 billion. In 2000, spectacular cases of corruption that demonstrated the extent of the problem within some of the higher party echelons again made the headlines. Equally, China is losing significant amounts of money through illegal asset stripping. China's financial sector has equally been ridden with corruption, with problems of 'temporary misappropriation' and downright 'embezzlement' (Ding 2000). Given that banks are facing substantial bad loan problems while increasingly becoming key decision-makers in resource allocation, China desperately requires appropriate banking surveillance and regulatory structures. It is difficult to see how the problem of corruption could be curbed. Imposing harsh penalties against those found guilty of economic crimes has so far also done little to reduce the scale of the problem. The prospect of clean government may thus be relatively distant at best.

China's future economic development, let alone its advance to becoming an economic superpower, is also handicapped by the high levels of environmental pollution that already affect the quality of life and health of many. In more ways than one, China has an environmental catastrophe in the making. For instance, with many waterways being heavily polluted China faces a threat that ground water might become toxic and unsuitable for human consumption. Available water resources are fast declining in any case. More than 400 of China's 668 cities are already said to face water shortages (*Quarterly Chronicle and Documentation* 2000c: 891). This has led engineers and policy-makers to plan for redirecting water flows. The task of addressing the environmental damage, to the extent this is at all possible, will also consume significant resources, not least because much of the requisite technology will need to be purchased from the advanced industrialised countries.

To the extent that China's continued economic success story is tied to the further increases in its foreign trade volume and in the amount of real foreign direct investment secured, the developmental strategy will be hostage to the well-being of other economies and the confidence of foreign businessmen. According to Chinese estimates, the PRC's accession to the WTO will approximately double its foreign trade volume to US$ 600 billion, as well as foreign direct investment to 100 billion, by 2005. However, a downturn or recession in the American and Japanese economy has at least the potential to temporarily slow and perhaps even reverse China's export growth. Perhaps even more importantly, Beijing also continues to depend on technological transfers from developed countries to be able to move up the value-added chain.

These are just some of the points that may lead one to adopt a cautious stance when assessing the ease with which China can turn into an economic superpower. No doubt many other problems, that could potentially also prevent the PRC from assuming economic superpower status soon, have not been mentioned; but then it is possible to raise or examine here only a very limited number of points. In sum, it would appear that the assumption of economic superpower status by Beijing in the near future is not a foregone conclusion. China may boast impressive growth figures, but these do not automatically imply significant economic development or increased influence in the global economy.

Prospects for continued social and political stability

Periods of rapid change often may well be followed by periods of relative stability. In the countries of Western Europe, for example, the years following the end of the Second World War saw unprecedented stability and along with it economic, social and political advance. The same might be said of parts of East Asia in the aftermath of the Pacific War. However, as recent events in Asia illustrate yet again, there is no intellectual reason to look primarily to stability as a core facet of human existence. Social and political stability is however generally viewed as the precondition for economic development. In China stability is already threatened from a variety of quarters.

As regards social stability, Beijing has for some time been confronted with both spontaneous and organised unrest and demonstrations. Grievances in relation to multiple issues have brought parts of the public out into the streets, and on occasions violence has flared. The question is whether the state is likely to be able to prevent or at least continue to contain such unrest. The answer must be ambiguous. On the one hand, the state seems very keen, for example, to pursue the reform of state-owned enterprises, a process that inevitably involves the laying-off of scores of workers. On the other hand, the government is committed to sustaining high economic growth rates to create a sufficiently large private sector that is able to absorb as many as possible of the workers made redundant. Notably, during the course of the Asian financial crisis, some SOEs rehired former employees. Nevertheless, in the first half of 1998, close to 1700 major protests – each involving more than 10,000 persons – took place in China, involving above all recently laid-off employees, long-term unemployed workers, and groups alienated by the thrust of social welfare reforms, such as ordinary pensioners.

To maintain social stability the Chinese government has decided, inter alia, to establish a social welfare system that is suitable to address the significant social welfare problems encountered by many citizens in the third decade of economic reform. The welfare system, in other words, is meant to provide a disincentive to protest. The steps introduced thus far are necessarily limited, however. The 'three guarantees' given to urban residents, which entail covering the basic cost of living allowances for laid-off SOE employees, making available unemployment insurance benefits and making available subsistence allowances, may be insufficient to stop further grievances from being generated. Indeed, these may ultimately translate into various forms of opposition to the regime. At the same time, however, it is a fact that more than 125 million people have bought basic retirement insurance and 100 million have purchased unemployment insurance (*Quarterly Chronicle and Documentation* 2000d: 1114), which suggests that many citizens play a part in the inevitable changes.

The possibility of major social instability, stemming not least from resentment of the unemployed, will remain for the time being. As long as the process of economic restructuring continues, millions of new job-seekers flood into the job-market, and the prospects for reducing unemployment and related problems are slim. Total urban unemployment is already said to stand at approximately 32–33 million, in contrast to an official figure of 15 million. According to official Chinese calculations 8 per cent growth simply creates roughly 6.4 million jobs. This compares to an additional labour force per year of more than 10 million (*Quarterly Chronicle and Documentation* 2000b: 611). In these circumstances, preventing workers from organising independently will remain a high priority for Chinese leaders.

A further threat to social stability arises in the context of change in rural areas. Relations between peasants and the local state have in places tended to be strained, due to the levy of excessive and illegal taxes on farmers. The grievances thus generated have led to instances of violent unrest and retaliation against officials. Significantly, the central authorities, as noted above, have empowered villagers to resist illegal practices by way of removing village officials through local elections. Indeed, the political centre has sought to offset the political power of the respective township and the village Party branch by promoting 'open-ticket elections' at the village level, i.e. anyone can run for office. The central authorities have also sought to strengthen transparency in financial matters, to curb the problem of local corruption. While these measures appear to have had some positive effect, the problem of the lagging growth of farmers' incomes, the increasing rural–urban income gap and rural unemployment and underemployment are of concern to the central government. This is particularly the case in geographical areas that have thus far been relatively neglected in China's modernisation drive, at least when compared to the coastal regions.

In short, a combination of alienation, perceived inequities, and exposure to corruption are likely to pose, or continue to pose, significant challenges to social stability in both urban and rural areas. The problem of social stability may be accentuated if an urban–rural alliance develops (Bernstein and Lü 2000). One reason why that has not happened so far is that the competition between job-seeking urban workers and rural migrants has been intensifying.

On the issue of organised resistance, it is instructive to note the government's attempt to suppress the activities of the Falungong. This is not surprising. Given that the Falungong has acted as a source of spiritual meaning at a point in time when many Chinese have become disoriented, Falungong has proved to possess quite remarkable organisational skills and cohesion. As such, the movement is a clear threat to the regime. At the same time, given its anti-Western undertones, Falungong is probably quite the opposite of the kind of political movement that certain Western governments have been keen to endorse. Having already outlawed the movement, the Chinese central government continues to accuse the Falungong of being allied with 'international anti-China forces' (that advocate Tibetan independence and accelerated democratisation in China) and decry it as an 'out-and-out cult opposed to science, society, mankind and the government'. Unsurprisingly, the Ministry of Public Security determined that, as of November 1999, concerts, mass meetings, *qigong* or other body exercises, and other mass congregations involving more than 200 participants require approval by public security departments (*Quarterly Chronicle and Documentation* 2000a: 333). The state can be expected to continue to use its coercive powers of suppression in an attempt to destroy the Falungong's organisational strengths, while using the state media to viciously denounce the movement. Whether the government will be able to avoid in all quarters the emergence of romantic views about the parallels between the Falungong and other social forces that possess an impressive record of resistance and rebellion in Chinese history remains to be seen. It is not unreasonable to expect similar treatment as that meted to out to the Falungong to be also meted out to other groups that may threaten the regime's security in other ways.

That said, it would not appear that Chinese leaders are unwilling to tolerate any form of protest, especially if local issues are at stake. Indeed, central leaders are likely to generally tolerate local protest and the rise of social movements, if those participating do not explicitly challenge the regime's claims to power. As mentioned above, this does not apply to attempts to organise workers independently. In this context, it is notable that the 'left' or 'moral left' within the Party, which has written a normative critique of the socio-economic conditions arising from reform, has thus far not been able to attract political support from the relevant sections of the population.

Still, few issues are able to agitate ordinary Chinese citizens as much as pervasive corruption by people in power. The implications for regime stability are likely to remain very serious even as the bureaucracy is exposed to the 'three stresses' campaign by which the government strives to establish a cleaner and more honest government. However, while alienation may lead to both individual and collective forms of resistance in the future, the resultant instability will not necessarily translate into major nationwide political instability in the short term. Certainly, we do not anticipate a near-term collapse of the state or the party. Indeed, we see a relatively orderly transition to the fourth generation of leaders. The new political leadership emerging as of 2002 is, however, likely to continue to reinforce measures designed to promote social and political security.

China – moving toward political liberalisation?

The issue of China's political development has been hotly debated over the years. Bringing Beijing to embrace political reform has for many years been an explicit policy objective of various Western countries. Most have justified China's integration into the global economy and its relevant institutions as leading to increasing political pluralism in China and, eventually, bringing about a regime change. That economic development and, in particular, the formation of a middle class will bring about political liberalisation has also been the contention of the influential approach of modernisation theory (Rueschemeyer 1992). Of course, the simple model admitted of exceptions – it was granted, for example, that the military within a developing polity could play a greater role that was the case in developed polities, and a politically important distinction between authoritarian and totalitarian systems came to be made. Nonetheless, notwithstanding the manoeuvres of mainstream advocates of modernisation theory, empirical evidence that would support their theoretical position has proved ambiguous. To see this, one only needs to look at political developments in Southeast Asia in the post-Cold War period.

Modernisation theory has also drawn criticism in a series of more recent debates. One of these explored the historical development of political systems and posited against the simplicities of modernisation theory the historical contingency of democratic systems (that is, they were difficult to establish and difficult to sustain). The second sought to problematise not merely the issue of historical trajectories, but also the putative end goal itself. In other words, it was suggested that the notion of 'democracy' not only could be unpacked in a variety of ways but also that it had been, in practical terms, throughout the particular historical development experiences of countries within the modern world. The implication here was that there was no single model of 'democracy' and that when political systems were inspected, other models could be found too. Some of these, as is well known, have emphasised 'good governance' rather than liberal democracy. These points raise the question of whether China is likely to liberalise politically anytime soon.

It is quite clear that the Chinese elite have moved a long way from the peasant-centred socialism espoused by Mao and, although attempts to introduce significant political reform failed in the 1980s, China is clearly, in general terms, no longer the oppressive state of the past. Tentative moves toward greater political participation and democratisation have taken place. The experiment of village-level democracy has proved relatively successful, evidenced perhaps by the consensus assessment that the Communist Party cannot always take the election of its preferred candidates for granted. Certainly, the responsiveness of elected candidates to the concerns of villagers has generally improved. In this context, democracy at the grassroots level has to some extent served to address the grievances held by sections of the rural population faced with rapacious and corrupt officials. From this point we may deduce that concerns for stability may not only translate into modes of repression, but that they can equally find expression in putative steps toward greater democracy.

However, if, as was suggested, even the fourth-generation leaders will continue to emphasise above all political stability, dramatic steps toward democratisation at much higher administrative levels should not be expected soon. In the medium to long term, societal changes, and changing state–society relations are nevertheless likely to raise more and more expectations that further political reforms will be enacted. For the moment, therefore, Zhao Chenggen's analysis in this volume that soft authoritarianism is likely to endure for some time longer may well be on target. To the extent that soft authoritarianism is seen as a legitimate form of governance by sections of the Chinese public, and of course the wider elite, radical political reforms – which most fear might bring about chaos (*luan*) – are likely to be opposed. At the same time, a reversion to strong authoritarianism is unlikely, as this would probably undermine the legitimacy of the Party, not least against the background of societal and political change experienced so far. The constituency calling for radical political reform is in any case probably rather small. There are at least two reasons for this. First, the regime has succeeded in drawing or co-opting non-threatening organisations into the party-state structures where some have registered a positive influence on decision-making processes. Second, social and economic interests that have emerged with the introduction of market capitalism also appear to have a clear preference for economic gain and social stability over political reform. The point here is that there is nothing inevitable about a rising middle class supporting political reform, especially along the lines of liberal democratic models. As Maurice Meisner (1996: 514–15) put it, '[a] bourgeoisie whose economic fortunes are so closely bound up with the political fortunes of the Communist state is not a social class that holds great democratic potential'.

China – a destabilising power?

The People's Republic has since its inception been regarded as a destabilising power. For many years China supported world revolution and to this effect provided material and financial assistance to a number of communist movements, especially in Southeast Asia. More importantly perhaps, China continues to be seen as a destabilising and non-status quo power because it has continued to pursue the full restoration of its territorial integrity. After the formal transfer of sovereignty of Hong Kong and Macao to the PRC, only unification with Taiwan still eludes CCP leaders. The PRC also has territorial and jurisdictional claims over large tracts of water, particularly in the South China Sea.

China might also be considered a destabilising power in the light of its apparent propensity to use force in international relations. Beijing has resorted to coercive diplomacy to influence politics in Taiwan and cross-Strait relations, and does not renounce the use of force against Taiwan in certain circumstances. As recently as 1979 the People's Liberation Army conducted a punitive military campaign against Vietnam. China has also resorted to the use of force in the South China Sea. Not surprisingly, many of China's neighbours are pursuing a dual strategy of engagement and containment (or hedging) *vis-à-vis* the People's Republic. Their security concerns are, among others, reinforced by China's ongoing modernisation programme, particularly the many double-digit increases in military spending in the last decade.

Meanwhile, as we saw, PRC leaders seek to undermine the American role in East Asia by ascribing to the continuation of military alliances between the United States and several East Asian countries a Cold War mentality. China has apparently also transferred missile and nuclear technology to Pakistan, and helped to upgrade the defence systems of Middle Eastern countries viewed with suspicion in the West.

While these points do testify to the quite considerable potential of the PRC to destabilise the regional order in East Asia and to weaken important international regimes, it is not clear that Beijing will choose to do so in the future. Indeed, in the medium term the prospects of China seeking to continue to promote a continuation of an era of peace and development are high. The recent bilateral agreements between Beijing and Washington and Beijing and Brussels on China's WTO accession are testimony to Beijing's appreciation that more economic interdependence is likely to be advantageous to China's development and long-term prosperity, notwithstanding the probable serious consequences for inefficient Chinese producers and service industries. The PRC is, moreover, dependent on markets in the United States, Japan and Europe as well as on access to foreign technology and capital.

China has, equally, integrated ever more fully into international society by joining existing international regimes and institutions, and by embracing their respective norms and rules. This includes global non-proliferation, as well as regional forums such as the ASEAN Regional Forum. While participation in all these endeavours serves to defend Chinese national interests, it seems plausible to argue that Chinese leaders also see part of the process of 'joining the world' as being consistent with, if not part of, their drive for greater security, economic prosperity and recognition.

Not least because China has largely sought to live up to the role of a 'regional good citizen' and 'responsible power', Beijing has been unhappy at efforts to constrain its future influence and the persistent disregard for what it takes to be its vital interests. On this score, China's relationship with the United States remains particularly conflict-prone. Whether something like a new Cold War could emerge between these two countries will depend not merely on what Beijing does, but also on what Washington does. The political and security effects of Washington's policies in relation to global arms control efforts, the significance of the U.S. and Japan alliance as the pillar of regional peace and security in East Asia and, of course, with respect to Taiwan, may be especially significant in this regard. If these effects, at least from the perspective of Beijing, are seen to conflict with the latter's vital interests and long-term ambitions, China's responses may well lead to added instability in East Asia. In the event of a conflict involving only Beijing and Taipei, the political-security and economic repercussions would be immense, and the entire East Asian region would be affected. If an armed conflict were to arise that led to U.S. intervention, the consequences would no doubt be even more serious and the fruits of decades of development would be at risk. We should therefore perhaps expect Beijing to do as much as possible to keep ties with the United States on an even keel, while simultaneously seeking to advance its interests in the region at Washington's expense.

However, apart from Sino-U.S. strategic competition and the strong likelihood that the PRC will continue to pursue coercive policies towards Taipei, the chapters in this volume do not suggest that China will necessarily destabilise regional order in other ways. That said, Sino-Japanese relations are complicated and mutual suspicions are deep. While 'history', as Caroline Rose has suggested in her chapter, may be less of an issue in bilateral relations than is usually argued, the political rivalry between the PRC and Japan has probably not yet peaked. Thus far, the two countries have not been terribly supportive of one another in core international organisations. The question of a permanent seat for Japan in the UN Security Council is particularly sensitive. The more successful Japanese politicians and the wider public are in making Japan play the role of a 'normal state' (with responsibility for regional and global peace and security), the less incentive there is for Beijing to support a continued U.S. strategic role in East Asia in its present form. Nevertheless, the recent visit by Zhu Rongji to Tokyo at least demonstrated that the Chinese side fully appreciates that continued insistence on the moral high ground can actually prove counterproductive if the objective is to keep relations stable and to benefit from access to the Japanese market and capital. To what extent Sino-Japanese rivalry will affect the broader international politics of East Asia may well depend on the resilience of the available 'coping mechanisms'.

Moreover, alone by the virtue of its size and its improving technological and economic base, neighbouring countries are bound to find China threatening. This is why many countries, especially in Southeast Asia, have adopted a strategy of forming a stable balance of power among all the majorregional players. Still, the Chinese leadership may well seek to push its own interests more than it has done in the past, while appreciating that many bilateral relationships remain delicate. However, Beijing is interested in seeing ASEAN remain coherent and relevant, not least in view of China's bilateral ties with the United States and Japan. At the same time, Chinese leaders are not interested in a strong ASEAN that opposes China on regional issues. The PRC has consequently sought to strengthen bilateral ties with individual member states. The likelihood that Southeast Asian states will face massive Chinese coercion is thus relatively unlikely.

In sum, China's foreign policy will probably pose new challenges for the region. On the other hand, a country that poses challenges is not necessarily thought of as an adversary, nor must it be, as evidenced by the foreign policy of other major powers.

Conclusion

On the basis of the analyses presented in this text it seems clear that the processes of change evident within contemporary China are set to continue into the future. It is also clear that the future will hold significant opportunities and major challenges for the government and people of China. The government will face the business of managing change. The citizens of China will have to deal with the uncertainties that accompany periods of pervasive change. Analysts and policy-makers meanwhile will no doubt continue to closely analyse and evaluate these changes.

Bibliography

Bernstein, Thomas P. and Xiaobo Lü (2000) 'Taxation without Representation: Peasants, the Central and Local States in Reform China', *The China Quarterly*, no. 163: 742–763.

Ding, X.L. (2000) 'Systemic Irregularity and Spontaneous Property Transformation in the Chinese Financial System', *The China Quarterly*, no. 163: 655–676.

Goodman, David S. and Gerald Segal (1994) *China Deconstructs: Politics, trade and regionalism* (London and New York: Routledge).

Meisner, Maurice (1996) *The Deng Xiaoping Era: An inquiry into the fate of Chinese socialism, 1978–1994* (New York: Hill and Wang).

Quarterly Chronicle and Documentation (2000a) *The China Quarterly*, no. 163: 332–352.

Quarterly Chronicle and Documentation (2000b) *The China Quarterly*, no. 162: 593–624.

Quarterly Chronicle and Documentation (2000c) *The China Quarterly*, no. 163: 883–904.

Quarterly Chronicle and Documentation (2000d) *The China Quarterly*, no. 164: 1105–1127.

Rueschemeyer, D. et al. (1992) *Capitalist Development and Democracy*, Cambridge, Polity.

Segal, Gerald (1999) 'Does China Matter?', *Foreign Affairs*, 78 (5): 24–36.

Index

For Product Safety Concerns and Information please contact our EU representative GPSR@taylorandfrancis.com
Taylor & Francis Verlag GmbH, Kaufingerstraße 24, 80331 München, Germany

www.ingramcontent.com/pod-product-compliance
Ingram Content Group UK Ltd.
Pitfield, Milton Keynes, MK11 3LW, UK
UKHW020931280425
457818UK00025B/196

* 9 7 8 0 7 0 0 7 1 6 3 7 1 *